IV

Rock Climbing

Red Rocks

NOV 0 2 2010

Todd Swain

FALCON®

HELENA, MONTANA

AFALCONGUIDE®

Falcon® is continually expanding its list of recreational guidebooks. All books include detailed descriptions, accurate maps, and all the information necessary for enjoyable trips. You can order extra copies of this book and get information and prices for other Falcon® guidebooks by writing Falcon, P.O. Box 1718, Helena, MT 59624 or calling toll-free 1-800-582-2665. Also, please ask for a free copy of our current catalog. Visit our website at www.FalconOutdoors.com or contact us by e-mail at falcon@falcon.com.

2 3 4 5 6 7 8 9 0 TP 05 04 03 02 01

All black-and-white photos by author unless otherwise noted.
All drawn topos by author unless otherwise noted.

Cataloging-in-Publication Data is on file at the Library of Congress.

CAUTION

Outdoor recreational activities are by their very nature potentially hazardous. All participants in such activities must assume the responsibility for their own actions and safety. The information contained in this guidebook cannot replace sound judgment and good decision-making skills, which help reduce exposure, nor does the scope of this book allow for disclosure of all the potential hazards and risks involved in such activities.

Learn as much as possible about the outdoor recreational activities in which you participate, prepare for the unexpected, and be cautious. The reward will be a safer and more enjoyable experience.

 Text pages printed on recycled paper.

WARNING:
CLIMBING IS A SPORT WHERE YOU MAY BE SERIOUSLY INJURED OR DIE. READ THIS BEFORE YOU USE THIS BOOK.

This guidebook is a compilation of unverified information gathered from many different climbers. The author cannot assure the accuracy of any of the information in this book, including the topos and route descriptions, the difficulty ratings, and the protection ratings. These may be incorrect or misleading and it is impossible for any one author to climb all the routes to confirm the information about each route. Also, ratings of climbing difficulty and danger are always subjective and depend on the physical characteristics (for example, height), experience, technical ability, confidence and physical fitness of the climber who supplied the rating. Additionally, climbers who achieve first ascents sometimes underrate the difficulty or danger of the climbing route out of fear of being ridiculed if a climb is later down-rated by subsequent ascents. Therefore, be warned that you must exercise your own judgment on where a climbing route goes, its difficulty and your ability to safely protect yourself from the risks of rock climbing. Examples of some of these risks are: falling due to technical difficulty or due to natural hazards such as holds breaking, falling rock, climbing equipment dropped by other climbers, hazards of weather and lightning, your own equipment failure, and failure or absence of fixed protection.

You should not depend on any information gleaned from this book for your personal safety; your safety depends on your own good judgment, based on experience and a realistic assessment of your climbing ability. If you have any doubt as to your ability to safely climb a route described in this book, do not attempt it.

The following are some ways to make your use of this book safer:

1. Consultation: You should consult with other climbers about the difficulty and danger of a particular climb prior to attempting it. Most local climbers are glad to give advice on routes in their area and we suggest that you contact locals to confirm ratings and safety of particular routes and to obtain first-hand information about a route chosen from this book.

2. Instruction: Most climbing areas have local climbing instructors and guides available. We recommend that you engage an instructor or guide to learn safety techniques and to become familiar with the routes and hazards of the areas described in this book. Even after you are proficient in climbing safely, occasional use of a guide is a safe way to raise your climbing standard and learn advanced techniques.

3. Fixed Protection: Many of the routes in this book use bolts and pitons which are permanently placed in the rock. Because of variances in the manner of placement, weathering, metal fatigue, the quality of the metal used, and many other factors, these fixed protection pieces should always be considered suspect and should always be backed up by equipment that you place yourself. Never depend for your safety on a single piece of fixed protection because you never can tell whether it will hold weight, and in some cases, fixed protection may have been removed or is now absent.

Be aware of the following specific potential hazards which could arise in using this book:

1. Misdescriptions of Routes: If you climb a route and you have a doubt as to where the route may go, you should not go on unless you are sure that you can go that way safely. Route descriptions and topos in this book may be inaccurate or misleading.

2. Incorrect Difficulty Rating: A-route may, in fact, be more difficult than the rating indicates. Do not be lulled into a false sense of security by the difficulty rating.

3. Incorrect Protection Rating: If you climb a route and you are unable to arrange adequate protection from the risk of falling through the use of fixed pitons or bolts and by placing your own protection devices, do not assume that there is adequate protection available higher just because the route protection rating indicates the route is not an "X" or an "R" rating. Every route is potentially an "X" (a fall may be deadly), due to the inherent hazards of climbing – including, for example, failure or absence of fixed protection, your own equipment's failure, or improper use of climbing equipment.

THERE ARE NO WARRANTIES, WHETHER EXPRESS OR IMPLIED, THAT THIS GUIDEBOOK IS ACCURATE OR THAT THE INFORMATION CONTAINED IN IT IS RELIABLE. THERE ARE NO WARRANTIES OF FITNESS FOR A PARTICULAR PURPOSE OR THAT THIS GUIDE IS MERCHANTABLE. YOUR USE OF THIS BOOK INDICATES YOUR ASSUMPTION OF THE RISK THAT IT MAY CONTAIN ERRORS AND IS AN ACKNOWLEDGMENT OF YOUR OWN SOLE RESPONSIBILITY FOR YOUR CLIMBING SAFETY.

DEDICATION

This book is dedicated to Paul Ross, Allen Steck, John Thackray, and other "mature" climbers who continue to enjoy the vertical world.

AUTHOR'S NOTE

The original guidebook to the area, *The Red Rocks of Southern Nevada*, by Joanne Urioste, contained 221 climbs. That guide was first published in 1984 and has recently been reprinted. It contains over 150 traditional routes that are not found in this guidebook.

This, the third edition of my original *Red Rocks Select*, contains more than 1,100 routes and also has a new title, *Rock Climbing Red Rocks*. We deemed it appropriate to drop the word "select" from the title because, due to the inclusion of more and more routes with each new edition, the book has clearly moved beyond the realm of a "select" guide. Still, there are so many routes at Red Rocks that even with 1,100 routes this book is by no means comprehensive.

No guidebook to an area like Red Rocks can be written without help. I'd like to thank everyone who has provided route information in the past. I encourage you to send me new route descriptions, corrections, and other comments for the fourth edition of this book.

My main climbing partners this time around were Jake Burkey, Kevin Campbell, Chris and Patty Gill, Teresa Krolak, Bob McCall, Paul and Marea Ross, and my wife, Donette Swain. They put up with my need to thrash through scrub oak and my whimpering while on the lead. Thanks to all!

Chris and Patty Gill and their wonder dog, Rosie, provided me with my own bedroom while in Las Vegas. In addition to lodging, Chris made sure I saw the latest episodes of the "World's Scariest Car Chases" and "When Good Animals Go Bad!"

The "knowledgeable locals" that have made these guides possible include Tom Beck, Pat Brennan, Wendell "the Dean" Broussard, Michael Clifford, Bob Conz, Robert Finlay, Randal Grandstaff, Richard Harrison, Leo and Karin Henson, Chuck and Merlise Liff, Mark Limage, Sal Mamusia, Randy Marsh and Pier Locatelli, Greg and "Chucky" Mayer, "Flyin' Brian" McCray, Dan McQuade, Danny Meyers, Nick Nordblom, Danny Rider, Brad Stewart, Mike Tupper, Paul Van Betten, Chuck Ward, and Mike and Tim Ward of Desert Rock Sports.

I would like to thank the following people at Falcon Publishing, who logged considerable time with me during the preparation phase of this edition: Nicole Blouin, John Burbidge, and Molly Jay.

Finally, I'd like to thank George Meyers and the former staff of Chockstone Press. Without their hard work, the first two editions of this guide would never have happened.

CONTENTS

Introduction 1

CALICO BASIN 15
Red Spring Area/Calico Basin South 15
  Moderate Mecca 15
  Jabba the Hut Rock 22
  Red Spring Rock 24
  Cannibal Crag 27
  Riding Hood Wall 30
  Ranch Hands Crag 31
  Dickies Cliff 32
  Gnat Man Crag 34
  Happy Acres 35
Calico Basin North/Gateway Canyon 36
  The Playground 39
  Caligula Crag 41
  Conundrum Crag 42
  Swirly Cliff 44
  Cannabis Crag 44
  Yin and Yang 46
  Meyers Cracks 48
  Sunny and Steep Crag 49
  Winter Heat Wall 51

FIRST PULLOUT 57
  Climb Bomb Cliff 58
  Velvet Elvis Crag 58
  Universal City 60
  Cactus Massacre 61
  Meat Puppets Wall 62
  Bowling Ball 64
  Circus Wall 64
  Dog Wall 65
  Fixx Cliff 67
  The Oasis 69
  Tuna and Chips Wall 71
  Tiger Stripe Wall 72
  Panty Wall 73
  Ultraman Wall 77

SECOND PULLOUT 81
  Tsunami Wall 81
  Trundle Wall 83
  Jane's Wall 84
  Truancy Cliff 85

The Arena 85
Rescue Wall 86
Magic Bus 86
Kitty Crag 88
The Sandbox 88
Ethics Wall 89
The Black Corridor 90
Hunter S. Thompson Dome 94
Poser Crag 97
Great Red Book Area 97
Meister's Edge Area 100
Sweet Pain Wall 102
Stone Wall 103
The Observatory 104
The Gallery 107
Wall of Confusion 109

SANDSTONE QUARRY 113
Sandstone Quarry East 113
  Front Corridor 113
  California Crags 116
  The Pier 117
  Americrag 119
Running Man Wall Area 120
  Boschton Marathon Block 122
  Running Man Wall 123
  Stratocaster Wall 126
  B/W Wall 132
Sandstone Quarry Central 133
  Sandy Corridor 133
  Sonic Youth Cliff 134
  The Asylum 138
  Broast and Toast Cliff 138
  Numbers Crag 140
  Common Time 141
  Wake Up Wall 141
Sandstone Quarry North 144
  The Twinkie 144
  The Marshmallow 145
  The Bull Market 145
  Satellite Wall 147
  Avian Wall 147
  The Trophy 148

Sandstone Quarry Northeast 150
   Blister in the Sun Cliff 150
   The Beach 151
   Mass Production Wall 152
   The Hall of Fame 154
   Holiday Wall 155
James Brown Area 157
   James Brown Wall 158
   Next Wall 158
   The Sweet Spot 159
WHITE ROCK SPRING AREA 161
   Angel Food Wall 161
   White Rock Springs Peak 165
WILLOW SPRING 169
   Nadia's Niche 169
   Lost Creek Canyon/Hidden Falls 169
   Ragged Edges Cliff 176
   Graduate Cliff 179
   The Case Face 180
   Sumo Greatness Slab 182
   Outhouse Wall 183
   The Dark Thumb 183
ICEBOX CANYON 185
   Sunnyside Crag 185
   Buffalo Wall 189
   Hidden Wall 192
   Icebox Canyon, South Wall 192
   Refrigerator Wall 192
   Smears for Fears Area 199
   Bridge Mountain 201
   Frigid Air Buttress 202
   The Necromancer 204
PINE CREEK CANYON 209
Bridge Mountain 209
   East Face 209
   The Abutment 214
   Flight Path Area 217
   Stick Gully 219
   Straight Shooter Wall 220
   Beer and Ice Gully 222
   Brass Wall 227
North Fork of Pine Creek Canyon 232
   Out of Control Area 232

Dark Shadows Wall 234
Mescalito, East Face 239
South Fork of Pine Creek Canyon 245
Mescalito, South Face 245
Crabby Appleton Area 247
Magic Triangle Area 249
JUNIPER CANYON 255
   Rose Tower 256
   Jackrabbit Buttress 256
   Brownstone Wall 259
   Rainbow Wall 264
   Cloud Tower 276
   Ginger Buttress 279
OAK CREEK CANYON 285
   Solar Slab Area 286
   Black Arch Wall 297
   Eagle Wall Area 299
   Upper Oak Creek Canyon 306
Mount Wilson 309
   Afterburner Cliff 309
   Ramen Pride Cliff 309
   East Face 312
   Willy's Couloir 317
FIRST CREEK CANYON 321
   Mount Wilson 321
   Indecision Peak 326
   Lotta Balls Wall 326
   Alcohol Wall 329
   Romper Room Area 331
   Slippery Peak Apron 335
BLACK VELVET CANYON 337
   The Monument 338
   Burlap Buttress 340
   Whiskey Peak 344
   Black Velvet Wall 358
   Western Spaces Wall 377
WINDY CANYON 386
ILLUSION CRAGS 393
   Left Side 393
   Main Cliff 394
OTHER AREAS 398
Index 404

LAS VEGAS CLIMBING AREAS

(MAP NOT TO SCALE)

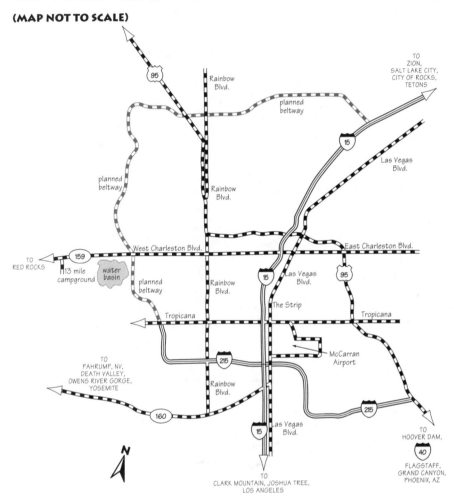

RED ROCKS

(MAP NOT TO SCALE)

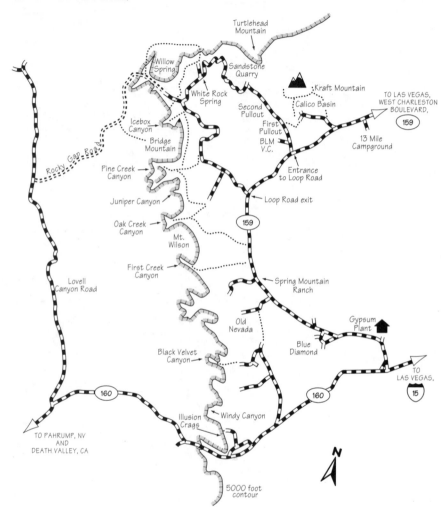

Turtlehead Mountain

Willow Spring

Sandstone Quarry

Kraft Mountain

White Rock Spring

Calico Basin

TO LAS VEGAS, WEST CHARLESTON BOULEVARD,

Second Pullout

159

Icebox Canyon

First Pullout BLM V.C.

13 Mile Campground

Bridge Mountain

Rocky Gap Road

Pine Creek Canyon

Entrance to Loop Road

Juniper Canyon

Loop Road exit

Oak Creek Canyon

159

Mt. Wilson

First Creek Canyon

Lovell Canyon Road

Spring Mountain Ranch

Old Nevada

Gypsum Plant

Black Velvet Canyon

Blue Diamond

TO LAS VEGAS,

15

160

Illusion Crags

Windy Canyon

160

TO PAHRUMP, NV AND DEATH VALLEY, CA

N

5000 foot contour

MAP LEGEND

Trail

Interstate

Paved Road

Gravel Road

Unimproved Road

State Line, Forest, Park, or Wilderness Boundary

Waterway

Intermittent Waterway

Lake/Reservoir

Building

Camping

Gate

Town

City

Climbing Area

Crag/Boulder

Cliff Edge

Mountain Peak

Trailhead

Parking

Interstate

U.S. Highway

State Highway

County Road

Forest Road

Mile Marker

KEY TO TOPO DRAWINGS

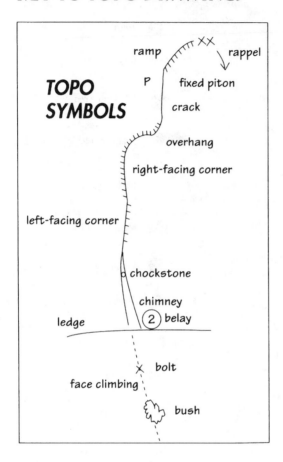

TOPO SYMBOLS

ramp

XX — rappel

P — fixed piton

crack

overhang

right-facing corner

left-facing corner

chockstone

chimney

2 belay

ledge

bolt

face climbing

bush

INTRODUCTION

Most climbers have now at least heard of Red Rocks and know that it lies just outside of Las Vegas, Nevada. While this guidebook contains more than 1,100 selected climbs, Red Rocks currently has an estimated 1,700 different routes of all grades and lengths.

From the popular sport climbs of the Calico Hills to the multiday routes in Juniper and Icebox canyons, the area hosts numerous climbs of world-class stature. The area is officially named Red Rock Canyon National Conservation Area and is administered by the Bureau of Land Management (BLM), a federal agency within the United States Department of the Interior.

GETTING THERE

Once you arrive in Las Vegas, you'll find that it's pretty simple to get around. McCarran Airport is right off the Strip, while Interstate 15 and U.S. Highway 93/95 divide the city roughly into quarters. The Red Rock escarpment is located about 15 miles west of Las Vegas and is typically approached from West Charleston Boulevard (Nevada 159).

With the exception of Black Velvet Canyon, Windy Canyon, and the Illusion Crags, all of the climbing at Red Rocks is accessed by NV 159 and a one-way scenic loop road. This loop road, within the National Conservation Area (NCA), is gated and closed at night. Typically, the road is open from early morning until just after dark. An entrance fee is required to use the loop road and Red Spring Area of the NCA. Check with the NCA Visitor Center or local climbing shops for current opening and closing times. Black Velvet Canyon, Windy Canyon, and the Illusion Crags are accessed via NV 160.

The introduction to each chapter of this guide describes how to get to the trailhead for that certain area. The individual route descriptions tell you how to get from your car to the base of the climb. Hiking approach times at Red Rocks range from a few minutes to four hours and are also mentioned in the chapter and route introductions.

THE LAND

Like all climbing areas, Red Rock Canyon National Conservation Area should be treated with the utmost respect. The area was first designated as Red Rock Canyon Recreation Lands in 1967, and the scenic loop road was completed in 1978.

Dan McQuade on *The Choad Warrior* (5.12c), Stratocaster Wall, Sandstone Quarry East.
MCQUADE COLLECTION

The current designation as a National Conservation Area came in 1990. It is defined as "An area of the public lands managed by the Bureau of Land Management which has been established by Congress for the purpose of protecting and conserving identified resource values of national interest. A Conservation Area is managed for multiple use and sustained yield in conformance with the Resource Management Plan and in accordance with a General Management Plan which reflects the dominant and compatible uses for specific tracts."

Red Rock Canyon NCA currently encompasses 196,000 acres and hosts nearly one million visitors each year. A very nice visitor center located just off the scenic loop road has interpretive displays, books, postcards, and a helpful staff. The visitor center is typically open from 8:30 a.m. to 4:30 p.m. For more information, call 702-363-1921.

The BLM has a number of useful handouts for planning your visit to Red Rocks. These include a park brochure and the following titles: *Climbing and Camping, Hiking, Mammals, Birds, Geology, Plants,* and *Archeology of Southern Nevada.* For more information, brochures, or a list of other publications available, contact the BLM at Las Vegas District Office, 4765 West Vegas Drive, Las Vegas, NV 89108; 702-647-5000.

REGULATIONS

As climber visitation increases, land managers at Red Rocks and other desert parks are becoming more concerned about a number of climbing impacts. Please abide by posted regulations and closure times, and be courteous to other user groups. The following climbing-related regulations are currently in effect at Red Rock Canyon National Conservation Area. (Note: The first three regulations are extremely important. Violations will most likely lead to the closure of climbing areas.)

- It is prohibited to chip, chisel, glue, or scar the rock.
- Climbing is not allowed within 50 feet of any Native American rock art site (petroglyphs and/or pictographs).
- Digging or in any way disturbing archaeological sites is prohibited.
- Camping is allowed only in designated camping areas, or, when backpacking, above 5,000 feet elevation (accessed only off the Red Rock Summit Road/Rocky Gap Road or Lovell Canyon Road). When backpacking, you must camp more than 200 feet from archaeological sites and water sources. **Note:** As of press time, roadside camping was only allowed at 13 Mile Campground.
- Vehicles must be outside the gated sections of the loop road before closing time. (If there's one thing that annoys the rangers at Red Rocks, it's waiting for tardy visitors to get back to their cars and exit the loop road.)

- Permits are required for backpacking, bivouacs, and early or late access to the loop road. Contact the NCA Visitor Center for more details.
- Fires are allowed only within furnished fire grates.
- Gathering of native vegetation is prohibited. Bring your own firewood.

LOW IMPACT

In addition, a number of very important low impact policies should be followed.

- Do not climb on wet sandstone! The rock becomes very brittle and typically needs at least 24 hours to dry.
- Pack out all trash, whether it's yours or not.
- Pack out all toilet paper and human waste using a Ziploc-type bag. At the least, bury waste 6 inches deep and always carry out toilet paper.
- Stay on maintained trails as much as possible and try to minimize impacts to plants and soil through erosion and trampling.
- New routes should be established away from the view of the general public. At Sandstone Quarry no new fixed anchors are allowed within 0.25 mile of the parking area.
- All bolts and anchors should be painted to match the color of the rock. If webbing is used, it should also match the color of the rock.
- To help keep the visual impacts of climbing to a minimum, remove all retreat (or bail) slings you encounter.
- Do not use chalk on areas visible to the general public. This definitely applies to the boulders at Willow Spring Picnic Area and Sandstone Quarry.

THE RULES OF THE GAME

How a route is established (whether from the ground up or on rappel) will never be as important as having the opportunity to climb. Do your part to minimize all impacts associated with climbing (noise, visuals, social trails, human waste, disturbing wildlife, etc.). Climb to have fun, not to aggravate others or upset land managers. Here are the ethics currently accepted by the majority of climbers at Red Rocks.

- Not all routes are worth bolting. Top-rope those routes that share anchors or are close to other established routes.
- Lead routes may be established from the ground up or on rappel. From a boldness and historical perspective, ground-up is more desirable. Hooks are typically used on ground-up ascents. If you do decide to rap-bolt, be sure to top-rope the route first, so that the bolts are in the proper place!

- Bolts should be at least $^3/_8$" in diameter. Anchors should be at least $^1/_2$" in diameter.

- All bolts and anchors should be painted to match the color of the rock.

- New routes should not be established within view of the general public.

- Climbs that are still in progress will have a red ribbon tied to the first bolt. Please do not attempt these routes until they have been completed or abandoned by the party that installed the bolts.

- A new route is completed when the leader starts at the bottom of the cliff and climbs to the top without falling, grabbing slings, or hanging on the rope.

RATINGS

The Yosemite Decimal System (YDS) is used throughout this book to rate climbs. Currently, technical rock climbs at Red Rocks range from 5.0 to 5.13. The higher the number, the more difficult the climb. Aid ratings go from A0 (tension or grabbing a sling) to A5 (long stretches of body-weight-only placements). To differentiate between true sport climbs (quickdraws only) and routes where gear is needed, I have used two different types of subgrading methods.

True sport climbs have ratings subdivided by letter grades (a–d), as was introduced by Jim Bridwell of Yosemite fame. Routes that require some amount of traditional gear have the subdivisions of minus and plus. These "gear subdivisions" are used on climbs 5.10 or harder, with a rating of 5.10- being equal in difficulty to 5.10a.

As with any rating system, the ratings are not meant to be definitive but are intended to give you a rough idea of the difficulty that may be encountered. Height, reach, finger size, and flexibility vary for each climber, thus making the rating system somewhat inaccurate. Just because a route is rated 5.9 doesn't mean it's really 5.9. Remember, I haven't done all of the routes in this guide; therefore, the information should be considered suspect.

I also have used the protection rating system first introduced by Jim Erickson in his climbing guide to Boulder, Colorado. This system is based on the movie rating system (G, PG, PG13, R, and X), with X-rated routes being very dangerous. There may be very dangerous climbs listed in this book that don't have an R or X rating. Use caution and good judgment when leading!

I have dropped the G ("safe") rating and use only the other four grades. These ratings assume the leader is competent at the grade, has the proper equipment for the route, and has an attentive belayer. Roughly, the ratings mean:

PG   Protection is usually considered adequate, although the leader may fall up to 15 feet. The leader will probably not get injured in the fall. These routes might seem a little bit sporty.

Chris Gill on *Atman* (5.10), Yin and Yang Cliff, Calico Basin.

PG13 This is somewhere between PG and R (as you might have guessed).

R Protection is usually considered inadequate and the leader will probably get injured if he/she falls. These routes are potentially dangerous and runout.

X Protection is nonexistent. A falling leader will probably suffer severe injuries and/or death. These are death routes or solos.

TERMS

One year and a day, twenty to life, life without parole . . . you get the idea! The following climbing terms are used throughout this guide. Note: Generally, the person whose name appears first led the crux of the route.

FA: First Ascent

FFA: First Free Ascent

FRA: First Recorded Ascent

FRFA: First Recorded Free Ascent

Directions: For left and right, assume the reader is facing the cliff.

Quality ratings: * "Thumbs up!" This symbol means the route is of very high quality.

GEAR

The joy of sport climbing is that you need only a rope, quickdraws, and strong fingers. For the traditional routes, you'll want a good selection of wires, TCUs, Friends, and slings. "Specialty" gear is noted in the description of the climb. For the longer canyon routes, you'll usually need two ropes to descend. Again, this is noted in the description.

WEATHER

Climbing is possible at Red Rocks all year, but most people visit the area in the spring and fall. For the latest forecast, check out the numerous weather sites on the Internet. The preferred weather telephone number is 702-736-3854. You can also call 702-734-2010. "Typical" weather for each season is detailed below.

Spring: While the weather can be good, it's likely that there will be windy and wet conditions in March. Shade combined with down-canyon winds can make places like Black Velvet seem much colder than the sunny cliffs of the Calico Hills. By May, the temperatures could reach 100 degrees Fahrenheit (F).

Summer: It is common for temperatures to reach 106 degrees F or higher. Thunderstorms are the norm for late July and all of August, and these rains frequently cause flash floods. Climb in the early morning and evening hours, and avoid the sun. Drink lots of water!

Fall: Although the days are getting shorter, it is probably the best time to visit the area. As November rolls around, expect it to get cold in the shady canyons. Places like The Gallery are warm enough for climbing in shorts and T-shirts.

Winter: Sunny cliffs, such as The Gallery and Trophy, are extremely popular. Snow is common at the higher elevations and forces the closure of the loop road on occasion. Shady canyon climbs are usually out of the question. Shaded descents (such as on *Solar Slab*) may remain icy for some time.

EMERGENCIES

The BLM and Las Vegas Metropolitan Police Department (Metro) provide emergency services at Red Rocks. Emergency telephones are located on the scenic loop road at Sandstone Quarry, White Rock Spring, and Icebox Canyon. Between 8 a.m. and 5 p.m., report the accident to the NCA Visitor Center if possible. After hours, call from pay phones at the entrance to the loop road, outside the NCA Visitor Center, or in the towns of Blue Diamond, Old Nevada (Bonnie Springs Ranch), and Las Vegas.

Emergency Telephone Numbers:

- BLM Emergency Dispatch: 702-293-8932
- Las Vegas Metropolitan Police: 911
- BLM Non-Emergency Dispatch: 702-293-8998
- NCA Visitor Center: 702-363-1921

Area Medical Facilities: The nearest hospital to the crags is Summerlin Medical Center (655 Town Center Drive; 702-233-7000). Head into town on West Charleston and turn left (north) on Hualapai Way. The hospital is about 1 mile north on Hualapai Way and is visible from West Charleston. It is a multistoried tan building on the northeast side of a traffic circle. Other local hospitals include University Medical Center (1800 West Charleston; 702-383-2000) and Valley Hospital Medical Center (620 Shadow Lane; 702-388-4000). Valley Hospital has Flight for Life capabilities.

WHERE TO STAY

Las Vegas has over 120,000 rooms available for its 32 million annual visitors. These rooms range from astonishingly cheap to astronomically expensive. Many of the huge casinos on The Strip offer great deals and are only minutes away from the crags. As a general rule, room prices are quite a bit higher on weekends and in the summer. At least one hotel offers discounts to climbers. Check with the climbing shops for details.

For those who want to camp, the choices are very limited. As of January 2000, 13 Mile Campground was the only convenient place to legally camp. This BLM campground is located on West Charleston (Nevada 159), roughly 1 mile east (toward town) from Calico Basin Road. The campground currently has individual sites that cost $10 per night (limited to two vehicles), walk-in sites ($5 per night), and group sites ($25 a night). Long-range plans include as many as 10 group sites with several of these sites able to accommodate up to 50 people. The campground has drinking water and restrooms. Check with the BLM or local climbing shops for the latest information. There are also commercial campgrounds in Las Vegas, some of which will provide showers to those staying elsewhere.

SUPPLIES AND OTHER IMPORTANT INFORMATION

Along West Charleston (Nevada 159), you find grocery, drug, and department stores, as well as numerous restaurants. Blue Diamond has a small convenience store with limited items. Water is available at the NCA Visitor Center and at various places in town.

Numerous movie theaters can be found in the local area. The Red Rock Cinema is about 1 mile east of Rainbow at 5201 West Charleston (702-870-1423). The Torrey Pines Theater at 6344 West Sahara (the intersection of Torrey Pines) offers cheaper, second-run movies (702-876-4334). There is a public library at 6301 West Charleston, just west of Jones. There is also a small branch library in Blue Diamond.

Showers are available at some commercial campgrounds and fitness centers. Check with the local climbing shops for the latest information. Do not use the NCA Visitor Center bathrooms for bathing.

LAS VEGAS

If you haven't been to Vegas yet, you're missing out! Before your trip, rent the following films at your local video store to get a feel for the area: *Bugsy* starring Warren Beatty, *Viva Las Vegas* starring Elvis, and *Honeymoon in Vegas* starring Nicholas Cage. Here's a list of my favorite things to show first-time visitors to Las Vegas.

Bellagio: The owners of this hotel intended it to be the most elegant in the world. If you can afford it, see the Cirque du Soleil show ($100/person), which features some amazing stuff. Several local climbers work as riggers on the show. Check out the free water fountain show in front of the casino as well.

Caesar's Palace: One of the more opulent casinos, you'll find a higher-class clientele here than at Circus, Circus. Take in a movie at the large-screen Omnimax

Theater and don't miss The Forum, an amazing shopping area featuring talking statues and a "sky" that changes.

Coca Cola World: Across from New York, New York and next to the MGM Grand is a relatively interesting complex featuring an indoor climbing wall (expensive), Coca Cola World (the tour price is worth it—check out the shooting soda fountain), and M&M World (not worth it). Downstairs are more video games than you have ever seen before!

Circus, Circus: A bit tacky, but the original casino designed to suck in the whole family. Check out the free circus acts (running from about noon to midnight), the midway, and "The World's Largest Buffet." Grand Slam Canyon is attached to the rear of the casino and features an indoor roller coaster and other stuff.

Excalibur: The biggest (and gaudiest) hotel in the world when it was built. It sports a medieval motif and was built by Circus, Circus. For those with money ($25), the dinner theater features jousting and other knightly derring-do.

"Glitter Gulch": This is the downtown part of Vegas. The buildings generally aren't as tall as those on the Strip, but their closeness makes the neon that much more impressive.

Las Vegas Hilton: The *Star Trek* show is expensive, but a must for sci-fi fans.

Luxor: It's shaped like a pyramid and has an Egyptian theme. Sooner or later, I think someone will attempt to BASE jump the interior. Check out just the first Episode and the buffet.

The Mirage: There are a bunch of free things to experience here. Don't miss the exploding volcano in front of the casino. It erupts on a regular basis all evening. Inside, you find rare white tigers (usually sleeping), a tropical jungle, and a huge tropical aquarium (behind the check-in desk).

MGM Grand: This huge, green casino/outdoor amusement park is across the street from New York, New York. It has all sorts of shows and rides to while away those long winter nights but is barely worth the entrance fee.

New York, New York: An interesting and realistic exterior and interior (once you see them, you know what I mean). The roller coaster is worth the money.

Treasure Island: Don't miss the free pirate battle in front of the casino (run multiple times each evening).

LOCAL CLIMBING SHOPS

Desert Rock Sports
8201 West Charleston Boulevard
Las Vegas, NV 89117
702-254-1143

Great Basin Outdoors
2925 North Green Valley Parkway
Henderson, NV 89014
702-454-4997

LOCAL AUTHORIZED GUIDE SERVICES

Jackson Hole Mountain Guides
P.O. Box 80875
Las Vegas, NV 89180
702-223-2176

Sky's The Limit
HCR 33 Box 1
Calico Basin, NV 89124-9209
702-363-4533

Contact the BLM for other authorized guide services.

GRIPES, COMPLAINTS, ETC.

Believe it or not, some people complain about my guidebooks. Should you have any of the following complaints, please refer to my standard responses (in brackets).

- Our approach took longer than the guidebook time. (I have longer legs than you do.)
- The description was wrong. (I haven't done all the routes. I'm only human.)
- My favorite route didn't get included. (This isn't an all-inclusive guidebook. I didn't know about the route.)
- This route does/doesn't deserve a * (thumbs up). (Use a pen to add the thumb yourself. Use white-out to remove the thumb.)
- The guidebook said the climb was in the sun/shade and when we got there it was in the shade/sun. We froze our @#$ off/fried our brains and it's your fault! (The earth rotates around the sun, causing extreme seasonal differences in what does/does not receive sunshine on any given day.)

Please remember that rock climbing is supposed to be fun and adventurous. I have made every effort to make this book as accurate as possible. Constructive criticism, corrections, and route information are greatly appreciated and should be directed to me at P.O. Box 826, Joshua Tree, CA 92252-0826.

FURTHER READING ABOUT CLIMBING AT RED ROCKS

Several other guidebooks, as well as numerous articles, have been written about climbing at Red Rocks. This is not meant to be a complete list of published material, but it will get you started in your quest for more routes to do (once you've done all of the climbs contained in this book!).

Books:

> *The Red Rocks of Southern Nevada* by Joanne Urioste; American Alpine Club, 1984 (red cover); reprinted 1999 (white cover).
>
> *Climber's Guide to North American Rock Climbs: West Coast Rock Climbs* by John Harlin III; Chockstone Press, 1987.
>
> *A Climber's Guide to the Red Rocks of Nevada* by Randy Faulk; RT Publications, 1992.

Periodicals:

> *Climbing*, issues 128, 131, 161, 167, 168, 179, 182, 186.
>
> *Mountain Magazine*, issue 140.
>
> *Onsight Magazine*, issues 1, 2.
>
> *Rock & Ice*, issues 18, 36, 49, 50, 53, 90, 94.
>
> *Sport Climbing*, volume 1 (#3), volume 2 (#4).Calico Basin

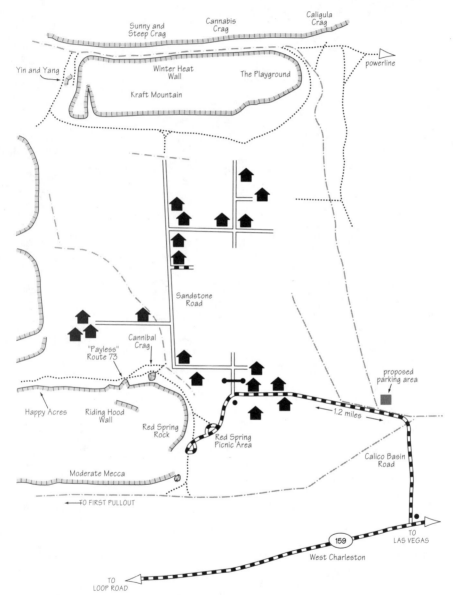

CALICO BASIN
OVERVIEW
(MAP NOT TO SCALE)

Sunny and
Steep Crag

Cannabis
Crag

Caligula
Crag

powerline

Yin and Yang

Winter Heat
Wall

The Playground

Kraft Mountain

Sandstone
Road

Cannibal
Crag

"Payless"
Route 73

proposed
parking area

1.2 miles

Happy Acres

Riding Hood
Wall

Red Spring
Rock

Red Spring
Picnic Area

Calico Basin
Road

Moderate Mecca

←TO FIRST PULLOUT

159

West Charleston

TO
LAS VEGAS

TO
LOOP ROAD

CALICO BASIN

The Calico Basin is a portion of the conservation area that has many private residences. In the past few years, climbers have not been particularly sensitive to these residents, despite warnings in previous editions of this guidebook. Consequently, parking and access have become an issue. Please keep a very low profile and park only in authorized areas!

RED SPRING AREA/CALICO BASIN SOUTH

The majority of the climbs in this chapter are in the area around Red Spring Picnic Area along the western side of the basin. Note: Numerous routes have been done on the outcrops directly above Red Spring but are not covered in this edition. To reach the picnic area, turn off West Charleston (Nevada 159) onto Calico Basin Road and follow it for 1.2 miles to a T-intersection. Turn left into the Red Spring Picnic Area and park.

MODERATE MECCA

This newly developed area should become quite popular due to the short approach and warmth. Park at the back (southern end) of the parking lot inside the Red Spring Picnic Area. Walk south up the obvious old road to the top of a dirt ridge (100 yards). Follow the road downhill into a valley for 20 yards, then angle right (west) onto a ledge that runs along the cliff (it'll seem like you're going to end up on top of the cliff). Routes are described from east (toward Las Vegas) to west as you encounter them. If you walk up the bottom of the valley, you'll eventually arrive at the First Pullout.

1. **Side Effects** (5.10+) FA: Mike Ward; circa 1991. At the extreme east end of the cliff is a freestanding pinnacle shaped a bit like an Easter Island head. The pinnacle begins at the lower level of the cliff and ends even with the main ledge system. This route climbs large huecos on the southeast face of the formation to a chain anchor. At press time, the bolts had been removed from this route for some unknown reason.

The following routes begin on the ledge system described in the approach to the area.

2. **Stew on This** (5.10 PG) FA: Kevin Campbell, Todd Swain; December 1998. Rope up about 250' from the right (east) edge of the formation at an arête on the main ledge system. Mantle past a low overhang (bolt) to a stance

Moderate Mecca
Right

Red Spring

below a steep varnished wall (#2–2.5 cam placement). Climb the varnished face past a bolt to easier climbing on light-colored rock. There is an anchor on the arête above.

3. **Is It Soup Yet?** (5.10 PG) FA: Kevin Campbell, Todd Swain; December 1998. Start 10' left of the last route on the west side of the arête. Pull past a low ceiling (bolt) then up a steep, shallow dihedral to a ledge. Continue up the short face to an anchor on the arête. Bring wires, TCUs, and small cams to protect the route.

4. **Chicken Soup for the Soul** (5.10- TR) FA: Teresa Krolak, Patty Gill, Todd Swain; January 1999. Begin 10' left of the last route and just right of a large, left-facing corner. Climb the steep face past a shallow left-facing corner and huecos to the top. Medium cams and long slings needed for the anchor.

5. **Chicken Gumbo for Your Dumbo** (5.6) FRA: Todd Swain, Patty Gill, Teresa Krolak; January 1999. A good little route. Same start as the last route at a varnished, left-facing corner that is just right of the main corner. Climb the small, varnished corner to the top. Bring gear to a #3.5 Friend. Walk off right. (No topo.)

6. **Soupy Sales** (5.6+) FRA: Patty Gill, Todd Swain, Teresa Krolak; January 1999. Harder than it looks. Climb the obvious crack/left-facing corner (5' left of the last route) to the summit. (No topo.)

Climbers on *Valentine's Day* (5.8+). MAREA ROSS PHOTO

7. **From Soup to Nuts** (5.7) FRA: Todd Swain, Patty Gill, Teresa Krolak; January 1999. Ascend the crack 5' left of the last route. The crux is at the bottom. Bring gear to a #4 cam, including a #2.5 and #3 Friend for the anchor. Walk off right (east). (No topo.)

8. **The Singing Love Pen** (5.9) FRA: Todd Swain, Patty Gill, Teresa Krolak; January 1999. Rope up 30' left of the last route at the left side of a black face. The route starts at a right-facing corner and follows a crack through a bulge. Finish up a lower-angle crack to a right-facing corner. Bring equipment up to a #3.5 Friend. (No topo.)

9. **Valentine's Day** (5.8+) FA: Randal Grandstaff, Danny Rider; circa 1988. You'll love this one. Rope up 20' left of *The Singing Love Pen* and about 100 yards from the east end of the ledge system at a varnished, left-facing corner. Carry gear up to a #3.5 Friend. Stem up the nice corner to a ledge. There are 2 belay bolts just to the left of the top of the route.

10. **Ace of Hearts** (5.10+ TR) FA: Unknown. FFA: Unknown; circa 1990s. It appears this route was aided with thin pitons (hence the route name) prior to being free-climbed. Start 20' left of the *Valentine's Day* corner below a varnished face. Climb up along thin, vertical cracks to the top. This can be toproped after doing *Valentine's Day*.

There is a large yellow recess 200' left of the last route. The ledge system traversing the cliff crosses a talus slope at this point.

11. **Pending Disaster** (5.9+) FA: Todd Swain, Kevin Campbell; December 1998. This is one of the better routes on the crag. Bring a full rack up to a #4 Camalot. Rope up at the right edge of a large yellow recess below an obvious crack system. Jam a left-slanting crack past a low overhang. Continue up obvious, steep cracks to a lower-angled face. Rappel with one rope from the belay anchor.

12. **Pending Project** (5.9 A2?) FA: Unknown; circa 1998. You can see pin scars and bolts on the steep wall to the left of the last route. The upper half of the route climbs a prominent, overhanging wide crack. Whether the route has been climbed in its entirety is unknown. (No topo.)

13. **Penny Lane** (5.3) FA: Unknown. About 200 yards from the right (east) edge of the cliff is a large recess with a huge corner in the back. Romp up the huge, left-facing corner system to the summit. Watch out for loose rocks. Walk off right (east). (No topo.)

14. **Abbey Road** (5.4) FA: Unknown. Bring wires, TCUs, and some long slings. Begin 10' left of the last route (the huge corner) and 75' left of *Pending Disaster* at prominent thin cracks on a slabby face. Face-climb up along the thin cracks to a small alcove. Pull over a small ceiling, then climb up another 10' to a ledge. Either continue to the top of the cliff or traverse 40' left to an anchor. You need two ropes for the rappel from the anchor. If you go to the top, walk off right (east).

15. **Fleet Street** (5.8 PG) FA: Kevin Campbell, Todd Swain; December 1998. If you are fleet-footed, this route won't seem bad. Carry some small wires to supplement the 2 bolts on this route. Climb the center of the black, varnished face just left of the last route. Belay and rappel from the communal anchor on a ledge about 100' up.

16. **Muckraker** (5.8) FRA: Todd Swain, Paul Ross; December 1998. Carry gear up to a #3 Friend. Start 25' left of the last route at the right-hand of two cracks leading through a roof. Climb the crack past the right side of the roof (crux), then up the lower-angled wide crack to its top. Angle up and left to the communal belay. Rappel with two ropes.

17. **Scalawag** (5.10) FA: Todd Swain, Paul Ross; December 1998. A wild route that protects well with multiple large cams. Rope up at the left-hand of two roof cracks in an alcove. Traverse out the crack to a stance, then up past the lip to lower-angle terrain. Finish up a crack system that forms an X. Rappel with two ropes from the communal anchor.

18. **Boodler** (5.8+ PG) FRA: Todd Swain, Teresa Krolak, Patty Gill; January 1999. An interesting and challenging route for the solid leader. Start 40' left (west) of *Scalawag* and around a nose of rock. The route climbs the

Climber on *Scalawag* (5.10). MAREA ROSS PHOTO

left-leaning ramp/corner to an anchor about 60' up. Bring small wires, lots of small TCUs, and cams to #3.5.

19. **Carpetbagger** (5.6+) FRA: Todd Swain, Winston Farrar, Jake Burkey; January 1999. Rope up 70' left of the last route at a huge openbook. Climb the large corner system to an anchor on a ledge. Carry gear to a #3 cam. Rappel with one rope.

20. **Mugwump** (5.10 TR) FA: Unknown. Start between *Carpetbagger* and *The Haj* in the middle of a pink overhang. Climb the loose overhang and lower-angled face above to the communal anchor. (No topo.)

21. **The Haj** (5.9) FA: Jake Burkey, Todd Swain, Winston Farrar; January 1999. A good route. Begin 30' left of *Carpetbagger* on the left side of a pink overhang. The route starts near an acacia bush and below a varnished, left-facing corner. Jam and stem up the steep corner to lower-angle terrain. Carry gear up to a #3 cam. Rappel from the communal anchor with one rope. (No topo.)

22. **Sir Climbalot** (5.7 PG) FRA: Winston Farrar, Jake Burkey, Todd Swain; January 1999. Winston was 13 years old at the time of this ascent. Begin in the same place as the last route on the left edge of a pink overhang (near an acacia bush on the traverse ledge). Climb the low-angle, left-facing corner that is just left of a steep, varnished corner. The crux is near the bottom, pulling a bulge (#1.5 Friend or Tri-Cam in a pocket). Bring gear to a #3 cam and rappel from the communal anchor with one rope. Watch for loose rock near the anchor. (No topo.)

23. **The Route to Mecca** (5.7) FRA: Todd Swain, Winston Farrar, Jake Burkey; January 1999. A pretty good route for the grade. Rope up 10' left of the last route at a short, pink, left-facing corner. This is just left of an acacia (cat's claw) bush. Bring gear to a #2.5 Friend. Climb the corner, then pull past a bulge at a varnished crack (crux). Continue up the low-angle, left-facing corner to its top. Wander up past several ledges (watch for loose rock) to a communal anchor. Rappel with one rope.

24. **Treacherous Journey** (5.9 R) FA: Todd Swain, Jake Burkey; January 1999. Beware of loose rock at the start of this route. Begin 8' left of the last route at the left end of the ledge system that traverses the cliff. Climb a dihedral for about 20' (#3 Friend in a pocket before you can get gear in the crack), then go up an obvious crack to the end. Continue up the face to merge with *The Route to Mecca*, which is followed to the communal anchor. Carry gear up to a #3 cam. Rappel with one rope. (No topo.)

JABBA THE HUT ROCK

Approach this crag from the first parking spot inside of the picnic area. Walk about 100 yards west across a flat field to the base of the obvious, rocky hillside. Scramble about 150 yards uphill through several small cliff bands to the base of an obvious, rounded crag with two thin, vertical crack systems. This cliff receives morning sun. Routes are described from left to right.

25. **Han Soloing** (5.4) FA: Unknown; probably 1970s. Start 15' left of the prominent finger crack at the left edge of the face (see variation 1 and 2). Climb the easy face to the top. **Variation 1** (5.8): Climb up the left side of the varnish patch at the bottom of the cliff. **Variation 2** (5.10): Start up the right side of the varnish patch at the bottom of the cliff, then angle up and left. (No topo.)

26. **Aliens Have Landed** (5.9+) FA: Unknown; probably 1970s. The best route on this cliff. Begin 40' to the right of the left edge of the crag at an obvious, vertical crack. Climb up about 15' to a small ceiling, then continue up the finger crack to the summit. Descend down the gully to the left.

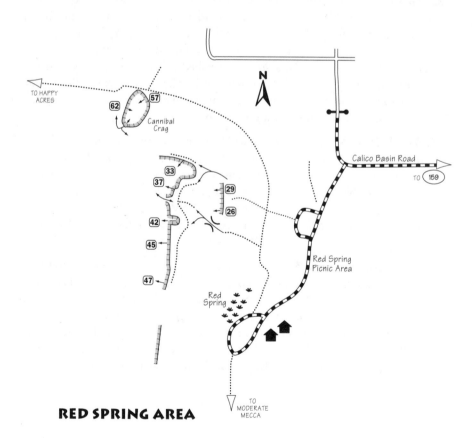

RED SPRING AREA

27. **Carrie Fissure** (5.8) FA: Unknown; probably 1970s. Bring gear to a #2.5 Friend. Start 10' right of the last route at a short, left-facing corner capped by an overhang. Climb past the overhang (crux), then up the crack to the end. Face-climb up to another short crack/flake and the summit.

28. **Obie-One Keone** (5.8 X) FRA: Chris Gill, Keone Kim; September 1998. Rope up 80' right of the last route near the center of the cliff. The climb starts at the base of an obvious vertical crack. Climb up and left on an easy ramp to a ledge 20' up. Climb straight up the varnished face to a short, shallow, left-facing corner. Angle up and right from the top of the corner to finish at the top of the crack system. Poor rock with equally poor protection (but a good route name!).

29. **Shallow Fried Cracken** (5.9 PG) FRA: Larry Ferber, Lesley Tarleton; November 1991. Poor rock and difficult protection make this a challenging route to lead. Same start as the last route at an obvious vertical crack with a hueco on the right side about 10' up. Climb the crack system to the top. Lots of little gear needed (RP's, wires, TCU's).

30. **Gold Bikini and Cinnamon Bun Hairdo** (5.10-) FA: Todd Swain, Patty Gill; November 1998. Begin 30' right of the last route at a left-leaning crack. This is just left of the graffiti "Janet Loves Todd" (I don't know her, really). Difficult initial moves lead to a bolt. Move left into double thin cracks, then up a left-facing corner/groove. You'll need wires, TCUs, and cams up to #3.

RED SPRING ROCK

The next routes are spread out across the hillside above Jabba the Hut Rock. The routes are described from right to left beginning about 75 yards up and right from the right edge of Jabba the Hut Rock. Most of these routes receive morning sun.

31. **Ruta de Roja** (5.7?) FA: Unknown; probably 1970s. Rope up about 80' up and right of the lowest point of the formation at a white flake. This right-facing flake is about 45' uphill of a chimney leading to a gap between the main cliff and a pinnacle. Climb the flake to a ledge 20' up. Traverse right to an obvious, varnished finger crack. Climb the crack past two ledges to the base of a gully (possible belay here). Finish up the gully. Descend off right. (No topo.)

32. **Fontanar de Rojo** (5.8?) FA: Unknown; probably 1970s. Start in the same place as the last route at an obvious, right-facing white flake. Ascend the flake to a ledge 20' up. Continue up a wider section of the crack to another ledge with a bush (possible belay here). A varnished corner above leads to a notch below a bush. Finish up the wide crack/gully past the bush. Descend off to the right. (No topo.)

33. **Hidden Meaning** (5.10 TR) FA: Randal Grandstaff, Danny Rider; late 1980s. Climb the steep varnished face to the left of the last route and right of a chimney formed by a freestanding pinnacle.

From the lowest portion of the formation, scramble up and left on a light-colored slab or climb the hillside to the left of Jabba the Hut Rock to reach the following routes. Routes are described from right (north) to left (south).

34. **Access Fun** (5.10+ TR) FRA: Mark Limage, Dave Melchior; November 1998. Climb the arête and varnished corner just right of *Welcome to N.I.M.B.Y. Town,* using the anchors on that route. (No topo.)

35. **Welcome to N.I.M.B.Y. Town** (5.8 R) FRA: Mark Limage, Dave Melchior; November 1998. This route begins about 40' right of *Classic Corner* at a steep, varnished wall that faces south. It is just left (west) of a chimney formed by a freestanding pinnacle and right of a right-facing corner. Climb up along a small right-facing flake/corner to an anchor. Traditional gear and 4 bolts provide protection. (No topo.)

36. **Flying Pumpkin** (5.9 R) FA: Randal Grandstaff, Danny Rider; circa October 1981. Named for a pumpkin-shaped block on the route. Start just left of *Welcome to N.I.M.B.Y. Town* on the left (south) side of a corner below a steep, varnished face. Climb up and slightly left on the face, then up past an area of white rock to the top.

*37. **Classic Corner** (5.8) FA: Unknown; 1970s. One of the best moderate routes at Red Spring. This route ascends a beautiful varnished dihedral that is located about 100' up and left from the lowest portion of the rock formation. It is clearly visible from the parking lot at Red Spring Picnic Area. Bring small to medium cams and some large stoppers to protect the route. If you get past the first 15', it'll be smooth sailing. After belaying near a prominent bushy ledge, descend the easy gully to the left.

38. **Badger's Buttress** (5.6) FRA: Todd and Donette Swain, Marea and Paul Ross; November 1998. This good, moderate route climbs the rounded arête to the left of *Classic Corner*. The route is named after the Ross' champion Jack Russell Terrier, Blencathra Badger. Badger fathered Wishbone, the dog of television fame. Bring Friends up to #3 and TCUs. Start 50' up and left of the base of *Classic Corner* at a short gully. Traverse out right on ledges, then do an exposed move out onto the arête. A #0 TCU and #2.5 Friend protect the first moves up the arête. Above, you'll find 2 bolts and some gear placements before reaching the top. Descend the easy gully to the left as for *Classic Corner*.

There is an obvious overhanging prow 150' to the left of *Classic Corner*. The right side of the formation has a varnished slab at the base.

39. **Rocky Road** (5.10-?) FA: Unknown. Scramble up between several huge blocks to the base of a huge right-facing corner. The start of the corner is a bit steep and wide, then the angle kicks back a bit and the crack narrows. Bring medium to large cams for protection. Descend the gully to the right.

40. **Love on the Rocks** (5.12+) FA: Mike Tupper 1986. An impressive route. Begin as for the last route on the right side of the overhanging prow below a very steep varnished face. This face is just right of an off-width crack. Climb past 5 bolts and a #1.5 Friend placement to the anchors.

41. **Love Hurts** (5.11) FA: Robert Finlay; circa 1986. Sport climbers beware! Wiggle up the off-width crack just left of *Love on the Rocks,* then continue up the left-facing corner system formed by a huge flake.

42. **Contempt of Court** (5.12-) FA: Mike Tupper 1986. Rope up as for the last three routes on the right side of an overhanging prow. Climb the overhanging arête just left of the prominent off-width crack, angling up and left past a ceiling to anchors. Bring a #1.5 Friend to supplement the 9 bolts on the route.

There are more routes 100 feet up and left of the overhanging prow.

43. **Habeas Corpus** (5.10?) FA: Unknown. There are two crack lines high on the left side of the previously described overhanging prow. Easy fifth-class scrambling is required to reach the base of the routes. This short route ascends the fist/off-width crack.

Calico Basin South

Shit Howdy

Risk Brothers Roof

Riding Hood Wall

The Fox

Cannibal Crag

Payless

To Red Spring

To Happy Acres

To main road

44. **Haberdasher** (5.10+?) FA: Unknown. This route climbs a short, overhanging corner just left of the last route.

45. **Boulder Dash** (5.10d PG) FA: David Parker, Raquel Speers; September 1994. A worthwhile route. Just left (southeast) and below the last two climbs is a bolted seam. Climb a low-angle face past 3 bolts to the base of the seam. Climb up along the seam past 4 more bolts to the anchor.

There is a prominent, varnished buttress with a dogleg seam on the north side located 175' left of the last route.

46. **Black Licorice** (5.9 PG) FRA: Todd and Donette Swain, Marea and Paul Ross; November 1998. Start 40' right of the varnished buttress and just right of a low ceiling. Climb up to a bolt, then continue up a shallow, right-facing corner to another bolt. Go up the varnished wall above, then finish the route by surmounting a bulge (bolt). Rappel from an oak tree on the obvious ledge. Bring some wires and TCUs to supplement the bolts.

47. **Red Vines** (5.8) FRA: Paul and Marea Ross, Donette and Todd Swain; November 1998. Rope up 10' left of the last climb and 30' right of the varnished buttress at a crack system above an oak tree. Jam up a short, left-facing corner (crux), then continue up a low-angle crack to the top. Rappel from an oak tree on the belay ledge. Bring medium to large gear to protect the route.

The next cliffs described are all on the north-facing hillside several hundred yards to the right of the picnic area. For the best approach, follow the well-worn path leading northwest along the base of the hillside from the Red Spring Picnic Area. The crags are described from left to right as viewed from the trail.

CANNIBAL CRAG

This huge boulder is about 300 yards to the northwest of Red Spring Picnic Area and just above the well-defined trail that contours along the hillside. The boulder is in the sun for a good part of the day and harbors some excellent climbs. Climbs are described from left to right starting on the extreme left end of the formation. As you approach the cliff along the trail, you arrive on the southeast face near *Caustic*. The first four climbs described are on the over-hanging south wall and face away from the trail.

48. **Maneater** (5.12a) FA: Dan McQuade; Spring 1992. Start just right of the easy descent route on the back of the formation. Four bolts lead to a cold-shut anchor.

49. **Wonderstuff** (5.12d) FA: Paul Van Betten, Richard Harrison, Sal Mamusia; July 1991. Rope up 8' right of the last route below the leftmost line of 6 bolts. There is an obvious hole in the rock between the second and third bolts. It seems like most people are now avoiding the first bolt by traversing

Cannibal Crag
East Face

in from the left. If you start from the very bottom of the route, bring a #1 or #1.5 TCU to get to the first bolt (or stick-clip). (Not shown.)

50. **New Wave Hookers** (5.12c) FA: Paul Van Betten, Richard Harrison, Sal Mamusia; July 1991. Rope up as for the last route just above a pit. Power past 6 bolts heading right, then up past honeycombed rock.

51. **Fear this Sport** (5.12b) FA: Paul Van Betten, Richard Harrison, Sal Mamusia; July 1991. Start 12' downhill of the last two routes. Angle out right toward the arête, passing 5 bolts.

The next routes are on the eastern side of the formation and are visible from the trail. There may or may not be anchors on top.

52. **Caliban** (5.8+ PG) FA: Sal Mamusia, Paul Van Betten; 1993. A bit contrived near the bottom, but an OK route nonetheless. Begin 20' left of the obvious left-leaning crack at a hole in the rock. Climb the low-angle face past 3 bolts to cold shuts. The 5.8+ (and most obvious) route moves right past the first bolt, then way back left to the second bolt (hence the PG rating).

53. **You Are What You Eat** (5.3) FA: Unknown; early 1990s. Climb the obvious left-leaning crack.

54. **Baseboy** (5.10d PG) FA: Paul Van Betten, Richard Harrison, Sal Mamusia; August 1991. Rope up at the base of a *You Are What You Eat*, the obvious left-leaning crack. Jam up the crack for 20', clip 2 bolts, and move right and up past 1 more bolt. Lower off the fourth bolt or go to the top.

55. **Save the Heart to Eat Later** (5.12a) FA: Sal Mamusia, Paul Van Betten, Shelby Shelton, Richard Harrison; August 1991. Begin 40' left of the arête and just left of some Native American petroglyphs (do not touch!). Angle up left past 3 bolts before lowering off.

56. **Pickled** (5.11c) FA: Paul Van Betten, Sal Mamusia, Richard Harrison; August 1991. Same start as the last route. Shoot up a slabby face to a bolt, then angle up right past 4 bolts. It's common to lower off the last bolt.

*57. **Caustic** (5.11b PG) FA: Paul Van Betten, Dan Krulevski, Shelby Shelton, Richard Harrison, Sal Mamusia; 1991. This route climbs the arête separating the east and west faces directly above the well-worn trail that contours along the hillside. Start to the right of the arête and climb easy rock out left (a bit scary; possible TCU placement before reaching the arête) onto the edge. Or, climb straight up the arête utilizing a bolt down low that was recently added. Most people lower off the fourth bolt.

The next routes (not pictured) are on the varnished west face of the formation. Because the majority of these routes are moderate in nature, this face is quite popular.

58. **Have a Beer with Fear** (5.11a) FA: Richard Harrison , Paul Van Betten; August 1992. Begin at the left edge of the wall. Climb past 4 bolts, either lowering off the last bolt or going to the summit. The height-related crux is by the first bolt.

59. **Fear This** (5.11+) FA: Sal Mamusia, Paul Van Betten; September 1992. Start 8' right of the last route. Follow 3 bolts to cold shuts.

60. **Elbows of Mac and Ronnie** (5.10d) FA: Todd Swain; June 1992. Begin 10' right of the last route at a right-leaning flake/ramp. Climb up and right past 4 bolts to the cold-shut anchor.

61. **What's Eating You?** (5.9+) FA: Todd Swain, Randy and Andy Schenkel; June 1992. Start 10' left of *Elbows of Mac and Ronnie* at a left-facing flake leading to a bulge. Saunter past 3 bolts to the top, where you need TCUs or Friends for the anchor.

62. **A Man in Every Pot** (5.8+) FA: Debbie Brenchley, Todd Swain; June 1992. Begin 8' right of the last route at the left edge of the white boulder leaning against the crag. Scamper up the face past 3 bolts to the top. Bring a couple of TCUs for pro and the anchor.

63. **Mac and Ronnie in Cheese** (5.10-) FA: Todd Swain, Debbie Brenchley; June 1992. Begin 3' right of the right edge of a white boulder leaning against the west face of the cliff. Climb to a bolt about 8' up (added recently), then continue straight up past 2 more bolts to the top. You may want to bring a few TCUs for the climb and the belay. Walk off right (southwest).

64. **Ma and Pa in Kettle** (5.7-) FA: Todd Swain, Randy and Andy Schenkel; June 1992. Start at a varnished, left-facing corner that is at the very right edge of the face and 20' right of a white boulder leaning against the cliff. There are 3 bolts for protection on the face above the corner, and TCUs make up the belay. Walk off right.

65. **Shishka Bob** (5.6 X) FA: Todd Swain; solo, June 1992. Climb the very short, varnished face on the upper right side of the wall.

The next route is located on the hillside above Cannibal Crag.

66. **Shit Howdy** (5.10+) FA: Paul Van Betten, Nick Nordblom; 1986. This unique climb lies above and right of Cannibal Crag on an obvious large boulder/cliff. On the right (northwest) face, climb a crack that arches right, paralleling the slope of the hillside. Bring pro to 3".

The next two routes are near the top of the hillside, midway between *Shit Howdy* and Riding Hood Wall. The cliff is visible from the trail and has a distinctive cleft in the middle. Approach via gullies on either side of the formation.

67. **Risk Brothers Roof** (5.11) FA: Paul Van Betten, Sal Mamusia, Richard Harrison; Winter 1985/86. Start on a flat ledge 20' to the left of the cleft dividing the formation in two. Climb a short dihedral to an obvious hand crack that goes out a flake/roof. Above, angle up and left on lower-angled rock, then up to the top. Scramble down the back (uphill) side of the formation. Bring a good selection of traditional gear and some long slings.

68. **Zona Rosa** (5.9) FA: Robert Finlay; solo, circa 1986. Named for the "Pink Zone" in Panama City where some American servicemen were killed. Rope up about 40' right of *Risk Brothers Roof* and 20' inside the cleft on the left (east) wall. Climb a low-angle, left-facing corner that leads to a prominent, pink off-width crack.

RIDING HOOD WALL

This cliff has several moderate long routes (not illustrated) that are in the shade in the afternoon. Walk northwest along the trail from Red Spring Picnic Area for about 450 yards (about 150 yards past Cannibal Crag). Go straight up the rocky hillside 150 yards to the biggest section of visible rock. Routes are described from left to right. Descend the gully to the right (west) of the formation.

69. **Riding Hood** (5.8) FA: John Williamson, Bob Logerquist; September 1970. Climb the obvious black corner system on the upper east side of the formation. This route doesn't look too great.

70. **Physical Graffiti** (5.6) FA: Jon Martinet, Randal Grandstaff, Scott Gordon; 1973. They aren't too many rolling stones on this one. Start at the northeast corner of the formation at a varnished dihedral with a crack running up and slightly right. **Pitch 1** (5.6): Follow the crack up about 130' to a belay anchor. **Pitch 2** (5.6): Move right into the main crack system of *Over the Hill to Grandmother's House*, then continue up the easy crack and face to the top, about 160'. **Variation:** It appears the low ceiling and varnished face to the right of the normal start has been climbed.

71. **Over the Hill to Grandmother's House** (5.9+) FA: Bob Logerquist, John Williamson; September 1970. Difficult to start no matter which way you go. Begin this journey 50' right of *Physical Graffiti* atop boulders and below a vertical crack running through a roof. A variation exists for the start. **Pitch 1:** Climb a short, smooth face to a roof, then over this at an obvious crack (crux). Follow the crack to a stance 40' up. Rappel off jammed slings or continue. **Variation 1** (5.9+): Climb the right-leaning crack 15' left of the normal start until it intersects with the main crack about 40' up. **Pitch 2:** Head up the easy but awkward crack for about 200' to the top of the buttress.

72. **Lil' Red** (5.9 PG) FA: Unknown. This route starts about 40' right of the last climb at an obvious right-leaning crack. Climb a varnished area (crux) to reach the crack system. Follow the main crack system up and right until it goes around a corner into a gully. **Variation:** Move left from the main crack system into a prominent, vertical crack and follow that to the top.

RANCH HANDS CRAG

From Red Spring Picnic Area, walk about 550 yards northwest along the obvious trail to a low, overhanging buttress. The cliff sits just above the trail and has two tiers. The lower tier faces east; the upper tier, north. The first seven routes are on the lower tier and are in the shade in the afternoon. For all of the routes on this buttress, walk off left (southeast) and bring gear for an anchor on top. (Routes are not shown.)

73. **Payless Cashways** (5.11a) FA: Richard Harrison, Sal Mamusia, Paul Van Betten, Shelby Shelton; June 1991. Shelby dropped Sal's Bosch and they had to go to Payless to buy another! Start at the left (south) edge of the lower tier at the base of a left-leaning crack that leads to a cave. Move up right past a hueco to the first bolt ($1/_2$" with blue hanger), then straight up the face past 4 more bolts. Bring #3.5 and #4 Friends for the belay.

74. **Spanky** (5.11-) FA: Richard Harrison, Sal Mamusia, Paul Van Betten, Shelby Shelton; June 1991. Begin 10' right of the last route and slightly downhill atop a boulder. A difficult boulder problem to a pocket leads to face climbing past 4 bolts. Finish up a short crack. Bring #3.5 and #4 Friends for the belay.

75. **Mexican Secret Agent Man** (5.11b) FA: Paul Van Betten, Richard Harrison; July 1991. Start 8' right of the last route off the same boulder. Climb past 4 bolts, trending slightly right. Many people lower off the last bolt or bring #3.5 and #4 Friends for the belay.

76. **Swilderness Experience** (5.11c) FA: Paul Van Betten, Richard Harrison, Shelby Shelton; July 1991. Rope up 10' right of the last two routes, near the bottom of the boulder. Traverse out right along flakes past 1 bolt, then go up past 4 more bolts to the top.

77. **Swilderness Permit** (5.12c) FA: Sal Mamusia, Paul Van Betten, Richard Harrison; July 1991. Begin 20' downhill from the last route at very overhanging, brown rock. Power past a bunch of moonscoops to lower-angle rock. There are 7 bolts. Most folks lower from the last one.

78. **Roman Meal** (5.11 TR) FA: Todd Swain; December 1994. This loose face 15' right of *Swilderness Permit* has been climbed.

79. **Roman Hands** (5.4 X) FA: Unknown; 1991. Good easy climbing, but unfortuately, there's no protection. Start 35' right of the last route at the

base of a lower-angle face leading to an overhanging wall. Climb the face to a ledge, then move left and up a crack system to the top.

The next three routes are on the upper tier, which is best approached by climbing *Roman Hands* to the base of the overhanging wall. These routes are in the shade all day.

80. **Jack Officers** (5.12c) FA: Paul Van Betten, Richard Harrison, Sal Mamusia; April 1991.

Angle up left from the center of the wall past 3 bolts.

81. **Ranch Hands** (5.12c) FA: Richard Harrison, Paul Van Betten, Bob Conz, Sal Mamusia; January 1991. Angle up and/or angle slightly up right from the center of the wall past 4 bolts to a 2-bolt rap station.

82. **Blood Stains** (5.10 R/X) FA: Richard Harrison, Sal Mamusia, Paul Van Betten; September 1990. Dangerously loose. If the block midway up comes off, there could be bloodstains! Same start as the last two routes on the ledges. Traverse out right to a loose crack and follow this up to an overhang formed by a loose block. Pull the ceiling, then go up the steep face past 1 bolt to another ceiling. Swing over this, then go left to the rappel anchor on *Ranch Hands*.

To approach the next route, walk about 100 yards right of the last routes. About 250 yards up the hillside is a striking crack in a right-facing corner. This climb is in the shade all day. Note: Apparently there is a bolted route just left of this next route (up the narrow rib), but no more is known.

*83. **The Fox** (5.10+) FA: Unknown; early 1970s. FFA: Unknown; mid-1970s. One of the finest pitches at Red Rocks. Bring a full set of camming devices with extra of the biggest sizes. Climb the widening crack in a right-facing corner for 150'. Descend to the left (east) down the rocky slope.

The next two routes are to the right of the top of *The Fox*. Approach this north-facing formation via a gully to the right of *The Fox*.

84. **Unknown** (5.11b) FA: Unknown; after 1995. This good-looking route follows a vertical seam up the center of the formation. Follow 5 bolts to a chain anchor. You may want to stick-clip the first bolt.

85. **Unknown** (5.11?) FA: Unknown; after 1995. Start 6' right of the last route. Climb past 5 bolts to a chain anchor.

DICKIES CLIFF

This short formation is about 200 yards right (west) of Ranch Hands Crag and 100 yards right (west) of *The Fox*. The cliff faces north and is at the level of the desert floor. Approach time from the picnic area is about 15 minutes. Routes are described from left to right.

DICKIES CLIFF
AND GNAT MAN CRAG

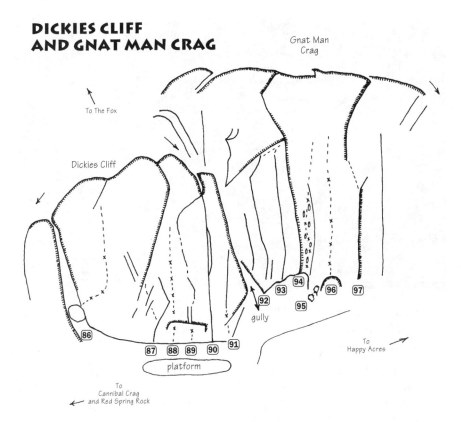

86. **Gigantor** (5.10) FA: Richard Harrison, Paul Van Betten, Wendell Broussard, Mike Forkash; July 1991. Start atop a boulder in a gully at the left edge of the crag. Move out right past 2 bolts (crux), then up past another bolt and a couple of small TCU placements to the summit. You will need medium Friends for the belay. Walk off either side.

87. **Guys and Ghouls** (5.6) FA: Donette and Todd Swain, George and Catriona Reid; Halloween 1994. Begin 18' right of *Gigantor* at the most obvious chimney/crack system in the center of the cliff. Climb disjointed cracks up and left to an easy, right-leaning chimney.

88. **Boobytrap** (5.12c PG) FA: Sal Mamusia, Paul Van Betten; July 1991. The first ascent party says no stick-clipping the first bolt! Rope up 8' right of the obvious crack system (*Guys and Ghouls*). After a very hard start, climb past 5 bolts to the summit. Some folks lower from the top bolt, others walk (or crawl) off either side.

89. **Stukas over Disneyland** (5.12-) FA: Paul Van Betten, Richard Harrison; July 1991. A wild ride! Begin 15' right of the last route at a section of

smooth rock below an 18-inch ceiling that is 15' up. Power past 2 bolts and the ceiling to the obvious, varnished, left-leaning cracks (5.10). Bring wires and TCUs.

90. **Lancaster Levels Luxor** (5.9+) FA: George Reid, Todd and Donette Swain; October 1994. Headline news. Start 15' right of *Stukas over Disneyland* below a prominent crack system. Scramble up to a bulge, then pull this (crux) into the main crack system and follow it to the top.

91. **Monster Island** (5.11) FA: Paul Van Betten, Sal Mamusia; July 1991. This route climbs a thin, vertical crack 5' right of the last route near the right edge of the cliff. Gear (up to #2.5 Friend) and 3 bolts are used for protection.

GNAT MAN CRAG

This escarpment is located 100 feet up and right of Dickies Cliff and is separated by a gully forming one of the descent routes for Dickies Cliff. The crag was named after a climber who supposedly looked like a gnat! The routes are described from left to right.

92. **P-Coat Junction** (5.9) FA: Todd and Donette Swain; December 1994. Climb the crack system 10' left of *P-Coat Sleeve* and just above the approach gully. Finish up a low-angle, right-facing corner as for *P-Coat Sleeve*. Bring gear up to 4".

93. **P-Coat Sleeve** (5.10-) FA: Paul Van Betten, Sal Mamusia; November 1991. An obvious finger crack that is 8' left of an easy-looking dihedral with a crack in the back. The start of this route is varnished and looks appealing.

The upper portion is a bit low-angle and on white rock. Climb the crack, eventually joining *Ghouls Just Wanna Have Fun* to the top. You need medium Friends for the belay. Scramble off right (west).

94. **Ghouls Just Wanna Have Fun** (5.7) FA: Donette Swain, Catriona Reid; Halloween 1994. Climb the central dihedral to the summit. Carry gear up to a #3.5 Friend. Scamper off right.

*95. **Gnat Man on Ranch Hands** (5.11) FA: Paul Van Betten, Sal Mamusia; November 1991. Rope up just right of the central dihedral at a series of neat-looking vertical huecos. Power past 5 bolts to easy slabs and the top. You will need medium Friends for the belay or you can lower off the fifth bolt. Bring a small TCU for the flake between the first and second bolt.

*96. **Knock the Bottom out of It** (5.10- PG13) FA: Paul Van Betten, Sal Mamusia; November 1991. Good climbing, but a bit scary getting to the first bolt. Begin 10' right of *Gnat Man* below a varnished face. Climb past 4 bolts to lower-angled rock (TCU and Friend placements) and the summit. Bring medium Friends for the belay, then walk off right.

*97. **Bottoms up** (5.7) FA: George and Catriona Reid, Todd and Donette Swain; October 1994. A good, moderate route. Climb the left-facing corner 10' right of the last route. Exit left at the top of the corner, then follow a lower-angle, right-facing flake/corner to the top. Use medium Friends for the belay, then scramble off right (west).

Across the canyon to the north of Dickies Cliff is a sunny, low-angle red formation with an obvious, left-leaning overlap/ceiling.

98. **Cow Lick Co. Crag** (5.7) FA: Todd and Donette Swain, Mike Dimitri; November 1993. A sunny, moderate slab route. Follow 4 bolts to a cold-shut anchor, passing the lower right edge of the overlap.

HAPPY ACRES

This obvious cliff sits on the left side of the canyon and gets sun in the morning. Other routes have been done here, but information was lacking at press time. The following routes (not shown) are located on the black, slabby face up and right from Gnat Man Crag.

99. **The Life Chuckle** (5.8?) FA: Nick Nordblom, Paul Van Betten; 1984. This is a traditional route with 1 bolt somewhere on the right side of the main, low-angle black face.

100. **Spontaneous Enjoyment** (5.8?) FA: Nick Nordblom, Paul Van Betten; 1984. A traditional route with 2 bolts somewhere on the right-hand portion of the cliff. This route is supposed to be up and right from the last route, presumably to the right of a huge, right-facing corner.

The next routes are located near the right edge of the cliff. Below this section of cliff are several pine trees. These trees are visible from Gnat Man Crag and are about 175 yards below the saddle leading to Ethics Wall and the Second Pullout.

101. **Mothers of Invention** (5.10c) FA: Randy Marsh, Pier Locatelli; 1998. Start about 30' left of an obvious dihedral on a ledge that is about 50' above the gully bottom. There is a hole the size of a beach ball at the start of the route. Climb the black face past 7 bolts with black hangers to an anchor on the skyline.

102. **Mom and Apple Pie** (5.9) FA: Randy Marsh, Pier Locatelli; 1998. Begin 10' right and downhill of the last route. Follow 8 bolts with black hangers up the face to an anchor.

103. **Mother's Day** (5.9-) FA: Randal Grandstaff, Danny Rider; circa 1988. This route was originally led without the bolt. Rope up just right of the last route and below an obvious left-facing corner that doesn't quite reach the ground. Face-climb to the corner, then follow it to the top. Walk off right.

104. **Happy Acres** (5.7 PG) FA: Unknown. Start 40' right of the last climb at the base of a right-facing chimney. There is a pine tree at the base of the climb. Ascend the varnished, right-facing chimney to an obvious bush about 50' up. Climb the varnished dihedral directly above the bush (5.7) to the top. **Variation** (5.10): The prominent hand crack above the finish of the route has been toproped.

105. **The Dividing Line** (5.11+) FA: Shelby Shelton, Danny Rider; circa 1994. Up-canyon of *Happy Acres* is a subsidiary gully that goes up and left (southeast) toward the First Pullout. At the corner of this gully and the main canyon (leading to the Second Pullout) is an overhanging buttress. This route ascends the overhanging buttress along a series of neat-looking pockets and huecos. For some unknown reason, the bolts had been removed as of press time.

CALICO BASIN NORTH/GATEWAY CANYON

Numerous formations are described on the north side of Calico Basin: The obvious south-facing cliffs are called Kraft Crags, and the large drainage on the back (north) side of Kraft Crags is called Gateway Canyon. Due to access issues, I have decided to leave out the crags that overlook private property (Kraft Rocks). Climbers should be considerate and unobtrusive when using these areas!

There are several acceptable ways to access this portion of Calico Basin. The overriding concern is to minimize your impact on the environment and the

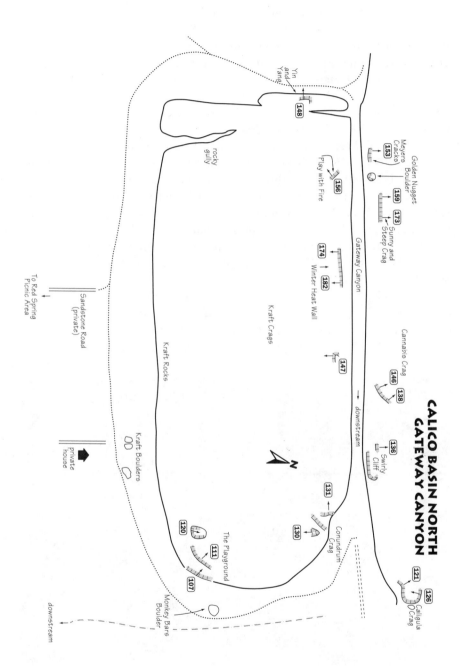

CALICO BASIN NORTH
GATEWAY CANYON

residents of Calico Basin. Choose one of the two following options, depending on your destination. See the maps of Calico Basin for more details.

1) Turn off West Charleston (Nevada 159) onto Calico Basin Road and follow it for about 0.5 mile to a point just past the large wash. Park on the side of the road and hike north for about 0.75 mile to the eastern end of Kraft Crags and the mouth of Gateway Canyon. Note: The BLM is considering building a public parking lot in this area to serve as a trailhead and constructing a formal trail. This approach is best for The Playground, Caligula Crag, Conundrum Crag, Swirly Cliff, and Cannabis Crag.

2) Turn off West Charleston (Nevada 159) onto Calico Basin Road and follow it for 1.2 miles to a T-intersection. Turn left into Red Spring Picnic Area and park. Follow the trail northwest from the picnic area for about 250 yards, then drop down onto the road heading toward the north side of the basin (Sandstone Road). Walk along this until it ends near the base of the rocky hillside (0.4 mile). From here, a well-worn trail meanders along the base of the mountain in both directions. It takes about 10 minutes to walk to this junction from Red Spring Picnic Area. To reach Yin and Yang, Meyers Cracks, Sunny and Steep Crag and Winter Heat, this approach is best.

It is best to follow the trail to the left (west) from the end of Sandstone Road. The trail (an old roadbed) goes up and over a vegetated saddle to the left of the leftmost rocks on the mountain and enters Gateway Canyon about 200 yards upstream of Sunny and Steep Crag (see map).

THE PLAYGROUND

The next routes (none of which is shown) are located at the right (east) end of Kraft Crags and face south (towards Las Vegas). The routes are sunny and take about 20 minutes to approach from Red Spring Picnic Area or the wash on Calico Road. From the end of Sandstone Road, follow the trail to the right (east) past the Kraft Boulders. The climbs are located on three separate tiers, all of which are southwest (left) and uphill of the Monkey Bars Boulder (the last prominent boulder as you turn the corner into Gateway Canyon). Climbs are described from right to left on each level, beginning closest to the trail and moving uphill.

LOWER TIER

106. **Show Burro** (5.10+ PG) FA: Shelby Shelton, Paul Van Betten; December 1993. Rope up about 150 yards southwest of Monkey Bars Boulder and 75 yards directly above the trail. This is a muddy-looking cliff with an obvious hand crack at the base. Climb the low-angle hand crack to its top, then move right around a nose to a bolt. Continue past 3 more bolts to a chain anchor. Bring several Friends up to #2.5.

107. **Lick It** (5.11) FA: Danny Rider, Luis Saca; December 1993. Same start as the last route, then climb the hand crack to its top. Go up and left along an easy crack to the end. Climb the steeper face above past 3 bolts to a chain anchor located on a bulge. Carry TCUs and Friends up to #2.5.

MIDDLE TIER

108. **The Figurine** (5.10-) FA: Dave Kruleski, Danny Rider; circa 1995. Above Monkey Bars Boulder is a curving crack that faces east. This is up and right of the last routes. The crack runs from off-width to hand-size and has a distinctive flake shaped like a figurine. Climb the crack to the top.

109. **Repo Man** (5.11a PG13) FA: Danny Rider, Dave Kruleski; January 1994. A good route. Begin directly above the last two routes at the base of a chimney filled with blocks. Move out left and up past 2 bolts (a bit dicey), then up the steeper face above past 3 more bolts to open cold shuts.

110. **Messie Nessie** (5.11d) FA: Danny Rider, Luis Saca; January 1994. Rope up 20' to the left and around a corner from the last route at a steep, pink section of rock with pockets. Climb past about 7 bolts to the anchor.

111. **Dirty Little Girl** (5.10d) FA: Danny Rider, Luis Saca; January 1994. Another good route. Start 8' left of the last climb at an arête with honeycombed rock. Climb up and left along the arête on big holds, then up the face past a total of 6 bolts to 2 open cold shuts.

112. **Gold-Plated Garlic Press** (5.11+) FA: Paul Van Betten, Shelby Shelton; December 1993. Rope up 8' left and around the arête from the last route at a short, left-leaning crack. This is just right of an obvious fist crack in a sentry box. Follow 4 bolts up the overhanging left side of the arête to an easier face and the top. You may want to bring wires and TCUs for the upper section.

113. **Electric Orange Peeler** (5.10) FRA: Todd Swain, Mary Hinson; October 1995. Climb the obvious fist crack in the center of the tier. Carry gear up to a #4 Camalot. Walk off left (west), then down an easy gully.

114. **Practice Crack** (5.9+) FA: Unknown; circa 1980s. Harder (and better) than it first appears. Climb the prominent dogleg crack system about 50' left of the last routes. Bring gear up to a #4 Friend. Scramble down the gully to the left of the summit boulder.

UPPER TIER

115. **Powder Puff** (5.10?) FA: Unknown; before October 1995. The next six routes are located on a very prominent (and large) boulder on the right shoulder of Kraft Crags. This route climbs an obvious wide dogleg crack at the right edge of the boulder, then follows varnished plates on an arête to the summit.

116. **Headmaster Ritual** (5.11c) FA: Paul Van Betten, Luis Saca; January 1994. Begin 20' left of the last climb behind a boulder at the base of the cliff. Climb up the center of the wall past 4 bolts to chains.

117. **Climb and Punishment** (5.12b) FA: Richard Harrison, Michelle Locatelli; January 1994. Rope up 10' left of the last route and 6' left of the prow. Angle up and left past 3 bolts toward the arête, then go up and right past 2 more bolts to a chain anchor.

118. **Project** A bolt is located at the base of the prow separating the southeast and southwest walls.

119. **Country Bumpkin** (5.11a) FA: Danny Rider, Dan Kruleski; January 1994. A good route, but watch out for breaking edges! Climb the center of the southwest face past 4 bolts to a chain anchor. The lower third of the route is on solid varnish; the upper section, on white rock with varnish patches.

*120. **City Slickers** (5.11-) FA (TR): Randy Marsh, Wendell Broussard; circa 1990. FA (lead): Unknown. An excellent climb. Carry TCUs and Friends to #2.5, plus a #4. Start in the chimney at the left edge of the face. Move out right under a ceiling to a vertical crack. Follow this crack up past a bolt and gear placements to a chain anchor.

CALIGULA CRAG

A sunny cliff located about 450 yards to the northeast of Monkey Bars Boulder (a huge, chalk-covered boulder with a cave on the southern side). This crag is on the hillside across the mouth of Gateway Canyon from the boulder and sits just above a dirt road. Routes are described from left to right (west to east).

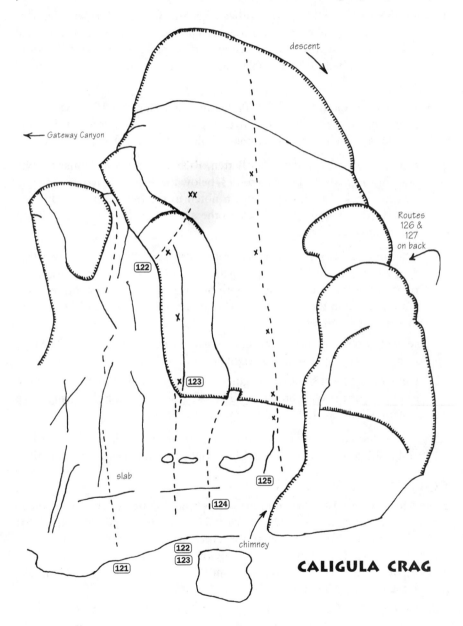

121. **Ms. October, 1995** (5.9) FA Todd Swain, Mary Hinson; October 1995. Rope up near the left side of the crag, just left of an acacia bush. Climb deceptive vertical cracks to a stance below a steep bulge. Pull the bulge along left-slanting cracks, then finish up a chimney. Bring gear up to a #3 Friend.

122. **Penthouse Pet** (5.11-) FA: Paul Van Betten, Richard Harrison; January 1990. Start at the center of a lower-angle face at the rightmost vertical seams. Follow seams and the face to a short, pink, overhanging dihedral. Climb the dihedral, then angle right past a bolt to the obvious rappel station.

123. **Disguise the Limit** (5.11d) FA: Paul Van Betten; January 1990. Same start as *Penthouse Pet*. Climb the lower-angled face to an overhang. Pull the overhang and climb the arête past 3 bolts to the rappel anchor.

124. **Caligula** (5.12-) FA: Paul Van Betten, Richard Harrison; January 1990. Start just right of the last two routes, below the center of an overhang and vertical crack. Climb the face to a notch in the overhang, pull this (#3 Friend), then climb a thin crack to the anchor for *Penthouse Pet*. Bring multiple pieces from 3/4" to 1".

125. **Guccione** (5.11) FA: Richard Harrison, Paul Van Betten; January 1990. This route is named for the publisher of *Penthouse* magazine. Begin 15' right of the last route, at the mouth of an obvious chimney formed by a pinnacle. Climb the left face of the chimney past 5 bolts and gear placements to the summit.

The next two routes are on the short north face of the formation. The best approach is to walk up around the right side of the cliff.

126. **Hefner** (5.7) FA: Unknown. Begin at the upper end of the chimney on the right side of the cliff. Step left off stacked blocks to a right-facing flake system. Climb the flake and face above to the top.

127. **Bonus Pullout Section** (5.6) FA: Unknown. Start 8' right of the last route and just left of the cliff's edge. Climb right-facing flakes to the summit.

CONUNDRUM CRAG

From Monkey Bars Boulder, continue on the trail up into Gateway Canyon to a point where the trail drops into the wash. Head left (south) directly uphill for about 150 yards, aiming for a small formation with a distinctive, curving ceiling near the base. The following climbs are on two small crags that face east. A gully separates the two formations. From the mouth of the canyon, the approach takes about 10 minutes.

128. **Drilling Miss Daisy** (5.11a) FA: Steve "Bucky" Bullock, 1992. Excellent climbing and a clever route name. The first two routes are on a pinkish,

Conundrum Crag

overhanging face that slants uphill. Start on a ledge 25' up a gully at a vertical seam. Muscle past 4 bolts on big holds to chains. You may wish to stick clip the first bolt or use TCUs for supplemental protection.

129. Satan in a Can (5.12d PG) FA: Jonathan Knight, 1992. Begin 20' farther up the gully at a brown, vertical seam. Difficult climbing past 3 bolts leads to a chain anchor. You may want to bring wires or TCUs to protect the section between the second and third bolts.

130. Arrowhead Arête (5.11d) FA: Leo Henson; January 1994. Climb the short, overhanging arête that is 80' left of the last two routes. There are about 4 bolts on the route and a chain anchor.

The next routes are about 50 yards to the right, on a southeast-facing crag. This cliff has an angular, overhanging wall on the downhill side.

131. Family Affair (5.8) FA: Danny Rider and family; Fall 1998. Start at the right edge of the southeast face, near the overhanging, downhill side of the formation. Climb just left of a rounded arête past 7 bolts to a cold-shut anchor.

132. Family Circus (5.9) FA: The Rider Family; Fall 1998. Begin 15' uphill from the last route behind some scrub oak bushes. Follow 5 bolts up the face to lower-angle climbing and the top.

133. Project (5.10-?) FA: Presumably the Riders; 1999. Another partial route is located 10' further uphill at the base of a chimney. At press time, there was 1 bolt in dark varnish.

SWIRLY CLIFF

This sunny cliff sits on the right (north) side of the drainage and is visible from the mouth of Gateway Canyon. It is about 200 yards up-canyon from the Conundrum Crag. As the name implies, the cliff looks like taffy or some type of ice cream. The area in front of the cliff is flat and grassy. Numerous routes have supposedly been done, but information is lacking.

134. **Old School** (5.11-) FA: Paul Van Betten, Danny Rider; March 1998. Climb the most obvious crack system, which goes over a small roof.

The following routes are located on the extreme upper left end of the formation.

135. **Saltwater Taffy** (5.11?) FA: Dave Burns; circa 1998. Start just right of a distinctive, curving crack/chimney at the left edge of the formation. Follow 5 bolts up a rib to a chain anchor.

136. **Turkish Taffy** (5.11?) FA: Dave Burns; circa 1998. Begin under a triangular ceiling 8' up and right of the last route. Climb past 5 bolts to a chain anchor.

137. **Chocolate Swirl** (5.11?) FA: Dave Burns; circa 1998. Gear up 15' right of the last route at the right edge of a triangular ceiling. Power past 6 bolts to the chains.

CANNABIS CRAG

This sunny escarpment sits on the right (north) side of the drainage, about 15 minutes upstream from Monkey Bars Boulder and the mouth of Gateway Canyon. It is about 250 yards upstream of Swirly Cliff and sits about 50 yards above the drainage floor. The cliff is partially hidden by a lump of rock in front of it. The easiest approach is to ascend a boulderfield comprised of limestone boulders from a point about 100 yards downstream of the right end of the crag. Routes are described from right to left.

138. **Smokin'** (5.12b) FA: Unknown; 1993. Start just right of an acacia bush on a ledge about 20' up. Climb past 4 silver bolts to open cold shuts. This route has a distinctive scar just down and right of the anchor where a huge flake fell off (almost killing Paul Van Betten!).

139. **One Man's Kokopelli Is another Man's Side Show Bob** (5.12d) FA: Paul Van Betten, Richard Harrison, Michelle Locatelli; November 1993. If you've seen the Simpsons and know anything about Anasazi rock art, this name will make sense! Begin 25' to the left (downhill) at a prominent, left-leaning thin crack. Climb the crack past 3 bolts, then up the steep face past 3 more bolts to the anchor.

140. **Freak Brothers** (5.13a) FA: Paul Van Betten, Shelby Shelton; October 1994. Rope up 10' down and left of the last climb. Climb a short slab to a ledge (bolt), then up the steep wall past 6 more bolts to cold shuts.

141. **KGB** (5.12a) FA: Dan McQuade, Jim Greg; Spring 1993. Same start as *Freak Brothers* but climb up and left past 2 bolts to a ledge. Continue up and slightly left past 4 more bolts to an anchor.

142. **Cannabis** (5.12a) FA: Dan McQuade, Jim Greg; Spring 1993. Start 40' down and left at the left edge of a prominent black waterstreak. Climb the left edge of the waterstreak past 5 black bolts to cold shuts halfway up the cliff. There is 1 bolt in the waterstreak to the right, but the route hasn't been completed yet.

143. **Synapse Collapse** (5.11d) FA: Dan McQuade, Jim Greg; Spring 1993. Begin just left of the last route and climb up and left past 4 silver bolts to another set of cold shuts.

CANNABIS CRAG

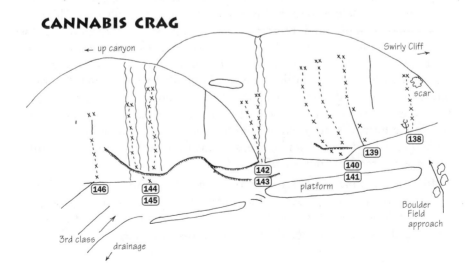

144. **The Fiend** (5.12c) FA: Dan McQuade, Jim Greg; Spring 1993. Rope up 45' to the left of the last two routes at the next black water streak. There is a belay bolt at the base. Six light-colored bolts lead up the water streak to an anchor.

145. **Cavity Search** (5.12d) FA: Dan McQuade, Jim Greg; Spring 1993. Same start as the last route. Move left and climb the black water streak past 6 bolts to an anchor.

146. **The Felon** (5.11c) FA: Dan McQuade, Jim Greg; Spring 1993. Begin 25' left of the last route at a point where the ledge begins to drop toward the wash. Climb past 4 black bolts to the anchor.

The next route is located on the left (south) side of the canyon about 100 yards upstream of Cannabis Crag.

147. **Horizontal Departure** (5.10-) FA: Paul Van Betten, Randy Marsh, Wendell Broussard; circa 1984. About 100 yards upstream of Cannabis Crag the drainage bends around a rock outcrop. Halfway up the left side of the canyon is a prominent dihedral with a protruding rib of rock on the right side. Just right of this is a small pinnacle on the skyline. The route climbs the prominent dihedral (5.9), then jams and underclings left around a roof (crux). Large gear is needed to protect the route.

The next crags are located in the upper reaches of Gateway Canyon and are best approached from Red Spring Picnic Area via the saddle to the west (left) of Kraft Crags. These crags are described as they are encountered heading downstream from the Yin and Yang saddle at the west end of Kraft Crags.

YIN AND YANG

Approach from Red Spring Picnic Area by hiking to the end of Sandstone Road (20 minutes). Go left (west) along the trail at the base of Kraft Crags. This trail, which follows an old road for part of its length, passes a rocky gully near the left edge of the hill, then ascends a vegetated slope to a saddle overlooking the upper portion of Gateway Canyon (15 minutes). The trail up the vegetated slope is clearly visible from the vicinity of Cannibal Crag. About 100 yards down from the saddle on the Gateway Canyon (north) side is a squat, lone formation on the right (east) side of the trail. Walk around the uphill (saddle) side of the formation to reach the climbs. The routes are described from left (uphill) to right (downhill) and face east (away from the trail) toward a brushy drainage and the main portion of Kraft Crags.

*148. **Yin and Yang** (5.11) FA: Unknown; circa 1980. An area classic. This is the right-curving crack in the center of a smooth wall. Bring a good selection of small to medium cams. Small gear will be needed for the anchors unless you go about 20' back from the edge.

Chris Gill and Donette Swain on *Atman* (5.10).

149. **Zoroaster** (5.8 X) FA: Unknown; circa 1980. Classic sandstone chimneying (if you're into that sort of thing). Climb the obvious chimney that forms a left-facing corner in the center of the cliff. Easily toproped.

*150. **Atman** (5.10) FA: Unknown; circa 1980. A classic hand crack. Jam up the slightly right-leaning hand crack 8' right of the chimney. Bring large cams for the anchor.

MEYERS CRACKS

The next two routes are across Gateway Canyon from Yin and Yang. Go about 200 yards up a sandstone gully on the north side of Gateway Canyon to reach these northeast-facing climbs. The routes are supposed to be good quality.

151. **Meyers Crack** (5.10) FA: Danny Meyers; circa 1992. Climb the left crack, which is about hand-size.

152. **Conz Crack** (5.11-) FA: Bob Conz; circa 1992. Climb the right-hand crack, which is flaring. Bring gear up to a #3 Camalot.

The next route is located on a south-facing formation across Gateway Canyon from the saddle. It is 75 yards to the left (up canyon) of the Golden Nugget Boulder. The formation is tall and yellow with prominent, parallel crack systems in the center.

153. **Chunder Bolt** (5.12a) FA: Shelby Shelton, Paul Van Betten, Danny Rider, Richard Harrison, Michelle Locatelli; January 1994. Climb the right-hand, vertical crack system past 9 bolts to a chain anchor.

The next two routes are on Gold Nugget Boulder, a freestanding boulder on the north side of Gateway Canyon. The boulder faces the drainage (south) and is about 75 yards downstream (east) of the saddle. It is about 150 yards to the left (upstream) of the main Sunny and Steep Crag.

154. **Edward Silverhands** (5.10a) FA: Todd and Donette Swain; April 1994. This sunny 3-bolt route faces the drainage and follows disjointed cracks.

155. **Golden Nugget** (5.11d) FA: Chris and Ward Smith; February 1994. This route is located 20' to the right (east) of the last route and climbs a steep face past 4 bolts to an anchor.

The next two routes are across the main drainage from Golden Nugget Boulder and are in the shade most of the day. Zigzag up a gully for about 120 yards to an overhanging pillar on the west (right) side of the gully.

156. **Play with Fire** (5.11c PG13) FA: Lynn Lee; circa 1996. Watch out or you may be burned. Start 6' left of a large chimney that forms a small pillar. Climb the steep face on the main, overhanging pillar past 4 bolts to an anchor.

157. **Judgment Day** (5.12a PG) FA: Lynn Lee; circa 1996. Beware, or you may be terminated. Begin 5' left and uphill of the last route at a thin, left-facing flake. Climb the left prow of the pillar past 4 bolts to an anchor.

SUNNY AND STEEP CRAG

This sport crag became instantly popular. As the name implies, the crag is in the sun most of the day, although it's steep enough to be shady on summer mornings when the sun is higher in the sky. Approach from Red Spring Picnic Area by hiking to the end of Sandstone Road (20 minutes). Go left (west) along the trail at the base of Kraft Crags. This trail, which follows an old road for part of its length, passes a rocky gully near the left edge of the hill, then ascends a vegetated slope to a saddle overlooking the upper portion of Gateway Canyon (15 minutes). Follow the trail down into Gateway Canyon from the saddle (300 yards). Sunny and Steep Crag is about 200 yards downstream of the saddle, on the left (north) side of the drainage. It faces south (toward the drainage) and is partially hidden by a large flat terrace that lies below it. Routes are described from left to right (upstream to downstream).

158. **Claimjumper's Special** (5.10d) FA: The Smith Brothers, Leslie Smith, Paula King; February 1994. The leftmost route on the crag. There are 5 bolts and the route climbs just right of a chimney.

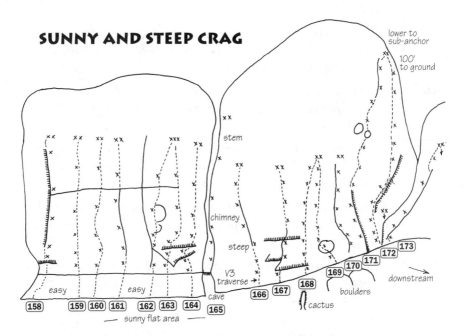

159. **Black Happy** (5.11d) FA: The Brothers Smith; February 1994. Follow 5 bolts that are 5' right of a chimney and 5' left of *Blackened.*

160. **Blackened** (5.11d) FA: Ward Smith; February 1994. Climb past 5 bolts beginning 10' right of an ugly chimney and 7' left of *Scorpions.*

161. **Scorpions** (5.11b) FA: Chris and Ward Smith, Leslie Smith, Paula King; February 1994. Follow overhanging huecos along the left-hand of two cracks past 5 bolts.

162. **Turtle Wax** (5.11b) FA: Dave Quinn, the Guys from Massachusetts; February 1994. A 5-bolt climb right of the last route. Although it's possible to climb the right-hand crack, it's easier to climb the huge huecos farther right. This route shares the same anchor as *Sunny and Steep.*

163. **Sunny and Steep** (5.12a) FA: Ward Smith, Dave Quinn; February 1994. Begin 7' left of *Tour de Pump* and follow 6 bolts to a shared 3-bolt anchor.

164. **Tour de Pump** (5.12a) FA: Ward Smith; February 1994. Rope up 20' left of the central chimney and climb past 6 bolts to the anchor.

165. **The Sport Chimney** (5.8) FA: The New England Dudes plus Steve Wood; February 1994. Face climb, wiggle, and stem up the obvious varnished chimney past 5 bolts.

*166. **Gimme Back My Bullets** (5.12a) FA: The Brothers from New England; February 1994. The excellent, 6-bolt route is 8' right of the obvious chimney that splits the formation.

167. **Steep Thrills** (5.12a) FA: Ward Smith; February 1994. Another over-hung route that is 16' right of a chimney and 10' left of *Turbo Dog.* Six bolts lead to a rest at the anchor.

168. **Turbo Dog** (5.12b) FA: Ward Smith; February 1994. A steep route that starts 8' left of *Peak Performance* and behind a boulder. If you can, climb past 7 bolts to the same anchor as *Peak Performance.*

169. **Peak Performance** (5.11d) FA: Chris and Ward Smith, Dave Quinn; February 1994. Rope up 8' right of the last route. Clip 7 bolts in route to a shared anchor.

170. **Solar Flare** (5.11d) FA: Dave Quinn, Ward and Chris Smith; February 1994. Begin 10' up and right of the last route at the base of a steep, left-leaning seam. Stick-clip the first bolt, then follow 5 more bolts to the anchor.

171. **Mr. Choad's Wild Ride** (5.11b) FA: Ward Smith, Steve Wood; February 1994. Start 10' right of the last route and 8' left of a chimney at a left-facing corner. Follow 10 bolts to the anchor. Either rappel 100' to the

ground with two ropes, or use one rope to lower to an intermediate anchor and then to the ground.

172. **Cirque du Soleil** (5.11b) FA: Paula King, Ward Smith, Steve Wood; February 1994. Named for the famous circus troupe that originated in Montreal and now performs regularly in Las Vegas. Begin right of the last route on the left side of a chimney. Stem up a few moves then follow a total of 10 bolts to the anchor. Either rappel 100' to the ground with two ropes, or use one rope to lower to an intermediate anchor and then to the ground.

173. **Working for Peanuts** (5.9 PG) FA: Ward and Chris Smith, Dave Quinn; February 1994. The Smith brothers have been putting up new routes in New England since the mid-1970s, and they currently live in Massachusetts. This route follows cracks and 5 bolts along a low-angle arête that is separated from the main formation by a chimney. Make sure you have an attentive belayer on the first few moves.

WINTER HEAT WALL

This excellent cliff is in the shade most of the day and features traditional routes. Approach from Red Spring Picnic Area by hiking to the end of Sandstone Road (20 minutes). Go left (west) along the trail at the base of Kraft Crags. This trail, which follows an old road for part of its length, passes a rocky gully near the left edge of the hill, then ascends a vegetated slope to a saddle overlooking the upper portion of Gateway Canyon (15 minutes). Follow the trail down into Gateway Canyon (300 yards), then go downstream about 230 yards. This formation is more cliff-like than most in the canyon and is characterized by dark desert varnish. The crag is divided into three sections by chimney/crack systems. Hike about 75 yards uphill from the streambed along one of two trails to reach the base of the formation. One approach trail contours across the hillside from a point in front of the Sunny and Steep Crag; the other starts directly below the wall. Please do not create additional social trails! Routes are described from right to left (upstream to downstream).

174. **Hole in the Pants** (5.7 PG) FRA: Gary Savage, Jake Burkey; June 1998. A nice line with a scary crux. This obvious line ascends the center of the rightmost section of Winter Heat Wall. Bring wires and cams up to about #3. **Pitch 1** (5.3): Either follow a crack straight up, or start to the right of the crack and climb up to a small ledge. Move up past a short off-width and easier climbing to a large ledge at the base of a steep face. Go up left along a ramp to the base of a right-facing corner and belay (small cams). Watch for rope drag. 120'. **Pitch 2** (5.7): Climb the cracks just to the right of the corner up to the point where the corner overhangs, then step into the corner and follow it to the top. The holds are sandy and sloping through the crux, but the crack takes good pro. 70'. Descend to the left

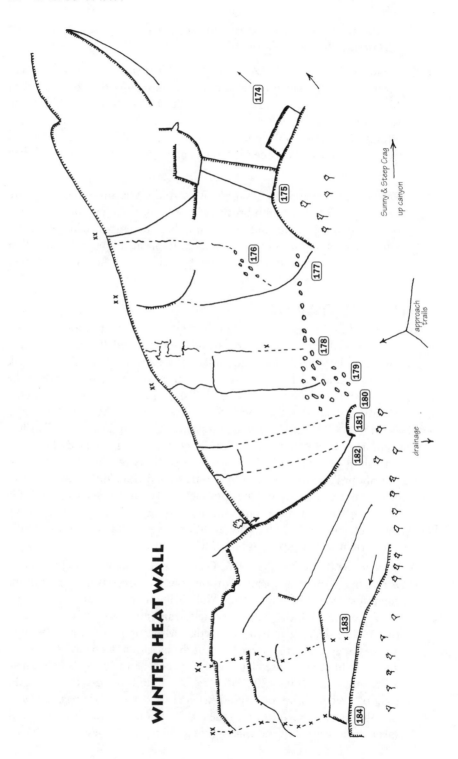

WINTER HEAT WALL

174

175

176

177

178

179

180

181

182

183

184

Sunny & Steep Crag

up canyon

approach trails

drainage

(east) and rap from either the anchors on *Winter Heat* or the tree at the top of *A-OK*.

The next routes are on the central section of the formation.

*175. **High Class Hoe** (5.10-) FA: Richard Harrison, Wendell Broussard, Paul Van Betten; Spring 1983. Carry gear up to a #2 Friend and some long slings. Start 20' up and right of *Winter Heat* at a short finger crack. This crack is just left of a huge crack/corner forming the right edge of the central section of the crag. Climb the finger crack to a ledge (crux), then angle left over a ceiling (intimidating) to a left-leaning groove/corner. Exit left at the top of the corner to an anchor and rappel with one rope.

176. **Vernal Thaw** (5.11 TR) FA: Bobby Knight, Todd Swain; October 1994. Climb *Winter Heat* for 10', then move right at some huecos to a thin, vertical seam. Climb the seam and face above, finishing through an overhanging, light-colored bulge.

*177. **Winter Heat** (5.11) FA: Paul Crawford, Jay Smith, Richard Harrison, Paul Van Betten; Spring 1983. Bring wires and TCUs. Begin 10' up and right of *Autumnal Frost* at some boulders sitting at the base of the crag. Climb the obvious vertical corner/groove to the end. Step right, then go up another overhanging corner/groove to an anchor.

178. **Autumnal Frost** (5.11+) FA: Todd Swain; October 1994. This route was originally attempted by Paul Crawford, who placed the bolt on the route. If you're under 6'3", you'll be in trouble on this one! Start in the center of the crag at a point 15' right of *Couldn't Be Schmooter* and 10' left of *Winter Heat*. Climb up and left along a series of huecos, aiming for a shallow groove that begins 35' up. When the huecos end, make very height-related moves up the smooth face past a bolt, then move left into the groove. Follow this to easier face climbing and the top.

*179. **Couldn't Be Schmooter** (5.9) FA: Wendell Broussard, Richard Harrison, Paul Crawford; Spring 1983. Bring gear to a # 3.5 Friend and some long slings for this excellent route. Climb the face along a very obvious crack, using huecos and the thin crack for protection. Finish in the right-hand of the two final cracks. Belay from an anchor.

180. **Nuttin' Could Be Finer** (5.7 R) FA: Bobby Knight, Donette and Todd Swain; October 1994. Begin at the base of the curving chimney (*A-OK*) that is 25' up and left from *Couldn't Be Schmooter* and just left of a block. Follow a small ramp up and right to its top. Follow the last route to the top of the ramp, then go straight up the face past numerous huecos to finish in the left-hand of two obvious vertical cracks.

181. **Mo Hotta, Mo Betta** (5.8 R) FA: Todd and Donette Swain; October 1994. Begin at the base of the curving chimney (*A-OK*) that is 25' up

Wendell Broussard on *Couldn't be Schmooter* (5.9).

and left from *Couldn't Be Schmooter* and just left of a block. Follow a small ramp up and right to its top. Step left, then climb straight up the face past honeycombed rock and huecos to finish in a thin, vertical seam that is just left of a nose.

182. A-OK (5.0) FA: Unknown; 1980s. Climb the short, left-curving chimney at the left margin of the central wall. This route ends at a small sapling. Walk off left or rappel.

The next two routes are on the left (east) section of the formation.

183. Cool Water Sandwich (5.10d) FA: Randy Marsh, Pier Locatelli; 1998. Begin on a ledge 100' left of a gully (*A-OK*) and 25' down and right of the next route. Climb up chocolate-colored rock past 2 bolts (contrived) to a ledge. Follow 6 more bolts past a small overlap and a small ceiling to an overhang. Pull the overhang near a right-facing corner (bolt), then continue up the yellow rock to the anchor.

184. Cool Whip (5.10c) FA: Randy Marsh, Pier Locatelli; 1998. Excellent quality, although the initial holds are a bit disconcerting due to their rounded nature. Start about 125' left of the gully dividing the left and central portions of the crag. This route begins at the left (highest) end of a ledge running along the base of this section of cliff. Climb a short, left-facing flake, then angle up and left past 5 bolts to an arch. A bolt protects moves out left past a smooth wave of rock. **Variation** (5.11): If you climb directly up and over the wave, the route is harder. Lower-angle climbing on varnished plates leads past another bolt to the anchor.

FIRST PULLOUT AREA OVERVIEW

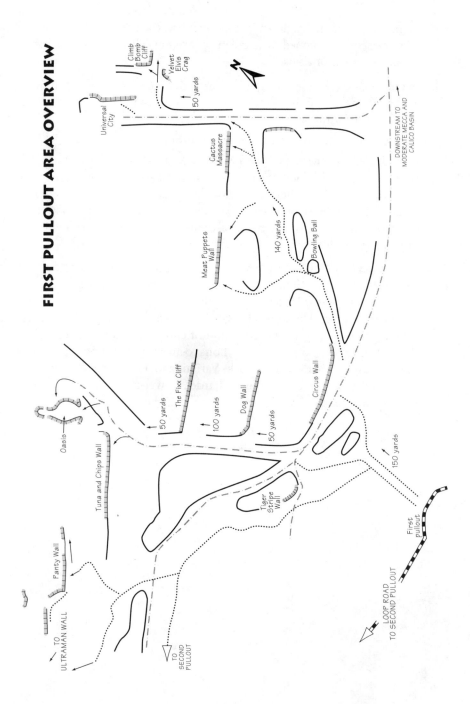

Climb Bomb Cliff

Velvet Elvis Crag

50 yards

Universal City

Cactus Massacre

Meat Puppets Wall

140 yards

Bowling Ball

The Fixx Cliff

50 yards

100 yards

Dog Wall

50 yards

Oasis

Tuna and Chips Wall

Circus Wall

Tiger Stripe Wall

150 yards

Panty Wall

TO ULTRAMAN WALL

TO SECOND PULLOUT

First pullout

LOOP ROAD TO SECOND PULLOUT

DOWNSTREAM TO MODERATE MECCA AND CALICO BASIN

N

FIRST PULLOUT

Numerous crags are described in this chapter, probably the best of which are Dog Wall and The Fixx Cliff. The Fixx Cliff was one of the first small, modern cliffs to be developed at Red Rocks and subsequently led to establishing popular cliffs like The Gallery. All of these routes have very short approaches and generally are in the sun most of the day. To reach First Pullout, drive the scenic loop road for 1.1 miles and park in the designated area on the right. The cliffs are generally described from right (toward the loop road entrance) to left (toward Second Pullout).

To approach the first four cliffs in this chapter (Climb Bomb Cliff, Velvet Elvis, Universal City, and Cactus Massacre), walk down the trail from the parking lot to the bottom of the wash (150 yards). Go up and right (southeast) on a ramp that is just right of Circus Wall (the somewhat rotten cliff that is right at the level of the wash and is characterized by a large arch/ceiling in the middle of the cliff). Continue for 50 yards to a small saddle (graffiti on the left side of this saddle says "T SOL").

Continue in the same direction, dropping down into a hole then scrambling back up to the same elevation (another 40 yards). The gray-colored wall Cactus

Massacre is now 50 yards toward the hillside (left/north) and is characterized by a right-leaning crack crossing the cliff at mid-height. Walk 30 yards right from Cactus Massacre to a gully and go up this for about 50 yards, passing an arch formed by boulders leaning across the gully. Universal City is up on the right, facing northwest (left).

Velvet Elvis Crag and Climb Bomb Cliff are to the right (toward Las Vegas) of Universal City and about 100 feet right of two boulders with right-leaning white stripes on them. Routes are described from left to right as you approach from Universal City.

CLIMB BOMB CLIFF

This cliff is 100 feet right and just down over the crest of the ridge from Universal City. It is a bulbous, overhanging boulder on the right side of a short gully and a patch of scrub oak. The cliff faces toward the road and is in the sun all day. Routes are described from left to right.

1. **Climb Machine** (5.9? PG13) FA: Unknown. Begin 30' uphill of *Climb Warp* in a wide gully. This route climbs an obvious C-shaped crack/seam on the right (east) wall of the gully. Small wires and TCUs provide some protection.

2. **Climb Traveler** (5.5) FA: Todd Swain; July 1992. Rope up 10' downhill of the last route at an arête on the right wall. Climb the arête and face just left of the arête past numerous varnished plates. Bring wires and slings for protection on the varnished plates.

3. **Climb Warp** (5.11-) FA: Paul Van Betten, Robert Finlay; December 1988. Start near the left edge of the formation at the right edge of the gully at some big boulders. Climb to the top of a pedestal then up an overhanging seam past 1 bolt. Walk off left toward the back of *Universal City*.

4. **Climb Bomb** (5.11+ R) FA: Paul Van Betten, Robert Finlay; December 1988. Rope up 15' right of *Climb Warp* at a left-leaning crack that is 5' left of a gully. Climb the broken crack to a ledge, then power out a roof past 2 bolts and a round hueco to overhanging seams and the summit.

VELVET ELVIS CRAG

The next buttress to the right (northeast) of *Climb Bomb* has a distinct gully on the left side. Routes are described from left to right starting about 75 feet up the gully.

5. **Black Tongue** (5.11?) FA: Paul Van Betten, Sal Mamusia; 1989. Too many crab legs causes black tongue! Carry wires and TCUs to supplement the bolts. Begin in the midst of oak bushes below a shallow crack/dihedral that has 2 bolts on the left aspect. Follow the crack/dihedral past a bulge to the top. Walk off toward the top of the gully.

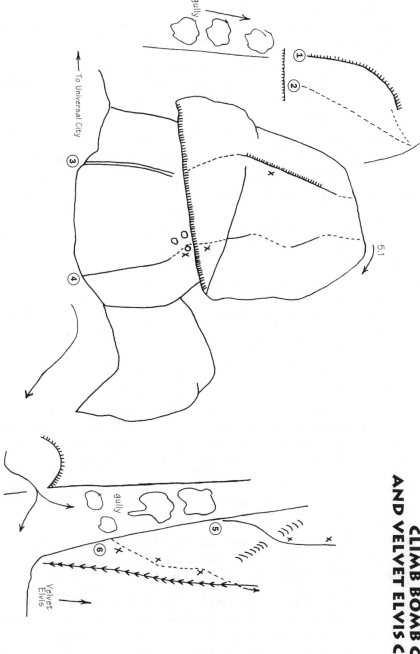

CLIMB BOMB CLIFF
AND VELVET ELVIS CRAG

6. **Isis** (5.11-?) FA: Sal Mamusia, Paul Van Betten; 1989. Rope up at the mouth of the gully and on the left (west) side of a rounded arête. This is the first route you see as you approach the crag from *Climb Bomb*. Climb the face to the left of the arête past 3 bolts. Wires and TCUs needed.

7. **Velvet Elvis** (5.12-) FA: Paul Van Betten, Don Welsh; November 1988. Start 15' right of the last route on the south face of the formation and below a vertical crack system. Climb the crack and seam system past 3 bolts. Bring wires, TCUs, and Friends. (No topo.)

8. **Climb Bandits** (5.10) FA: Paul Van Betten, Sal Mamusia; 1989. This route is about 30 yards to the right of *Velvet Elvis*. It climbs a hand crack to a roof, then finishes up a face. (No topo.)

9. **Claw Hammer** (5.9?) FA: "Frodo" Lybarger; 1989. This route is somewhere down and right of the last climb and goes up a face with 1 bolt (which was hand-drilled using a claw hammer, hence the name). (No topo.)

UNIVERSAL CITY

This shady crag is located near the top of the hillside and to the right (east) of the parking area. To find the cliff, hike about 50 yards above Cactus Massacre and just left of two boulders with right-leaning stripes on them. The cliff faces northwest and the routes are described from right to left as you approach up the gully. (No topos.)

10. **Prime Ticket** (5.11b) FA: Randy Faulk; November 1991. Start atop a boulder just left of a crack/alcove. Follow 7 bolts to cold shuts.

11. **Cameo Appearance** (5.11c) FA: Randy Faulk; November 1991. Begin 15' left of the last route between two bushes. Climb up right to a horizontal crack (bolt), then cruise along a vertical seam past 3 bolts. Continue up the steep face past 2 more bolts to a shared cold-shut anchor.

12. **Celebrity Roast** (5.12b) FA: Leo Henson, Randy Faulk, Dan McQuade; November 1991. Same start as the last route, then move left at the horizontal crack and power past 7 bolts to an anchor.

13. **Star Search** (5.11c) FA: Randy Faulk, Doug Henze; November 1991. Rope up 5' left of *Celebrity Roast* by a block on the ground. There are 6 bolts along a vertical seam that lead to the anchor.

14. **Quiet on the Set** (5.10c) FA: Louie Anderson, Bart Groendycke; December 1991. Begin 5' left of the last route and climb the arête that is just right of a corner. There are 5 bolts with black hangers on this somewhat contrived route. If you step into the corner, the route is about 5.8.

15. **Ed MacMayonnaise** (5.8) FA: Todd Swain; July 1992. Climb the obvious left-facing corner on the left (north) side of the face. Gear to #3 Friend needed.

CACTUS MASSACRE

This gray-colored crag has three steep and somewhat loose routes. The cliff is about 200 yards right (east) of Dog Wall and at about the same level on the hillside. It is slightly below and to the right of the parking lot and is characterized by a right-leaning crack crossing the cliff at one-third height. The climbs are in the shade in the morning.

CACTUS MASSACRE

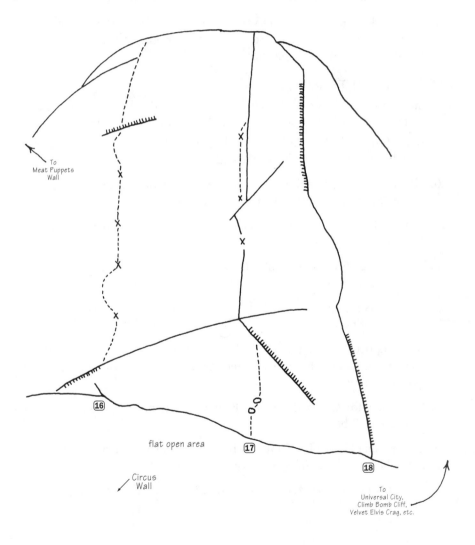

To
Meat Puppets
Wall

16

flat open area

17

Circus
Wall

18

To
Universal City,
Climb Bomb Cliff,
Velvet Elvis Crag, etc.

16. **Cactus Massacre** (5.11) FA: Paul Van Betten, Sal Mamusia, Mike Ward; December 1987. The left route. Begin in the center of the cliff just right of obvious parallel, varnished vertical seams. Scamper up 15' to a ledge, then climb past a bolt (left, right, or center), continuing past 3 more bolts to a ledge. Either continue to the top, or downclimb and lower off the last bolt. Bring a #2.5 Friend and TCUs.

17. **Cactus Root** (5.11+) FA: Paul Van Betten, Sal Mamusia, Jim Olsen; December 1987. Bring a smattering of gear, including a #2.5 Friend. Start 30' right of the last route at a left-slanting crack/corner that leads to a vertical crack. Follow the crack system past 3 bolts to the top.

18. **Cactus Head** (5.9) FA: Paul Van Betten, Don Welsh; 1989. This route starts up a left-facing corner (right of *Cactus Root*), follows a crack, and finishes up a right-facing corner.

MEAT PUPPETS WALL

This short brown wall sits to the left (west) and slightly above Cactus Massacre. Routes are described from left to right. All routes require gear for anchors.

19. **Blanc Czech** (5.11c) FA: Nick Nordblom, Paul Van Betten; 1989. Climb past 4 bolts at the left edge of the wall.

20. **Hodad** (5.12-) FA: Paul Van Betten; 1989. Angle out left to a bolt, then go up the face past 2 more bolts to finish in a crack.

21. **Crawdad** (5.11?) FA: Paul Van Betten; 1989. A 3-bolt route to the right of *Hodad*.

22. **Yellow Dog** (5.11-) FA: Paul Van Betten; 1989. Climb past 1 bolt, then place gear to the summit.

23. **Ranger Danger** (5.10-) FA: Bob Conz, Dr. Bob Yoho; 1989. Climb the left-hand of two crack systems in the center of the cliff.

24. **Meat Puppet** (5.11-) FA: Paul Van Betten, Mike Ward, Sal Mamusia; 1989. Start behind a boulder in the center of the cliff. Climb the right-hand of two crack systems.

25. **Gay Nazis for Christ** (5.12) FA: Paul Van Betten; 1989. Climb a crack system past 2 bolts.

26. **Green Eagle** (5.12-) FA: Paul Van Betten; 1989. Climb a crack system on the right side of the cliff past 1 bolt.

27. **The Max Flex** (5.11c) FA: Craig Reason; 1989. Climb past 6 ring bolts on the extreme right side of the crag.

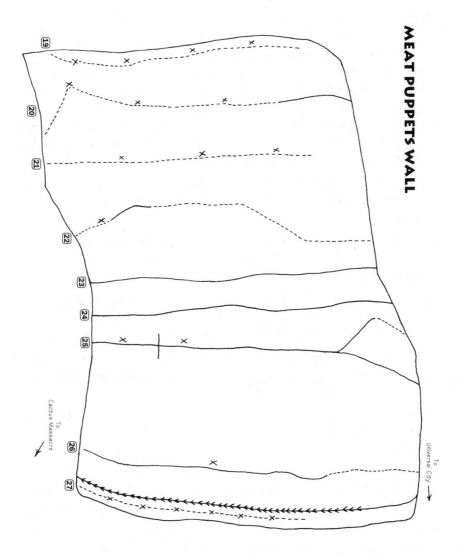

MEAT PUPPETS WALL

To
Cactus Massacre

To
Universal City

BOWLING BALL

This small, overhanging wall is located about 50 yards right (downstream) of Circus Wall and faces north toward Cactus Massacre.

28. **Take the Skinheads Bowling** (5.12) FA: Paul Van Betten; June 1988. You need 3 bolts and wires to get up this route. The start uses finger pockets similar to those found on a bowling ball.

CIRCUS WALL

This is the cliff that is right at the level of the wash and is characterized by a large arch/ceiling in the middle and a smaller arch on the right. It is not quite visible from the parking lot, but as you walk down the trail toward the wash, it will become obvious. Climbs on this sunny cliff (no topos) are listed from left to right (upstream–downstream).

29. **Human Cannonball** (5.8?) FA: Kurt Mauer; 1980s. Begin in the wash at graffiti that says "Black Panthers Local 431" and 5' left of a finger crack. Climb past 1 bolt to a ledge then up to the top.

30. **High Wire** (5.10-) FA: Unknown. Climb the finger crack just right of the graffiti mentioned above and 50' left of the big arch in the center of the cliff.

31. **Carful of Clowns** (5.10?) FA: Unknown. Start 30' right of the last route and 20' left of the central arch at a white water streak above "Patrick Loves Michelle Feb. 23 90." Climb past 2 bolts to the top.

32. **Lion Tamer** (5.11? TR?) FA: Unknown. Begin 10' right of *Carful of Clowns* at a short crack that leads to the left edge of the central arch. Follow the crack to a small ceiling, then straight up the face to a vertical seam.

33. **Circus Boy** (5.11+) FA: Paul Van Betten, Sal Mamusia; December 1987. Scamper up ledges to the left end of the central arch, then climb past 2 bolts and finish up a thin seam.

34. **Main Attraction** (5.12+) FA: Paul Van Betten, Sal Mamusia; December 1987. Climb out the center of the roof using 1 bolt. There are chains for rappelling.

35. **Midway** (5.12) FA: Paul Van Betten, Nick Nordblom; December 1987. Rope up 20' right of the last climb, near the right edge of the main arch. Climb past 3 bolts, staying just right of a seam, to a chain anchor.

36. **Crowd Pleaser** (5.12-) FA: Paul Van Betten, Sal Mamusia; December 1987. Starting 15' right of the right edge of the arch, below a left-leaning crack. Climb up the crack, then follow a seam past 4 bolts.

37. **Elephant Man** (5.11-) FA: Jay Smith; circa 1987. Same start as the last route, but move up right into a vertical crack. Climb the face above past a drilled angle piton and a bolt.

38. **Big Top** (5.10) FA: Jay Smith; circa 1987. Start 5' right of the last route at the left end of the small arch on the right side of the wall. Climb over the arch to a flaring crack, then past a bolt to the top.

DOG WALL

A popular sport cliff with a quick approach. Walk down the trail from the parking lot to the wash, then go left 200 feet to the edge of Circus Wall. The Dog Wall is about 150 feet up a gully to the right on the next level above Circus Wall. This cliff is plainly visible from the trailhead, appearing as the lowest good face. Routes are described from left to right. To access the top, continue up the gully about 50 feet, then go right. From the top of the routes, walk off left.

39. **Wok the Dog** (5.7) FA: Todd Swain; January 1992. Bring your pooper-scooper. Near the left edge of the crag and above the approach gully, climb a low-angle, right-leaning ramp to the top of the wall.

*40. **Cat Walk** (5.10a) FA: Don Burroughs, Alan Busby; January 1992. Begin 40' right at the left end of a right-leaning ramp/flake and about 75' up from the drainage. Climb past 4 bolts to a chain anchor.

First Pullout (Left)

Ultraman
Panty Wall
Oasis
The Fixx Cliff
Tuna and Chips Wall
Dog Wall

DOG WALL

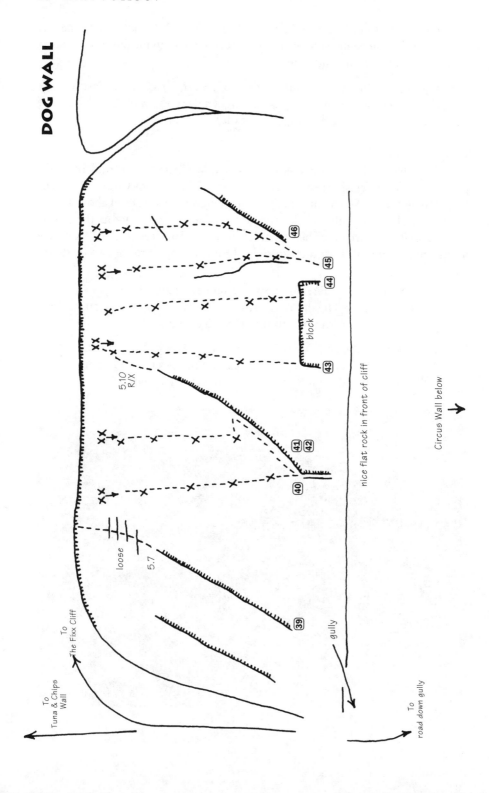

5.10 R/X

block

46

45

44

43

41 42

40

loose

5.7

39

To
Tuna & Chips
Wall

To
The Fixx Cliff

nice flat rock in front of cliff

Circus Wall below →

gully

To
road down gully

*41. **It's a Bitch** (5.10b) FA: California Dudes; circa 1987. Start 5' right of *Cat Walk* and crank past 4 bolts to a cold-shut anchor. Rebolted by Randy Faulk and Leo Henson in 1991 after going many years with chopped bolts.

42. **Man's Best Friend** (5.10 R/X) FA: Todd Swain; January 1992. Not exactly. Climb the right-leaning ramp/flake noted in the last two routes and finish up the unprotected face.

43. **Here Kitty, Kitty** (5.11c) FA: Geoff Weigand; circa 1987. Begin 30' right of the ramp/flake, atop a block. Power past 4 bolts to a cold-shut anchor. Rebolted in 1991 after having been chopped long ago.

44. **K-9** (5.12b) FA: Geoff Weigand; circa 1987. Gear up 8' right of the last route at the right end of a block at the base of the cliff. Climb past 5 bolts to the bolt anchor on top. Rebolted in 1991.

45. **Cujo** (5.11d) FA: Geoff Weigand; circa 1987. Rope up 5' right at a white streak and just left of a large flake. Climb past 5 bolts to a cold-shut anchor. Rebolted in 1991.

46. **Poodle Chainsaw Massacre** (5.11c) FA: Randy Faulk, Karin Olson; October 1991. Start at a right-leaning flake 5' right of the last route. Climb past 4 bolts to a cold-shut anchor.

THE FIXX CLIFF

The first semi-sport cliff to be developed in the area. Bring traditional gear for the routes here. Follow the trail from the parking lot down to the wash, then turn left (northwest) and follow the drainage about 200 feet until it turns uphill. About 250 feet up from the bottom of the wash (and 100 feet above the turnoff for Dog Wall) the drainage is split by a rock shaped like the prow of a ship. Take the right fork (straight ahead) and scramble up about 300 feet. The cliff is on your right. Like Dog Wall, this cliff is plainly visible from the trailhead, level with the road, and just left of center as you view the cliff bands. Routes are described from left to right. Descend off the right side.

47. **The Whiff** (5.10- PG) FA: Jay Smith, Mike Ward; March 1987. This finger-and-hand crack is near the left edge of the cliff. The climb is a bit hard to protect.

48. **Snow Blind** (5.11 R) FA: Paul Crawford; March 1987. Start 10' right of *The Whiff* and climb steep huecos past 1 bolt to a vague arête.

49. **Stand or Fall** (5.11-) FA: Paul Van Betten, Jim "Frodo" Lybarger; March 1987. Begin 5' right of the last route and climb steep huecos past 1 bolt to a crack.

*50. **Crack** (5.11) FA: Paul Crawford, Jay Smith; March 1987. Crank up the obvious finger crack 8' right of the last route.

THE FIXX CLIFF

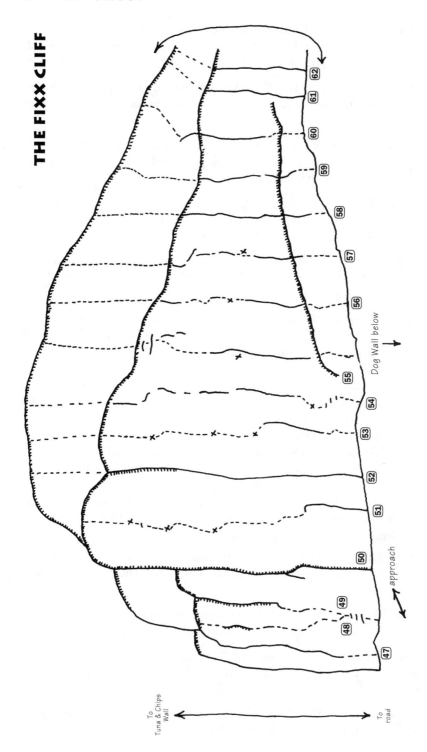

Dog Wall below →

approach

To Tuna & Chips Wall ←→ To road

*51. Free Base (5.11) FA: Paul Crawford, Paul Van Betten, Jay Smith, Nick Nordblom; March 1987. Rope up 10' right of *Crack* and climb a vertical crack to 3 bolts along an overhanging seam.

*52. Saved by Zero (5.11) FA: Nick Nordblom, Danny Meyers; May 1986. Climb the steep finger-and-hand crack that is 10' right of *Free Base*.

53. Red Skies (5.11+) FA: Paul Van Betten, Paul Crawford; March 1987. Follow a seam and 3 bolts 5' right of *Saved by Zero*.

54. The Geezer (5.11) FA: Jay Smith, Paul Crawford; March 1987. Starting 10' right of the last route, climb the pink face past a drilled angle.

55. Cocaine Hotline (5.11) FA: Paul Crawford, John Rosholt, Jay Smith; March 1987. Begin 8' right and climb a thin seam up varnished rock past 1 bolt.

56. Reach the Beach (5.11) FA: Nick Nordblom, Jenni Stone, Paul Crawford, Jay Smith; March 1987. Rope up 6' right of *Cocaine Hotline* at the left edge of a low boulder and bushes. Climb a thin, varnished seam past 1 bolt.

57. Eight Ball (5.11) FA: Paul Crawford, Jay Smith, Nick Nordblom, Jenni Stone; March 1987. Start 10' right of *Reach the Beach* and face climb to a thin seam and a bolt.

58. One Thing Leads to Another (5.11) FA: Nick Nordblom, Jenni Stone, Paul Crawford, Jay Smith; March 1987. Climb the thin seam 8' right of *Eight Ball*.

59. The Skagg (5.11) FA: Mike Ward, Paul Van Betten, Paul Crawford, Jay Smith; March 1987. Power up the 30-foot-high seam that is 10' right of the last route.

60. Running (5.11-) FA: Nick Nordblom, Jenni Stone; March 1987. Climb the next seam 10' to the right of the last route. This seam is also about 30' long.

61. Outside the Envelope (5.11) FA: Nick Nordblom; solo, March 1987. Crank up the seam 8' right of the last route. This seam is about 20' high.

62. The Bindle (5.11) FA: Unknown; 1987 or later. Shoot up the very short seam 10' right of the last route, near the crag's far right edge.

THE OASIS

Up and right of the Tuna and Chips Wall is a hanging valley/alcove that is visible from the parking area. This sunny area requires a bit of fourth-class scrambling to reach. Follow the trail from the parking lot down to the wash, then turn left (northwest) and follow the drainage about 200 feet until it turns uphill. About 250 feet up from the bottom of the wash (and 100 feet above the turnoff for Dog Wall), the drainage is split by a rock shaped like the prow of a ship. Take the right fork (straight ahead) and scramble up about 300 feet. The Fixx Cliff is on your right. Continue up the drainage past The Fixx Cliff about 150 feet to a big, plated cliff blocking the drainage. You arrive at the center of the cliff (Tuna and Chips Wall), just right of a low-angle crack and directly below a water streak. Go up and right in the large, bushy gully about 100 feet, weaving around boulders and bushes. From here, you have two scrambling options on the left (north) side of the main, bushy gully. Scramble up a low-angle chimney past an obvious pine tree, or continue a bit farther up the main gully, then face-climb up a rounded buttress. The routes (not shown) are described from the mouth of the alcove inward, beginning with the right (east) wall.

63. **Hang Ten** (5.11d) FA: Brian McCray, Mike Lewis; March 1998. Start at the right edge of the right (east) wall. Follow a thin vertical seam and 3 bolts to a stance on a slab. Climb a varnished corner past 2 more bolts to a cold-shut anchor.

64. **Tropicana** (5.12b) FA: Brian McCray, Mike Lewis; March 1998. Begin 5' left of the last route. Climb past 7 bolts.

65. **The Sands** (5.12a) FA: Brian McCray, Mike Lewis; March 1998. Rope up 5' left of the last route. Climb past 7 bolts to shuts.

66. **Pad's Passion** (5.8) FA: Tim Henkles; March 1998. Start 15' up and left of the last route, at the narrowest portion of the alcove. Follow 4 bolts up to chains.

67. **Lizardry** (5.8 TR) FA: Elizabeth Craig; March 1998. Top-rope the face just right of *Diamond Dance*.

68. **Diamond Dance** (5.7) FA: Chris Lowry; March 1998. There is a prominent finger crack 10' up and left of *Pad's Passion*. Climb the crack to an alcove, then go up and right to a chain anchor. Bring gear to a #2 Friend.

The next routes are on the left (west) wall of the front alcove.

69. **Crack Bar** (5.8) FA: Unknown. Climb the obvious right-leaning crack at the mouth of the alcove.

70. **Casino** (5.12a) FA: Brian McCray; March 1998. Start about 30' up and right of a prominent, right-leaning crack. Climb left of a vertical seam past 5 bolts to shuts.

71. **My Thai** (5.12a) FA: Brian McCray; March 1998. Rope up 10' right of the last route and climb past 5 bolts to another shut anchor.

72. **Snack Crack** (5.11d) FA: Brian McCray; March 1998. Begin 5' right of the last climb. Power past 4 bolts along a vertical seam to an anchor.

73. **The Warming** (5.10d) FA: Brian McCray; March 1998. This route is across from the obvious finger crack (Diamond Dance) and 6' uphill of the last route. Climb along a crack past 3 bolts to an anchor.

The next two routes are about 50 feet uphill of the main alcove. The rock is gray in color and the climbs are just left of a short waterfall.

74. **Money** (5.10c) FA: Mike Lewis; March 1998. An interesting-looking route. There are 3 bolts protecting moves up and left along a crack/corner system.

75. **Insecure Delusions** (5.12b) FA: Mike Lewis; March 1998. Begin in the same spot as the last route. Angle up and right past 4 bolts to chains.

TUNA AND CHIPS WALL

Follow the trail from the parking lot down to the wash, then turn left (northwest) and follow the drainage about 200 feet until it turns uphill. About 250 feet up from the bottom of the wash (and 100 feet above the turnoff for Dog Wall), the drainage is split by a rock shaped like the prow of a ship. Take the right fork (straight ahead) and scramble up about 300 feet. The Fixx Cliff will be on your right. Continue up the drainage past the Fixx Cliff about 150 feet to a big, plated cliff blocking the drainage. You will arrive at the center of the cliff,

just right of a low-angled crack and directly below a water streak. Routes on this sunny cliff are described from right to left. Walk off to the right (east) and then follow a gully back to the base of the cliff.

76. **Chips Ahoy!** (5.9 R) FA: Mike Ward, Paul Van Betten; 1986. Start 50' right of the crack/gully in the center of the cliff and atop boulders below left-slanting seams. **Pitch 1** (5.8): Climb steep varnished rock above the left-slanting seams and continue up the plated face above, passing 2 bolts to a 2-bolt belay. 120'. **Pitch 2** (5.9): Power through the roof above (bolt, crux) to easier ground and the top of the formation. 100'. Descend off right.

77. **Tuna Cookies** (5.7 R) FA: National Outdoor Leadership School (NOLS) staff; 1987. If you've seen the movie *Traxx*, this route name will make sense. Begin just left of the last route, at several left-arching seams. Bring wires and gear to a #3 Friend. **Pitch 1** (5.7): Climb up left to a bolt 30' up, then continue up the center of the long face past 1 more bolt to the ceiling. Climb past the left edge to a big ledge. 150'. **Pitch 2** (5.2): Scramble to the top. 100'. Descend off right.

*78. **Waterstreak** (5.8 PG) FA: Jim Kessler; 1987. The difficulty is dependent on exactly where you climb. Going directly up the streak could be as hard as 5.10. Gear up 30' left of the last route at the base of an obvious water streak, which is 20' right of a low-angle crack. Climb past 3 bolts to join the main crack/chimney system (bolt and drilled piton in the alcove). Rappel, or continue up the crack to the top.

79. **Chips and Salsa** (5.3) FA: Unknown; 1980s. Rope up at the base of the central crack/chimney system and directly behind a block. Follow the crack for about 200' to the top. Descend off right.

80. **Tuna and Chips** (5.7 R) FA: Bob Conz, "Frodo" Lybarger; January 1987. Start 20' left of the central crack at the left edge of a block. Bring up to a #2 Friend. **Pitch 1** (5.7 R): Climb a low-angle face, keeping right of a black, left-facing flake. Follow 3 bolts to a belay in a vertical crack (small gear needed). 150'. **Pitch 2** (5.3): Continue up the crack and face to the top. 60'. Descend off right.

TIGER STRIPE WALL

This cliff is clearly visible from the parking area and, as the name implies, has tigerlike stripes. Even though the climbing is less than stellar, the crag was immortalized in Stefan Glowacz's book *Rocks around the World*. At least three routes appear to have been done on the formation.

Approach this sunny cliff from First Pullout, but do not follow the main trail to the bottom of the wash as for all the other cliffs. Instead, cut off left on a subsidiary trail (toward Second Pullout), aiming for the wash bottom to the left of the rock outcrop closest to the road (about 40 yards). The routes are on the aspect facing the road, but begin behind a large boulder/pillar. Routes are described from right (east) to left (west). (No topo.)

81. **Shere Khan** (5.10) FA: Paul Van Betten, Don Welsh; 1988. Start in the center of the cliff between two obvious, vertical crack systems. Climb past at least 8 bolts to an anchor.

82. **Tigger** (5.10 R) FA: Paul Van Betten, Don Welsh; 1988. A bolt appears to lead right into the central crack system. There are 2 shuts at the top of the crack.

83. **White Tigers** (5.11?) FA: Dan McQuade, S. Fischbacher, R. Horn; circa 1990. Begin 30' left of the last route (the central crack). Follow 4 bolts to an anchor.

84. **Bengal** (5.9+) FA: Paul Van Betten, Sal Mamusia; 1988. Climb an off-width crack on the right side of the face.

PANTY WALL

The obvious black cliff that sits 150 yards up and left from Tuna and Chips Wall is known as Panty Wall. The 30-foot pine tree that sits in front of the blackest portion of the cliff easily identifies it. Three separate cliffs are listed here; they are all considered part of Panty Wall.

Approach this sunny cliff from First Pullout, but do not follow the main trail to the bottom of the wash as per all the other cliffs. Instead, cut off left on a subsidiary trail (toward Second Pullout), aiming for the wash bottom to the

Panty Wall

PANTY WALL

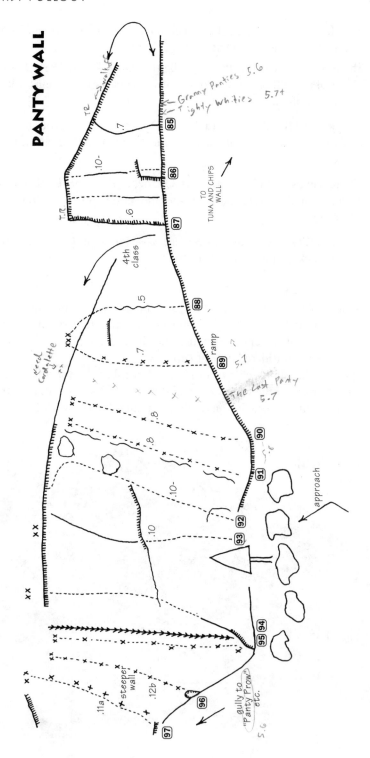

Granny Panties 5.6
Tighty Whities 5.7+

TO TUNA AND CHIPS WALL

The Last Party 5.7

Keel Cookielette

ramp

4th class

approach

steeper wall

gully to "Panty Prow" etc.

left of the rock outcrop closest to the road (about 40 yards). Follow the trail up around the left side of this formation (Tiger Stripe Wall), going up over a short hill (100 yards), then contouring above another wash (150 yards). Take a subsidiary trail off the main trail and go down to the bottom of the wash (100 feet). From here, you should see several right-trending ribs of rock leading up toward Panty Wall. Scramble up the right flank of the red slab directly in front of you, then wander 100 yards up boulders to the base of the cliff. You arrive at the center of the crag, near the prominent pine tree. Climbs are described from right to left, starting at a short buttress 200 feet up and right along a ramp.

85. **Thong** (5.7 PG) FA: Todd Swain, Marion Parker; February 1994. The next three routes are located on a small buttress about 200' up a ramp from the prominent pine tree mentioned in the introduction to the crag. Start 12' left of a left-facing flake at a vertical crack system. Crux moves off the ground lead to easier climbing up the crack. Walk off right.

86. **Butt Floss** (5.10- TR) FA: Todd Swain; February 1994. Begin 10' left of *Thong* at a right-facing flake capped by a small ceiling. Pull past the ceiling and follow vertical seams to the top. Use medium Friends for the belay.

87. **Cover My Buttress** (5.6) FA: Todd Swain; solo, February 1994. Climb the obvious left-facing corner that makes up the left edge of the buttress. Bring large gear to protect the route. Walk off right.

The next two routes are located midway up the ramp, about 100 feet up from the prominent pine tree. Start 50 feet down and left of the last route and 5 feet left of an oak bush.

88. **Scanty Panty** (5.5 X) FA: Todd and Donette Swain; February 1994. Face-climb up along vertical seams, finishing right of a small ceiling. Angle left to the anchor on *Silk Panties*.

89. **Silk Panties** (5.7) FA: Donette and Todd Swain; February 1994. Begin 12' downhill of the last route and climb past 5 bolts with black, home-made hangers to a belay anchor.

90. **Boxer Rebellion** (5.8) FA: Albert Newman, Leo Henson; November 1996. Start 45' down and left of the last route, where the ramp transitions to a flat ledge. Climb past 6 bolts to a chain anchor.

91. **Brief Encounter** (5.8) FA: Albert Newman, Leo Henson; October 1998. Begin 20' left of the last route and 10' right of *Panty Line* below a line of bolts. There are 6 bolts leading to a chain anchor that is barely visible from the base of the route.

92. **Panty Line** (5.10- R) FA: Nick Nordblom, Paul Van Betten; 1987. Rope up directly behind the rightmost of the boulders lying at the base of the

cliff and just right of the pine tree. Wander straight up the right side of the black-plated face aiming for a gap in the varnish at the top of the wall. Bring extra of the larger-sized wires. There is a 2-bolt anchor on a ledge above the route and a rap anchor just to the left.

*93. **Panty Raid** (5.10) FA: Paul Van Betten, Nick Nordblom; 1987. A quality route that's not as scary as it first appears. Begin 8' left of the last route and climb straight up the face to a ceiling formed by the varnish. Follow a slightly right-leaning thin crack to the top. The 2-bolt belay anchor is directly above on a ledge.

94. **Edible Panties** (5.10 R/X) FA: Todd and Donette Swain; February 1994. Scary to lead due to the looseness, but still worth toproping. Start 40' left of the last route at a short, right-leaning flake/crack. Climb up and right along the fissure, then up the plated wall, finishing at a small notch. The crux is the transition from the flake to the steeper wall above. There are 2 cold shuts on a ledge above the route.

95. **Viagra Falls** (5.12a) FA: Leo Henson, Albert Newman; October 1998. At a point where the wall changes from less than vertical to overhanging is a line of bolts. This is about 10' left of *Edible Panties*. Power past 7 bolts to an anchor.

96. **Wedgie** (5.12b) FA: Leo Henson, Albert Newman; November 1996. In the middle of the overhanging wall is a short pedestal. Follow 8 bolts up this steep varnished wall to cold shuts. The first bolt was placed in the early 1990s.

97. **Totally Clips** (5.11a) FA: Scott "Jimmy Dean" Carson, Steve "Bucky" Bullock (both from Salt Lake City); 1990. Begin 50' uphill of *Edible Panties* near a freestanding block. Follow 6 bolts to a chain anchor.

There is another cliff with four very good routes about 60 yards up and left from the prominent pine tree. (No topo.)

*98. **Panty Prow** (5.6) FA: Donette and Todd Swain; February 1994. Climb the right arête of the formation past 5 bolts to the same cold-shut belay as *Victoria's Secret* and *Panty-Mime*.

99. **Victoria's Secret** (5.10 TR) FA: Todd and Donette Swain; February 1994. No need to bolt this one because it can easily be toproped. Climb the face between *Panty Prow* and *Panty-Mime* starting at a small block leaning against the cliff.

*100. **Panty-Mime** (5.10c PG) FA: Todd and Donette Swain; February 1994. Start atop a block 40' left of *Panty Prow* and 20' right of a right-facing corner (*Panty Shield*) at a line of bolts trending up and right. Dance past 6 bolts to an anchor.

*101. **Panty Shield** (5.10d R) FA: Nick Nordblom, Paul Van Betten; 1987. Good climbing, but a bit dangerous to reach the first bolt. Follow the obvious right-leaning corner system past 4 bolts. A small TCU and a #2 Friend could be carried to supplement the bolts. Bring large Friends for the belay then scramble down left.

Above Panty Prow is another cliff with a huge roof split by a crack.

102. **The Great Red Roof** (A1) FA: Paul Van Betten, Sal Mamusia, Nick Nordblom; 1987. This huge roof crack was aided without pins or bolts. Have at it!

ULTRAMAN WALL

This sunny, low-angle formation has numerous moderate routes. It is located at the far left (west) margin of First Pullout and may also be approached from Second Pullout. The cliff is identified by a waterstreak that runs down the cliff from a large, curving ledge.

Approach this sunny cliff from First Pullout, but do not follow the main trail to the bottom of the wash as for all the other cliffs. Instead, cut off left on a subsidiary trail (toward Second Pullout), aiming for the wash bottom to the left of the rock outcrop closest to the road (about 40 yards). Follow the trail up around the left side of this formation (Tiger Stripe Wall), going up over a short hill (100 yards), then contouring above another wash (150 yards). Take a subsidiary trail off the main trail and go down to the bottom of the wash (100 feet). Go up the other side of the wash past several small, red rock ridges. Zigzag up slabs to the left of center past many dark varnished boulders, then traverse right (east) below the routes. Allow about 20 minutes for the approach. Routes are described from left to right as you approach the cliff. (No topo.)

103. **Clutch Cargo** (5.9) FA: Pier Locatelli, Dan McQuade; circa 1996. Same start as *Ultraman*, at small, left-facing corners. Follow 7 bolts up and slightly left to anchors on the skyline. You need at least a 60-meter rope for the rappel.

*104. **Ultraman** (5.8+ PG13) FA: Jon Martinet, Scott Gordon; 1970s. Begin in the center of the slab at a waterstreak that leads to an obvious ledge. Follow 8 bolts up and slightly right to an anchor on the big, bushy ledge. You can either walk off right or rappel with at least a 60-meter rope. **Note:** The top of this route can be approached via Calico Basin by going up the gully past *The Dividing Line*.

105. **Speed Racer** (5.8+ PG13) FA: Ed Prochaska; circa 1990. Start about 50' up and right of *Ultraman* at a line of bolts with silver hangers. There is a bolt with a homemade hanger just right of the first bolt on this route. Climb the red face past 8 bolts to a cold-shut anchor. Rappel with two ropes.

106. Godzilla (5.7 PG13) FA: Ed Prochaska; circa 1990. Rope up about 100' up and right of *Ultraman* at an oak bush growing against the base of the cliff. Climb past 7 bolts with silver hangers to an anchor. You need two ropes for the rappel.

107. Rodan (5.7+ X) FA: Unknown. Begin about 50' uphill and right of the last route. Climb straight up the face to an anchor under a large overlap.

108. Science Patrol (5.8 PG) FA: Jon Martinet, Nick Nordblom; 1970s. Start 100' uphill of *Rodan* at a short, shallow, left-facing corner. Climb past 9 bolts with homemade hangers to an anchor on a ledge. Rappel with two ropes.

109. The Hex Files (5.6) FA: Unknown; 1970s. Bring gear up to a #4 Friend and many long slings to reduce rope drag. This route climbs the obvious, left-facing corner system at the right edge of the cliff. From the alcove about 80' up, traverse left to reach a vertical crack and the top. Traverse left to the anchor atop *Science Patrol* and rappel with two ropes.

The next route is located about 50 yards right of the main formation in a gully. The climb is on a short, squat formation with a huge, varnished depression in the center. By continuing past this formation for 50 yards, you can easily access the upper Panty Wall.

110. Telletubby Scandal (5.11?) FA: Tinky Winky, J. Fallwell; February 1999. Bring your magic purse. A 4-bolt route climbs the smooth face just right of the huge depression in the middle of the southwest face.

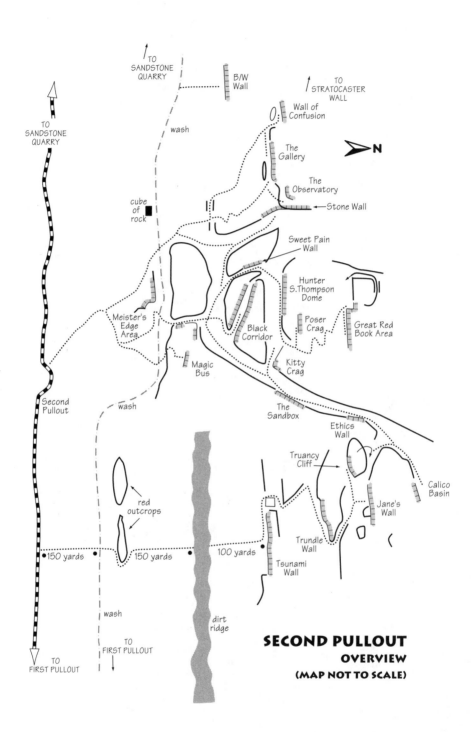

TO
SANDSTONE
QUARRY

B/W
Wall

TO
STRATOCASTER
WALL

TO
SANDSTONE
QUARRY

wash

Wall of
Confusion

The
Gallery

N

The
Observatory

cube
of
rock

Stone Wall

Sweet Pain
Wall

Hunter
S.Thompson
Dome

Meister's
Edge
Area

Black
Corridor

Poser
Crag

Great Red
Book Area

Magic
Bus

Kitty
Crag

Second
Pullout

wash

The
Sandbox

Ethics
Wall

Truancy
Cliff

Calico
Basin

red
outcrops

Jane's
Wall

Trundle
Wall

•150 yards   •   150 yards   •   100 yards   •

Tsunami
Wall

wash

dirt
ridge

TO
FIRST PULLOUT

TO
FIRST PULLOUT

TO
FIRST PULLOUT

SECOND PULLOUT
OVERVIEW
(MAP NOT TO SCALE)

SECOND PULLOUT

This area has some of the best sport climbing cliffs at Red Rocks. The Gallery, Wall of Confusion, and Black Corridor are of excellent quality and extremely popular. They are so popular, in fact, that the disposal of human waste and other environmental issues are of great concern to land managers. Please do your part to reduce impacts, not only here but at every climbing area you visit!

Park at Second Pullout, 1.7 miles from the start of the scenic loop road, to approach any of these crags. The cliffs at this pullout are described from right to left (from the direction of First Pullout, moving left toward the Sandstone Quarry).

Tsunami Wall, Trundle Wall, Jane's Wall, and Truancy Cliff are all within 150 yards of each other and are located about 500 yards to the northeast of Second Pullout. All face toward the road and sit fairly high up on the hillside. The approach described here is not the most direct way to reach the cliffs, but once you've made it to the climbs, you can figure out a better way back to the parking lot.

To reach these cliffs, walk down the road from Second Pullout toward First Pullout for about 300 yards until you reach the red rock outcrops within the drainage on your left. Looking at the larger hillside behind these outcrops, you can now see all of the aforementioned cliffs lined up in a row.

Tsunami Wall is the lowest crag and is easily recognized by its rectangular boxcar shape and the huge, detached block on its left side. The other three cliffs are about 100 yards directly above. From this point along the loop road, walk down into the drainage, then up the other side to the top of the dirt ridge right above the outcrops (about 300 yards total). Tsunami Wall is now about 100 yards in front of you.

TSUNAMI WALL

Routes on this wildly overhanging wave of rock are about 40 feet long, face the road, and are in the shade in the morning. The right-hand part of the wall is smaller and less steep. Climbs are described from left to right. All routes have anchors on top.

1. **Poseidon Adventure** (5.12b) FA: Chris Knuth, Leo Henson; January 1993. This route climbs a very overhanging block just left of the main Tsunami Wall. Follow 4 bolts to open cold shuts.

*2. **Barracuda** (5.13b) FA: Chris Knuth, Leo Henson; January 1993. Start 30' right of the huge detached block at a seam that runs out a low ceiling, then up left along the wall. Follow 4 bolts to chains.

3. **Land Shark** (5.12b) FA: Leo Henson; January 1992. Rope up 40' right of the huge detached block at a boulder under the low roof running along the base of the cliff. Three routes start here and share the same first 2 bolts. Climb up and left past a total of 6 bolts to the anchor. (Not shown.)

4. **Angler** (5.12c) FA: Leo Henson; January 1992. Same start as *Land Shark*, but continue straight up after the third bolt to an anchor. (Not shown.)

5. **Threadfin** (5.12c) FA: Leo Henson; January 1992. Same start as *Land Shark*, then follow the line of bolts straight up to chains. (Not shown.)

6. **SOS** (5.13a) FA: Leo Henson; January 1992. You may need help on this one! Start 10' right of *Land Shark* on the left edge of a block under the low roof. Move left to a horn, then up the seam past 5 bolts. (Not shown.)

7. **Man Overboard!** (5.12d) FA: Leo Henson; January 1992. Begin 5' right of *SOS* in the center of the block under the low roof. Follow 6 bolts to chains. (Not shown.)

8. **Aftershock** (5.12b) FA: Randy Faulk, Leo Henson; January 1992. Rope up 4' right of the last route at the right end of the block under the low roof. Strong fingers and 5 bolts will get you to the cold-shut anchor.

*9. **Abandon Ship** (5.12b) FA: Randy Faulk, Leo Henson; January 1992. Start 10' right of the last route at a dihedral that marks the right edge of the wave. Climb up and left past 5 bolts.

10. **Women and Children First** (5.6+) FRA: Donette and Todd Swain; Spring 1993. Climb the dihedral just right of *Abandon Ship*. Bring a full set of

Friends. Walk off to the right (toward First Pullout), then scramble down onto a ledge below the start of the two 5.10 routes. (Not shown.)

11. **Tremor** (5.10b) FA: Leo and Karin O. Henson; February 1992. Begin 25' right of the *Women and Children First* dihedral on a smaller, broken section of cliff. Locate 4 bolts and chains to identify the route.

12. **Low Tide** (5.10b) FA: Leo and Karin O. Henson; February 1992. Start 30' right of the last route, on the right side of a low ceiling and climb up along a varnished seam past 4 bolts. (Not shown.)

TRUNDLE WALL

To reach this crag, walk down the road from Second Pullout toward First Pullout for about 300 yards until you reach the red rock outcrops within the drainage on your left end. Looking at the larger hillside behind these outcrops in the drainage, you can now see several cliffs lined up in a row.

Tsunami Wall is the lowest crag and is easily recognized by its rectangular boxcar shape and the huge, detached block on its left side. Trundle Wall can clearly be seen about 100 yards directly above. From this point along the loop road, walk down into the drainage, then up the other side to the top of the dirt ridge right above the outcrops (about 300 yards total). Tsunami Wall is now about 100 yards in front of you. Walk past the left (west) edge of Tsunami Wall, then continue about 100 yards up the hillside to the next obvious cliff (Trundle Wall). These sunny routes are described from left to right as you approach the cliff.

13. **Before Its Time** (5.12b) FA: Leo Henson; November 1994. Start to the left of a big, rotten corner and climb past about 8 bolts to the anchor.

14. **Standing in the Shadows** (5.12a) FA: Greg Mayer; Winter 1990. Begin 10' right of a big, rotten, right-facing corner. Climb up and left past 2 bolts to a left-facing flake/corner, then straight up past 4 more bolts to the chain anchor.

15. **Master Beta** (5.13a) FA: Scotty Gratton; October 1994. Rope up 5' right of the last route and 5' left of a rotten corner and zip past 5 bolts with homemade hangers to chains.

16. **Pocket Rocket** (5.11d) FA: Mike Tupper; Winter 1990. Start 15' right of the last route, on the other side of the rotten corner. Power past 2 bolts with homemade, tan-colored hangers, then go up and slightly left to the chains.

17. **Life out of Balance** (5.11c) FA: Mike Tupper, Greg Mayer; Winter 1990. Begin 6' right of the last route and just left of an obvious right-facing flake/corner leading to a huge hole. Finger-traverse left, then up past 4 bolts to an anchor left of the hole.

18. **Bone Machine** (5.11c) FA: Danny Meyers, Scotty Gratton; October 1994. This line is to the right of the right-facing flake/corner. Bolts lead to a chain anchor.

JANE'S WALL

Jane's Wall is a large, dark, rounded formation near the top of the ridge with a huge, black roof just up and right of it. To reach this crag, walk down the road from Second Pullout toward First Pullout for about 300 yards until you reach the red rock outcrops within the drainage on your left end. Looking at the larger hillside behind these outcrops in the drainage, you can now see several cliffs lined up in a row.

Tsunami Wall is the lowest crag and is easily recognized by its rectangular boxcar shape and the huge, detached block on its left side. Jane's Wall is the second obvious cliff about 150 yards directly above. From this point along the loop road, walk down into the drainage, then up the other side to the top of the dirt ridge right above the outcrops (about 300 yards total). Tsunami Wall is now about 100 yards in front of you. Walk past the left (west) edge of Tsunami Wall and continue about 100 yards up the hillside to the next obvious cliff (Trundle Wall).

Go to the right (east) end of the wall, then scramble 150 feet up a gully to the base of Jane's Wall, which is characterized by a smooth black face capped by an overhang on its left side. The cliff faces the road and is in the sun the majority of the day. All routes have anchors and are described from right to left (east to west).

19. **See Dick Fly** (5.10d) FA: Greg Mayer; Spring 1991. Begin atop a block near the right edge of the crag. Climb a slab to steeper rock and the belay. The route has 5 bolts with homemade hangers.

20. **Idiots Rule** (5.11b) FA: Don Welsh; Fall 1990. Rope up 15' left of the last route. Scramble up a slab, step right, then up and slightly left past 6 bolts to a hook and chain.

21. **Pigs in Zen** (5.12b) FA: Don Welsh; Fall 1990. Same start as *Idiots Rule*. Scamper 40' up the slab to a cave. Exit left out of the cave, clipping a total of 6 bolts. (Not shown.)

22. **Naked and Disfigured** (5.12b) FA: Don Welsh; Fall 1990. Begin 25' left at the mouth of a small corridor. Go up a low-angle, right-leaning ramp to the lowest point of the overhang and pull this, then power up the steep face to the anchor. (Not shown.)

23. **Stealin'** (5.12b) FA: Don Welsh; Winter 1991. Done after *Every Mother's Nightmare*; it's really a variation. Start at the mouth of the small corridor and zip up to a left-leaning crack under a sculptured arête. Follow bolts up the arête, then escape right and clip 1 more bolt before reaching the anchor. (No topo.)

*24. **Every Mother's Nightmare** (5.12b) FA: Greg Mayer; Fall 1990. Climb the overhanging, sculptured arête of *Stealin'*, then continue up left through roofs to the anchor. There is a total of 6 bolts on the route. (No topo.)

TRUANCY CLIFF

The routes on this small cliff aren't too inspiring, but because they're within 50 feet of Jane's Wall, you can conveniently tick them off. To reach this crag, walk down the road from Second Pullout toward First Pullout for about 300 yards until you reach the red rock outcrops within the drainage on your left. Looking at the larger hillside behind these outcrops in the drainage, you can now see several cliffs lined up in a row.

Tsunami Wall is the lowest crag and is easily recognized by its rectangular boxcar shape and the huge, detached block on its left side. Jane's Wall is the second obvious cliff about 150 yards directly above. From this point along the loop road, walk down into the drainage, then up the other side to the top of the dirt ridge right above the outcrops (about 300 yards total). Tsunami Wall is about 100 yards in front of you. Walk past the left (west) edge of Tsunami Wall and continue about 100 yards up the hillside to the next obvious cliff (Trundle Wall).

Go to the right (east) end of the wall, then scramble 150 feet up a gully to the base of Jane's Wall, which is characterized by a smooth black face capped by an overhang on its left side. Truancy Cliff is 50 feet to the left (west), faces the road, and is in the sun the majority of the day. Routes are described (but not shown) from right to left (east to west).

25. **Ditch Day** (5.7) FA: Todd Swain (solo); July 1991. Start near the right edge of the cliff below some very varnished huecos and horizontal cracks. Climb straight up the face using traditional pro (up to a #3 Friend). No anchors; walk off to the rear, then down the corridor between Truancy Cliff and Jane's Wall.

26. **Playing Hooky** (5.10a) FA: Greg Mayer; Fall 1990. Begin 8' left at the base of a scoop/groove with 3 bolts. Wander up the face past the bolts, then move left to the chain anchor.

27. **Doctor's Orders** (5.10b) FA: Greg Mayer; Fall 1990. Climb the line of 3 bolts 6' left of *Playing Hooky* to the same chain anchor.

28. **Iron Man** (5.10+) FA: Jay Smith, Paul Van Betten; 1983. This route is down and right of Jane's Wall. It climbs a right-facing, right-arching corner past 1 bolt to a bolted belay. The arch separates red and white rock and faces the road. Carry gear to a #3 Friend.

THE ARENA

This big, brown, overhanging wall sits on the top left side of the gully on Rescue Wall. It's about a 15-minute approach from the parking area. (No topo.)

29. **Shadow Warrior** (5.13a) FA: Leo Henson; June 1994. Climb the left route past about 6 bolts to a shared anchor.

30. **Gladiator** (5.12c) FA: Leo Henson; April 1994. Climb the right route, also with about 6 bolts.

RESCUE WALL

This steep, east-facing cliff is hidden in a gully between Tsunami Wall and Magic Bus. Follow the trail from the parking lot down to the wash level, then go downstream about 200 yards to a gully running north-south on the left (north) side of the drainage.

The routes are about 100 yards straight north of a bend in the main drainage on the left (west) side of the gully. The wall is noted for its mushroomlike summit block. The approach takes 10 minutes.

31. **Airlift** (5.11c) FA: Randy Faulk, Bart Groendycke; before 1992. Start at the left (south) edge and climb past 2 bolts. Traverse right in a horizontal crack, then up the face past 6 more bolts to the anchor.

32. **Jaws of Life** (5.12a) FA: Leo and Karin Henson; March 1998. Climb past 7 bolts up the face between *Airlift* and *911*. The route shares an anchor with *Airlift*.

33. **911** (5.11d) FA: Randy Faulk, Bart Groendycke; before 1992. Begin just left of a gully and about 35' right of *Airlift*. Climb the right arête of the wall past at least 6 bolts.

MAGIC BUS

This small crag hosts a number of moderate routes and has become a popular cold-weather spot for intermediate climbers. It is visible directly to the north of Second Pullout about halfway up the rocky hillside. The crag is an obvious black block with a small, red triangle near its lower right corner. There are several dark, angular boulders at the top of the ridge just above this wall.

From Second Pullout, follow the main trail down to the wash level. Cross the wash and walk straight north toward the red outcrop. Follow a hidden gully with a smooth south wall up and right (east) for 250 feet to a fault. Scramble up left (north) along the fault/gully for 75 feet to an open, relatively flat area. The formation is located about 150 feet up and right (northeast) from this point. Routes are described from left to right as you approach. The approach takes about 15 minutes. (No topo.)

34. **Electric Koolaid** (5.9+ TR) FA: Donette and Todd Swain; February 1994. The loose face just right of the formation's left edge has been toproped via the anchors on *Blonde Dwarf*. (Not shown.)

35. **Blonde Dwarf** (5.10-) FA: Nick Nordblom, Paul Van Betten; 1988. The obvious thin crack that curves right and up. When the crack ends, follow 2

Second Pullout (Central)

Great Red Book Area

Magic Bus

To Calico Basin

Poser Crag

bolts up left on steep rock to a cold-shut anchor. Bring a good selection of small to medium protection for the crack. The bolts were added in 1993.

*36. **Neon Sunset** (5.8) FA: Kevin Pogue, Craig Dodson; January 1993. Climb the center of the wall past 9 bolts with red hangers to a chain anchor. This route is 15' right of *Blonde Dwarf* and is very well protected (some might say overbolted). (Not shown.)

37. **Zipperhead** (5.8 PG13) FA: Paul Van Betten, Nick Nordblom; 1988. Rope up 8' right of *Neon Sunset* at a thin, vertical crack in varnished rock. Follow the crack for 20', then step right and go up another seam to a bolt. Angle either left or right to reach an anchor on one of the adjoining routes. Bring gear to a #1 Friend. (Not shown.)

38. **Technicolor Sunrise** (5.8 PG) FA: Todd and Donette Swain; December 1993. Begin 6' right of the last line at the left edge of a smooth, triangular section of rock. Climb the left edge of the triangle, then straight up the face past 4 bolts to 2 cold shuts. Small wires are helpful near the bottom of the route.

39. **Ken Queasy** (5.8 PG13) FA: Donette and Todd Swain; December 1993. Start 12' right of the last climb and 8' left of the cliff's edge. Climb a thin, vertical seam in steep, black rock to a bolt, then straight up to another bolt. Angle up left to join *Technicolor Sunrise* from its last bolt. A small TCU and RPs will help you reach the first bolt. (Not shown.)

KITTY CRAG

This sunny cliff is located in a large gully to the right (east) of the Black Corridor. A gully immediately left (downhill) of Kitty Crag provides an alternate approach for Poser Crag and *The Great Red Book*.

Follow the trail down from Second Pullout and take the second left (the first goes to The Gallery/Wall of Confusion). Follow this trail across a red sandy area, then turn slightly right into a drainage (the main wash curves left/west toward The Gallery). Scramble over rocks for 100 yards (you may have to avoid water) to an open sandy area. Walk about 100 yards up the obvious gully to the right of center (east). Kitty Crag is on the left wall of the gully (the sunny side) and slightly downhill of The Sandbox. There is a distinctive boulder the shape of a ship's prow above the routes. Routes are described from left to right as you approach up the gully. (No topos.)

40. **Suffering Cats** (5.11c) FA: Randy Marsh, Pier Locatelli; 1994. This route climbs a beautiful flake system with a red-and-black, smooth wall on its left side. At the top of the flake, move right past the third bolt (crux) then up past 3 more bolts to an anchor. Holds broke at the crux after the first ascent making this more difficult.

41. **Titty Litter** (5.10d) FA: Randy Marsh, Pier Locatelli; 1994. Same start as *Suffering Cats*. Climb a right-facing, bulbous corner past 4 bolts, then up a face past 1 more bolt to shuts.

42. **Nine Lives** (5.11d) FA: Leo and Karin Henson; Fall 1993. Begin on the right side of a ledge, 6' right of the last two routes. Climb a shallow dihedral past 5 bolts to the same anchor as *Titty Litter*.

THE SANDBOX

A pretty cliff that hosts a number of difficult climbs. It is in the shade all day. Follow the trail down from Second Pullout and take the second left (the first goes to The Gallery/Wall of Confusion). Follow this trail across a red sandy area, then turn slightly right into a drainage (the main wash curves left/west toward The Gallery). Scramble over rocks for 100 yards (you may have to avoid water) to an open sandy area. Walk about 100 yards up the obvious gully to the right of center (east). Kitty Crag is on the left wall of the gully (the sunny side) and has a distinctive boulder shaped like a ship's prow above the routes. The Sandbox is on the right side of the canyon, just uphill of a large pine tree. Scramble up a short red cliff band to reach the bottom of the routes. The climbs are described from right (downhill) to left. (No topos.)

43. **Sand Wedge** (5.11b) FA: Leo and Karin Henson; November 1997. Start at the right end of a ledge and about 75' from the large pine tree mentioned in the approach. Two silver bolts protect moves up a black bulge to reach a ledge, and 3 more bolts lead past a left-slanting crack. A final bolt on the face above gets you to an anchor.

44. **Sand Buckets** (5.11b) FA: Leo and Karin Henson; November 1997. Rope up 10' left of the last route. Climb brown huecos past 6 bolts to an anchor.

45. **Sand Rail** (5.12b) FA: Leo Henson; December 1997. Begin 6' left of the last route at a bolt on a low bulge. Climb up and left into a small corner capped by a ceiling. There are 6 bolts on the route and a chain anchor.

46. **Sandblaster** (5.12b) FA: Leo Henson; Fall 1993. Start by an oak bush that is 8' left of the last climb. Follow 7 bolts to an anchor.

47. **Sand Boxing** (5.12d) FA: Leo Henson; December 1997. Rope up 5' left of an oak bush at the center of a low overhang. Climb up and slightly left past 7 bolts to chains. At the third bolt, the rock looks like brown taffy.

48. **Crimson Crimp** (5.12b) FA: Leo Henson; November 1997. Begin 90' up and left of the last route and just right of a black waterstreak. There are red huecos by the first and second bolts. Climb past 6 bolts to chains.

49. **Rubber Biscuit** (5.13a) FA: Leo Henson; April 1994. Start between two black waterstreaks on pink rock. This is at a point 25' left of the last route, where the bottom of the cliff is scooped out. Power past 7 bolts to chains.

ETHICS WALL

This shady cliff is located about 130 yards up-canyon of The Sandbox at the third of three prominent pines. The cliff is at the saddle that leads into Calico Basin above Happy Acres. The rock is gray and burgundy and is in the shade all day. Routes are described from right (downhill) to left as you approach. (No topos.)

50. **Ethical Behavior** (5.11?) FA: Unknown; early 1990s. Bring some traditional gear to supplement the bolts on the route. It appears that the first bolt is missing. Start 40' from the right edge of the cliff at a pink cave with left-slanting fissures above. Climb up to a bolt, then up to an obvious, vertical crack (bolt). Go up a line of gray huecos past 2 more bolts to lower-angle rock. Rappel from the anchor atop the route.

51. **Mind Field** (5.11c) FA: Unknown; early 1990s. Begin 25' left and uphill of the last route at rotten pink rock with gray, slanting rock above. Follow 7 bolts to an anchor.

52. **The Laying on of the Hands** (5.11d) FA: Unknown; early 1990s. Rope up 30' left of the last route behind a cube of rock. There are 2 bolts protecting moves up a smooth face to some huecos and 3 more bolts leading up honeycombed rock to the base of a red band. Continue up and slightly left on overhanging red rock past 3 more bolts to an anchor.

53. **Rafter Man** (5.12a) FA: Unknown; nearly 1990s. Start at the base of an ugly slanting chimney 15' left of the last climb. Climb up grayish brown rock past 8 bolts to an anchor.

THE BLACK CORRIDOR

This corridor, which runs southeast-northwest, currently hosts a total of 25 routes on both walls. The climbs are generally of a moderate nature, making this a popular destination. For an added challenge, try to do all of the routes in a day! This is also a good place to experience the true meaning of generic sport climbs. We can only hope this sort of development won't be repeated in too many other places. The approach is quite simple, although the corridor or its entrance can't be seen from the parking lot. Follow the trail down from Second Pullout and take the second left (the first goes to The Gallery/Wall of Confusion). Follow this trail across a red sandy area, then turn slightly right into a drainage (the main wash curves left/west toward The Gallery). Scramble over rocks for 100 yards (you may have to avoid water) to an open area.

Continue north for 50 yards until your progress is blocked by a bush-filled corridor. Traverse 75 feet right (east) on a ledge system just above the bushes, then curve left toward trees at the entrance of the corridor. This sounds complicated, but once you've done it, the whole approach takes less than 10 minutes. These climbs are in the shade most of the time and are described from the lower entrance moving up the corridor. All routes have anchors on top. (No topos.)

LEFT/SOUTH WALL, LOWER LEVEL

54. **Bonaire** (5.9) FA: Jim Steagall, Kevin Sandefur, Chris Werner, Dave Sobocan (all from Phoenix, Arizona); Fall 1990. Start 75' in from the lower corridor entrance. Climb past 6 bolts with homemade hangers to an anchor. The first bolt is stupid.

55. **Bon Ez** (5.9+) FA: Steagall, Sandefur, Werner, Sobocan; Fall 1990. Begin 20' right of the last route and climb past 7 bolts to an anchor. Again, the first bolt isn't needed.

*56. **Crude Boys** (5.10d) FA: Steagall, Sandefur, Werner, Sobocan; Fall 1990. Rope up 15' right of the last route, then clip 6 bolts en route to an anchor on top. There is an overhang in the middle of the route.

57. **Black Corridor Route 4 Left** (5.11a) FA: Unknown; 1991 or later. This route shares the anchor with the last route. Deceptively difficult. Start 8' right of *Crude Boys* and climb the slippery rock past 2 bolts to a horizontal crack. Move left and finish on *Crude Boys*.

58. **BCR 5L** (5.10+) FA: Steagall, Sandefur, Werner, Sobocan; Fall 1990. Begin 10' right of the last route and 20' left of the boulders that divide the corridor into two levels. Climb past 1 bolt to a thin, vertical crack and follow it to the top.

59. **Vagabonds** (5.10a) FA: Steagall, Sandefur, Werner, Sobocan; Fall 1990. Climb the groove and face 6' right of the last route, clipping 8 bolts on your way to the anchor.

60. **Crude Control** (5.12a) FA: Steagall, Sandefur, Werner, Sobocan; Fall 1990. Contrived and difficult at the start. Begin 12' right of *Vagabonds* and just left of the boulders that divide the corridor into two levels. Follow 6 bolts to the anchor.

RIGHT/NORTH WALL, BASEMENT

61. **Adoption** (5.11b) FA: Leo Henson, Karin Olson; November 1991. Stiff climbing right off the ground. Start at the entrance to the corridor and climb the plated face past 6 bolts.

62. **Burros Don't Gamble** (5.10c) FA: Harrison Shull, Todd Hewitt; December 1994. Begin near a tree about 20' left of *Adoption*. Climb a huecoed face to a flake, then on to the top, passing 7 bolts to a shared anchor.

63. **Burros Might Fly** (5.10a R) FA: Harrison Shull, Todd Hewitt, Dane Cox; December 1994. Start about 30' left of *Adoption* and 10' left of the last route. Climb a right-leaning ramp to a bolt. Go straight up on thin edges

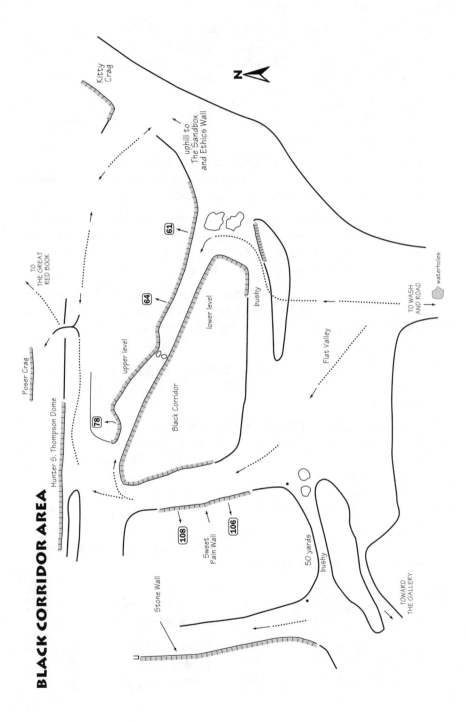

BLACK CORRIDOR AREA

Kitty Crag

uphill to
The Sandbox
and Ethics Wall

N

61

64

lower level

bushy

upper level

Black Corridor

Flat Valley

waterholes

TO WASH
AND ROAD

TO
THE GREAT
RED BOOK

Poser Crag

Hunter S. Thompson Dome

78

108

106

Sweet
Pain Wall

50 yards

bushy

TOWARD
THE GALLERY

Stone Wall

to a flake. Make a long runout across a flake to the fourth bolt, then on up to the shared anchor.

*64. **Nightmare on Crude Street** (5.10d) FA: Jim Steagall, Kevin Sandefur, Chris Werner, Dave Sobocan; Fall 1990. A little loose, but that gives it some character! This route is directly across from *Bonaire* (the route with home-made hangers) and climbs overhanging, red rock past 5 bolts to an anchor. Climbing directly between each bolt makes the climb about 5.11b and contrived.

LEFT WALL, UPPER LEVEL

65. **Thermal Breakdown** (5.9+ PG) FA: Steagall, Sandefur, Werner, Sobocan; Fall 1990. Begin atop the dividing boulders and cruise past some big ledges and 6 bolts.

66. **Crude Street Blues** (5.9+ PG) FA: Steagall, Sandefur, Werner, Sobocan; Fall 1990. Start at a stupidly placed bolt 15' right of the last route. Climb past ledges and 4 bolts to the anchor.

67. **Crude Behavior** (5.9+) FA: Steagall, Sandefur, Werner, Sobocan; Fall 1990. Rope up at a ramp 8' right of *Crude Street Blues*. Scamper past 4 bolts to an anchor.

*68. **Dancin' with a God** (5.10a) FA: Steagall, Sandefur, Werner, Sobocan; Fall 1990. One of the better routes in its grade. Start 12' right of the last route and 35' right of the dividing boulders. Follow 6 bolts to an anchor.

69. **Live Fast, Die Young** (5.10d) FA: Steagall, Sandefur, Werner, Sobocan; Fall 1990. This one may be harder for tall folks. Start 8' right of *Dancin' with a God*. Follow 5 bolts to the anchor—if you can do the mantle at the start.

70. **Black Gold** (5.10b) FA: Dudes from Phoenix; Fall 1990. Begin at a small flake 6' to the right of the last route. Follow 5 bolts with hangers to chains.

71. **Texas Tea** (5.10a) FA: Guys from Phoenix; Fall 1990. From the route names, you can tell these guys watched *The Beverly Hillbillies*! Start at the left edge of a large flake 8' right of the last route. Climb the smooth face to a small ceiling (bolt), then up past 4 more to an anchor. The crux is at the bottom and is contrived.

72. **Fool's Gold** (5.10b) FA: Steagall, Sandefur, Werner, Sobocan; Fall 1990. A broken hold has made this climb harder. Same start as the last route, but walk up right on a ramp. Face-climb past numerous huecos and 5 bolts to an anchor.

RIGHT WALL, SECOND STORY

73. **Oils Well that Ends Well** (5.11a) FA: Steagall, Sandefur, Werner, Sobocan; Fall 1990. Start about 10' left of the dividing boulders and just left of a right-leaning crack system. Climb past 5 bolts (if you get past the second, you should be home free) to the anchor.

74. **Sandstone Enema** (5.11b) FA: Steagall, Sandefur, Werner, Sobocan; Fall 1990. Begin 10' left of the last route, below a short, right-leaning ramp and 10' right of a sentry box. Tricky moves past the first 2 bolts lead to easier climbing past 4 more on the slabby face above. If you start on the left and climb by the hangerless bolt, the route is 5.10d/.11a.

75. **Lewd, Crude, and Misconstrued** (5.9+ PG) FA: Steagall, Sandefur, Werner, Sobocan; Fall 1990. One of the longer routes in the corridor. Start at a sentry box/left-facing corner that is 10' left of *Sandstone Enema* and just left of a boulder in the corridor. Power up the corner and arête past 6 bolts to the anchor.

76. **Texas Lite Sweet** (5.11b PG) FA: Rad Men from Phoenix; Fall 1990. Rope up 6' left of the last route and climb past 3 bolts with hangers to a chain anchor under a ceiling.

77. **Livin' on Borrowed Time** (5.11c) FA: Steagall, Sandefur, Werner, Sobocan; Fall 1990. Begin 3' left of the last route at smooth, varnished rock with a crescent-shaped hold by the first bolt. Follow 4 bolts to the anchor.

*78. **Rebel without a Pause** (5.11a) FA: Steagall, Sandefur, Werner, Sobocan; Fall 1990. Probably the best route here. Climb the overhanging huecos 50' left of the last route and just right of the upper entrance to Black Corridor. Follow 4 bolts to a chain anchor.

HUNTER S. THOMPSON DOME

This cliff is named for the author of *Fear and Loathing in Las Vegas*. To approach this south-facing cliff, follow the trail down from Second Pullout and take the second left (the first goes to The Gallery/Wall of Confusion). Follow this trail across a red sandy area, then turn slightly right into a drainage (the main wash curves left/west toward The Gallery). Scramble over rocks for 100 yards (you may have to avoid water) to an open area. Slightly left of center is an obvious gully with a steep wall facing east. This is Sweet Pain Wall, about 80 yards up the gully from the open area. Continue up the gully past Sweet Pain Wall for another 150 feet to a saddle. The large, plated face directly in front is Hunter S. Thompson Dome. This crag may also be accessed via Black Corridor. The routes are more traditional in nature and are described from left (west) to right (east).

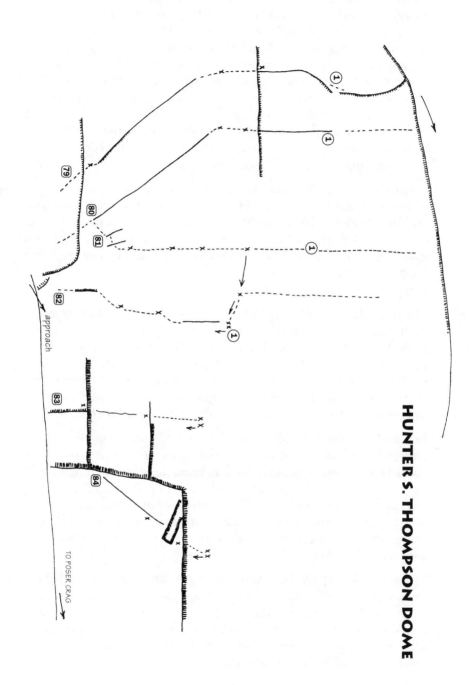

HUNTER S. THOMPSON DOME

79. **Walking the Vertical Beach** (5.9+ PG13) FA: Karen and Don Wilson, Jack Marshall; March 1988. This takes the left of two left-slanting cracks on the far left side of the wall. Bring wires and TCUs to supplement the 4 bolts on the route and a #2.5 and #3 Friend for the belay. **Pitch 1** (5.9+): Starting in a small corridor on the left side of the face, climb up to a bolt, then follow the left-slanting crack to its end. Go up the face past a bolt to a ceiling (bolt), then follow a lower-angle crack up. Belay when you run out of rope (#2.5 and #3 Friends just below a small bush). 150'. **Pitch 2** (5.1): Climb the easy crack and left-facing corner to the top. 50'. **Descent:** Head uphill, then go right and around the right side of the cliff (reversing part of the approach to *The Great Red Book*).

80. **Gonzo Dogs** (5.10-) FA: Jack Marshall, Dave Wonderly; December 1987. Some traditional gear will probably be needed to supplement the bolts on the route. **Pitch 1** (5.10): Begin 20' right of the last route at the right-hand of two left-slanting cracks. Follow the crack to its end at a big hueco (bolt). Go up steep brown rock past another bolt, then up to a crack in a small ceiling. Follow the crack to a belay stance. 140'. **Pitch 2:** Continue to the top.

81. **Runout Rodeo** (5.10 PG) FA: Unknown. Double ropes would be great for the first few moves on this route. Bring RPs, wires, and TCUs. Same start as the last route at the right-hand of two left-slanting cracks. Climb the left-slanting crack for 10', then move right past two thin cracks and up to the first bolt (scary). Continue up the steep face past 3 more bolts to lower-angle terrain. At the last bolt, you can either continue up to the summit or traverse and tension right to the anchor atop *Fear and Loathing II*.

82. **Fear and Loathing II** (5.10+ PG13) FA: Jack Marshall, Dave Wonderly, Warren Egbert; December 1987. A steep and sporty route. Carry wires and a #1 Friend to supplement the 2 bolts on the route. Start at a small, right-facing corner 10' right of the last two routes. This is at the entrance of a corridor at the base of the cliff. Climb the shallow corner, then move up and right to lower-angle rock. Climb up past 2 bolts, then move right and finish up a vertical seam. Rappel with one rope from the anchor or continue to the top.

83. **Liquid God** (5.11) FA: Jack Marshall, Dave Wonderly, Warren Egbert; December 1987. Rope up at a short, clean, right-facing corner capped by a 3-foot ceiling 40' right of the last climb. Stem up the corner to a bolt, then turn the ceiling onto the varnished face. Follow a seam in varnished rock up to another ceiling. Climb past the left edge of this ceiling and another bolt. Belay above from slings.

84. **Pretty in Pink** (5.12a) FA: Paul Van Betten, Don Burroughs; 1990s. A wild-looking route! Begin 25' right of the last route, at the next right-facing corner system. Climb up the right-facing corner for 15', then go up a right-slanting crack/flake past a bolt to a huge block underneath a roof. Clip a bolt above the block, then pull through the roof to lower-angled rock and an anchor.

POSER CRAG

This wall is technically part of Hunter S. Thompson Dome but is up and right of the main face. It is directly above and behind Black Corridor. To approach this south-facing cliff, follow the trail down from Second Pullout and take the second left (the first goes to The Gallery/Wall of Confusion). Follow this trail across a red sandy area, then turn slightly right into a drainage (the main wash curves left/west toward The Gallery). Scramble over rocks for 100 yards (you may have to avoid water) to an open area. Slightly left of center is an obvious gully with a steep wall facing east. This is Sweet Pain Wall, about 80 yards up the gully from the open area. Continue up the gully past Sweet Pain Wall for another 150 feet to a saddle. The large, plated face directly in front is Hunter S. Thompson Dome. Walk right (east) along the base of this wall until you can scramble back up left to the base of Poser Crag. A large, dark patch of varnish near its right edge characterizes Poser Crag. (No topo.)

85. **Special Guest Posers** (5.11a) FA: Randy Marsh, Pier Locatelli; Fall 1990. This is the left-hand route and climbs past 4 bolts to chains.

86. **Tin Horn Posers** (5.11c) FA: Randy Marsh, Pier Locatelli; Fall 1990. This 5-bolt route climbs near the right arête of the formation.

GREAT RED BOOK AREA

This is a traditional area with numerous sunny climbs. *The Great Red Book* is one of the better moderate routes at Red Rocks. Due to a lack of route re-searching/reporting, it appears that older, poorly protected routes have recently received bolted "first ascents."

To approach this south-facing cliff, follow the trail down from Second Pull-out and take the second left (the first goes to The Gallery/Wall of Confusion). Follow this trail across a red sandy area, then turn slightly right into a drainage (the main wash curves left/west toward The Gallery). Scramble over rocks for 100 yards (you may have to avoid water) to an open area. Slightly left of center is an obvious gully with a steep wall facing east. This is Sweet Pain Wall, and it is about 80 yards up the gully from the open area. Continue up the gully past Sweet Pain Wall for another 150 feet to a saddle. The large, plated face directly in front is Hunter S. Thompson Dome. Walk right (east) along the base of this wall until you can scramble up through a large boulder-field to the base of the cliff. Routes are described from left (west) to right (east). Approach time is about 30 minutes from the parking area at Second Pullout.

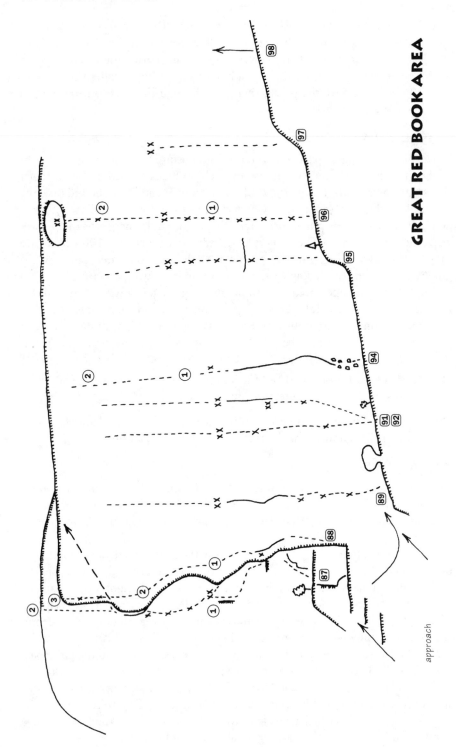

GREAT RED BOOK AREA

approach

*87. **The Great Red Book** (5.8 PG) FA: Bob Logerquist, John Williamson; October 1971. This route has a bit of everything on it. Bring a full rack, including cams up to a #4 Camalot and lots of slings. Rope up below the huge, left-facing corner on a nice ledge. **Pitch 1** (5.8 PG): Scramble up past two ledges with bushes then move right into the corner. Go up about 10', then move left and climb the face and features to a belay stance with 2 bolts. Watch out for rope drag! 130'. **Pitch 2** (5.8 PG): Angle up and slightly left on the smooth face past 2 bolts, then angle right back into the corner. Lieback up a wide section (bolt) past a bulge, then into a low-angle chimney. Either finish up the chimney or climb directly up the face to the top. 150'. **Descent:** Scramble down gullies to the left (west) of the formation.

88. **Animal Boy** (5.11+) FA: Don Wilson, Jack Marshall; March 1988. A difficult route up the right arête of *The Great Red Book*. Bring wires, TCUs, and cams to supplement the bolts. Start on the ledge as for *The Great Red Book*. **Pitch 1** (5.11+): Move onto the arête to reach a thin, left-leaning crack (bolt). Pull the bulge, then continue up lower-angle rock on big plates. **Pitch 2:** Continue up the arête. **Pitch 3** (5.10-): Follow the arête out over *The Great Red Book* past 2 bolts.

89. **Tomato Amnesia** (5.9 PG13) FA: Don and Karen Wilson, Jack Marshall; January 1988. Begin 75' down and right of *The Great Red Book* and just down and left of a mushroom-shaped boulder. Bring wires, TCUs, small cams, and long slings to supplement the bolts. **Pitch 1** (5.9 PG13): Three silver bolts lead to a varnished, curvy seam. Follow the seam past steep rock to an anchor. 100'. **Pitch 2:** Easier climbing leads straight up to the summit of the formation.

90. **Abandoned Line** (5.10+ R) FA: Nick Nordblom, Jenni Stone; 1986. From the start of *Tomato Amnesia*, angle up and right across the face.

91. **See Spot Run** (5.6 X) FRA: Mark Limage and friends; January 1998. Start between the mushroom-shaped boulder and some oak bushes. Climb the face past 2 bolts to an anchor.

92. **Question of Balance** (5.9 R) FA: Nick Nordblom, Jon Martinet; 1979. Begin in the same spot as the last route. Angle up and right to a bolt 40' up. Continue past double bolts just left of a vertical seam. Follow the seam to belay slings. A second pitch goes to the top of the formation.

93. **Elementary Primer** (5.7+ X) FRA: Mark Limage and friends; November 1998. Rope up between two bushes 30' right of the last two routes. These bushes are at a point where the gully at the base of the cliff begins to rise. Climb the poorly protected face to an anchor.

94. **Stone Hammer** (5.8 R) FA: Alan Bartlett, Eliza Moran; 1984. Climb the obvious curving crack system 25' right of the last route. There should be one bad bolt somewhere on the first pitch. This bolt was drilled using a rock, hence the route's name. Belay from gear, then continue to the top of the cliff.

95. **Chips Away** (5.10+ R) FA: Nick Nordblom, Jenni Stone; 1986. Start 40' up and right of the last route and just below a small pine tree. There should be a tiny corner just right of a horizontal white streak. Climb up the face to a silver bolt 40' up and just below a horizontal crack. Continue past at least 2 more bolts to an anchor. Climb to the top.

96. **Ground-up Vocabulary** (5.8+ R) FRA: Mark Limage and Friends; January 1998. Start just above the small pine tree. **Pitch 1** (5.8+): Five bolts with black hangers lead to an anchor. 90'. **Pitch 2** (5.6): Face-climb past 1 bolt to an anchor in a cave.

97. **Chairman Mao's Little Red Book** (5.8? X) FA: Unknown. Begin 40' right of the last route at a solid band of varnish in the chasm. Climb the face to an anchor.

98. **Sandstone Cowboy** (5.10 X) FA: Jack Marshall, Dave Wonderly; December 1987. Here is what the first ascent party wrote about this route: "This is a serious route up discontinuous cracks on the far right side of this wall. The first pitch is protected by lassoing a horn far above the leader's head from halfway up the pitch." Rope up 20' right of the last route at the right edge of a varnish patch in the chasm. **Pitch 1:** Angle up right to a bolt with an old SMC hanger about 30' up. Go straight up to another bolt, then angle left to a bolt and drilled piton. **Pitch 2:** Wander up the face between modern anchors past at least 1 more bolt.

MEISTER'S EDGE AREA

Numerous routes have been done where the trail from Second Pullout first meets the wash. Seven routes are described in this edition. Follow the trail down from Second Pullout and take the second left (the first goes to The Gallery/Wall of Confusion). Follow this red, sandy trail for 50 yards along the base of a red, crumbly cliff.

99. **Sand Man** (5.11 TR) FA: Paul Van Betten; 1987. This neat route climbs an obvious series of huecos and pockets directly above the trail and to the left of *Meister's Edge*.

*100. **Meister's Edge** (5.11a) FA (TR): Joe Herbst; early 1970s. This short but striking arête is located just above the wash as you approach Black Corridor or Sweet Pain Wall. It was bolted in 1988 after being soloed by at least a couple of brave locals. The route starts off giant angular blocks and has 3 bolts but no anchor.

MEISTER'S EDGE AREA

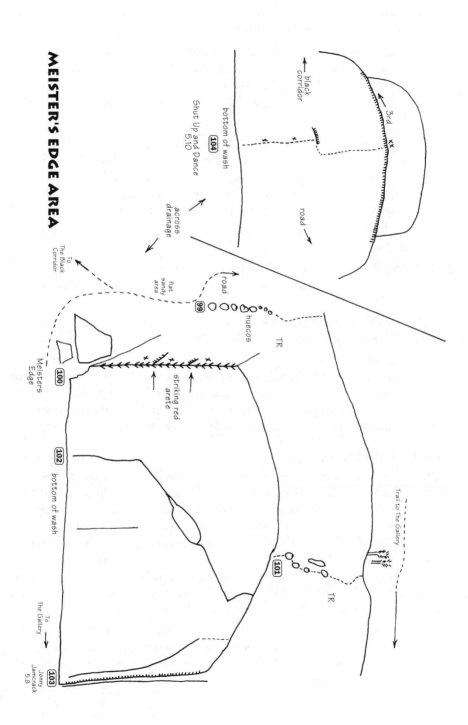

black corridor

3rd

xx

road

bottom of wash

104 Shut Up and Dance 5.10

across drainage

To The Black Corridor

flat sandy area

road

99

huecos

TR

Meisters Edge

100

striking red arete

102

bottom of wash

Trail to The Gallery

101

TR

To The Gallery

103 Jonny Jamcrack 5.8

101. **Yucca** (5.11+ TR) FA: Paul Van Betten; 1987. Climb a series of huecos on the wall above *Jonny Rotten.*

102. **Jonny Rotten** (5.11-) FA: Paul Van Betten, Sal Mamusia; January 1986. A typical Navajo sandstone crack climb. Not as good as *The Fox,* but maybe you'll like it. Climb the steep, loose, right-leaning crack that is 50' right of *Meister's Edge* and right above the streambed. Like its neighbor, *Jonny Jamcrack,* it's in the shade most of the day.

103. **Jonny Jamcrack** (5.8 R) FA: Sal Mamusia, Paul Van Betten (both solo); January 1986. Begin 75' right of *Jonny Rotten* and just left of a low-angle chimney/gully. Climb the left-curving hand crack to a ledge, then follow a left-slanting seam to an unprotected face and the top. Bring gear to 4" for the crack and small TCUs for the belay.

The following route is located on the sunny face directly across the wash from *Sand Man* (#99).

104. **Shut up and Dance** (5.10) FA: Danny Meyers; 1985. Follow a seam system past 2 bolts to a 2-bolt anchor. Walk off left (toward Black Corridor).

The following route is located in an east-west running corridor to the left (north) of *Shut up and Dance.* (Not shown.)

105. **Malice Alice** (5.10) FA: Sean Ward, Chuck Carlson; April 1996. Bring gear up to a #1.5 Friend. Start on the right (south) wall of the corridor below a finger crack leading through ceilings. Climb up and right along the finger crack past several ceilings. At the final roof, traverse right past a hueco to an easier face and the top. Walk off left.

SWEET PAIN WALL

Although this small crag can't be seen from the parking lot, the approach is fairly straightforward. Follow the trail down from Second Pullout and take the second left (the first goes to The Gallery/Wall of Confusion).

Follow this trail across a red sandy area, then turn slightly right into a drainage (the main wash curves left/west toward The Gallery). Scramble over rocks for 100 yards (you may have to avoid water) to an open area. Slightly left of center is an obvious gully with a steep left wall facing northeast. This is Sweet Pain Wall, and it is about 80 yards up the gully from the open area. Routes are described from left to right as you approach the cliff. (No topos.)

*106. **Sweet Pain** (5.12a) FA: Leo Henson, Randy Faulk; 1991. Start in the center of the cliff, at the bottom of a rotten, right-leaning crack with blocky ceilings above. Follow 5 bolts up and left through angular ceilings to a chain anchor.

107. **Glitter Gulch** (5.11b) FA: Guys from Colorado; 1991. Begin 40' right on a ledge 15' off the ground. Angle up and left past 6 bolts to chains. Holds broke on this former 5.10 route, making it more difficult.

108. **Slave to the Grind** (5.11b) FA: Guys from Colorado; 1991. Same start as *Glitter Gulch*, but climb straight up, passing a right-leaning gash with a bush at mid-height. Follow bolts to a cold-shut anchor.

109. **Sister of Pain** (5.11c) FA: Leo and Karin Henson; Fall 1992. Rope up 15' right of the last two routes at the right edge of a low scoop that is just left of a chocolate-colored streak. Climb past 4 bolts to an obvious right-leaning crack, then follow 3 more bolts up the steep, rounded arête above to cold shuts.

110. **Lee Press-on** (5.12b) FA: Leo and Karin Henson; Fall 1992. Start 6' right of the last route at the blankest section of the wall. Clip 6 bolts en route to the obvious right-leaning crack, then pass 1 more bolt while climbing a left-leaning crack above.

111. **Pain in the Neck** (5.10a PG13) FA: Unknown; pre-August 1993. A contrived start leads to better climbing. Begin at an obvious right-leaning crack near the right end of the cliff. Climb into a bowl (bolt), follow the obvious big holds up and slightly right, then move back left just above the second bolt. A total of 5 bolts leads to chains. If you climb up and left from the first bolt to the second, it's 5.10c.

112. **A-Cute Pain** (5.8) FA: Todd and Donette Swain; November 1993. Named for my sweetie. Rope up 8' right of the last route at a shallow, left-facing, varnished corner. Climb past a bolt to the obvious right-leaning crack and follow that up right for 15' (small TCUs needed). Break out left and climb the plated face past 2 more bolts to a cold-shut anchor.

STONE WALL

This cliff faces east and receives sun in the morning. It is located in the first gully running north-south to the west (left) of Sweet Pain Wall. The Stone Wall approach is fairly straightforward, although, like Sweet Pain Wall, it can't be seen from the parking lot. Follow the trail down from Second Pullout and take the second left (the first goes to The Gallery/Wall of Confusion).

Follow this trail across a red sandy area, then turn slightly right into a drainage (the main wash curves left/west toward The Gallery). Scramble over rocks for 100 yards (you may have to avoid water) to an open area. Slightly left of center is an obvious gully with a steep left wall facing northeast. This is Sweet Pain Wall, about 80 yards up the gully from the open area.

Continue west past the mouth of the Sweet Pain gully to a narrow, bushy gully running east-west. Follow this west for 50 yards until a narrow gully opens up on your right (uphill/north). Go up this gully about 100 yards to reach Stone Wall, which is on your left. Routes are described from left to right as you approach the cliff. (No topo.)

113. **Purple Haze** (5.10d) FA: Don Burroughs, Alan Busby; 1993. The leftmost line on the wall. Start 25' right of a left-facing corner at a point where the solid desert varnish ends. Climb past 6 bolts to chains.

114. **Haunted Hooks** (5.10d) FA (TR): Brad Stewart; August 1992. FA: (lead) Don Burroughs, Alan Busby; 1993. Begin 15' right of the last route, at the smaller of two left-leaning arches located at the base of the crag. Follow 9 bolts to rappel bolts.

115. **Roto-Hammer** (5.10c) FA: Daryl Ellis; August 1992. Rope up 12' right of *Haunted Hooks,* at the larger of two left-leaning arches at the base of the wall. Follow 7 bolts with colored hangers to chains, passing the left side of a small ceiling between the fifth and sixth bolts.

116. **Nirvana** (5.11a) FA: Don Burroughs, Alan Busby; 1993. Start at a vertical, left-facing flake 12' right of the last route. The first bolt on this route has a colored hanger. A total of 7 bolts lead to rappel bolts.

117. **Stonehenge** (5.11b) FA: Don Burroughs, Mike Ward, Alan Busby; 1993. Begin at a small, left-facing flake that is just left of a bush 8' right of *Nirvana.* Following 8 bolts will (hopefully) get you to the chains.

118. **Stone Hammer II** (5.10) FA: Mike Ward, Mike Clifford; 1986. The original route on the wall. You'll need traditional gear to supplement the bolts. About 25' to the right of *Stonehenge* is a vertical crack with an oak tree in front of it. Climb this crack for 35' to reach the first bolt, then climb past more bolts to the rappel anchor, which is to the right of the climb.

119. **Birthstone** (5.10d) FA: Leo and Karin Henson, Karl Williamson; April 2, 1993. Completed on Karin's birthday. Climb straight up to the anchors on *Stone Hammer II.*

120. **April Fools** (5.10b) FA: Don Burroughs, Alan Busby; 1993. Start 40' right of the oak tree and crack at the base of *Stone Hammer II* and between two scooped caves at the base of the cliff. Clip 6 bolts en route to the rappel bolts.

THE OBSERVATORY

This section of cliff was included under the Gallery listing in the first edition of this guide, but further development and the difference in climbing experience have warranted a separation. Bring a selection of gear to protect the climbs and two ropes for rappelling.

Climber on *April Fools* (5.10b).

From the parking area, walk down the main trail, then take the first trail leading off to the left (about 120 yards from the lot as for The Gallery). Follow this lesser-used trail about 400 yards up and over a red outcrop (the top of the Meister's Edge Area and *Jonny Rotten*), then down to a wash and pine tree.

Cross the wash immediately (well before another pine and a large, red cube of rock) and follow a well-trodden path up broken slabs for 100 yards to a small corridor running parallel to the hillside. Scramble up the far wall of the corridor (about 30 feet of scrambling), then angle right across slabs for 35 yards to the base of the slabby wall.

The right (east) end of the crag has the best staging area, which is under an overhanging section of rock. This approach takes about 15 minutes and involves some scrambling. The cliff is visible from the road, characterized by its prominent right arête, and in the sun most of the day. Routes are described from left to right (west to east). (See photo on page 90.)

121. **Witches' Honor** (5.8 R) FA: Danny Meyers: rope solo, circa 1988. A good but scary route; you need to be very solid leading 5.8. Gear up at a human-sized hueco that is almost directly above the scrambling in the approach corridor. This hueco is located on a low-angle slab about 60 yards left of the cliff's right edge. From the hueco, scramble about 60' up along a right-leaning crack to a pedestal on the right side of a vertical crack. Follow the vertical crack past a horizontal crack to a bolt, then up to another bolt. Traverse right and up to a third bolt, then up and left on a slab to a 2-bolt anchor. Rappel with two ropes down to a point just above the initial hueco, or use one rope to reach the pedestal, then downclimb the right-leaning crack to the hueco.

122. **Which Hunters?** (5.10- R) FRA: Todd and Donette Swain; February 1994. An unknown party placed the first 4 bolts but apparently did not finish the climb. Bring small TCUs, a #1.5 Friend, the two smallest Tri-Cams, some long slings, and your rabbit's foot. You can back up the highest bolt with all of the gear mentioned, but you still have to run it out above. Begin 40' left of the flat staging area (located below an overhang at the right edge of the cliff) on a low-angled slab. Climb past 4 bolts, then angle up and right (no protection) to the shared anchor. Rappel with two ropes. (Not shown.)

123. **Warlock** (5.9 R) FA: Todd and Donette Swain; February 1994. Have your protective spells and incantations ready in case of a fall! Carry gear to 1.5", lots of slings, and a #3.5 Friend. Start about 20' left of the overhang and flat ledge. Climb straight up the face past a bulge to a vertical crack that passes between two overhang/cave formations. At a horizontal crack, either traverse straight right or climb up and right to the arête. Belay at the anchor for *Which Hunters?* and *Bewitched*. Rappel with two ropes. This route can easily be toproped after doing *Bewitched*.

*124. **Bewitched** (5.3) FA: Unknown; 1970s. This route was soloed long before it was developed as described here. An excellent outing for moderate climbers. Bring long slings for the climb and two ropes for rappelling. Rope up on a large terrace at the very right (southeast) edge of the Observatory/Gallery face, approximately 200' right of the man-sized hueco on *Witches' Honor*. Climb the slab just left of a big overhang, aiming for the right side of a cavelike formation above. Pass 2 bolts, moving up and left past the second bolt into the cave. Move straight right from the cave (bolt) to the arête, then up past 3 more bolts to an anchor that is just right of another, smaller cavelike formation.

THE GALLERY

This is the most popular sport climbing cliff at Red Rocks and probably the best place to meet climbers. Human waste is a *big* problem here! Do your part: pack it out, and chastise those who don't.

From the parking area, walk down the main trail, then take the first trail leading off to the left (about 120 yards from the lot). Follow this lesser-used trail about 400 yards up over a red outcrop (the top of the Meister's Edge Area), then down to a wash and pine tree. Cross the wash immediately (well before another pine and a large, red cube of rock) and follow a well-trodden path up broken slabs for 100 yards to a small corridor running parallel to the hillside. Either scramble up the far wall of the corridor (about 30' of scrambling) and then angle up left across slabs for 75 yards to the base of the wall, or go left in the gully, then walk up slabs.

You should arrive at the right (east) end of the crag under the most overhanging section of rock if you did the scrambling, and at the left (west) end if you took the easy way. This approach takes about 15 minutes. The cliff is visible from the road (although it looks very small and insignificant) and is in the sun most of the day. Routes are described from right to left. All routes have anchors from which to grab, lower, rappel, or toprope. (No topo, but see photo on page 90.)

125. **Glitch** (5.12c) FA: Mike Tupper; Winter 1990. Start 10' left of an alcove on the right side of The Gallery. Follow a right-leaning flake past 4 bolts, then continue up right past a hueco and 2 more bolts to the anchor.

126. **Nothing Shocking** (5.13a) FA: Don Welsh; Winter 1989/90. Climb *Glitch* to the third bolt, then power straight up past 3 more bolts to join the end of *The Sissy Traverse*.

127. **Who Made Who** (5.12c) FA: Mike Tupper; Winter 1989/90. Climb *Glitch* to the second bolt, then continue up past 3 more bolts.

128. **Where the Down Boys Go** (5.12d) FA: Mike Tupper; Winter 1989/90. Start at the bottom of the flake that the last three routes climb and go up and slightly left past 5 bolts.

*129. **The Gift** (5.12d) FA: Boone Speed; Winter 1989/90. Start at the base of *Yaak Crack* and climb up very steep rock past 6 bolts.

*130. **Yaak Crack** (5.11d) FA: Bill Boyle; Winter 1989/90. Begin 8' left of the last four routes and below the obvious left-leaning crack. Climb the crack past 6 bolts.

*131. **The Sissy Traverse** (5.13b) FA: Don Welsh; Fall 1991. Start in the corridor behind the right edge of a huge boulder that is 15' left of *Yaak Crack*. The bolts on this route have been painted black so that you know you're on the right route! Climb up to the first bolt (see variation), then angle right and up past 8 more bolts. **Variation:** Start at the base of *Yaak Crack* and climb past the first 3 bolts on *The Gift* before going up right past 5 more bolts. This seems to be the more logical line.

132. **Minstrel in the Gallery** (5.12b) FA: Mike Tupper; Winter 1989/90. The first route on the cliff. Same start as *The Sissy Traverse*, then climb the face just left of *Yaak Crack* past 5 bolts.

133. **A Day in the Life** (5.11b) FA: Bill Boyle; Winter 1989/90. Begin 10' left of the last route, behind the huge boulder and on the left side of a cat's claw bush. Cruise out the right side of the pod past 5 bolts.

134. **Social Disorder** (5.11d) FA: Scott (a.k.a. Jimmy Dean), "Bucky," Bullock, and Jonathan Knight; 1991. Rope up as for the last route, then climb straight up from the pod past 5 bolts.

135. **Gridlock** (5.11c) FA: Greg Mayer; Spring 1990. Same start as the past two routes but exit out the left side of the pod, passing 4 bolts with homemade hangers. It's a little easier to go left, then back right between the second and third bolts.

136. **Running Amuck** (5.10c) FA: Greg Mayer; Spring 1990. Rope up 10' left of the last route below a short, left-facing flake and up on a ledge. Run past 4 bolts to the same anchor as *Gridlock*.

137. **Pump First, Pay Later** (5.10b) FA: Greg Mayer; Spring 1990. Don't run out of gas before you get to the anchor! Start 6' left of the last route, clipping 4 bolts.

138. **Gelatin Pooch** (5.10a) FA: Greg Mayer; Spring 1990. Begin 6' left and climb past 4 bolts (3 have homemade hangers) to chains.

139. **Buck's Muscle World** (5.9-) FA: Greg Mayer; Spring 1990. Start 8' left of *Gelatin Pooch* to climb this 3-bolt route with homemade hangers.

140. **Sport Climbing Is Neither** (5.8) FA: Unknown; Winter 1991. Start 10' left of *Buck's Muscle World* at a short, curving crack. Follow 3 bolts to an anchor.

141. **Range of Motion** (5.10d) FA: Todd Swain, Dick Peterson, Peggy Buckey; May 1990. Start about 75' left of *Buck's Muscle World* and 20' left of a right-facing corner that doesn't reach the ground. Climb up through a pod, passing 4 bolts.

WALL OF CONFUSION

This cliff is about 150' left of The Gallery on the same level. Routes are described from right to left because the normal approach is from The Gallery. All routes have anchors. Believe it or not, these routes were done before The Gallery was developed.

142. **Resin Rose** (5.11+) FA: Paul Crawford, Jay Smith; April 1987. Named for a model of climbing shoe that was popular in the 1980s. This traditional route climbs the right-leaning crack/roof that is up and right of the bolted routes. (Not shown.)

143. **Body English** (5.12c) FA: Mike Tupper; Winter 1988. Start 30' up and right from *Fear and Loathing III* at the very right end of the cliff. Climb the steep corner past 4 bolts to chains (or go left to the anchor on *Fear and Loathing III*).

*144. **Fear and Loathing III** (5.12a) FA: Bill Boyle, Boone Speed; Winter 1988. One of the steepest routes you've seen until you go to *The Trophy*. This is at least the third *Fear and Loathing* at Red Rocks. Start atop a boulder in an alcove and power past several roofs on an overhanging wall. There are 9 bolts providing convenient places to hang and rest.

145. **Promises in the Dark** (5.12b) FA: Mike Tupper; Winter 1988. Begin 12' left of the last route at a short dihedral capped by a ceiling. Zip past 7 bolts to the anchor.

146. **Big Damage** (5.12b) FA: Boone Speed; Winter 1988. Start at a right-curving crack 6' left of *Promises in the Dark* and climb up and slightly left past 6 bolts.

147. **Sudden Impact** (5.11c) FA: Boone Speed, Bill Boyle; Winter 1988. Climb the face 8' left of the last route, passing 5 bolts.

148. **Desert Pickle** (5.11b) FA: Bill Boyle, Boone Speed; Winter 1988. Power up the wall 6' left of the last route, using 4 bolts.

149. **American Sportsman** (5.10c) FA: Boone Speed, Bill Boyle; Winter 1988. Another 4-bolt route 6' left of the last route.

150. **The Runaway** (5.10b PG) FA: Greg Mayer; Spring 1989. The farthest left route on the cliff. It starts up on a ledge. There are 4 bolts with homemade hangers for pro.

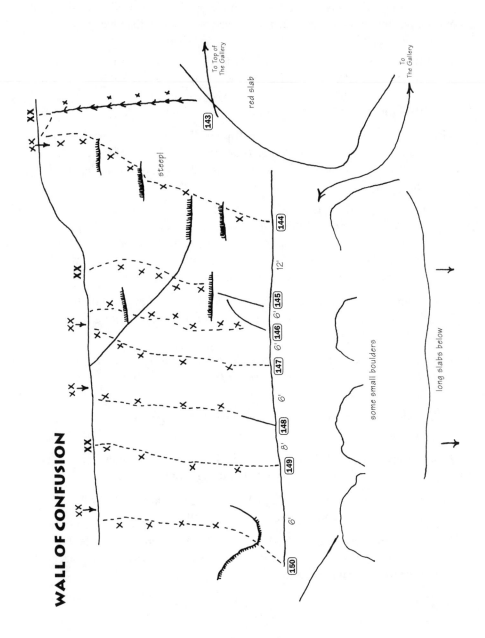

WALL OF CONFUSION

SANDSTONE QUARRY
OVERVIEW

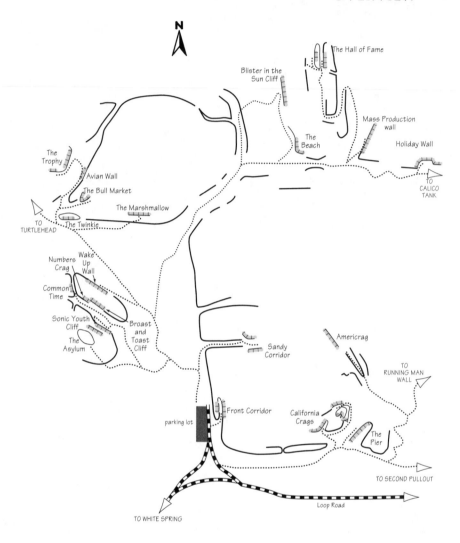

N

The Hall of Fame

Blister in the
Sun Cliff

Mass Production
wall

The
Beach

Holiday Wall

The
Trophy

Avian Wall

TO
CALICO
TANK

The Bull Market

The Marshmallow

TO
TURTLEHEAD

The Twinkie

Wake
Up
Wall

Numbers
Crag

Common
Time

Sonic Youth
Cliff

Broast
and
Toast
Cliff

The
Asylum

Sandy
Corridor

Americrag

TO
RUNNING MAN
WALL

parking lot

Front Corridor

California
Crags

The
Pier

TO SECOND PULLOUT

Loop Road

TO WHITE SPRING

112

SANDSTONE QUARRY

This area has a host of worthwhile crags containing climbs of all difficulties. The approaches range from 1 to 25 minutes. The best cliffs here include The Trophy, Holiday Wall, and Sonic Youth Wall. Follow the scenic loop road for 2.7 miles and park in the large lot at Sandstone Quarry. The first routes described are to the right (southeast) of the parking lot (toward the Second Pullout), and they are listed as you encounter them from left to right (west to east).

SANDSTONE QUARRY EAST

FRONT CORRIDOR

Walk 75 yards due east from the Sandstone Quarry parking lot to reach this obvious north-south running corridor. Routes in this corridor are good but certainly not the best sport climbs at Red Rocks. Some routes may need some traditional gear to supplement the bolts, as well as some courage. The climbs are described from right to left as you enter the corridor. Some of the ones on the right (east) wall get sun in the afternoon. (No topos.)

1. **Sicktion** (5.9) FA: Nick Nordblom, Randy Marsh; Fall 1988. Start at the mouth of the corridor on the right (east) wall below a flake 10' up and near an oak tree. Follow a vertical seam past 3 bolts to the top. Belay in a large recess (a TCU; #2.5 and #3 Friends), then walk off right. Easily toproped.

2. **Prescription Gription** (5.10 R) FA: Nick Nordblom, Jenni Stone; Spring 1988. Begin 20' left of the last route. Climb past 2 bolts to a left-leaning seam/corner, then up a vertical crack, passing 1 more bolt. Bring a #2.5 or bigger Friend for the belay. Walk off right.

3. **Friction Addiction** (5.10 PG13) FA: Bob Conz, Shelby Shelton; Spring 1988. Start at the right edge of a tree clump, which is 15' left of the last climb. Power past 3 bolts, then follow a seam up left past 2 more bolts. Bring a #2.5 or bigger Friend for the belay. Walk off right.

4. **Affliction for Friction** (5.11a R) FA: Mike Ward, Danny Meyers; Fall 1989. Begin at a horizontal oak tree in a clump of four trees that is 10' left of *Friction Addiction*. Make a difficult mantle, then climb past 2 bolts, angling way left (dicey crux) to a seam. Continue up the seam past 3 more bolts. Bring a #2.5 or bigger Friend for the belay. Walk off right.

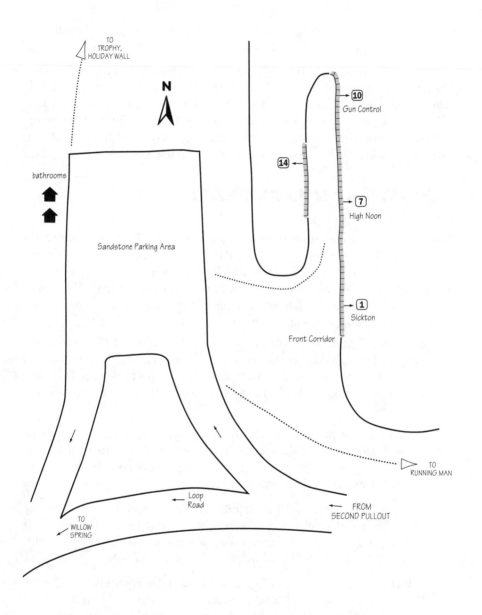

5. **Crumbling Community** (5.10 PG) FA: Paul Van Betten, Danny Meyers; 1989. Start at a gray waterstreak 15' left of the last route. Dance up the streak past a low bolt to a seam, then follow a left-leaning crack to its top. Angle up right past 2 more bolts to the top. Walk off right.

6. **A Thousand New Routes** (5.11 R) FA: Paul Van Betten, Nick Nordblom; Summer 1986. The first route, done in the corridor. Climb the left-leaning diagonal crack, then go up right from the last bolt to the belay station. 3 bolts.

7. **High Noon** (5.11 R) FA: Nick Nordblom, Jenni Stone; Spring 1988. Begin 10' left of the last route, below a right-facing corner with varnish on its right side. There are 6 bolts on the route. Rappel with two ropes.

8. **Hair Today, Gone Tomorrow** (5.11a) FA: Nick Nordblom, Paul Van Betten; Spring 1988. Start near a shrub 25' left of *A Thousand New Routes*. Climb along a left-trending seam past 7 bolts, the first of which is a Metolius about 30' up. A 120-foot rappel will get you back to the ground, or you can traverse off right.

9. **To Bolt or Toupee** (5.10c) FA: Mike Ward, Paul Van Betten; Spring 1988. Rope up 40' left of *Hair Today* and 30' right of the end of the corridor. Climb up to a right-facing corner capped by a ceiling, then follow bolts up and right to the rappel anchor. 7 bolts.

10. **Gun Control** (5.11b) FA: Bob Conz, Shelby Shelton, Nick Nordblom; Summer 1988. Start 10' left of the last route and 20' right of where the corridor narrows down. Follow bolts up into a large scoop, then exit out the left side (crux) to the belay anchor. 8 bolts. Rappel with two ropes.

The next routes are on the left (west) wall of the corridor and are in the shade all day.

11. **Churning in the Dirt** (5.12b) FA: Mike Tupper, Craig Reason; November 1988. Start across from *High Noon*. This is the left-hand route that ends at a chain anchor.

*12. **Sound of Power** (5.12a) FA: Craig Reason, Mike Tupper; November 1988. The right-hand route that follows thin flakes to a chain anchor.

13. **Sunsplash** (5.13c) FA: Dan McQuade; April 1995. One of the hardest routes at Red Rocks. Follow the bolts (if you can) between *Sound of Power* and *Monster Skank*.

*14. **Monster Skank** (5.13b) FA: Dan McQuade; January 1993. This route is located 30' right of *Sound of Power* roughly across from *Hair Today Gone Tomorrow*. Climb past 8 bolts to chains.

CALIFORNIA CRAGS

This sunny cliff is a very short walk from the Sandstone Quarry parking area. Approach via the trail leading east (toward Second Pullout) from the entrance to the Sandstone Quarry parking area. Walk about 200 yards on the trail to a point where the trail touches white rock. Go another 100 yards above several small red outcrops to just before a long red buttress that protrudes into the drainage (The Pier). Turn left (north) across the drainage at a varnished triangular boulder, then go up red slabs to the base of the formation. Routes are described from left (toward the parking lot) to right and begin on a white slab to the left of a large, red recess. (Not all routes are shown in photo.)

15. **Cal. West** (5.10c) FA: Albert Newman, Leo Henson; March 1998. Begin about 80' left of a large red recess on a white slab. Find a prominent red arête about 30' right of a waterstreak. Climb the face just left of the red arête past 6 bolts to an anchor.

16. **Hurricane** (5.11b) FA: Leo Henson, Albert Newman; March 1998. Start at the base of a deep gully/corner just right of the last route. Climb the overhanging, right side of the red arête past 8 bolts to an anchor.

17. **Quicksand** (5.11d) FA: Louie Anderson; circa 1996. Start 75' right of the last two routes on the left side of a large, red recess. The route begins on a ledge that is 15' right of a broken corner. Climb past 5 bolts to an anchor. There is a ceiling between the second and third bolts.

18. **Far Cry from Josh** (5.10c) FA: Louie Anderson; circa 1996. This route gets sun in the afternoon. Start across the recess from *Quicksand* and atop a block. Angle up and left past 4 bolts to an anchor.

19. **Just in from L.A.** (5.11b) FA: Louie Anderson; circa 1996. Rope up in the same place as *Far Cry from Josh* on top of a boulder. Climb up along a crack past 2 bolts, then up the face past 2 more bolts to an anchor.

20. **The Staircase** (5.5) FA: Unknown; 1990s. This route provides an exposed approach to the upper level of the formation. Bring Tri-Cams and long slings to place protection in pockets on the face. Begin at a gray cave about 100' around and right from the last routes. Climb a red slab just right of the cave, then traverse up and left across a gray, pocketed face to the top.

21. **The Escalator** (5.10?) FA: Unknown; circa 1995. Directly above the gray cave and *The Staircase* is a huge boulder. On the side of this block facing the loop road is a brown varnished face. Climb up and right along the edge of a varnished, slabby face past 2 bolts. Bring wires, Tri-Cams, and small cams to place in pockets on the route.

22. **People Mover** (5.8?) FA: Unknown; circa 1995. There is a right-facing corner 10' left of *The Escalator*. Climb up and right along the corner to the top of the block. Bring gear up to a #3.5 Friend.

The next three routes are above *Quicksand*. You can approach via *The Staircase* or via a gully on the back (northeast) side of the formation.

23. **Nevadatude** (5.12b) FA: Leo Henson; January 1998. Start directly above the back of the lower red recess. Climb along vertical seams past 5 bolts.

24. **Serious Leisure** (5.12a) FA: Louie Anderson; circa 1996. Rope up 30' right of the last route and directly across from *The Escalator* block at a 6-foot-long finger crack. Follow 6 bolts along a left-curving crack to an anchor.

25. **Orange County** (5.11b) FA: Leo Henson; January 1998. Begin 12' uphill of *Serious Leisure*. Climb past 6 bolts to an anchor.

Note: To avoid descending *The Staircase*, follow a gully (10' right of *Orange County*) that leads down from the saddle between the cliff and the huge boulder.

THE PIER

This sport climbing area is similar to Black Corridor, but it has routes that are more difficult. The climbs are generally in the shade, but the sun is never far away. Approach via the trail leading east (toward Second Pullout) from the entrance to the Sandstone Quarry parking area. Walk about 200 yards on the trail to a point where the trail touches white rock. Go another 100 yards above several small red outcrops to just before a long red buttress that protrudes into the drainage (The Pier). Follow a side trail down into a small canyon. The routes are on the right (east) wall of the canyon and are described from right to left as you descend the gully. (No topo.)

26. **Scantily Clad Bimbo** (5.11b) FA: Leo and Karin Henson; January 1996. Start on a ledge at the right end of the cliff and just left of some green lichen. There are several large solution holes at the base of the cliff. Climb past 4 bolts along a vertical seam to an anchor.

27. **Seventh Hour** (5.11a) FA (TR): Unknown. FA (lead): The Hensons; January 1996. Rope up at a left-facing corner 15' left of the last route. Climb a vertical crack system past 5 bolts. There is an old toprope anchor atop this route.

28. **This Is the City** (5.12a) FA: Leo and Karin Henson; January 1996. Begin at an oak bush 8' left of the last climb. Four bolts and a vertical seam mark the route.

29. **Desert Oasis** (5.12d) FA: The Hensons; January 1996. Start at a dark varnished section of rock 5' left of *This Is the City*. Clip 4 bolts as you go up along a vertical seam.

30. **How Do Ya Like them Pineapples?** (5.13a) FA: Leo Henson; January 1996. This route begins near an oak bush and below overlaps that are 6' above the ground. Follow 5 bolts to the anchor.

31. **False Alarm** (5.12c) FA: The Hensons; January 1996. Rope up directly above some yuccas 8' left of the last route. Climb past 5 bolts to an anchor.

32. **Geometric Progression** (5.12b) FA: Leo and Karin Henson; January 1996. In the middle of the crag is a prominent, slightly right-leaning crack. Climb the left side of the crack past 5 bolts.

33. **Drug Sniffing Pot-Bellied Pig** (5.12d) FA: Leo Henson; January 1996. Start at a vertical seam 8' left of the last climb and just left of some bushes. Follow 5 bolts to get to the anchor.

34. **Thirsty Quail** (5.12b) FA: The Hensons; January 1996. Rope up below a small ceiling that is 8' off the ground 6' left of the last route. Pull the ceiling (bolt), then go up along a dark varnished seam past 4 more bolts.

35. **Cling Free** (5.12b) FA: Leo and Karin Henson; January 1996. Same start as *Thirsty Quail*, then angle up and left past 6 bolts to an anchor.

*36. **Under the Boardwalk** (5.11b) FA: The Hensons; January 1996. The best route on the cliff. Start 10' left of the last two routes and just right of a large clump of bushes. The rock on this route is very featured. Climb up scoops and scallops past 6 bolts.

37. **Pier Pressure** (5.12b) FA: The Hensons; January 1996. Begin 6' down and left of the last climb and behind a scrub oak. Trend up and slightly left along a seam past 8 bolts.

38. **Almost, but Not Quite** (5.12c) FA: Leo Henson; January 1996. Climb past the first 3 bolts on *Pier Pressure*, then angle up left past 6 more bolts to an anchor.

39. **Poco Owes Me a Concert** (5.12c) FA: Leo Henson; January 1996. Begin at the right edge of a boulder 20' left of the last route. Climb the steep face past large huecos to a vertical crack. 8 bolts.

40. **Destiny** (5.12c) FA: Leo Henson; January 1996. Rope up atop a boulder at some large scoops. Follow 6 bolts up a brown face.

41. **Basement** (5.12a) FA: Leo and Karin Henson; January 1996. Start in the same spot as *Destiny*, then go up and left toward the edge of the cliff. Continue up the face just right of the left edge of the cliff, passing 6 bolts.

42. **Long Walk on a Short Pier** (5.9+) FA: The Hensons; January 1996. Start at the very left end of the cliff. Move out left around the corner and up the face past 8 bolts. This route gets morning sunshine.

AMERICRAG

For a while, the patriotic first ascent party had an American flag flying on the wall! The crag faces northeast, is visible from the loop road, and has a fairly straightforward approach. It receives some morning sunshine. From the southeast corner of the Sandstone Quarry parking lot, walk along a trail back toward Second Pullout, aiming for the outermost section of exposed white rock (about 200 yards).

Continue east on this trail along the right (south) slope of a small canyon, then drop down left (north) between two red outcrops to the bottom of the drainage. You pass a large, mushroom-shaped boulder just before reaching the drainage bottom. About 100 feet downhill of the mushroom boulder is a red cube of rock. At this point, you can see the crag for the first time. It is a large, tan, overhanging wall on the left (west) side of a canyon near the skyline. Go north up the canyon, through bushes to a fork in the drainage. Take the red rock rib up the middle of two gullies (the right/east one is narrow) to reach the bottom of the cliff. Routes are listed from left to right as you approach. The approach takes about 15 minutes. (No topo.)

43. **Stuck on You** (5.8?) FA: Unknown; 1990s. This sunny, 3-bolt route is on the approach to Americrag. It is on the right side of the gully, directly right of the start of the red rock rib mentioned in the approach. The route ascends a red slab with black varnished plates.

44. **That Wedged Feeling** (5.10+) FA: Jay Smith, L. Erickson; February 1990. This route is also on the approach to Americrag. As you approach up the red rib of rock separating the gullies, you can see a prominent red crack system on the left (west) that faces away from the road. The climb starts as a left-facing corner, then enters a wide pod. It finishes through an overhang. Bring wires and a double set of Friends up to #4.

45. **Toxic Playboy** (5.12) FA: Paul Van Betten, Richard Harrison, Sal Mamusia, Bob Conz; April 1990. Quite a testpiece, as the pitch ratings imply. Start at the base of a long, left-slanting crack/seam system that is 50' uphill from a pine tree in the gully. This is the leftmost route on Americrag. **Pitch 1** (5.12): Climb the face and vertical seam using 4 bolts and traditional gear to reach a bolt anchor. 80'. **Pitch 2** (5.12b): Power past 6 bolts to a bolted belay. 80'. **Descent:** Rappel the route.

46. **Mr. Moto** (5.11) FA: Paul Van Betten, Richard Harrison, Shelby Shelton; April 1990. Begin at a short, curving crack leading to a ceiling 15' uphill of the last route. Start up the crack and move left under the ceiling to a bolt, then pull the ceiling. Climb a left-leaning seam past 3 more bolts to the first belay on *Toxic Playboy*. You need gear to supplement the bolts on the route.

47. **Jimmy Nap** (5.11c) FA: Paul Van Betten, Richard Harrison, Sal Mamusia; April 1990. Same start as the last route at the curving crack that leads to a ceiling. Zoom up the face right of *Mr. Moto,* past 5 bolts, and rap from a 2-bolt anchor.

48. **Americragger** (5.12-) FA: Paul Van Betten, Richard Harrison; April 1990. Begin 20' uphill of the last two routes and directly across from a short, gnarled pine tree. Ascend overhanging slots using dynos and other neat tricks. There are 4 bolts for pro and a bolted belay for the rappel.

49. **Rebel Yell** (5.11+) FA: Paul Van Betten, Danny Meyers, Jenni Stone; September 1990. Start 40' uphill of *Americragger* and 25' uphill of a vertical thumb of rock in the gully. Follow 3 bolts out left along a seam, then up to a fourth bolt in a varnished plate. Step left and climb a vertical seam, then go up the face past 3 more bolts to a 2-bolt belay.

RUNNING MAN WALL AREA

This collection of sunny cliffs is located to the southeast of the parking lot and back toward Second Pullout. From the southeast corner of the Sandstone Quarry parking lot, walk along a trail back toward Second Pullout, aiming for the outermost section of exposed white rock (about 200 yards).

Continue east on this trail along the right (south) slope of a small canyon, then drop down left (north) between two red outcrops to the bottom of the

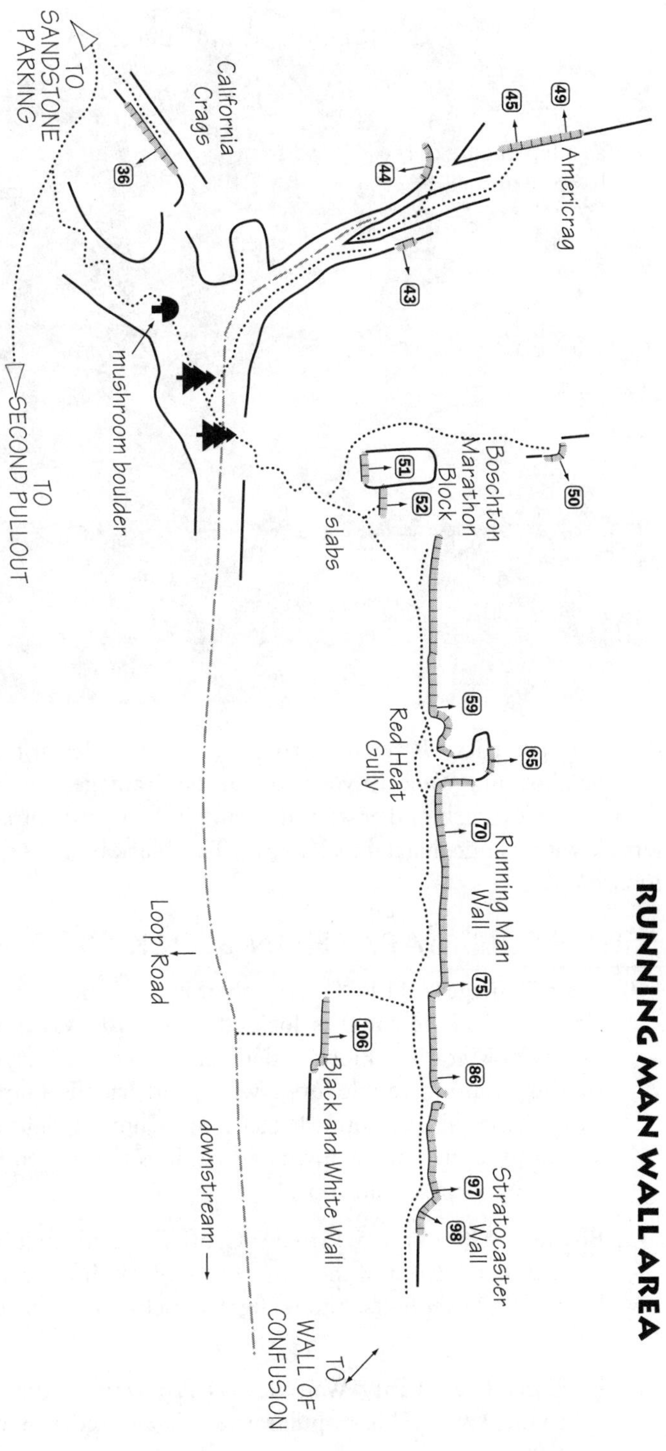

RUNNING MAN WALL AREA

TO
SANDSTONE
PARKING

California
Crags

36

49
45
44

Americrag

43

TO
SECOND PULLOUT

mushroom boulder

Boschton
Marathon
Block

51
52

50

slabs

Red Heat
Gully

59

65

70
Running Man
Wall

75

Loop Road

106
Black and White Wall

86

downstream

Stratocaster
Wall
97
98

TO
WALL OF
CONFUSION

Running Man Wall (Left)

To
Parking Lot

drainage. You pass a large, mushroom-shaped boulder just before reaching the drainage bottom. Walk 50 yards down the drainage, passing two pine trees, then veer left (north and east) and scramble 100 yards up red slabs to a huge terrace with a large, black block above. This black block is the *Boschton Marathon Block*.

BOSCHTON MARATHON BLOCK

50. **Brain Damage** (5.11 R/X) FA: Robert Finlay, Mike Ward, Paul Van Betten; circa 1987. This route is located about 400 yards north of (behind) Boschton Marathon Block and ascends a very striking dihedral that faces southwest. Bring double ropes, wires, and Friends. Start to the right of the base of the dihedral on a ledge/ramp. Climb a right-arching flake to a small ramp, then move down and left into the corner. Finish up the dihedral using your second rope.

51. **Boschton Marathon** (5.12b) FA: Geoff Wiegand; circa 1987. This route is located on the front of the large, black block. It is clearly visible from the loop road, has 6 bolts, and is slightly tricky to downclimb from the summit.

*52. **Frictiony Face, Panty Waist** (5.8+) FA: Danny Meyers, Brad Stewart; February 1989. This popular route is located just right of *Boschton*

Marathon, on a red slab. Start 20' up above the huge terrace on a ledge that is just right of the huge black block and behind a large cat's claw (acacia) bush. The route has 6 bolts and ends at a 2-bolt belay station 85' up.

RUNNING MAN WALL

From the Boschton Marathon Block, angle right (east) on the terrace for 125 yards to Running Man Wall, which faces the loop road (south). A long, low roof running along the majority of the crag characterizes it.

Routes are described from left to right, and the majority of routes in this guide are near the right edge of the formation. You will need two ropes to get off most routes. (Not all routes appear in photo on page 122.)

53. **True Lies** (5.9?) FA: Unknown; 1990s. As you reach the left edge of the Running Man Wall, locate a gully, that goes up behind the Boschton Marathon Block. About 20' up this gully, on the right (main) wall is a yucca. Directly above the yucca is a right-facing corner leading to a roof 40' up. Climb the corner for 20', then step left and climb up and left past 2 bolts to an anchor. Bring wires and cams to supplement the bolts.

54. **Calico Terror** (5.11) FA: Mike Ward, Paul Van Betten; December 1987. Sounds appealing, huh? Start near the left edge of Running Man Wall and climb past 2 bolts into a varnished, right-leaning crack. Follow the crack up and right past 1 more bolt to a 2-bolt rap station.

55. **There Goes the Neighborhood** (5.11+) FA: Greg Mayer; 1989. Start in the center of the cliff about 15' right of a tree near the right edge of the long, low roof. The route is marked by a block and cheater stones. Climb past 11 bolts with black, homemade hangers to an anchor. Bring a #1.5 Friend to supplement the bolts.

56. **Second Fiddle to a Dead Man** (5.11d) FA: Greg Mayer; November 1993. Start atop the right edge of the block where *There Goes the Neighborhood* starts and climb past 10 bolts to a chain anchor.

57. **New Traditionalists** (5.11d) FA: Mike Tupper; 1989. Begin 20' right of the last route and below a line of bolts with SMC hangers on very smooth rock. Climb straight up past 11 bolts to the anchor. There is a superfluous bolt without a hanger just left of the start of the route.

58. **Predator** (5.10+ R) FA: Nick Nordblom, Paul Van Betten; 1988. Same start as *Running Man,* then follow a prominent left-leaning crack that leads to a 2-bolt belay.

*59. **Running Man** (5.11) FA: Paul Van Betten, Sal Mamusia, Mike Ward; November 1987. Definitely better than the movie! One of the classic pitches at Red Rocks. Start 40' uphill and right of *New Traditionalists* and below an obvious vertical seam system that trends slightly up and left. Use your Schwarzenegger-like muscles to power past lots of bolts to a bolt anchor. You may want to bring a few TCUs and small wires to supplement the bolts.

60. **Graveyard Waltz** (5.11d PG) FA: Mike Tupper; 1989. Rather sporty, but great climbing. Same start as *Running Man,* but climb straight up past 9 bolts with homemade hangers.

61. **Commando** (5.12b) FA: Louie Anderson, Bart Groendycke; 1992. Begin at the left edge of a low ceiling that is just left of a right-facing corner 10' right of the last route. Follow 9 bolts that lead to an anchor. At press time, there was an unfinished route just right of this.

62. **Galloping Gal** (5.11a) FA: Folks from Spudland (Idaho); 1990. Being tall helps on this one. Rope up 45' right of the last route and 3' left of a left-facing chimney/corner. Starting atop a pink pedestal, climb past 10 bolts to a chain anchor 85' up.

63. **Vile Pile** (5.10 PG) FA: Mike Ward, Danny Meyers, Jessie Baxter; Fall 1989. Bring #1.5 and #2 Friends to place between the fourth and fifth bolts. Start 5' right of *Galloping Gal* and 10' left of an oak bush atop a pink pedestal. Zip past 6 bolts to the top of the block. Rap from an anchor.

Right of the *Vile Pile* formation is a gully leading up into a recess. The next 4 routes are in this gully.

64. **Unknown** (5.11c?) FA: Mike Ward; Spring 1995. Roughly 9 bolts go up the wall 30' left of *Red Heat.*

65. **Red Heat** (5.10+) FA: Nick Nordblom, Mike Ward, Danny Meyers; Fall 1989. Another excellent route. Scramble 100' up the obvious gully, to the right of *Vile Pile,* to ledges. Climb a right-facing, varnished groove past 5 bolts, then continue up the face past 4 more bolts to an anchor in a hueco. Bring some cams and plan on a two-rope rappel.

66. **Synthetic Society** (5.11a) FA: Mike Ward, Louie Anderson, Bart Groendycke; December 1990. A bit contrived. Scramble up the *Red Heat* gully for 40'. On the right (east) wall of the gully, climb past the left edge of a ceiling and 7 bolts to a chain anchor shared with *Plastic People.*

67. **Plastic People** (5.10b) FA: Louie Anderson, Bart Groendycke; December 1990. Same start as the last route, 40' up the *Red Heat* gully. Trend out right to the arête, then up to the shared chain anchor, clipping 8 bolts en route.

68. **Fibonacci Wall** (5.11+) FA: Paul Van Betten, Don Welsh; 1987. If you're not a math major, you'll need to look this one up in the dictionary. The

name should go with a 5.8 climb. No hooks were used on the first ascent, and all the bolts were placed free on the lead. Climb the rounded arête on the right edge of the *Red Heat* gully past 7 bolts.

69. **Northern Lights** (5.11d) FA: Folks from Idaho; 1991. Begin 40' down and right of the *Red Heat* gully on a slab and just right of a rounded overhang at the base of the cliff. Stick-clip the first bolt, then zoom past 8 bolts to chains, keeping 10' left of a vertical crack (*Falstaff*).

70. **Falstaff** (5.10- R) FA: Nick Nordblom, Paul Van Betten; 1985. Begin at a line of bolts 30' right of the last route. Climb past 2 bolts, then angle left to the obvious sickle-shaped crack, which is followed to the top. You'll probably have to finish the route with a short second pitch. Descend a gully to the west with one short rappel.

71. **Yodritch** (5.11 R) FA: Paul Van Betten, Mike Ward; Fall 1987. Gear up in the same spot as *Falstaff*. Climb up and right past 3 bolts on a slab to a varnished crack (traditional pro here), then past 1 more bolt in steep rock to the belay. The second pitch has only 1 bolt and is runout (5.8) to the top.

72. **Split Crack** (5.7) FA: John Williamson, John Taylor; October 1973. Rope up just right of a lone pine tree and left of a huge round boulder at the base of the cliff. These features are about 200' right of *Falstaff*. Swim up the prominent chimney system. The route was apparently first done starting at the level of the wash below the huge traverse ledge.

73. **Split Ends** (5.10-) FA: Unknown; early 1990s. Start just right of *Split Crack* and above the huge round boulder at the base of the cliff. This red face has numerous vertical seam systems and two established routes. Starting 15' right of the edge of *Split Crack*, climb the face past about 7 bolts to an anchor.

74. **Split Infinitive** (5.9) FA: Unknown; early 1990s. Begin above the huge, round boulder just right of the last route. Climb past at least 6 bolts to an anchor. Some gear may be needed to supplement the bolts.

75. **Nevada Book** (5.8) FA: John Taylor, John Williamson; October 1973. This prominent route ascends a huge left-facing corner about 30' right of *Split Crack*. It is presumably 2 pitches long. Scramble up and left on an easy red face to reach the base of the huge corner. Climb the corner to the top.

76. **Supernova** (5.10+ R) FA (Pitch 1): Paul Van Betten, "Frodo"; 1988. FA (Pitch 2): Nick Nordblom, Jay Smith; 1988. This 2-pitch route is supposed to be scary on both pitches. Begin about 300' right of *Falstaff* and *Yodritch*, at a short, right-facing corner at the lower left margin of a large face. There is a small cat's claw bush at the base of the 15-foot-high corner. **Pitch 1** (5.9+ R): Climb the right-leaning, right-facing corner to its

top. Angle up right on a slab to a bolt, then up the steepening face past at least 2 more bolts to a belay anchor near a horizontal crack. 150'. **Pitch 2** (5.10+ R): Pull the bulge above the belay and follow a seam/crack to a bolt, then continue up to the top. Belay at some holes and fixed slings. 150'. **Descent:** Rappel the route with two ropes.

77. **Spikes and Twine** (5.9) FA: Nick Nordblom, Jenni Stone; 1988. How do they get the rope up there? Rope up below a vertical seam/crack that is just left of a cat's claw bush 40' right of the last route. **Pitch 1:** Climb the crack for 40', then step left to the base of another crack. Follow this crack up to a belay at a horizontal crack below a bulge. 100'. **Pitch 2:** Pull the bulge (bolt) then move up left into an obvious crack, which is followed to the top.

78. **Swedish Erotica** (5.10-) FA: Paul Van Betten, Katja from Sweden; 1988. Bring gear to a #3 Friend, including wires and TCUs. Start 10' right of the last route, on the right side of the cat's claw bush. There are basketball-size huecos on either side of the cat's claw bush. **Pitch 1** (5.10-): Climb a low-angle face past 2 bolts to an obvious crack. Go up this crack, traverse right (crux), then up the easier crack/ramp to a belay niche. 100'. **Pitch 2:** Continue up the easy crack above, traverse left, and climb the second pitch of *Spikes and Twine*, or traverse 30' right and rappel with two ropes from the *Flame Ranger* anchor.

79. **Flame Ranger** (5.12-) FA: Bob Conz, Paul Van Betten, Sal Mamusia, Shelby Shelton; February 1991. Begin at a slightly left-leaning finger crack about 30' right of *Swedish Erotica* and 45' left of a chimney/chasm. Bring wires for the initial crack. Climb the finger crack to a right-leaning fissure. Move right 8', then climb past 7 bolts to an anchor. Rappel with two ropes.

80. **Tier of the Titans** (5.12) FA: Paul Van Betten, Bob Conz, Shelby Shelton, Sal Mamusia; February 1991. Climb the *Flame Ranger* finger crack, then angle up and right about 20'. Power past about 7 bolts to an anchor. Rappel with two ropes.

81. **Titan Rocket** (5.12a) FA: Paul Van Betten, Bob Conz, Sal Mamusia, Shelby Shelton; October 1991. Begin at the left edge of a varnished chimney/chasm about 20' right of the last two routes. Climb the face just left of the gully past 8 bolts to an anchor. You will need two ropes for the rappel.

The next routes are about 100 yards to the right, past a lower-angled, broken area.

STRATOCASTER WALL

This excellent cliff can be approached from either Second Pullout or the Sandstone Quarry. It is located about 400 yards right (east) of the Running Man Wall on the same level. Stratocaster Wall has two sections. The left side is char-

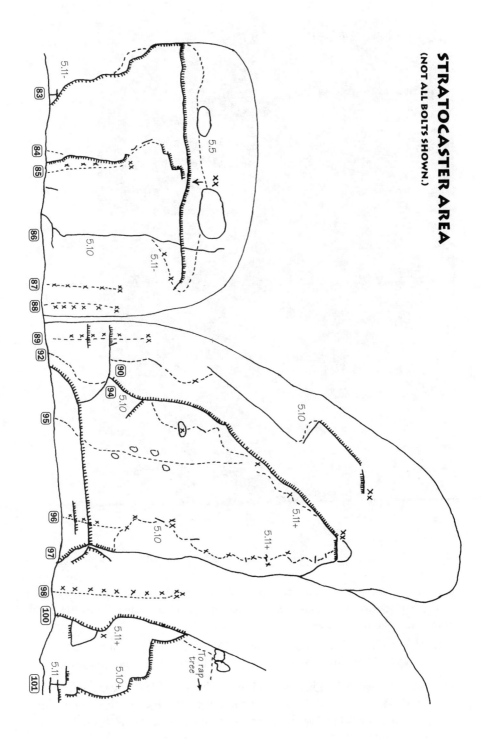

STRATOCASTER AREA
(NOT ALL BOLTS SHOWN.)

Stratocaster Wall

acterized by a deep chimney/corridor on its left side and a large roof in the center. Routes are described from left to right as approached from the Sandstone Quarry parking area.

82. Project (5.12?) FA: Unknown. Start 25' right of a chasm at the left edge of the cliff. There are 2 bolts heading out the bulge thus far. (No topo.)

83. Break Loose (5.11-) FA: Jay and Jo Smith; Spring 1988. Rope up 20' right of the last route and 40' from the left edge of the cliff. This route climbs the wide, slightly left-leaning crack system that goes up through the left side of the giant roof.

84. **Diablo** (5.10 A2+) FA: Paul Van Betten, Sal Mamusia; 1988. This route was done originally without pins or bolts. Start 40' right of *Break Loose* under the center of the roof. Free and aid the left-facing, left-slanting corner to the center of the giant roof, then out the tongues in the roof to a huge hueco.

85. **Pablo Diablo** (5.12d) FA: Paul Van Betten, Sal Mamusia; Spring 1993. A wild route up the arête just right of the *Diablo* corner system. This route has 5 bolts and meets *Diablo* at mid-height with a 2-bolt belay. The giant roof has been worked on as a free climb!

*86. **Cut Loose** (5.11-) FA: Jay Smith, Nick Nordblom; Spring 1988. An excellent line. Bring gear up to a #2.5 Friend. Start 20' right of *Diablo*. Jam and lieback up the obvious dihedral to a roof 40' up. Traverse out right past 2 bolts (crux), then back left to a chain anchor.

87. **One-Eyed Jacks** (5.11b) FA: Donny Burroughs, Alan Busby; 1993. The route is named after the eyelike formation above the first bolt (which can be used as a natural thread). Begin at the right edge of a cave about 35' right of *Cut Loose* and 8' left of a chasm. Follow 4 bolts to a chain anchor. A second pitch can be done up the arête to connect with the *Footloose* belay.

88. **Footloose** (5.11b) FA: Craig Reason, K. Bacon; 1991. Start 42' right of *Cut Loose*, at the right edge of the buttress and just left of a rotten, gray gully with huge huecos. Climb up a short arête, then up the steep, blank face past a total of 7 bolts to an anchor.

89. **Flying V** (5.11b) FA: Kelly Rich, Mark Swank; December 1993. Scramble about 30' up on ledges just right of *Footloose*. Climb the left margin of the face past about 7 bolts.

90. **Party Line** (5.10+ R) FA: Nick Nordblom, Jay Smith, Jo Bentley, Jenni Stone; 1988. Scramble up about 30' (as for the last route) into the bottom of the gully until you are below a crack system shaped like a lightning bolt on the right wall of the gully. Climb a thin, slabby face (dicey) past bolts, then follow the dogleg thin crack, which ends at an enormous hueco with a 2-bolt rap station. Another short pitch leads onto the terrace above (5.10-).

91. **Party Down** (5.12b TR) FA: Dan McQuade; May 1995. Begin 60' right of *Footloose* at the left edge of an amphitheater. This is about 15' right of bushes at the base of a gully and 10' left of *Choad Hard*. Horizontal slashes and pockets will get you to a 2-bolt anchor on a ledge. (No topo.)

92. **Choad Hard** (5.12c) FA: Tim Roberts; February 1995. Start at a boulder midway between the left edge of the wall and the first obvious crack system in the amphitheater. This is at a point where red and gray rock meet.

Dan McQuade on *Stratocaster Direct* (5.12a). MCQUADE COLLECTION

Follow 4 bolts up a bulging wall to a shoulder. Climb past 5 more bolts up the next bulge.

93. **The Choad Warrior** (5.12c) FA: Dan McQuade; Spring 1992. Steep! Rope up 75' right of *Footloose* at the left side of an amphitheater and 8' left of two rotten, gray, right-slanting cracks. Follow 5 bolts to a ledge (chain anchor), then climb out a huge bulge past 6 more bolts.

94. **When the Shit Hits the Fan** (5.11+ R) FA: Jay Smith, Paul Crawford; April 1987. This 3-pitch route climbs an obvious crack/corner system just right of *The Choad Warrior*.

95. **Marshall Amp** (5.11) FA: Bob Conz, Shelby Shelton, Jay Smith, Paul Van Betten; March 1991. Begin 50' right of *The Choad Warrior* and 30' left of the deepest part of the cave at a right-slanting crack. Large holds will get you to a ledge 20' up, then climb huecos past 7 bolts to a belay station. **Descent:** Rappel with two ropes.

*96. **Stratocaster Direct** (5.12b) FA: Dan McQuade; Spring 1992. Being monkeylike would be useful on this one! Begin 15' left of *Stratocaster* and just right of the deepest part of the cave. Power past 5 bolts to join *Stratocaster* at 2 cold shuts.

*97. **Stratocaster** (5.11+) FA: Jay Smith, Nick Nordblom; Spring 1988. You'll be wired after doing this one! Bring a variety of gear and two ropes. Start 65' right of *Marshall Amp* at the base of a chimney with a prominent black waterstreak. **Pitch 1** (5.10): Climb the chimney/corner to a pod 20' up, then move left (above 2 cold shuts) and go up past 3 bolts to a belay station. 80'. **Pitch 2** (5.11+): Follow cracks and huecos up the right arête of the wall, using bolts and natural gear for pro. Belay in the big hueco. 100'. **Descent:** Rappel the route.

*98. **Beyond Reason** (5.13b) FA: Dan McQuade; Spring 1992. One of the testpieces of Red Rocks. The route was originally bolted by Craig Reason without working it first, hence it's a bit of a mess. Start 15' right of *Stratocaster*, and climb past 7 bolts to a 3-bolt anchor that is 40' up. You may want to stick-clip the first 2 bolts, the lower one is a ring bolt.

99. **Purple Haze II** (5.12c) FA: Dan McQuade; February 1995. Start off a block as for *The Bristler*. Traverse out right to the arête, then up and left on the face to rejoin *The Bristler*. Cross that route onto the overhanging prow and go up to an anchor. A thread and 7 bolts provide the protection. (Not shown.)

100. **The Bristler** (5.12-) FA: Sal Mamusia, Paul Van Betten; 1987. Richard Harrison's term for a bolt, among other things (e.g. "Black Corridor is chock full of bristlers"). This route starts just right of *Beyond Reason* on a block below a triangular alcove. Climb out the overhanging corner/alcove past a bolt, then up and over the next corner/overhang. To descend, traverse right and scramble down around to the base.

101. **Telecaster** (5.11) FA: Jay Smith, Paul Crawford; circa 1988. Climb the overhanging crack/corner 10' right of *The Bristler*, then follow the left-facing arch/roof around left to a notch. Join *The Bristler* through the notch to the top. To descend, traverse right and scramble down.

102. **Cowboy Café** (5.12a) FA: Don Welsh; 1990. This route climbs a dark, south-facing boulder directly above The Observatory (described under Second Pullout). It is about 400 yards to the right of *Stratocaster*. Follow 6 bolts to a chain anchor.

B/W WALL

This sunny wall has at least four climbs and all have apparently been led. As of press time, I had done only one of the routes, hence the sketchy descriptions.

Located directly below *Cut Loose*, this cliff has a prominent black waterstreak on it. The crag is clearly visible from the loop road but is best approached from above at the level of Stratocaster Wall. Scramble down from the huge terrace below Stratocaster Wall to the lowest ledge. Walk right (west) and downclimb a short crack to a ramp. Follow this down until you can cut back east along the base of the cliff (you'll be about 75 feet above the drainage bottom). The routes are described from left to right (west to east) as you encounter them.

103. **The Negative** (5.10 R) FA: Jack Marshall, Dave Wonderly; January 1988. Near the left edge of the wall is a left-facing corner. Climb the corner until it ends, then continue up the face above to the top.

104. **The Darkroom** (5.9) FA: Wendell Broussard, "Little Rick"; 1982. This was originally led without the bolts. Bring a #2.5 Friend and some Tri-Cams for solution pockets. Climb the obvious black waterstreak to an alcove just below the top of the cliff.

105. **Snapshot** (5.10- R?) FA: Don and Karen Wilson, Jack Marshall; February 1988. A sparsely bolted face route located atop a boulder to the right of the waterstreak. It begins at a right-leaning crack and requires a belay somewhere before the top (no anchors visible). Good luck!

*106. **Red Light** (5.10- R) FA: Don and Karen Wilson, Jack Marshall; February 1988. A very good route, but not for the faint of heart! Bring gear to a #2 Friend, including several small TCUs, small Tri-cams, long slings, and wires. Begin in a corridor running north-south at a shallow dihedral with 2 bolts on its varnished left half. There may be a pool of water at the base of the dihedral. **Pitch 1** (5.10- R): Climb the dihedral past 2 bolts to a stance in a scoop. Move right (bolt) and up over a scary bulge to a belay stance with 2 bolts. 80'. **Pitch 2** (5.8 R/X): Follow a crack to face climbing past 2 bolts, and eventually, to the top. Belay by sitting down in a chasm (no anchors). 130'. **Descent:** Walk left (west) and downclimb a short crack to a ramp. Follow this down until you can cut back east along the base of the cliff (you'll be about 75' above the drainage bottom).

SANDSTONE QUARRY CENTRAL
SANDY CORRIDOR

There are dozens of climbs in this corridor, but only five routes are described in this guide. To reach this area, walk 150 yards north from the parking lot, staying close to the base of the obvious west-facing cliff on your right and walking past numerous quarried blocks. Continue across slabs for another 50 yards, then turn right (east) into the first corridor you encounter (Sandy Corridor). Walk to the back of the corridor, then scramble up the drainage about 100 yards, passing a few pine trees. Just before the red rock ends on the left (north) wall of the canyon, head up left on a ramp toward two huge detached boulders. The southwest face of the right (east) boulder is Requiem Wall. Approach time is about 15 minutes; routes are in the shade in the early morning. The three routes on this crag are described from left to right.

107. **Integrity of Desire** (5.12a) FA: Mike Tupper; Spring 1991. Start 10' right of the gap between the huge boulders and below a vertical white seam that begins in a corner. Follow 6 bolts to chains. This route was done for the movie *Moving Over Stone II*.

108. **Flying Cowboys** (5.12d) FA: Don Welsh; Spring 1991. Rope up 45' right and around the corner from the last route. Start up a vertical seam, then move left and up to the anchor (6 bolts).

109. **Plastic Pistol** (5.12b) FA: Don Welsh; Spring 1991. Begin 6' right of the last route and 20' left of the east edge of the boulder. Climb past 5 bolts to shuts.

To approach the next two routes, walk 150 yards north from the parking lot past numerous quarried blocks. Continue across slabs for another 50 yards, then turn right (east) into the first corridor you encounter (Sandy Corridor). Walk to the back of the corridor, then scramble about 200 yards up the canyon until you reach a large, left-leaning pine tree (this is about 30 yards before the canyon chokes off). Turn right (south) and go up a gully for 50 feet until it narrows into a corridor. Scramble out right (west) onto a ledge, then continue up and right past bulges and ledges for 150 feet to the base of the route.

*110. **Chrysler Crack** (5.9) FA: Randal Grandstaff, Jon Martinet; 1970s. This fine off-width (some might say those two words shouldn't appear in the same sentence) is high on the right wall of the gully, across from and above Requiem Wall. Bring Big Bros, the very largest Big Dudes, or be brave! You can get good wires about two-thirds of the way up, but you will need other huge gear to make the route truly safe. The climb ascends an amazing varnished corner with a pine tree at its base. Descend off left.

111. **The Deep West** (5.12b) FA: Geoff Wiegand; 1987. Climb the bolted face right of *Chrysler Crack*. You might be able to get a stopper in before the first bolt, or you might have to stick-clip it.

SONIC YOUTH CLIFF

This crag faces north and really can't be seen from the parking lot, although the rock formation is clearly visible. From the parking lot, follow the main trail 200 yards northwest past a white boulder in the main wash toward an old roadway. Turn left about 50 yards from the boulder at the right end of a low, white rock formation. Follow a faint path up a hill, then across a plateau for about 300 yards to some pine trees. Angle slightly left toward a canyon with a large, steep, brown wall on its right. About 100 yards from the pines, you'll see Sonic Youth Cliff on your left. It is dark brown, overhanging, and in the shade all day. Most of the routes do not have rappel anchors, and they finish on a ledge system dividing the cliff into lower and upper tiers. Routes are described from left to right.

112. **Hooligans** (5.11c) FA: Greg Mayer; July 1992. Begin about 25' left of a bush and just right of a left-leaning crack/ramp. Follow 6 bolts to a rap station that is about 15' below a bush on a ledge.

BROAST AND TOAST AREA

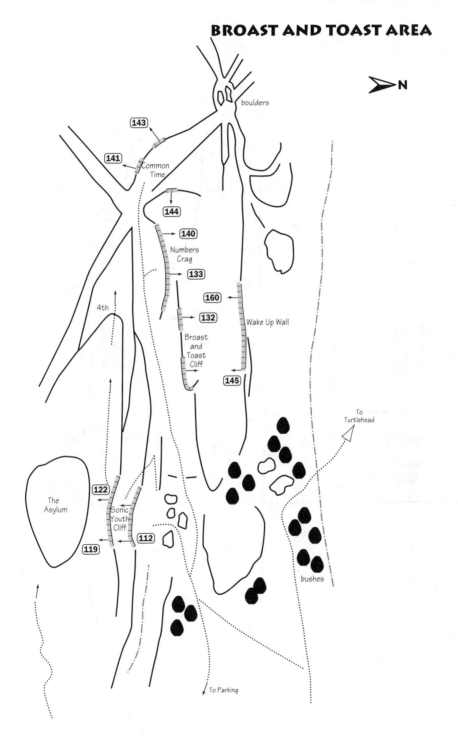

SONIC YOUTH CLIFF

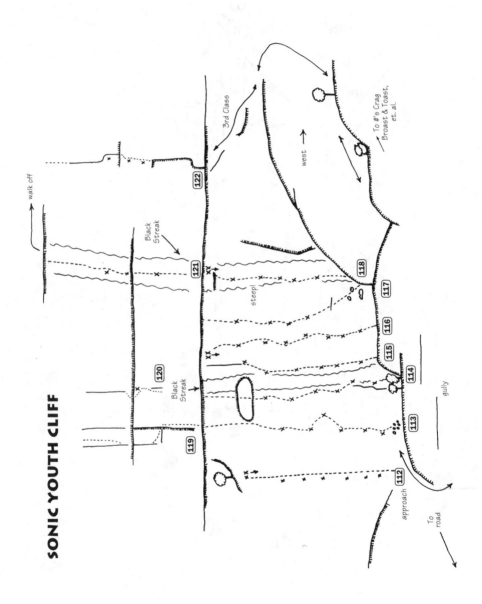

walk off

3rd Class

122

Black Streak

121

steep!

118

117

116

115

114

Black Streak

120

Black Streak

gully

113

119

112

approach

To road

west

To #'s Crag Broast & Toast, et. al.

113. **GBH** (5.11d) FA: Richard Harrison, Kevin Biernacki, Paul Van Betten, Don Burroughs; September 1989. Named for the band Great Bodily Harm—not the scary nature of the climb! Start about 10' left of a bush near the left end of the ledge system at the base of the cliff. Climb past numerous holes and 6 bolts to the ledge. Walk and scramble off right.

114. **Black Flag** (5.11c) FA: Paul Van Betten, Bob Conz; June 1989. Rope up 15' right of *GBH* at the right side of a bush. Ascend the cliff, passing 6 bolts en route.

115. **Loki** (5.12a) FA: Don Welsh; April 1991. Named for a *Star Trek* character that was half black and half white. Begin at the right edge of an obvious black streak 5' right of *Black Flag*. Climb past 6 bolts to a chain anchor.

116. **Agent Orange** (5.12b) FA: Paul Van Betten, Bob Conz; June 1989. Start 10' right and cruise past 7 bolts to the top.

*117. **Sonic Youth** (5.11+) FA: Paul Van Betten, Sal Mamusia, Bob Conz; May 1989. Begin at an assortment of huecos near the left edge of a black streak 20' right of the last route. Bring a couple of small Friends to give you the courage to reach the first bolt and the top! Four bolts lead to the ledge system. Walk off right.

*118. **Everybody's Slave** (5.11c) FA: Don Welsh; April 1991. A very good route; luckily, the holds get bigger the higher you get! Rope up about 8' right of *Sonic Youth* in the middle of a black streak, then climb past 5 bolts to a chain anchor.

The next four routes start on the ledge system splitting the cliff and can be approached by either doing a climb on the lower level or scrambling up to the ledge from the right (west). The scramble is a little bit dicey but obvious. You'll angle up and left from the terrace to a big ledge.

119. **Hip-Hoppin' with the Hutterites** (5.8 PG) FA: Todd and Donette Swain; August 1994. Carry gear up to a #3.5 Friend and some long slings to reduce rope drag. Begin at an obvious 40-foot-high right-facing corner that is 50' left of the *Crankenstein* waterstreak. Climb the corner for 20', then traverse left around the corner to a crack. Climb 20' up to a bulge, pull this (crux), then wander up the easier face above, following seams. Use a #1 Friend and TCUs for the belay, then walk off right.

120. **Seka's Soiled Panties** (5.11) FA: Richard Harrison, Paul Van Betten; September 1989. Start 30' left of *Crankenstein* and 20' right of an obvious right-facing corner. Climb vertical seams to the ceiling. Pull through the ceiling, moving slightly left at a bolt, then up along more seams to the top. Carry gear to a #3 Friend, using a #2.5 and #3 for the belay. Walk off right.

*121. **Crankenstein** (5.10c) FA: Danny Meyers; rope solo, April 1988. This route is well worth doing. Climb the central, black waterstreak past 3 bolts. This route is located directly above *Everybody's Slave*. Use #2.5 to #3.5 Friends for the anchor then walk off right (west).

*122. **Slam Dancin' with the Amish** (5.9+) FA: Paul and Pauline Van Betten; June 1989. A route as good as its name! Start about 60' right of the *Crankenstein* waterstreak and just above the end of the scramble up to this tier (you can start this route on the large, lower terrace and include the scramble as part of the route). Bring extra TCUs and Friends to #2.5. Climb an obvious right-facing corner/flake to its top, then follow 3 bolts and some seams to the summit. Save #1.5 to #2.5 Friends for the belay anchor, then walk off right.

THE ASYLUM

This shady, north-facing cliff sits on the very top of the Sonic Youth formation and is clearly visible from the parking area. Not much information was available about the three routes that had been done as of press time. Approach via slabs on the southeast side of the formation. You can walk off the tops of all three routes. (No topo.)

123. **Lounge Tomato** (5.12b) FA: Chris Burton and Jeremy Taylor; May 1998. The leftmost sport route with 4 bolts.

124. **Comforts of Madness** (5.11b/c) FA: Daniel Hudgins (D.T.) and Jeremy Smith; September 1997. The middle bolted route with 5 bolts.

125. **Flip the Switch** (5.10d) FA: Chris Burton, Jeremy Taylor, and Jeremy Smith; September 1997. The right-hand sport climb with 5 bolts.

BROAST AND TOAST CLIFF

This sunny cliff is visible from the parking lot and is located about 100 yards above Sonic Youth Wall on the right-hand side of the canyon. It is the highest and most prominent cliff in the canyon. These are traditional routes, and they are described from right to left as you approach up the canyon. (No topo.)

126. **Fairy Toast** (5.10) FA: Richard Harrison, Paul Van Betten, Wendell Broussard; November 1989. Begin 10' left of a low-angle, right-facing corner that forms the right margin of the cliff. Climb a seam through the left side of a ceiling (bolt), then follow the rightmost seam/crack system past another bolt to the summit.

127. **Burnt Toast** (5.10) FA: Paul Van Betten, Bob Conz, Sal Mamusia, "Frodo" Lybarger; December 1988. Start down and left of *Fairy Toast* at a left-slanting overhang/corner with a boulder at the base. Climb up the face

Broast and Toast
Area

Broast and Toast
Cliff

Common Time

Numbers
Crag

132

Sonic Youth

140 139

126

129

To Parking

past the very left edge of the *Fairy Toast* ceiling to a prominent, curving seam. Follow the seam/crack past at least 2 bolts.

128. **Rap Bolters Need to Be Famous** (5.11) FA: Richard Harrison, Paul Van Betten; November 1989. Named during the height of the trad/sport controversy. Rope up 50' left of *Burnt Toast* at the left side of a smooth, varnished section of rock. Step out right from some boulders at the right edge of a cave then climb up the face past a horizontal band of varnish. Follow a left-leaning crack to the top. There are supposed to be 5 bolts on this route.

129. **Roasted Ramen** (5.9+) FA: Sal Mamusia, Paul Van Betten, Don Burroughs; November 1988. Follow the last route to the horizontal band of varnish, then trend left and follow an obvious, jagged crack system. It looks like you'll need TCUs and wires to supplement the bolts on the route.

130. **Calico Jack** (5.11-) FA: Richard Harrison, Paul Van Betten, Don Burroughs; November 1989. Start at the left edge of the cave mentioned in the last two routes (or up and left off a higher ledge) and climb up to an obvious notch formed by a left-leaning crack. Follow the crack up a few feet above the notch, then climb up the steep varnished streak past 3 bolts.

The next two routes begin on a series of left-sloping ledges up and left from the cave at the base of the cliff. Scramble up about 50 feet to reach the base of the rightmost of the two routes described.

131. **Desert Sportsman** (5.11) FA: Paul Van Betten, Sal Mamusia; December 1988. From the right (lowest) edge of the sloping ledge, scramble out right on blocks, then go back left to a brown, varnished streak. Follow the streak past numerous bolts, finishing in a crack. There should be 7 bolts on the route, plus an anchor.

132. **C.H.U.D.** (5.11c) FA: Paul Van Betten, Bob Conz, Richard Harrison, Sal Mamusia, Shelby Shelton; April 1989. Rope up 25' up and left of *Desert Sportsman*. Climb up the steep, varnished face along right-facing flakes past 6 bolts.

NUMBERS CRAG

This sunny cliff sits down and left from Broast and Toast Cliff. Routes are described from right to left as you approach up the canyon. Walk off to the right (toward Broast and Toast Cliff) after doing any of the climbs here. (No topo.)

133. **#6** (5.11d) FA: Paul Van Betten, Sal Mamusia, Richard Harrison; January 1992. Start in a huge hueco at the right side of the crag. Follow 3 bolts up good-looking varnished rock.

134. **#5** (5.12b) FA: Paul Van Betten, Sal Mamusia, Richard Harrison, Bob Conz; January 1992. Begin in the hueco as for #6, but climb up and left past 5 bolts. A single belay bolt is located on top, about 40' back from the cliff edge.

135. **#4** (5.12a) FA: Paul Van Betten, Sal Mamusia, Richard Harrison; January 1992. Rope up 15' left of the huge hueco. Follow 4 bolts up a seam and waterstreak.

136. **#3** (5.11d) FA: Shelby Shelton, Richard Harrison, Paul Van Betten; 1991. Begin 8' left of #4 at a short white slab that leads to 4 bolts.

137. **#2** (5.11d) FA: Richard Harrison, Shelby Shelton, Paul Van Betten, Sal Mamusia; Winter 1990. Start 8' left of #3 and just right of a ledge that is 6' off the ground. Zoom past 4 bolts to a belay bolt on top with a large, homemade hanger.

138. **#1** (5.11d) FA: Sal Mamusia, Paul Van Betten, Richard Harrison; January 1992. Rope up 8' left of #2 on a ledge that is 6' above the ground. There are several huecos below the first bolt. Climb along an overhanging seam past 5 bolts.

139. **#.5** (5.12c) FA: Sal Mamusia, Paul Van Betten; January 1992. Begin at the base of right-leaning cracks 20' left of the last route. Clip 3 bolts along an overhanging seam.

140. **#0** (5.10 PG) FA: Paul Van Betten, Sal Mamusia, Richard Harrison; January 1992. Start at a line of scoops near an arête 20' left of the last route. Follow 2 bolts to a vertical seam that will provide some thrilling moves

before you reach the top (or lower off!). There's a pine tree way back from the cliff edge for an anchor.

COMMON TIME

From the left edge of Numbers Crag, take the first gully on the right (north) and go up about 75 yards. Common Time is the small cliff on the left (west) side of the gully and is visible before you go up the gully. Routes are described from left to right as you approach up the gully. (No topo.)

141. **Time Off** (5.11a) FA: Leo and Karin Henson, Albert Newman; March 1998. Start between two crack systems at the left (south) edge of the cliff. The left crack has a bush two-thirds of the way up. Follow 5 bolts to an anchor.

142. **Paradiddle Riddle** (5.11b) FA: Phil Bowden; July 1992. Rope up 5' right of *Time Off* at the left side of a tan section of rock. Follow 4 bolts to an anchor.

143. **Myxolidian** (5.11b) FA: Greg Mayer; July 1992. Begin at the right side of a light tan section of rock 25' right of the last route. There is a bush 20' farther right. Follow 4 bolts with homemade hangers to an anchor.

144. **One-Move Number** (5.12a) FA: Leo and Karin Henson, Albert Newman; March 1998. Directly across the gully from the left edge of Common Time is a short, varnished cliff. This is actually the back of Numbers Crag. Climb up a series of overhanging, varnished corners past 4 bolts. This climb is shady in the morning.

Note: There are two excellent boulders 50 yards up the canyon from the last two routes.

WAKE UP WALL

As the name implies, you have to get there early (at least in the winter) to have much sunshine. The routes are short, and they all have rappel/lowering anchors. This crag caused another uproar between the two local climbing factions, due to its large number of bolts. To get there, walk 200 yards northwest from the parking lot on the main trail, past a white boulder in the main wash, to an old roadway. Follow the roadway for about another 200 yards to an obvious oak bush on the left side of the trail. Turn left off the roadway onto the trail that goes to Turtlehead (sign). After about 200 yards, this footpath goes up over a dirt hump. Follow the trail along the top of the dirt mound until you reach white rocks. At this point, Turtlehead Trail turns right and goes down into the wash. Rather than dropping down to the wash, go slightly left across the white rock for about 50 yards to reach Wake Up Wall. The cliff faces north (toward Turtlehead–the prominent limestone peak), and there is a nice flat area in front of the crag. The climbs are described from left to right, beginning from the direction of your approach.

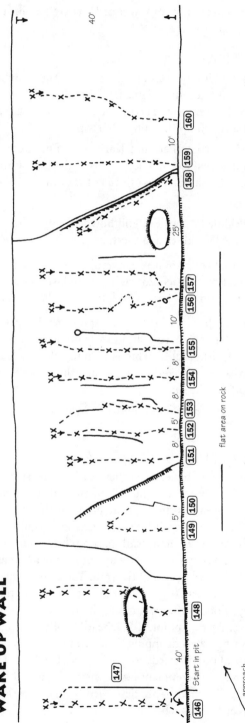

145. **Monkey Rhythm** (5.10+) FA: Paul Van Betten, Robert Finlay; 1983. At the crag's extreme left end is a shallow dihedral with a varnished crack in the back. (Not shown.)

146. **First Born** (5.10b) FA: Ed Prochaska; 1990. This is the first route on the central portion of the cliff. Start in a pit 8' right of boulders at a right-trending flake and climb past 5 bolts to the anchor.

147. **Elder Sibling** (5.10 TR) FA: Ed Prochaska; 1990. Same start as *First Born*. Follow *First Born* to the horizontal crack, then move right to a vertical crack. Climb the vertical crack to the anchor.

*148. **Just Shut up and Climb** (5.11b) FA: Randy Faulk, Rick Denison; June 1991. The best route on the cliff. Begin 40' right of the last route and clip 5 bolts as you climb past the right side of a hole.

149. **Poundcake** (5.8) FA: Jay and Gail Mueller; May 1997. Begin between two chimneys 30' right of *Just Shut up and Climb*. From a ledge above the chasm, climb past 3 bolts with red hangers to an anchor.

150. **Crack of Noon** (5.8 PG) FA: Jay and Gail Mueller; April 1997. Rope up on the right edge of a ledge and 5' right of the last route. Climb a thin, dogleg crack to the same anchor as the last route. Bring TCUs and small Friends.

151. **Shape of Things to Come** (5.11a) FA: Greg Mayer; Winter 1989. Rope up just right of an obvious left-leaning ramp. Power past 3 bolts to the anchor.

152. **The Healer** (5.11d) FA: Greg Mayer; Spring 1990. Start 8' right and climb past 4 bolts to a shared belay with *Rise and Whine*.

153. **Rise and Whine** (5.12a) FA: Mike Tupper; Spring 1990. Begin behind an oak bush 5' right of the last route. Climb along seams, clipping 4 bolts on the way.

154. **Pain Check** (5.12a) FA: Bill Boyle; Spring 1990. Begin 8' right and hobble past 5 bolts to the rap station.

155. **Good Mourning** (5.11b) FA: Bill Boyle; Spring 1990. Another 5-bolt route that begins 8' right of *Pain Check*.

156. **Native Son** (5.11c) FA: Mike Tupper; Spring 1990. Start at a vertical brown streak 10' right of the last route. Stroll past 5 bolts.

157. **Where Egos Dare** (5.12a) FA: Greg Mayer; Summer 1991. Same start as *Native Son*, but climb up right, passing the left side of a large hole and 5 bolts.

158. **XTZ** (5.9) FA: Greg Mayer; Spring 1990. Rack up 25' right, at the base of a left-leaning ramp. Climb past 3 bolts to the rappel anchor. This route is a bit of a grovel.

159. **Onsight Flight** (5.12b) FA: Don Welsh; Spring 1990. Start 4' right of the ramp and fly past 5 bolts.

160. **Stand and Deliver** (5.12b) FA: Mike Tupper; Spring 1990. Rope up 10' right of *Onsight Flight* and climb up and right past 5 bolts that are slightly right-trending.

SANDSTONE QUARRY NORTH
THE TWINKIE

These routes aren't all that great, but you walk right by them to get to good routes. This is a small, white formation that gets sun all day and is visible from the parking area. It is north of the parking lot, at the left end of the biggest white lump of rock (The Marshmallow).

To get there, walk 200 yards northwest from the parking lot on the main level past a white boulder in the main wash to an old roadway. Follow the roadway for about another 200 yards to an obvious oak bush on the left side of the trail. Turn left off the roadway onto the trail that goes to Turtlehead (sign). After about 200 yards, this footpath goes up over a dirt hump. Follow the trail along the top of the dirt mound until you reach white rocks. At this point, Turtlehead Trail turns right and goes down into the wash. Continue on the trail, which goes diagonally across the wash/valley toward white rocks and Turtlehead itself. The first white formation that the trail reaches is The Twinkie. Routes are described from right to left and begin in the wash. (No topo.)

161. **Like Mom Used to Make** (5.11c) FA: Anthony Williams, John and Ralph Day; Winter 1988. Start below 4 bolts just left of an easy-looking bulge at the base of the cliff. The route begins with difficult moves and finishes in a very short crack. There is a rappel anchor on top.

162. **Flake Eyes** (5.10+) FA: Anthony Williams, John and Ralph Day; Winter 1988. Begin 10' left of the last route and behind a bush. Climb up and slightly left past 3 bolts. There are belay bolts on top. Walk off the rear of the formation, then around left to regain the base of the route.

163. **Short but Sweet** (5.10 R/X) FA: Anthony Williams, John and Ralph Day; Winter 1988. Start 30' left at a right-leaning ramp/corner and just left of a low cave. Climb to the top of the corner, then move up and right about 10' to the first bolt (scary). Continue past 1 more bolt to the top. Belay from bolts, then walk off as on the last route.

THE MARSHMALLOW

At least two routes have been done on the large white formation that is up and right (northeast) of The Twinkie. This sunny formation has a distinctive horizontal band running across it and is visible from the parking lot. Scramble about 150' above the wash to get to the base of the routes.

164. Mojave Green (5.8+ PG13) FA: Jim Lybarger, Bob Conz; late 1980s. The left route on the formation climbs a slabby white face past 3 bolts. It is located about 100' left (west) of *Dime Edging*. The route starts on the left side of some oak bushes. Bring a #0 TCU for the climb, plus a #3.5 Friend for the anchor. Make difficult moves up to the first bolt (scary), then climb past 2 more bolts to the summit. Belay from a bolt and #3.5 Friend. Walk off left (west) toward The Twinkie, then cut through a drainage to a ramp that leads back up to the base of the route.

165. Dime Edging (5.10 R) FA: Bob Conz, Mike Ward; 1989. Rope up on the highest ledge below numerous varnish patches in the center of the cliff. Move out right from the ledge onto the varnish patches, then go up past 2 bolts to the ceiling formed by the horizontal band. Get gear in the vertical seam at the lip of the ceiling, then pull this (crux) to another bolt. Friction up the face above to a single drilled angle on top. There is a TCU placement 25' farther back toward Satellite Wall. Bring a long rope!

THE BULL MARKET

To get to this sunny cliff, walk 200 yards northwest from the parking lot past a white boulder in the main wash to an old roadway. Follow the roadway for about another 200 yards to an obvious oak bush on the left side of the trail. Turn left off the roadway onto the trail that goes to Turtlehead. After about 200 yards, this footpath goes up over a dirt hump. Follow the trail along the top of the dirt mound until you reach white rocks. At this point, Turtlehead Trail turns right and goes down into the wash. Continue on the trail, which goes diagonally across the wash/valley toward white rocks and Turtlehead itself. The first white formation that the trail reaches is The Twinkie. Walk just past the Twinkie, then turn right toward a smooth, brown wave of rock (The Drive-In). The Bull Market is a large, brown bulbous formation that is up and right (northeast) from the rear of the Twinkie (The Trophy and Avian Wall will be to the northwest). The Bull Market sits between two obvious gullies and has routes on three aspects. These lines are described from left to right starting in the left gully.

166. Twentieth Century Ultra (5.11c) FA: Mike Tupper; 1992. Start up the chimney at the left edge of the cliff, then step right and follow 8 bolts up the overhanging wall. (Not shown.)

The Trophy Area

Satellite Wall

Bull Market

The Trophy   Avian Wall

175

167 168 169   171

167. **Scudder Global** (5.11b) FA: Mike Tupper; 1992. Start above a bush 10' right of the last route and on the left edge of a smooth recess. Follow 4 bolts up the left side of an arête to chains.

168. **Fidelity Select** (5.12b) FA: Mike Tupper; 1992. Begin on a ledge in a smooth recess 25' up. Climb up the right side of the arête on smooth rock past three ceilings. There are at least 6 bolts.

169. **Liar's Poker** (5.11b) FA: Mike Tupper; 1992. This is the first route you come to as you approach up the gully. Start at the lower left end of the right gully. Follow 5 bolts out left then up to a communal chain anchor.

170. **Leveraged Buyout** (5.11b) FA: Mike Tupper; 1992. Same start and end as the last route, but climb past a different set of bolts in the middle. 5 bolts.

171. **Hostile Takeover** (5.11c) FA: Mike Tupper; 1992. Rope up 10' uphill from the last route. Climb along a vertical seam, passing 4 bolts to a communal chain anchor.

172. **Pinkies for the Dean** (5.11c) FA: Mike Tupper; 1992. The route name refers to "Jimmy Dean" of Salt Lake City, not Wendell Broussard of Las Vegas! Same start as *Hostile Takeover*, then branch right after the first bolt and go up a vertical seam past 4 more bolts to the shared anchor.

SATELLITE WALL

This crag sits about 100 feet uphill from the Bull Market. Approach up the right-hand gully that runs past the base of *Liar's Poker* et al. Routes are described from left to right on this sunny escarpment. (No topo.)

173. **Stargazer** (5.12c) FA: Leo and Karin Henson; Winter 1993. This 7-bolt route goes by numerous huecos on the left end of the formation.

174. **Sputnik** (5.12a) FA: Leo and Karin Henson; Winter 1993. Start 5' right of *Stargazer* and climb up brown rock past 6 bolts to a chain anchor.

*175. **Supernova II** (5.12c) FA: Randy Faulk, Jim Tobish, Tony Becchio; December 1991. An excellent route. Begin 5' right of the last route and 10' left of a large flake. Follow 8 bolts up the edge of brown rock to cold shuts.

176. **Cosmos** (5.12d) FA: Leo and Karin Henson; Winter 1993. Clip the first 3 bolts of *Supernova II*, then head up right past 5 more to chains.

AVIAN WALL

These routes are located on a north-facing wall just below The Trophy. They all are on primarily white rock and have anchors from which to lower. To get there, walk 200 yards northwest from the parking lot on the main trail, past a white boulder in the main wash, to an old roadway. Follow the roadway for about another 200 yards to an obvious oak bush on the left side of the trail. Turn left off the roadway onto the trail that goes to Turtlehead. After about 200 yards, this footpath goes up over a dirt hump. Follow the trail along the top of the dirt mound until you reach white rocks. At this point, Turtlehead Trail turns right and goes down into the wash. Continue on the trail, which goes diagonally across the wash/valley toward white rocks and Turtlehead itself. The first white formation that the trail reaches is The Twinkie. Walk just past The Twinkie, then turn right toward a smooth, brown wave of rock (The Drive-In). Go northeast up the canyon about 100 yards to the cliff, which makes up the right (east) wall of the canyon. The Trophy (described next) is 200 feet up slabs to the left. Routes are described from right to left as you head up the gully. Approach time is about 15 minutes. (No topo.)

177. **Spotted Owl** (5.11a) FA: Don Burroughs, Alan Busby; March 1992. No redwoods here! Start 20' right of a large oak tree at a flat sandy spot. Climb up along vertical seams, clipping 5 bolts before you reach the chain anchor.

178. **Thunderbird** (5.11b PG) FA: Don Burroughs, Alan Busby; March 1992. Not your typical crimper. This one requires a bit of technique. Begin in a pit 80' left of the last route and follow 6 bolts along a vertical seam to chains.

179. **Coyote Moon** (5.9) FA: Don Burroughs, Dr. Alan Busby; March 1992. Start at a block in the pit 15' left of the last route and 8' right of an oak tree. Zip past 4 bolts to chains.

180. **Spotted Eagle** (5.10a) FA: Don Burroughs, Alan Busby; March 1992. Rope up 25' left, at the left end of the pit and 10' right of a large, right-facing flake. Clip 4 bolts on your way to the chains.

THE TROPHY

This sunny cliff redefines the word steep! To get there, walk 200 yards northwest from the parking lot on the main trail, past a white boulder in the main wash, to an old roadway. Follow the roadway for about another 200 yards to an obvious oak bush on the left side of the trail. Turn left off the roadway onto the trail that goes to Turtlehead. After about 200 yards, this footpath goes up over a dirt hump. Follow the trail along the top of the dirt mound until you reach white rocks. At this point, Turtlehead Trail turns right and goes down into the wash. Continue on the trail, which heads diagonally across the wash/ valley toward white rocks and Turtlehead itself. The first white formation that the trail reaches is The Twinkie. Walk just past The Twinkie, then turn right toward a smooth, brown wave of rock (The Drive-In). Go northeast up the canyon about 150 yards to the obvious, overhanging wall on the left (north)

The Trophy

side of the canyon. Routes are described from left to right. Total approach time is about 15 minutes.

181. **Fifi Hula** (5.11a) FA: Don Burroughs, Alan Busby; January 1992. This sunny route isn't on the main wall of The Trophy but is about 150' left in the middle of a large white face. Start 40' left of a gray waterstreak and climb past 6 bolts to a chain anchor. There is at least one route to the left of this, a bolted arête, but no more is known. (Not shown.)

182. **Project** (5.12?) FA: After May 1999. At the left end of the main cliff is a cave with an oak bush. There is 1 bolt directly above the left edge of the cave at the base of a brown fin of rock. (Not shown.)

*183. **Shark Walk** (5.13a) FA: Mike Tupper; February 1992. Start just right of a cave and a scrub oak at the left (west) end of the main cliff. Climb past 6 bolts to the anchor. (Not shown.)

184. **Indian Giver** (5.12c) FA: Mike Tupper; January 1992. Begin 6' right of the last route and climb past 5 bolts to a chain anchor.

185. **Unknown** (5.12?) FA: Greg Mayer 1995. Begin at the base of a left-slanting crack 25' right of *Indian Giver*. Climb past 7 bolts with home-made hangers to chains.

186. **Unknown** (5.12?) FA: Don Welsh; 1995. Rope up at the left edge of a bowl about 30' right of *Indian Giver* at the base of the cliff. Follow 5 bolts (4 have black hangers) to a left-slanting crack or right into *Midnight Cowboy*.

187. **Midnight owboy** (5.13a) FA: Mike Tupper; March 1992. Start 40' right of *Indian Giver* on a rounded pedestal. Trend out left along cracks, then up a brown streak past 9 bolts.

*188. **Twilight of a Champion** (5.13a) FA: Mike Tupper; February 1992. An unsuccessful attempt to "steal" this route was made by a famous climber, hence the route name. Same start as the last route atop a pedestal. Climb pretty much straight up past 8 bolts to a chain anchor.

*189. **Pet Shop Boy** (5.12d) FA: Mike Tupper; February 1992. Named after Tupper's hairdo at the time. Begin 10' right of the last route and 8' left of a black recess at the base of the cliff. Stick-clip the first bolt, then climb straight back (!) past 5 more bolts.

*190. **Keep Your Powder Dry** (5.12b) FA: Mike Tupper; January 1992. Rope up 6' right of the last route, at the left side of the central cave. Follow 9 bolts up very overhanging rock to chains.

191. **The Trophy** (5.12c) FA: Mike Tupper; January 1992. Makes *Fear and Loathing III* look like a slab climb! Starting 8' right, climb out the center of the cave along a right-slanting crack past 10 bolts to the anchor.

192. **Caught in the Crosshairs** (5.12a) FA: Greg Mayer; March 1993. Begin on a ledge 30' uphill of the central cave. Power past 7 bolts to the safety of the anchor.

193. **Dodging a Bullet** (5.12a) FA: Greg Mayer; Spring 1991. Start about 45' right of the central cave. Climb along vertical seams, clipping 5 bolts en route.

194. **Meatlocker** (5.13?) FA; Unknown; after May 1999. Begin below a flat ceiling at the very right edge of the cliff. Follow 5 bolts to chains.

SANDSTONE QUARRY NORTHEAST
BLISTER IN THE SUN CLIFF

From the Sandstone Quarry parking area, follow the trail markers for CalicoTank. The trail goes something like this: Walk 200 yards northwest from the parking area, past a white boulder in the main wash, to an old roadway. Follow the roadway for 250 yards past a bush and small drainage to an interpretive sign about Native Americans. Turn right (northeast) into the obvious pebbly wash and follow it between two rock formations. You reach some pine trees after another 140 yards.

The main wash curves left (north) at this point with a subsidiary wash continuing east. Follow this sandy wash east (there may be a trail marker here) for

about 300 yards, then continue straight east along the same wash through a canyon with red rock for another 300 yards.

This large, white formation faces south and has a distinctive right-leaning crack/ramp system on it. It is about 500 yards to the left (north) of the approach to the Mass Production Wall and up and left of the Beach. Not much is known about these routes, which are described from left to right. (No topo.)

195. **Teenage Mutant Ninja Turtles** (5.11-) FA: "Frodo," Bob Conz, Sal Mamusia; December 1989. This is the leftmost of the routes. You need traditional gear to supplement the bolts and get you to the fixed anchor.

196. **Blister in the Sun** (5.11b) FA: Bob Conz, Shelby Shelton; December 1988. Follow 7 bolts to the top. Bring #2.5 and #3 Friends for the belay.

197. **Tortugas Mutante** (5.11d) FA: Richard Harrison, Jimmy Dunn (of New Hampshire and Colorado fame); 1989. The rightmost route, which also has bolts.

198. **High Scalin'** (5.7) FA: Paul Van Betten, Nick Nordblom; both solo, 1987. A fun outing whether you use a rope or not! Bring gear up to a #4 cam with extra of the larger sizes. This 2-pitch route ascends the prominent right-leaning ramp/crack that is visible from much of the Sandstone Quarry. Climb the face to the bottom of the crack system, then follow that up and right to the summit. Scramble down the gully to the right (southeast).

THE BEACH

This sunny crag sits just to left of the approach to Mass Production Wall and Calico Tank. It is just above the drainage bottom and has an overhanging, red-colored right side (southeast) and a shorter, white left side. Routes are described from right to left (starting closest to the drainage and moving toward Blister in the Sun Cliff). (No topo.)

199. **Southern Comfort** (5.12d) FA: John Heiman; circa 1997. This route was partially bolted in the early 1990s and later finished by Heiman. Begin at an obvious right-facing corner 40' to the left of the cliff's right edge. Follow 8 bolts to chains.

200. **Southern Cross** (5.12b) FA: Leo Henson; October 1994. Start at a bulging arête that forms the right side of a left-arching crack/corner 30' left of the last route. Follow 7 bolts to chains.

201. **Looks Like Craps** (5.9?) FA: Unknown. Climb the obvious left-leaning crack/corner in the center of the cliff. Watch out for loose rock.

202. **Wizard of Odds** (5.12a) FA: Greg Mayer; Winter 1992. Begin 100' left of the prominent crack/corner, at the left edge of a many-layerd bulge and just right of an arête. Starting at a small pine, climb along a vertical crack system past 7 bolts with homemade hangers to chains.

203. Static (5.6) FA: Unknown; 1980s. Rope up in a left-facing corner just left of the last route. This climb ascends the wide crack in a corner just right of a huge boulder.

*204. Squelch (5.10+) FA: Kurt Mauer; 1987. This route is to the left of *Static*, starts bhind the huge boulder, and climbs a varnished crack and a small right-facing corner.

*205. RF Gain (5.10 PG13) FA: Nick Nordblom (rope solo); 1987. Climb the smooth, brown arête 5' left of *Squelch* and at the right edge of a low-angle gully past 2 bolts.

Note: The cliff continues to the left about 100 yards and becomes smaller and white in color.

MASS PRODUCTION WALL

From the Sandstone Quarry parking area, follow the trail markers for Calico Tank. The trail goes something like this: Walk 200 yards northwest from the parking area, past a white boulder in the main wash, to an old roadway. Follow the roadway for 250 yards past a bush and small drainage to an interpretive sign about Native Americans. Turn right (northeast) into the obvious pebbly

wash and follow it between two rock formations. You reach some pine trees after another 140 yards.

The main wash curves left (north) at this point with a subsidiary wash continuing east. Follow this sandy wash east (there may be a trail marker here) for about 300 yards, then continue straight east along the same wash through a canyon with red rock for another 300 yards. Just before the red layer of rock ends, you see Mass Production Wall uphill to the left center (northeast). The cliff is in the shade most of the day and is primarily a white-colored rock with pine trees at its base. This approach takes about 15 minutes from the parking area. Routes are described from right to left, running uphill from the drainage bottom. (No topo.)

206. **Some Assembly Required** (5.10c) FA: Greg Mayer; Spring 1991. Start behind a gnarled pine tree and climb along parallel, left-leaning seams, then up the face right of a cave. Follow 6 bolts to chain anchors.

207. **Kokopelli** (5.10c PG) FA: Don Burroughs, Alan Busby; April 1992. Named for the hunchbacked flute player commonly seen in Native American rock art. Begin 50' uphill of the last route and below the right center of a cave. Face-climb past bolts, then out the ceiling at a right-facing corner to chains.

208. **Parts Is Parts** (5.8) FA: Todd Swain, Jeff Rickerl; April 1992. Greg Mayer installed the chain anchor in 1991, then bolted the route in 1993 after Swain and Rickerl had done the route using only traditional gear (5.8 X). Begin behind two pine trees 100' uphill of *Some Assembly Required*. Wander up the face past 4 bolts to reach the chain anchor.

209. **Battery Powered** (5.9) FA: Greg Mayer; Spring 1991. Rope up 10' left of the last route and 10' right of a right-facing corner. Climb past 6 bolts to the chain anchor.

210. **Foreman Ferris** (5.11b) FA: Leo Henson; October 1994. This bolted route follows a thin seam that goes through the right side of the large varnished patch shaped roughly like Australia. There are 7 bolts on the climb.

*211. **Trigger Happy** (5.10a) FA: Greg Mayer; Spring 1991. Start 90' uphill of *Battery Powered*, below a seam leading through the left edge of a large varnished patch shaped roughly like Australia. Scamper past 5 bolts to a chain anchor.

212. **Hit and Run** (5.9) FA: Greg Mayer; Spring 1991. Begin behind a pine tree with a broken top 10' left of *Trigger Happy*. Climb past 5 bolts to a chain anchor, keeping just right of a seam/crack.

THE HALL OF FAME

From the Sandstone Quarry parking area, follow the trail markers for Calico Tank. The trail goes something like this: Walk 200 yards northwest from the parking area, past a white boulder in the main wash, to an old roadway. Follow the roadway for 250 yards past a bush and small drainage to an interpretive sign about Native Americans. Turn right (northeast) into the obvious pebbly wash and follow it between two rock formations. You reach some pine trees after another 140 yards.

The main wash curves left (north) at this point with a subsidiary wash continuing east. Follow this sandy wash east (there may be a trail marker here) for about 300 yards, then continue straight east along the same wash through a canyon with red rock for another 300 yards. Just before the red layer of rock ends, you see Mass Production Wall uphill to the left center (northeast).

For The Hall of Fame, head up left (northeast) along a gully for 300 yards to the base of a large, white, south-facing cliff with a steep gully/cleft running north-south. From the base of the cleft, contour around left (west and then north) on ledges above one cliff band and below another for 100 yards (there should be cairns along this section). Scamper 50 yards up the first gully you reach, and you should be at the lower entrance to the Hall of Fame.

The Hall runs in a north-south direction with the routes all on the right (south) wall. They are in the shade all day, although it's very easy to reach sunshine to warm up on cooler days. The approach to this cliff is an additional 10 minutes from Mass Production Wall or a total of 25 minutes from the parking area. Routes are described right to left, running up The Hall of Fame from the approach. (No topo.)

213. **Yearnin' and Learnin'** (5.11a) FA: Don Burroughs, Alan Busby; April 1992. Begin about 15' inside the corridor, below two lines of bolts with a common start. Climb up and right past 5 bolts to chains.

214. **Repeat Offender** (5.10d) FA: Greg Mayer; Spring 1991. Same start as the last route, but climb slightly left past 6 bolts to a chain anchor, moving left then back right between the second and third bolts. **Variation** (5.11c): If you climb straight between the bolts, the route is harder.

215. **Armed and Dangerous** (5.10d) FA: Phil Bowden; Spring 1991. Begin 6' left of *Repeat Offender*. After a difficult lieback move, climb past huecos to the left side of a bulge. Follow a total of 6 bolts to the chain anchor.

216. **Bad Reputation** (5.11b) FA: Phil Bowden, Guy Pinjuv; Spring 1991. Climb the face 15' left of *Armed and Dangerous* past 6 bolts to the same chain anchor. There is a difficult ceiling down low, but the crux is up higher.

217. **Innocent Bystander** (5.10a) FA: Greg Mayer; Spring 1991. Start 30' uphill of *Bad Reputation* and power past 5 bolts to a chain anchor.

218. Ms. Adventure (5.7) FA: "Chucky" Mayer; Spring 1991. Begin 30' left of the last route and about 20' downhill from the upper entrance to the corridor. Climb past 3 bolts to the anchor. The crux is off the ground.

At least four routes have been done to the left (north and west) of The Hall of Fame. The first two routes are located just left (west) of the upper entrance to The Hall of Fame.

219. Hero Worship (5.10b) FA: Liz Tupper; December 25, 1993. Since the Tuppers were newlyweds at the time, one could presume Liz named the route for Mike! This is the left route, which climbs near an arête and has 4 bolts.

220. Computer Virus (5.12c) FA: Mike Tupper; December 25, 1993. Tupper was ill on the first ascent, hence the name. This is the right route, which has 9 bolts.

221. Sand Illusion (5.11c) FA: Greg Mayer; Spring 1991. This route climbs a prominent arête about 150 yards to the west of The Hall of Fame. It faces southeast and has 3 bolts and a chain anchor.

222. Unknown Arête (5.12a) FA: Jim Greg; Fall 1993. Somewhere to the right of *Sand Illusion* is an arête with 5 bolts.

HOLIDAY WALL

This crag has a number of very good sport routes that are in the sun most of the day. Total approach time is about 20 inutes. From the Sandstone Quarry parking area, follow the trail markers for Calico Tank. The trail goes something like this: Walk 200 yards northwest from the parking area, past a white boulder in the main wash, to an old roadway. Follow the roadway for 250 yards past a bush and small drainage to an interpretive sign about Native Americans. Turn right (northeast) into the obvious pebbly wash and follow it between two rock formations. You reach some pine trees after another 140 yards.

The main wash curves left (north) at this point with a subsidiary wash continuing east. Follow this sandy wash east (there may be a trail marker here) for about 300 yards, then continue straight east along the same wash through a canyon with red rock for another 300 yards. Just before the red layer of rock ends, you see Mass Production Wall uphill to the left center (northeast).

Continue up the main drainage beyond Mass Production Wall, heading slightly right to gain a trail that goes up along the hillside. About 200 yards beyond the end of the red rock, the trail drops down into a drainage and the red rock reappears. Continue up the valley another 200 yards to reach Holiday Wall, which is on the left (northeast) side of the drainage. The trail to Calico Tank continues for about another 500 yards. Routes at Holiday Wall are described from left to right as you approach up the drainage. (No topo.)

HOLIDAY WALL AREA

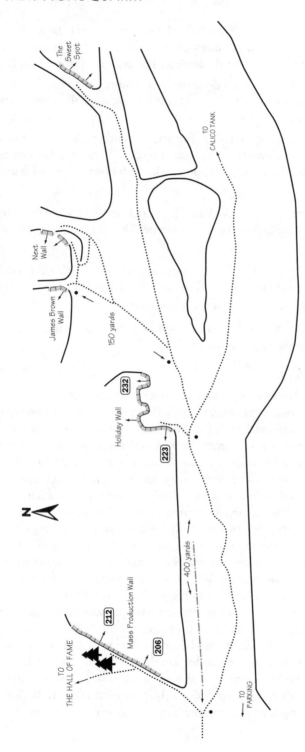

The Sweet Spot

TO CALICO TANK

Next Wall

James Brown Wall

150 yards

N

232

Holiday Wall

223

400 yards

212

Mass Production Wall

206

TO THE HALL OF FAME

TO PARKING

223. **Presents of Mind** (5.12a) FA: Unknown; after 1995. Begin at the left edge of the wall, about 50' right of a medium-sized oak and below left-slanting cracks. Climb past 4 bolts with red hangers to an anchor.

224. **The Grinch** (5.12c) FA: Mike Tupper; Christmas 1990. Start jut right of the last route, at smooth, overhanging, varnished rock. Climb past 3 bolts (there were 4 bolts, but the first one is missing) to chains.

225. **Death before Decaf** (5.12b) FA: Don Welsh; January 1991. Bolted by Kevin Lawler and Sandy Carrick, then led by Welsh much later. Begin at a thin zigzag crack in varnished rock 15' right of *The Grinch*. Fire past 6 bolts to chains.

226. **Gift Rapped** (5.11b) FA: Karen Peil; Christmas 1990. "Given" to Peil by Tupper as a Christmas present! Start 8' right of the last route, at a shallow, left-facing corner by a small pine and oak. Clip 6 bolts as you climb along seams to a chain anchor.

227. **Red Sky Mining** (5.11a) FA: Karen Peil; December 1990. Climb past 7 bolts to chains, starting 3' right of *Gift Rapped*.

228. **Red Storm Rising** (5.11b) FA: Karen Peil; December 1990. Rope up at the base of a chimney 3' right of the last route. Climb up along a left-facing flake/corner past 5 bolts to chains.

*229. **When the Cat's Away** (5.11b) FA: Greg Mayer; December 1990. Rope up 15' right at the base of a buttress with a small ceiling at the bottom. Pull the ceiling and clip 6 bolts as you climb up small, opposing flake systems.

230. **Saddam's Mom** (5.11d) FA: Karen Peil; December 1990. Could it be Mrs. Grinch? Begin 6' right of the last route, at the right arête of the buttress. Shoot past 6 bolts to a chain anchor.

231. **Moments to Memories** (5.11a) FA: Greg Mayer; December 1990. Start 40' right of *Saddam's Mom* and 30' right of a striking dihedral (a future testpiece) at the left arête of a short buttress. Climb the arête past 4 bolts to chains.

*232. **Fast Moving Train** (5.11a) FA: Greg Mayer; December 1990. Begin just right of *Moments to Memories* and climb past 5 bolts up the right arête of the buttress.

JAMES BROWN AREA

From the Sandstone Quarry parking area, follow the trail markers for Calico Tank. The trail goes something like this: Walk 200 yards northwest from the parking area, past a white boulder in the main wash, to an old roadway. Follow the roadway for 250 yards past a bush and small drainage to an interpretive sign about Native Americans. Turn right (northeast) into the obvious pebbly wash and follow it between two rock formations. You reach some pine trees after another 140 yards.

The main wash curves left (north) at this point with a subsidiary wash continuing east. Follow this sandy wash east (there may be a trail marker here) for about 300 yards, then continue straight east along the same wash through a canyon with red rock for another 300 yards. Just before the red layer of rock ends, you see Mass Production Wall uphill to the left center (northeast).

Continue up the main drainage beyond Mass Production Wall, heading slightly right to gain a trail that goes up along the hillside. About 200 yards beyond the end of the red rock, the trail drops down into a drainage and the red rock reappears. Continue up the valley another 200 yards to reach Holiday Wall, which is on the left (northeast) side of the drainage. The trail to Calico Tank continues for about another 500 yards.

JAMES BROWN WALL

The James Brown Wall is 150 yards diagonally up right (east) from the right edge of Holiday Wall and 200 yards above the level of the wash. The cliff forms the left side of a corridor and is characterized by a prominent brown waterstreak on the left arête of the corridor. Total approach time to this sunny crag is about 25 minutes. Routes are described from left to right. (No topo.)

*233. **James Brown** (5.11b PG) FA: Randy Marsh, Pier Locatelli; Winter 1991. An excellent climb that ascends the brown waterstreak. Dance up the waterstreak on the left arête of the corridor, clipping 7 bolts en route to chains.

234. **Brand New Bag** (5.10d) FA: Randy Marsh, Pier Locatelli; Winter 1991. Until you reach the anchor, this route isn't in the bag. Start 20' right and uphill from *James Brown* and just left of a bush. Follow 4 bolts to chains.

235. **Soul Power** (5.11d) FA: Randy Marsh, Pier Locatelli; Winter 1991. You'll feel good after completing this one! Begin 10' uphill, between two bushes. Climb past 8 bolts to a chain anchor.

NEXT WALL

This cliff has two sections and is immediately right (east) of James Brown Wall. The upper section of this cliff forms a terrace that slopes down and right (east) and drops off into space. Two routes climb the overhanging wall above this terrace. The other routes are located to the right of the terrace and are approached from below.

236. **Nexus** (5.12?) FA: Greg Mayer; circa 1995. Near the right edge of the terrace is a gray cave at the base of the wall. Follow 10 bolts along a vertical seam to chains.

237. **Connect the Dots** (5.12?) FA: Greg Mayer; circa 1995. A good-looking route that climbs an obvious line of huecos. Begin at the right edge of a gray cave 15' right of the last climb. Power past 11 bolts to an anchor.

The next routes are down and around to the right of the last route and must be approached from below.

238. **They Just Don't Make Outlaws Like They Used To** (5.12a) FA: Greg Mayer; Spring 1993. Start at the right edge of a rotten cave that is beneath a pod located 10' up the cliff. Climb past the right side of the pod and up the face above. There are 11 bolts total and a chain anchor.

239. **The Heteroclite** (5.11c) FA: Greg Mayer; Spring 1993. Begin atop a white boulder at the mouth of a gully 10' right of the last route. The climb has 10 bolts and a separate chain anchor.

240. **Mirage II** (5.10c) FA: Greg Mayer; circa 1996. Rope up on a white ledge above an oak bush that is 20' right of the last climb. Ten bolts lead up the face just to the left of a vertical seam system.

THE SWEET SPOT

When looking up canyon (east) from Holiday Wall, the canyon is divided roughly in half by a red rock formation. The trail to Calico Tank passes to the right (south) of this formation, while the established routes are approached via the north side of the formation. From Holiday Wall, take the left fork of the drainage for about 200 yards, going past red rock into the white layer. Go up and left (northeast) in a side gully for about 100 yards into a corridor. The right wall of the gully/corridor is brown and overhanging. The routes are in the shade most of the day and are described from right (downhill) to left. (No topo.)

241. **Absolute Zero** (5.12a) FA: Greg Mayer; Summer 1993. Start by an oak tree at the lower end of a cave that is located at the base of the cliff. Climb up and slightly left past 7 bolts to an anchor.

242. **Disposable Blues** (5.11c) FA: Greg Mayer; Summer 1993. Begin 30' uphill of the last route, at the narrowest part of the corridor. Climb along a vertical seam past 5 bolts.

WHITE ROCK SPRING AREA
(MAP NOT TO SCALE)

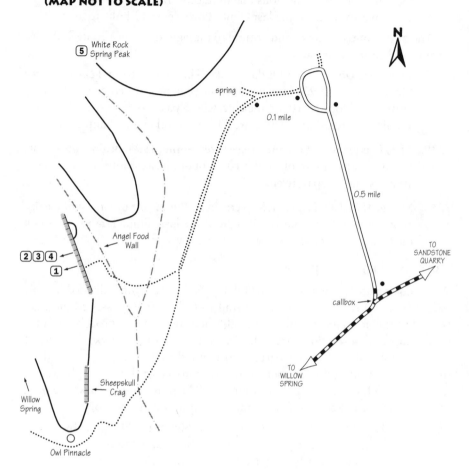

5 White Rock Spring Peak

N

spring

0.1 mile

0.5 mile

Angel Food Wall

2 3 4

1

TO SANDSTONE QUARRY

callbox

Sheepskull Crag

Willow Spring

TO WILLOW SPRING

Owl Pinnacle

WHITE ROCK SPRING AREA

ANGEL FOOD WALL

While numerous routes have been climbed and documented on this crag, only a few are described in this guidebook. To reach the parking area for White Rock Spring, drive 5.8 miles along the scenic loop road to the sign for White Rock Spring. Turn right off the loop road (emergency telephone here) and drive 0.5 mile to a parking area at a cul-de-sac.

From the cul-de-sac, walk down the obvious dirt road. Take the first left (White Rock Spring is about 150 yards down the main road) on a lesser-used road and follow this until you are almost to a drainage. Go cross-country toward the big cliff to the west, entering another drainage that runs parallel to the cliff. Head up this drainage for about 100 yards, then go up the hillside to the base of the wall. Aim for a point at the base of the wall that is roughly 100 feet left of the right end of a pink rock band. The approach takes about 30 minutes.

White Rock Spring Overview

Tunnel Vision

Angel food Wall

White Rock Spring Peak

Rosie's Day Out

To Parking Lot

To Willow Springs

*1. Tunnel Vision (5.7) FA: Joe Herbst, Randal Grandstaff; 1974. This unique route involves a bit of spelunking and is similar in nature to *The Tunnel* at Skytop Cliff in the Shawangunk Cliffs of New York. Bring a good selection of gear, including large Friends. Start 30' above the ground on a cleared section of ledge and 15' right of a chimney/alcove. **Pitch 1** (5.6): Climb a short corner to a ceiling 15' up, then traverse right 8' to an obvious crack system. Stem up the crack past loose blocks forming a roof, then continue up to a ledge (60'). Climb the chimney above to another ledge and belay in an alcove. 120'. **Pitch 2** (5.4): Continue up the chimney system, belaying on the flattest section you can find (large gear needed for the anchors). 100'. **Pitch 3** (5.7): Continue up the steep and exposed chimney to a spacious ledge below an overhanging wall. There's room for 15 people to sit comfortably here! 120'. **Pitch 4** (5.5): Climb straight up past an overhang to a lower-angle face. Ascend the delightful varnished face and right-facing corner to another huge ledge at the mouth of the tunnel. 130'. **Pitch 5** (5.3): Turn on your headlamps! Angle up left through the tunnel on water-polished rock to a ledge. A Friend or Tri-Cam in a pocket and some small wires provide protection for the chimney. Walk left to reach daylight, then climb the obvious crack system to a belay ledge. 150'. **Pitch 6** (5.5): Climb either of two cracks above, escaping left below a final ceiling or continuing straight up to the top. 150'. **Descent:** Head down and left (southeast) in a series of easy chimney/gullies for 100 yards. Contour around right (west) to the top of a huge gully leading southeast. Go down this to an obvious dropoff (possible 60-foot rappel here) and move right over a small saddle into a parallel gully. This will easily take you down to the open slope at the left (southeast) end of Angel Food Wall. The descent should take about 15 minutes.

2. Group Therapy (5.7) FA: Joe and Betsy Herbst, Randal Grandstaff, Matt McMackin; Spring 1974. This route starts quite a bit to the right of *Tunnel Vision* in a large recess/chasm with a pine tree. **Pitch 1:** Scamper up an easy face to a belay. 145'. **Pitch 2:** Jam up a wide crack in the center of a white face. 130'. **Pitch 3** (5.6): Climb up cracks, then move left and climb a left-facing corner to a belay. 90'. **Pitch 4:** Continue up cracks and the face above to a belay at a tree. This is about 80' below a prominent left-facing corner with a roof. 90'. **Pitch 5** (5.7): Climb the crack through the roof, then continue up to a belay. 150'. **Pitch 6:** Go off to the left to reach the summit. **Variation 1** (5.8): Continue up a vertical crack to the summit. **Descent:** Head down and left (southeast) in a series of easy chimney/gullies for 100 yards. Contour around right (west) to the top of a huge gully leading southeast. Go down this to an obvious dropoff (possible 60-foot rappel here) and move right over a small saddle into a parallel gully. This will easily take you down to the open slope at the left (southeast) end of Angel Food Wall. The descent should take about 15 minutes.

TUNNEL VISION (5.7)

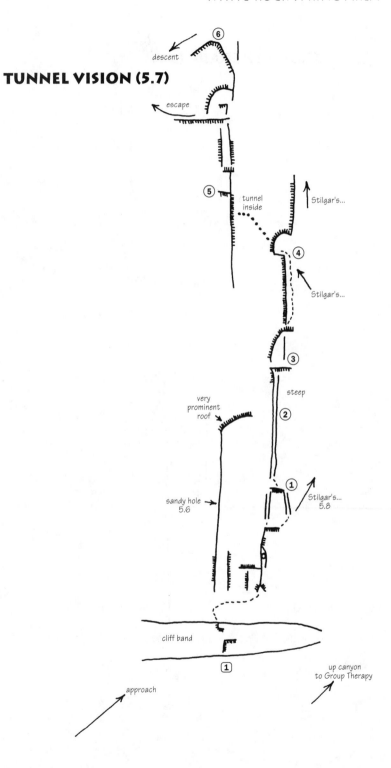

descent

escape

⑥

⑤

tunnel inside

Stilgar's...

④

Stilgar's...

③

steep

②

very prominent roof

①

sandy hole
5.6

Stilgar's...
5.8

cliff band

①

up canyon
to Group Therapy

approach

GROUP THERAPY (5.7)

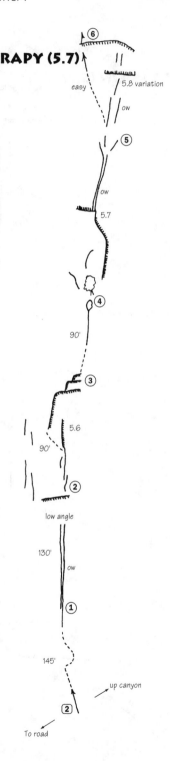

easy

5.8 variation

ow

ow

5.7

90'

6

5

4

3

5.6

90'

2

low angle

130'

ow

1

145'

up canyon

2

To road

*3. **Goobies for Gumbies** (5.10+) FA: Paul Van Betten, Randal Grandstaff, Nick Nordblom; 1985. A classic pitch of crack climbing. Bring lots of Friends (from #2 to #3) and two ropes. Same start as *Group Therapy* in a chasm. Climb the striking hand crack on the left wall of the chasm to an anchor about 140' up.

4. **Healy's Haunted House** (5.7) FA: Bob Healy, Joe Herbst; Spring 1974. Start on a bushy ledge at the base of a huge chimney just uphill (right) of *Group Therapy*. **Pitch 1** (5.7): Climb the inside of the chimney, utilizing face holds. Pass a ceiling and continue up to a belay in a narrower portion of the chimney. 135'. **Pitch 2** (5.7): Continue up the chimney, then exit right onto easier ground. Go up and right (see variation) to a belay ledge at the base of a left-facing corner. 150'. **Pitch 3** (5.6): Climb the corner, then step right and follow a crack past an overhang. Continue up the main chimney/crack system to a belay stance. 165'. **Pitch 4** (5.7): Continue up the crack system to the summit. 165'. **Variation** (5.7): Instead of going up and right to the belay, it is possible to climb straight up a crack, then angle right to a point just below the overhang. If you decide to do this variation, you may wish to belay soon after exiting the chimney, then climb the variation. **Descent:** Go southeast (toward the road) and go down a gully as for the other routes in this area.

WHITE ROCK SPRINGS PEAK

This formation is clearly visible from the trailhead and is in the sun all day. Numerous traditional lines exist on the cliff, but only one is described here. None of them are of particularly good quality.

From the cul-de-sac, walk down the obvious dirt road toward White Rock Spring. When the dirt road begins to angle left (south), go right across a small wash, then begin contouring west toward a prominent gully. This gully leads up to the southwest face of White Rock Springs Peak. Approach time is about 1 hour. (No topo.)

5. **Rosie's Day Out** (5.9) FRA: Rosie the Dog and friends; January 1999. This route generally climbs the skyline of White Rock Springs Peak as viewed from the trailhead. Start about 40' left of a huge detached block that is near the right edge of the main face. Bring wires, TCUs, and cams up to #4. **Pitch 1** (5.9): Traverse out left on a ledge to an obvious, vertical finger crack. Climb the crack to its top, then step up and right to a stance. Angle up and left along two corners to a ledge on the skyline (watch for rope drag). Step left and climb an easy crack to a huge ledge just above a prominent pine tree. 120'. **Pitch 2** (5.8): Starting above the pine tree, climb the right-hand of two obvious varnished cracks. Follow thinner cracks above to a belay at a tree. 130'. **Descent:** Rappel with two ropes straight down the cliff using trees for anchors. You may want to bring some webbing or pieces of rope to make your ropes pull more easily.

HEALY'S
HAUNTED HOUSE (5.7)

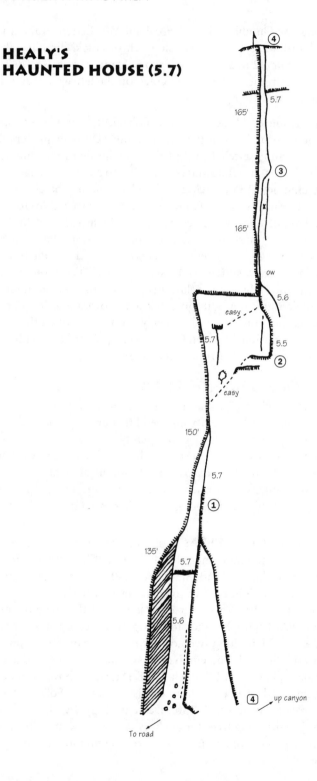

WILLOW SPRING

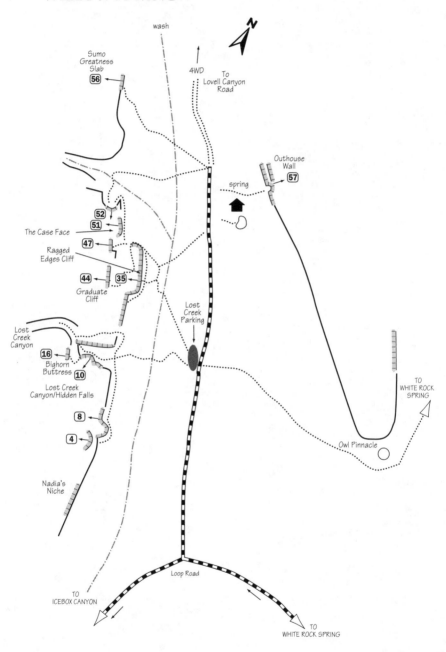

wash

N

Sumo
Greatness
Slab
56

4WD

To
Lovell Canyon
Road

Outhouse
Wall
57

spring

52

51

The Case Face

Ragged
Edges Cliff

47

44   **35**

Graduate
Cliff

Lost
Creek
Parking

Lost
Creek
Canyon

16

Bighorn
Buttress   **10**

Lost Creek
Canyon/Hidden Falls

TO
WHITE ROCK
SPRING

8

Owl Pinnacle

4

Nadia's
Niche

Loop Road

TO
ICEBOX CANYON

TO
WHITE ROCK SPRING

WILLOW SPRING

While not as in vogue as The Gallery or Wall of Confusion, Willow Spring offers many short routes of good quality. The turnoff for Willow Spring is 7.3 miles along the scenic loop road. This spur road is paved for 0.6 mile; after that it's four-wheel-drive territory.

Most of the routes described are one-pitch, though at times you may need two ropes to easily get back to your gear. Those longer convenience rappels are noted. The typical rack for Willow Spring includes a set of Friends, TCUs, and wired stoppers. It's mostly a traditional area.

At the end of the pavement is a picnic area on the right. There are a few picnic tables under the big cottonwood trees, a natural spring (no potable water, though), and an outhouse. Just to the right (east) of the outhouse building is some excellent bouldering, but stay off the Native American rock art!

NADIA'S NICHE

Three routes are described just outside the mouth of the Willow Spring canyon. These routes are located roughly halfway between Lost Creek Canyon and Icebox Canyon at the base of the hillside. The best view (and approach) is from the intersection of the scenic loop road and the Willow Spring Road. From here, walk straight west toward the hillside. All three routes are on a dark, northeast-facing formation. The routes are described from left to right.

1. **Nadia's Nine** (5.9+) FA: Joe Herbst, Mark Moore; Spring 1977. This route gets rave reviews in the Urioste guide, but I have yet to do it. It climbs a left-facing (toward Icebox Canyon) crack and corner system in 2 pitches. The first pitch is supposed to be harder than the second pitch. (Not shown.)

The next two routes are on a varnished face to the right of *Nadia's Nine*.

2. **Dark Star** (5.11+) FA: Paul Van Betten, Bob Conz; September 1988. After a hard start, climb a thin flake with bolts. 80'.

3. **Wheat Thick** (5.11b) FA: Paul Van Betten, Sal Mamusia; October 1988. This is supposed to be a thick version of Yosemite's *Wheat Thin*. Start to the right of *Dark Star* and climb a flake system and black huecos to an anchor.

LOST CREEK CANYON/HIDDEN FALLS

After turning off the scenic loop road into Willow Spring, you come to a dirt pullout on your left after 0.2 mile. This is the parking for Lost Creek Canyon

and Hidden Falls. Follow the obvious trail for about 300 yards, passing a spring en route to the mouth of the canyon. To the left (southeast) are routes *N'Plus Ultra* through *Buffalo Balls*. These routes are in the shade all day. To the right of the dry waterfall are routes *The Threat* through *Hot Climb*. These routes get sun in the morning, then move into the shade in the afternoon.

*4. **N'Plus Ultra** (5.10-) FA (TR): Joe Herbst; 1975. FA (lead): Randal Grandstaff; 1976. This route sits on the second tier of cliff bands about 300 yards left (southeast) of the trail. Turn off the trail at the spring (and a couple of wooden benches) and follow a faint path toward the cliff. Approach this route by scrambling up an easy gully with a pine tree at the base. The route climbs out a huge roof via a fist crack. Bring multiple #4 Friends. Descend by walking off right (northwest) around to the base of the roof, then back down the approach gully. (No topo.)

5. **The Abdominizer** (5.11) FA: Paul Van Betten, Richard Harrison, Shelby Shelton; April 1990. No spare tires allowed. Climb the roof just left of *N'Plus Ultra* along flakes. There are 2 bolts in the roof for protection. (No topo.)

6. **Pillar Talk** (5.7 R) FA: Joe Herbst; 1970s. Turn off the trail to Hidden Falls as for *N'Plus Ultra* (in the vicinity of a couple of wooden benches) and follow the faint trail about 200 yards to the base of a pillar with an

obvious hand-and-fist crack on its right side. **Pitch 1** (5.7 PG): Climb the crack to a roof (large protection needed; see variation), then hand-traverse left (scary) to the arête. Climb up the easy face and belay in one of many cracks. 100'. **Pitch 2** (5.4 R): Continue up the easy face to the top of the pillar. 80'. **Variation** (5.10-): Continue up the crack through the roof above, then rejoin the regular route. Large Friends needed. Descent: Walk right (west) and rappel with two ropes from a pine tree atop *Sleeper*.

7. **Big Iron** (5.11c) FA: Paul Van Betten, Bob Conz; Summer 1990. Climb the steep face just around the corner to the right of *Pillar Talk* past 7 bolts. Rappel *Sleeper* with two ropes.

8. **Sleeper** (5.9) FA: Wendell Broussard, Rocky Paravia; 1981. Start 30' right of *Pillar Talk* below an obvious finger crack leading to a pine tree. Climb flakes to a bulge (about 50' up) that is split by a crack. Pull the bulge (crux) and follow the crack to the top. Rappel from the pine tree with two ropes.

The next five routes are on the varnished buttress just left of the trail to Hidden Falls, near some big pine trees at the mouth of the canyon. These trees are several hundred yards along the main trail from the wooden benches. They are in the shade all day.

9. **Killer Klowns** (5.10+) FA: Paul Van Betten, Sal Mamusia, Richard Harrison, Kevin Biernacki; September 1989. Climb an easy ramp on the left edge of the steep, varnished wall to an alcove 20' up. Struggle up through a bomb bay slot, then up the face and cracks above to the top. Descend by scrambling over the highest part of the buttress, then down a gully just right (south) of the varnished wall. (Not shown.)

*10. **Left Out** (5.10+) FA (TR): Unknown. FA (lead): Joe Herbst; circa 1975. An excellent route that climbs a thin crack on the left side of the varnished face. Not to be left out! Climb steep huecos just left of the obvious central crack on the formation (see variation), thenup the thin crack to its top. Climb the easier face to the top of the formation. Same descent as *Killer Klowns*. **Variation** (5.11- R/X) FA: Bobby Rotert; 1983. Start up *Black Track*, then follow a left-leaning seam into *Left Out* (3 bolts lead up from this seam, but the route is apparently incomplete).

*11. **Black Track** (5.9) FA: Joe Herbst; early; 1970s. The obvious line on the wall and a good follow-up climb to *Ragged Edges*. Climb the central crack on the wall to a ledge two-thirds of the way up. Either rappel with one rope from the chain anchor, climb the short off-width to the top, or climb the steep face directly above past 2 bolts (5.11c). (Not shown.)

*12. **Bigfoot** (5.10a) FA: Yeti and A. Snowman; 1990. A very good face-climb just right of *Black Track*. Climb the steep face past 4 bolts to the chain anchor. One of the huccos on the route is shaped like a foot, hence the name. (Not shown.)

13. **Buffalo Balls** (5.11c) FA (TR): Bob Yoho; 1989; FA (lead): Don Burroughs, Alan Busby; May 1992. Follow 4 bolts up the steep face just right of *Bigfoot*. (Not shown.)

UPPER TIER

The next two routes are roughly above the *Black Track* buttress. They are located about 200 yards left of *Bighorn Buttress* at the top of a gully near a large, dead pine tree. Information is sketchy.

14. **Possum Logic** (5.9 R) FA: Nick Nordblom, Shelby Shelton; 1988. Climb the face left of the tree past 4 bolts. (No topo.)

15. **The Pocket Philosopher** (5.10-) FA: Nick Nordblom, Danny Rider; 1988. This route goes up behind the dead tree and has 2 bolts. (No topo.)

*16. **Bighorn Buttress** (5.11 PG13) FA: Nick Nordblom, Jenni Stone; Spring 1987. This good and scary route is on the left (south) side of upper Lost Creek Canyon and starts about 300' up and left from the dry waterfall (the top of *The Threat*). The start of the route faces the road, but the majority of the climbing faces right, toward Ragged Edges Cliff. Approach

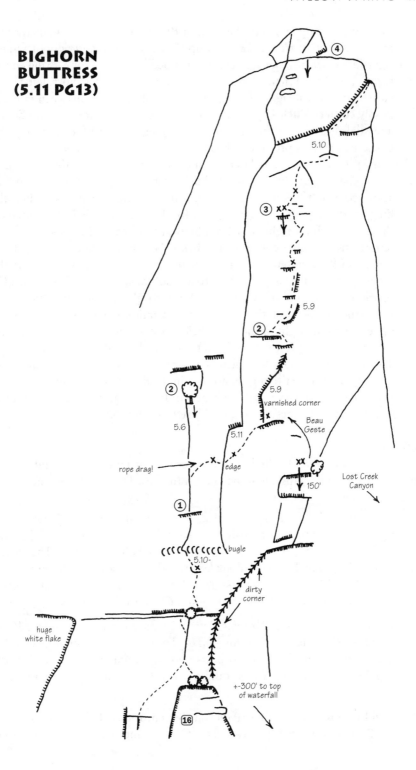

BIGHORN BUTTRESS (5.11 PG13)

(4)

5.10

(3)

5.9

(2)

5.9
varnished corner

(2)

Beau
Geste

5.6

5.11

rope drag!   edge

XX

150'

Lost Creek
Canyon

(1)

bugle

5.10-

dirty
corner

huge
white flake

+-300' to top
of waterfall

(16)

by scrambling up ledges to the right of *Buffalo Balls* or follow the trail up around the top of *Heatwave*. Gear up about 50' down and right of a huge, right-facing white flake at a section of chocolate brown rock. Bring equipment up to a #3 Friend and some long slings. Start at a short, left-facing corner that is just right of a mossy section of rock and between two opposing corners. **Pitch 1** (5.10- PG): Climb the short corner then wander up and slightly right on the brown face, aiming for a 20-foot-long vertical crack leading to a prominent bush in a horizontal crack (see Variations 1 and 2). Follow the vertical crack and the face just left to the horizontal crack, then step right toward the bush. Climb straight up the brown face above to a bolt below a bulge with a thin, vertical seam/crack. Pull the bulge and belay above on a ledge. 140'. **Pitch 2** (5.11 PG): Continue up the crack, exiting right to a bolt. Step around the arête, passing a bolt (crux), then climb a corner to the belay. Watch out for rope drag. 150'. **Pitch 3** (5.9): Climb up past a couple of left-facing corners and finish the pitch by face-climbing past a bolt to a 2-bolt belay. 80'. **Pitch 4** (5.10): Go up right past a bolt, turn a small roof into a right-facing corner and go up this to the top. Belay on the summit. 80'. **Variation 1:** You can also scramble up ledges to the right of the start (below a vegetated corner) and step left to the base of the vertical crack that leads to the bush. **Variation 2** (5.9+): The original route up this buttress was called *Beau Geste* and climbed up the vegetated corner that is mentioned in the first variation until you could traverse left into the varnished corners of Pitch 3. **Descent:** Rappel straight down with two ropes, ending to the right of the route.

LOWER TIER

The next routes are all located on the other side of Hidden Falls and are described starting at the falls and moving right (north). These routes are in the sun in the morning.

17. **The Threat** (5.10+) FA: Joe Herbst, Randal Grandstaff; 1975. Just to the right of the dry falls is an obvious water-polished crack. Move left into the crack (bolt, crux), then up this past another bolt to the top. The easiest descent is to walk left (east) along ledges and scramble down the gully to the right of the *Black Track* buttress. It is also possible to walk off right (north) by *Heatwave*, then circle back around the base of the cliff. (Not shown.)

18. **Flight Line** (5.12c) FA: Paul Van Betten, Richard Harrison; Summer 1990. Climb smooth flakes 10' right of *The Threat* to a very smooth wave of rock above. Clip the doubled bolts and surmount the wave to gain the top. Don't expect to get this route quickly. It's technical and tricky. (Not shown.)

19. **Mind Bomb** (5.11+ R) FA: Paul Van Betten, Richard Harrison; Summer 1990. A good route if you can get off the ground! Climb the 3-bolt arête

50' right of the dry falls and just right of a cave. Bring some natural gear and be prepared to run it out above the top bolt. (Not shown.)

*20. **Little Big Horn** (5.9+) FA: Jay Smith, Randal Grandstaff, Doug MacDonald; 1981. A great route. Hopefully you won't get massacred by the crux! Walk 100' to the right of *Mind Bomb*, past three ugly cracks, until the trail enters the trees. Start in the trees and climb a left-facing corner past an overhang (crux) to the varnished face and the top.

21. **Grippitty Gravity** (5.10) FA: Jon Martinet, Randal Grandstaff; mid-1970s. A short crux leads to an easy dihedral above. Start atop boulders 100' right of *Little Big Horn* and below a low roof split by a crack. Climb out the roof (crux), then up the low-angled, varnished corner above. Finish up easy cracks and a short face.

22. **Sportin' a Woody** (5.11+) FA: Paul Van Betten, Sal Mamusia, Bob Conz; February 1990. About 120' to the right of *Little Big Horn* is another good-looking, left-facing corner protected by bolts and RPs.

Roughly 160 feet to the right of *Little Big Horn* is a large, steep face with two bolted routes.

23. **Captain Hook** (5.11+ R) FA: Paul Van Betten, Jay Smith; Fall 1988. This climbs the left side of the face past 2 bolts to a thin seam/flake. Follow this and clip 2 more bolts on your way to the top.

24. **Captain Curmudgeon** (5.11- R) FA: Nick Nordblom, Jenni Stone, Paul Van Betten; Spring 1986. Climb loose flakes up the center of the steep face just right of *Captain Hook*, passing 3 bolts en route. (No topo.)

25. **Captain Crunch** (5.10- X) FA: Nick Nordblom, Jenni Stone, Paul Van Betten; Fall 1988. Bring a few small wires (not that you'll get many in!). Climb the right edge of the buttress, ending on the shoulder. Scary and loose.

26. **Tuckered Sparfish** (5.10 PG13) FA: Paul Van Betten, Don Burroughs; June 1992. Rope up 20' right of *Captain Crunch* on the next buttress and climb past 4 bolts to a tree on the top. Bring some wires and TCUs to get you to the first bolt. (No topo.)

27. **Rock Rastler** (5.12+ R) FA: Paul Van Betten; Summer 1985. Climb a hand crack to a roof, then struggle up an off-width to the top. (No topo.)

28. **Heatwave** (5.10- R) FA: Paul and Pauline Van Betten; 1988. Located at the far right (north) end of Hidden Canyon and 200' right of *Captain Curmudgeon*. Climb the center of a slabby face past 3 bolts. (No topo.)

29. **Hot Climb** (5.10- R/X) FA: Nick Nordblom, Wendell Broussard; 1989. This short route climbs a little, black, varnished wall up and right of *Heatwave*. You'll need some small wires. Note: The hiking trail leading into upper Lost Creek Canyon passes just to the right of this route. This may also be used as the descent. (No topo.)

RAGGED EDGES CLIFF

This is probably the most obvious cliff in the Willow Spring area. Either park as for Lost Creek Canyon or continue driving down the spur road toward Willow Spring for another 0.3 mile (0.5 mile total from the scenic loop road). On the left side of the road is a large, varnished wall with an obvious vertical crack system in the center. This crack is the classic *Ragged Edges*. After deciding where to park, follow one of the clearly defined trails to the base of the cliff. The following routes are shaded most of the day.

30. **Kemosabe** (5.10- PG) FA: Sal Mamusia, Richard Harrison, Paul Van Betten, Wendell Broussard; 1983. An exciting climb. Bring small gear. Begin at the base of an arch 100' left of *Ragged Edges*. Climb the face and thin cracks up the arête of the arch to a bolt. Continue up the arête (scary), or weenie out and traverse off left, then up to the top. Walk off to the right (west) as on *Ragged Edges*.

31. **Tonto** (5.5) FA: Joe and Betsy Herbst; 1972. Climb the obvious crack in the slab that is 90' left of *Ragged Edges* and just right of the arch mentioned in *Kemosabe*. At the top, move out right onto the face or continue up the crack past a roof (5.7).

32. **Vision Quest** (5.12d) FA: Paul Van Betten, Sal Mamusia; October 1988. Start 75' left of *Ragged Edges* and just right of an ugly chimney/corner. Climb up a short crack, then move slightly right to a bolt. Continue up the overhanging wall above, past 3 more bolts to a chain anchor. The second

pitch climbs a left-leaning crack to the top (5.10+). The 2 ring bolts below were placed by Craig Reason in a failed attempt to do a direct start.

33. **Bodiddly** (5.10 PG) FA: Robert Finlay, Richard Harrison; 1985. A very good route, but a tiny bit scary. Start 30' left of *Ragged Edges* on the left, front corner of the wall. Climb up the arête and face to a bolt, then follow more bolts up left (see variation) past a steep flake. Continue up the easy face above. Walk off right as for *Ragged Edges*. **Variation/Bodacious** (5.10): FA: Sal Mamusia, Richard Harrison, Wendell Broussard; Spring 1983. From the second bolt, it is possible to traverse straight left, then up past a bolt to rejoin the route. This was how this section of rock was first climbed. *Bodiddly* is the straighter (and perhaps more logical) line.

34. **Plan F** (5.11- PG) FA: Sal Mamusia, Richard Harrison, Paul Van Betten, Nick Nordblom; April 1983. The initial finger crack is often done by itself, rapping off the anchor in the *Ragged Edges* crack. Begin below an obvious finger crack 8' left of *Ragged Edges*. Jam up the crack (5.10-), then angle left up the smooth, slippery face past a few bolts to the top.

*35. **Ragged Edges** (5.8) FA: Joe Herbst; early 1970s. The classic route at Willow Spring. Bring lots of large gear. Climb the central crack on the varnished wall in 2 pitches. Walk off to the right (west), then back along the base of the crag.

*36. **Chicken Eruptus** (5.10 PG) FA: Richard Harrison, Wendell Broussard, Paul Van Betten, Sal Mamusia; Spring 1983. Named to commemorate Broussard's meal at Caesar's Palace the previous night! An excellent but sporty route for solid 5.10 leaders. Start 5' right of *Ragged Edges* and climb up a right-leaning ramp for 40' to horizontal cracks. Move out right to the nose, then climb straight up the face past a bolt to the summit. Bring #1.5 and #2 Friends for the belay.

37. **Gun Boy** (5.11+ PG) FA: Paul Van Betten, Sal Mamusia, Richard Harrison, Danny Meyers; March 1991. Start 30' right of *Ragged Edges* in a yellow band of rock. Climb past 1 bolt to a rounded, brown dihedral. Continue straight up the face, keeping just left of a black streak, passing 2 more bolts to the top. There's a rather scary section that requires some dicey moves off small RPs.

*38. **Sheep Trail** (5.10- PG) FA: John Bachar, Mike Lechlinski, Richard Harrison; Spring 1983. Wonderful climbing, but make sure you're solid at the grade. This was originally rated 5.8! Begin 40' right of *Ragged Edges* at a black streak and a clearing in the vegetation. Weave up past numerous horizontal cracks to a shallow, left-facing corner about 50' up. Continue basically straight up the face, exiting the brown rock at a short, vertical crack. Belay on the terrace (small to medium Friends), then walk off right.

39. **Dense Pack** (5.10 PG) FA: Nick Nordblom, Robert Finlay; Spring 1984. Another excellent but sporty route. Traverse out left on a ledge system 150' right of *Ragged Edges* to a right-facing corner. Lieback and stem up the corner, then swing out left (see variation). Weave up the varnished face above, angling slightly left. Belay on the terrace above, then walk off right. **Variation/Twelve Pack** (5.10+) FA: Paul Van Betten, Luis Saca; April 1990. From atop the corner, follow an undercling flake out right. Climb up the face past 1 bolt to the terrace. (Not shown.)

40. **Why Left** (5.11b) FA: Sal Mamusia, Paul Van Betten, Luis Saca; August 1992. Begin below a line of bolts about 30' to the right of *Dense Pack*. Climb up and left past 4 bolts to the terrace. (Not shown.)

41. **Why Right** (5.11b) FA: Paul Van Betten, Sal Mamusia, Luis Saca; August 1992. Clip the first 2 bolts on *Why Left*, then climb up and right past 2 more bolts. Walk off right on the terrace. (Not shown.)

42. **Sheep Dip** (5.11- R/X) FA (TR): Randy Marsh; 1981; FA (lead): Richard Harrison, Robert Finlay; 1986. Same start as *Dense Pack* at a black waterstreak about 150' right of *Ragged Edges*. Climb up the black streak on obvious holds (#4 Friend in the horizontal crack) to gain a white, left-facing corner. Follow this up to the terrace. **Note:** More topropes have been done to the right but aren't included here.

GRADUATE CLIFF

This crag is 100 yards directly above *Ragged Edges* and has huge, bulging roofs on its right side. It's easiest to approach these routes by walking up past the right side of Ragged Edges Cliff, then up a trail to the left of the top of *Ragged Edges*. All three hard routes have rappel anchors and start partway up the cliff, atop a varnished, water-streaked slab. The routes are in the shade in the afternoon and are described from left to right.

43. **Walk to School** (5.7) FA: Jon Martinet, Randal Grandstaff, Scott Gordon; 1975. Bring medium gear and some long slings. Climb the straight-in crack 40' left of *The Graduate* and 10' right of large white blocks at the mouth of a corridor. At a ledge about 50' up, traverse right to the anchor on *The Graduate*. Rappel with one rope.

*44. **The Graduate** (5.10) FA: Randal Grandstaff, Jon Martinet, Scott Gordon; 1975. Making the dean's list isn't necessary to do this fine route. Bring a good selection of gear, including extra #3 Camalots and a few long slings. This climb forms the left margin of the varnished wall and climbs a large, right-facing corner (see variation) to the ceiling. There is a natural thread rappel anchor above the ceiling to the left of the top of the corner. **Variation/G.E.D. (General Equivalent Diploma)** (5.9): Escape left before the final, steep corner, then up the easy face to the anchor.

Graduate Cliff and the Case Face

45. **Acid Jacks** (5.11) FA: Richard Harrison, Kevin Biernacki, Jerry from Colorado; Summer 1989. Start on the varnished slab below a line of bolts 20' right of *The Graduate*. Bring a #2 Friend, some wires, and a long sling to protect the moves above the fourth bolt. Rappel with one rope from a 2-bolt belay above the ceiling. This anchor is 15' right of the anchor on *The Graduate*.

46. **Circle Jerks** (5.11d) FA: Paul Van Betten, Richard Harrison, Kevin Biernacki; Summer 1989. Power past 6 bolts, starting 25' right of *Acid Jacks* and just left of some white corners above the varnished slab. There is a 2-bolt belay over the roof.

THE CASE FACE

The next routes are 150 yards right and about 50' above the top of Ragged Edges Cliff. They are to the right (northwest) and slightly below Graduate Cliff. *Hard Case* is easy to spot from the road. It climbs a left-leaning crack on a cliff that has a brown upper and white lower (The Case Face). Approach by walking up the bushy slope just right of Ragged Edges Cliff.

47. **Territorial Imperative** (5.10 R/X) FA: Kurt Reider, Randal Grandstaff; 1980. This scary but excellent route is located in a recess to the left of The Case Face and climbs a black waterstreak on small edges. Bring small

RPs. With a bit of luck (and talent), you can get some in just before the crux, which is between the first and second bolts. Traverse off left.

48. **Just in Case** (5.5) FA: Donette and Todd Swain, George and Catriona Reid; October 1994. Rope up next to a pine tree at the extreme left edge of The Case Face. Climb up to a bolt, step left (crux), then follow the arête and face up to a short flake/crack. Belay atop the flake, then traverse left across a slab to a corner and downclimb to your pack.

49. **Space Case** (5.7) FRA: Randy Marsh, Pauline Schroeder; 1983. Originally done without the bolt. Begin 10' right of *Just in Case* and climb past a bolt into a crack that leads up and slightly left. Traverse left across a slab into a gully/corner, then easily downclimb the gully and low-angled slab.

50. **Head Case** (5.8) FRA (TR): Todd and Donette Swain; March 1994. FA (lead): Todd and Donette Swain, George and Catriona Reid; October 1994. Start 25' right of *Space Case* and 35' left of *Hard Case* atop a long, narrow boulder. Climb the white and brown face past 4 bolts and a few gear placements to an anchor. Rap with one rope.

51. **Hard Case** (5.9) FA: Joe Herbst, Matt MacMackin; circa 1975. Bring large gear to protect the wide sections. Start 35' right of the last route, below an obvious varnished, left-leaning crack with a ceiling 20' up. Follow the crack past an alcove (crux) until it leads to face-climbing. Continue up to and around the right side of the summit roof. Walk off right (or traverse left below the roof and rappel from the anchor on *Head Case*).

The next two routes are located down and right from *Hard Case* and can be approached from that route or from the end of the paved section of Willow Spring Road. To approach from *Hard Case*, traverse 75 feet down and right on a rock rib, then scramble left (west) around some corners. To approach from the end of the pavement, walk 200 yards west into an obvious drainage that has three large pine trees on its left side. Scramble up to the highest pine tree (about 200 feet above the drainage bottom) and rack up.

*52. **Soylent Green Jeans** (5.9+) FA: Paul and Pauline S. Van Betten; 1985. Bring many TCUs, including at least two of the very smallest. Additionally, bring a good selection of gear up to a #4 Friend and some long slings. Much better than it may first appear. Start at a clean, right-facing corner left of *Sterling Moss* and just above the huge pine tree. Climb the cleaved, right-facing corner passing just left of a small pine tree to a yellow, triangular ceiling. Pull the ceiling (intimidating, but not too hard) into a lower-angled dihedral. Stretch the rope to belay at the top of the dihedral off #2 and #3 Friends in a horizontal crack above a ceiling (180'). Scramble down a gully just to the left (north) of the climb. (Not shown.)

53. **Sterling Moss** (5.10 R) FA: Richard Harrison, Randal Grandstaff, Wendell Broussard, Nick Nordblom, Sal Mamusia; Spring 1982. Named for the famous race car driver. Start 40' right of the prominent pine tree and climb the face to a bolt (scary). Move a bit right, then up to an obvious left-facing flake (pro here). Step right and climb an easy dihedral to a ceiling. Follow the left-leaning fissure (crux) up into the low-angle dihedral. Stretch the rope to belay at the top of the dihedral off #2 and #3 Friends in a horizontal crack above a ceiling (180'). Scramble down a gully just to the left (north) of the climb.

SUMO GREATNESS SLAB

From the end of the pavement on the Willow Spring Road, walk 200 yards up the dirt road. About 200 yards to the left (southwest) is a cliff band with a prominent black waterstreak in its center and a smooth, slabby face at its right end. These climbs are located on the slabby face about 180' right of the waterstreak and are in the shade all day. There is Native American rock art right of the waterstreak, and like all rock art, it should not be climbed on or disturbed in any way. Dozens of routes have been done to the left of the black streak, but due to the rock art, the routes are not listed here. (No topo.)

54. **Sumo Greatness** (5.9+ R) FA: Richard Harrison, Nick Nordblom, Wendell Broussard, Sal Mamusia, Paul Van Betten; Winter 1982. Start behind a pine tree, at a right-leaning crack/groove with dark varnish on its left side. This is about 120' right of the waterstreak. Climb up the crack/groove for 40', then angle right to a bolt. Climb up past a white splotch to another bolt and the top. Walk off right (west).

55. **Ice Climb** (5.9+ R) FA: John Long, Lynn Hill, Doug Robinson, Randal Grandstaff; 1981. Bring some TCUs and wires. Start at a short, overhanging wide crack 20' right of *Sumo Greatness*. Climb the face just left of the crack, then follow the thinner, right-leaning crack to a red band. Clip a bolt, then climb up a short seam through a bulge (fixed pin) to an alcove (#3 Friend). Step left and finish up the face above. Walk off right.

56. **Dean's List** (5.11 PG) FA: Paul Van Betten, Richard Harrison, Wendell "the Dean" Broussard, Druce Finlay (eight years old!); 1990. Can you make the grade? Bring some small wires to protect the moves to the first bolt, and bring very thin fingers for the pockets past the last bolt. Start atop boulders 45' right of *Sumo Greatness*. Move out left onto a ledge above some low roofs, then angle back right on the slab to a bolt at the right edge of the dark streak. Face-climb past 2 more bolts to the top. Walk off right.

OUTHOUSE WALL

To access this sunny cliff, park at the end of the pavement on the Willow Spring road. On the north (right) side of the road and above the outhouse building is a south-facing cliff. Go directly uphill for 50 yards to an alcove formed by a huge detached boulder. Many other routes have been done here, but only these few are listed. Routes are described from right to left. (No topo.)

57. **Tricks Are for Kids** (5.10- PG13) FA: Paul Van Betten; rope solo, 1982. Bring your bag of tricks for this one. Start in the alcove above the outhouse building and climb a flake to a ledge at 20'. Continue up the left-leaning corner/crack above (cheater stones may be needed to get off the ledge), moving right when the crack doglegs. Walk off right (south).

58. **Spiderline** (5.7 PG) FA: Unknown; circa 1980. Start in the alcove as for *Tricks Are for Kids* and climb an easy, wide crack on the left to a platform 40' up. Climb the left edge of the varnish above, finishing at a notch in a small ceiling. Walk off right (south).

59. **Rasting Affair** (5.10-) FA: Richard Harrison, Wendell Broussard; 1983. The face just left of *Spiderline*, which has some fixed gear on it.

60. **Sin City** (5.11- X) FA: Paul Van Betten, Sal Mamusia; 1983. This route climbs the left edge of the face, about 75' left of the *Spiderline* alcove. Start on a ledge and climb over a bulge, protecting in a right-leaning seam. Bring small wires.

61. **Jam Session** (5.11-) FA: Paul Van Betten, Sal Mamusia; 1984. An overhanging crack around the corner and left of *Sin City*.

THE DARK THUMB

This sunny formation sits directly across the canyon from the Lost Creek/Hidden Falls parking area. The two climbs listed here are about 175 yards up and left of Owl Pinnacle (the prominent, squat, freestanding formation at the mouth of the canyon). As you may have guessed, this formation looks like a dark thumb. (No topo.)

62. **Land of the Free** (5.11c) FA: Greg Mayer; 1986. The left-hand route, which has 6 bolts and a shared anchor.

63. **Home of the Brave** (5.11+) FA: Mike Tupper; 1986. The right-hand route, which has at least 5 bolts and a shared anchor. Bring a small Friend to supplement the bolts.

ICEBOX CANYON

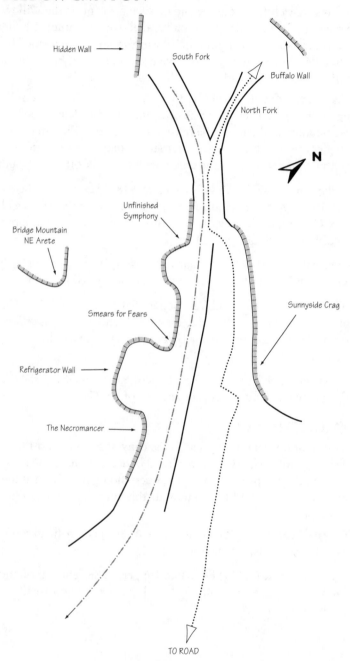

Hidden Wall →

South Fork

Buffalo Wall

North Fork

N

Unfinished Symphony

Bridge Mountain NE Arete

Sunnyside Crag

Smears for Fears

Refrigerator Wall →

The Necromancer →

TO ROAD

ICEBOX CANYON

The Icebox Canyon routes described here are primarily 1-pitch routes, although numerous multi-pitch routes exist. I've also included a few adventure climbs for people wishing for true wilderness experiences. Drive 7.8 miles along the scenic loop road until you reach the Icebox Canyon parking area. A well-maintained trail leads from the parking lot into the canyon, and the majority of routes are within 25 minutes of the road. Routes are described from right to left (counter clockwise) throughout the canyon.

SUNNYSIDE CRAG

Despite its name, this cliff is not very sunny during the winter months. As you look at the canyon from the parking lot, there are prominent, orange roofs at the bottom of the right (north) wall of the canyon. The climbs described on this crag start about 200 yards to the left of these low, orange roofs. They are farther

into the canyon at a point where the trail comes closest to the cliff. Approach time is about 15 minutes to this crag. Routes are described from right (east) to left (up-canyon) as you approach on the trail. (Not all routes are shown.)

1. **Whipper** (5.10) FA: Unknown; circa 1987. This route ascends a prominent roof crack about 100' left of a huge boulder with pine trees behind it. Climb the crack out a roof, then up the vertical crack to an anchor. Rappel with one rope.

2. **Backlash** (5.11) FA: PaulVan Betten, Jay Smith; October 1987. Begin 45' left of *Whipper* at a crack system through a large, bulging roof and just right of a nose. Climb the flake/right-facing corner to a 2-bolt anchor.

3. **Whiplash** (5.12-) FA (Pitch 1): Paul Van Betten, Jay Smith; October 1987. FA (Pitch 2): Paul Crawford, Paul Van Betten; Spring 1988. **Pitch 1:** Rope up as for the last route, but trend out left around a corner/nose to a left-leaning crack. Belay above in an alcove. **Pitch 2** (5.10+): A second pitch has been done and follows thin cracks on an arête to an anchor under a roof. **Descent:** Descend the route with two 75-foot rappels.

4. **Meteor** (5.11) FA: Unknown. FFA: Les Hutchinson, Paul Van Betten; 1988. FA (Pitch 2): Jay Smith, Paul Van Betten; 1988. The second pitch was done at a later date and is named *Meteorite*. Start in a cave 40' left of

Whiplash, up on a ledge. **Pitch 1** (5.11): Power outof the cave along an obvious roof crack to a belay stance in a shallow, left-facing corner. This corner is 10' left of a larger left-facing corner. 60'. **Pitch 2** (5.10+): Climb the vertical seam directly above the belay, then move right into a more pronounced crack/corner system. Climb up toward a roof, then angle about 30' up and right to an alcove under the roof. Pull the roof just left of the anchor on *Whiplash's* second pitch to broken ground and fixed gear (supposedly). **Descent:** Rappel with two ropes.

5. **Cold September Corner** (5.8) FA: Joe Herbst, Stephanie Petrilak, Bill Bradley; Fall 1978. About 20' to the left of *Meteor* is an obvious right-facing dihedral. Climb the dihedral to a belay anchor under a ceiling. At least 1 more pitch has been done, but no more is known. If you climb to the top of the crag, it appears you can descend off to the left (as for *Shady Ladies*).

6. **Mr. Freeze's Face** (5.10?) FA: Unknown; 1990s. Start at the bottom of a relatively smooth, varnished face just right of *Shady Ladies.* Climb up the center of the face along disjointed cracks past 1 bolt to the ledge 120' up. Bring wires, TCUs, and Friends up to #2. Rappel wit two ropes.

7. **Shady Ladies** (5.7) FA: Jineen Griffith, Barbara Euser; May 1978. Bring long slings and gear up to a #4 Friend. Start 75' left of *Cold September Corner* at a varnished dihedral that is just left of a brown face with a bolt on it. Climb the large dihedral for about 90', then traverse straight left along horizontal cracks to a fixed anchor on a ledge (120'). Rappel with

two ropes. The first ascent party apparently continued up for 3 more pitches. If you elect to do this, descend by heading left (up canyon) and rappelling from boulders and trees.

*8. **Magellanic Cloud** (5.9+ PG) FA: Unknown; 1980s. Probably the best moderate route on this crag. Carry gear to 4" plus some long slings. Same start as *Shady Ladies* at a varnished corner, but after 20' of climbing, angle up and left along a crack to the arête. Join *Van Allen Bet* for 10', then traverse straight right from a ceiling to a varnished, left-facing corner. Follow this clean corner straight up to the belay ledge. Rappel 120' to the ground with two ropes.

9. **Van Allen Belt** (5.7) FA: Unknown; 1980s. Bring up to a #4 Camalot, plus lots of slings. Begin at a smooth, 20-foot-high dihedral 20' left of the last two routes. Climb the dihedral and crack to a ceiling 40' up. Move left under the ceiling above to the arête, then climbthe crack and face up and right to the communal belay ledge (120'). Rappel with two ropes.

10. **Knotty Behavior** (5.10) FA: Randy Marsh, Greg Child; 1989. Start 75' left of *Van Allen Belt,* at a cave with a very nice-looking varnished nose just to its left. Climb past 2 bolts and horizontal cracks on the left side of the varnished nose, then up left to a chain anchor.

11. **Tie Me Tightly** (5.10) FA: Nick Nordblom, Jenni Stone; 1988. Start on varnished rock with numerous pockets and huecos 20' left of the last route. Climb 15' up, then move right to a right-facing flake. Climb the flake, then move right and up to the chain anchor on the previous route. Either rap from there or continue up a crack and the face to a 2-bolt belay anchor.

12. **Mercedes** (5.11-) FA: Jay Smith; circa 1988. Same start as the last route, but climb straight up the steep face past 4 bolts to a ceiling. Either move right to the chain anchor or continue up to the anchor above.

13. **Water Dog** (5.11+) FA: Paul Van Betten, Jay Smith, Paul Crawford; October 1987. Rope up 10' left of *Mercedes* at a thin, slightly left-leaning crack that is 10' right of a corner. Follow the crack up to a thread at the roof (see Variations 1 and 2), then up and left through more ceilings to an obvious fixed anchor. **Variation 1/Pit Bull** (5.10): Climb the crack just left, joining the regular route at the thread. **Variation 2/Hot Dog** (5.10 TR): A toprope up the thin arête/flake just left of *Pit Bull.*

14. **Water Logged** (5.9?) FA: Unknown; circa 1987. The obvious dihedral 4' left of *Hot Dog.* Rap from the anchor on *Water Dog* with one rope.

15. **Mister Masters** (5.9+) FA: Paul Van Betten, Danny Meyers; 1987. This route may be used to set up a toprope for the next three route. Start just left of the obvious dihedral and climb a varnished face up and left to the arête. Traverse left to a fixed anchor in the horizontal crack.

The next three routes climb the front of an appealing, varnished buttress that is just left (west) of *Water Logged*. They appear to be the best routes on the crag. (No topo.)

16. **Gotham City** (5.12- PG13) FA: Paul Van Betten, Robert Finlay; October 1987. This route climbs the right side of the face, using a thin seam for protection, to the communal anchor in the horizontal crack.

*17. **Spring Break** (5.11+) FA: Paul Van Betten, Sal Mamusia; Spring 1986. Ascend the center of the buttress along a thin, vertical seam, then up the face past horizontal cracks, keeping just left of a right-curving fissure.

*18. **Tarantula** (5.12-) FA: Paul Van Betten, Sal Mamusia; Spring 1986. Get Peter Parker to lead this one! The first ascent party found a tarantula in a horizontal crack about 40' up. This route climbs the left arête of the varnished buttress, following very thin seams to the communal belay.

Note: A bolted route has been attempted to the left of *Tarantula*, but as of press time it hadn't been completed.

19. **Crossfire** (5.11) FA: Jay Smith, Nick Nordblom; 1989. Begin at a thin, left-leaning crack that is about 40' left of the *Tarantula* arête and 20' right of a dirty, broken corner. Follow the left-leaning crack to a ceiling, then up past a bolt to horizontal cracks. Move right into an obvious left-facing corner and follow this to its top. Continue up the short, plated face to the anchor. A two-rope rappel will get you to safety.

BUFFALO WALL

This wall is apparently much steeper and more difficult than the Rainbow Wall in Juniper Canyon. Approach by hiking up the canyon beyond the Sunnyside Crags, then take the right (north) fork of the canyon up to the base of the wall. The approach up the north fork will at least require hauling packs up several dry falls. This cliff supposedly looks like a buffalo (hence the name) and is characterized by a huge dark section of rock in its middle.

20. **Buffalo Wall** (5.11 A3) FA: Paul Van Betten, Richard Harrison, Sal Mamusia; April 1991. The first ascent party took three days of climbing and used portaledges. The route climbs the center of the wall, finishing on the hump of the buffalo. The free climbing crux was a flaring off-width arch on the third pitch; the aid crux, the sixth pitch. There are eight pitches total. To descend, hike north to the dirt road running from Willow Spring toward Pahrump (Rocky Gap Road).

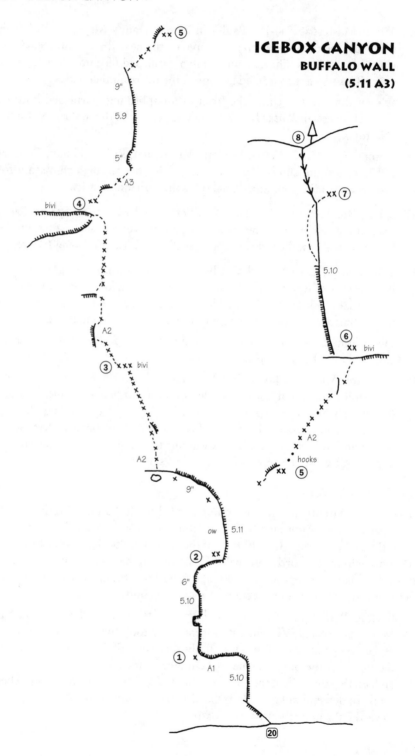

ICEBOX CANYON
BUFFALO WALL
(5.11 A3)

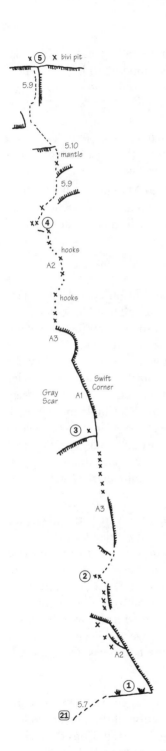

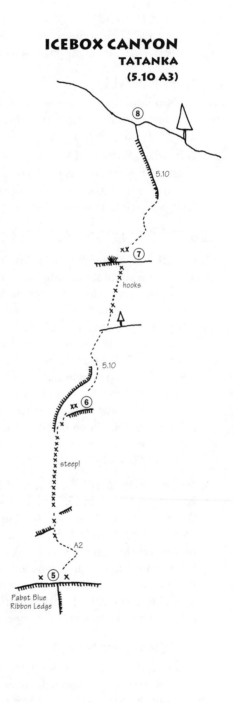

ICEBOX CANYON
TATANKA
(5.10 A3)

21. **Tatanka** (5.10 A3) FA: Richard Harrison, Paul Van Betten, Sal Mamusia; April 1993. This route took two days and is supposed to be of excellent quality. There are eight pitches, most of which require aid.

HIDDEN WALL

Like Buffalo Wall, this cliff is not easy to approach and may only have been climbed once. It sits quite a distance up the south fork of Icebox Canyon and is visible from the loop road in the vicinity of White Springs.

22. **Blitzkrieg** (5.10+ R) FA: Richard Harrison, Sal Mamusia; 1982. Follow prominent waterstreaks up the middle of the wall for seven pitches. There are no bolts on the route. To descend, hike north, then go down all of Icebox Canyon. (No topo.)

ICEBOX CANYON, SOUTH WALL

23. **Quiggle's Wiggle** (5.9 R) FA: Dave Gloudemans, Jason Quiggle; February 1996. This route supposedly starts near the waterfall that blocks nontechnical progress up Icebox Canyon. Start above some pools just down and left of the waterfall. Bring RPs, wires, TCUs, and cams to #3. **Pitch 1** (5.8 R): Face-climb up to an obvious, short, right-facing corner. Follow the corner to the left side of a major ledge. Swing off the left side of the ledge (TCU) and belay on another ledge. **Pitch 2** (third class): Move the belay about 80' left to the base of a crack. **Pitch 3** (5.9 R): Climb an easy crack past a tree, then step off a block onto the face (crux). Climb up the face to the right of a seam along pockets, then pull through a juggy section to a belay from nuts. **Pitch 4** (5.8): Angle left to a crack and follow this past some bushes to the summit. **Descent:** Follow a gully marked with cairns down and left (east) to the canyon floor.

*24. **Weenie Juice** (5.10) FA: Richard Harrison, Paul Van Betten, Wendell Broussard, Sal Mamusia, Lynn Cronin; 1983. An excellent 1-pitch route. Bring several #4 Camalots (or bigger units if you have them) and two ropes to rappel. Follow the Icebox Canyon Trail past Sunnyside Crag until it enters the main drainage. Walk up-canyon for about 300 yards until below an obvious right-facing arch on the left (south) wall of the canyon. Bushwhack 50 yards up the steep hillside to a platform below the route. Scramble about 50' up easy rock to a bushy ledge and belay. Follow the crack/arch/flake to a belay anchor. Rappel with two ropes. (No topo.)

REFRIGERATOR WALL

The routes on this cliff are in the shade most of the day (hence the name) and have about a 25-minute approach. To reach this section of the canyon, follow the trail from the parking lot past Sunnyside Crag. The trail drops down into the wash, at which point you cross the wash and head about 100 yards up the

ICEBOX CANYON
QUIGGLE'S WIGGLE (5.9 R)

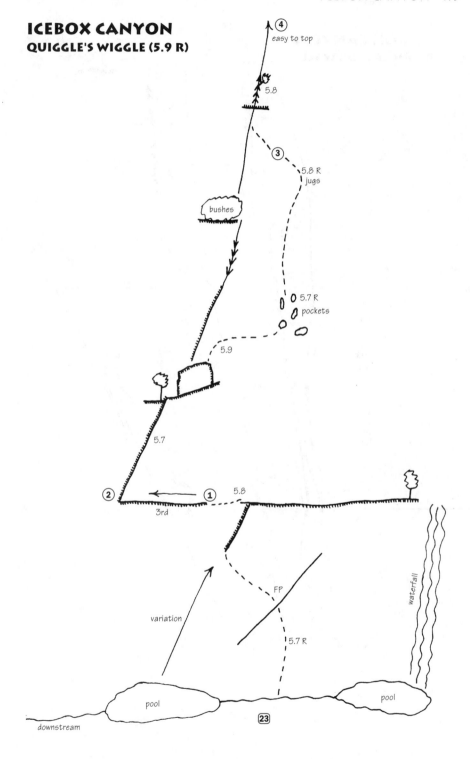

④ easy to top

5.8

③ 5.8 R jugs

bushes

5.7 R pockets

5.9

5.7

② ← ① 5.8

3rd

FP

variation

5.7 R

waterfall

pool

pool

23

downstream

ICEBOX CANYON
REFRIGERATOR WALL

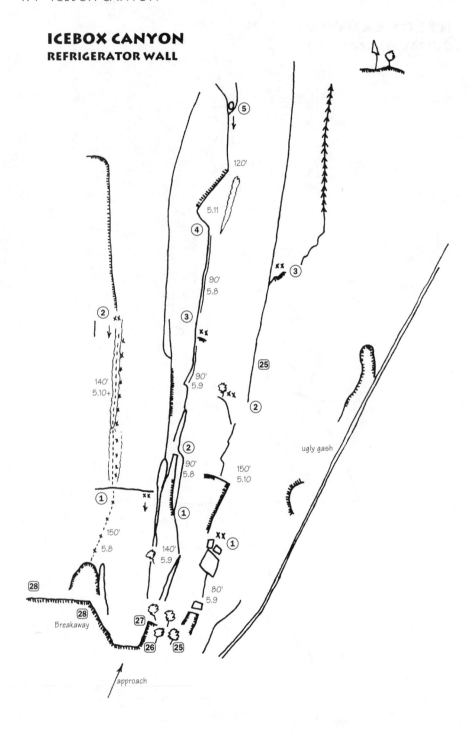

(5)

120'

5.11

(4)

90'
5.8

(2) XX

(3)

140'
5.10+

90'
5.9

(25)

(2)

(2)

90'
5.8

ugly gash

(1) XX

(1)

150'
5.10

140'
5.9

(1) XX

(1)

(28)

80'
5.9

(28)

Breakaway

(27)

(26)

(25)

approach

150'

5.8

(3) XX

(3)

Refrigerator Wall
Breakaway Area

bushy hillside on the left (southwest) side of the canyon. The routes are described from right to left; the first four routes are on the right side of a nose about 100 yards right of three obvious pine trees. The climbs begin roughly across the canyon from *Crossfire*.

25. **Music to My Fears** (5.10) FA (Pitch 1 and 2): Robert Finlay, Brad Ball; 1984. Only two pitches of this route are described, although at least five have been done. Nick Nordblom, Paul Van Betten, Jay Smith, and Paul Crawford have all turned back on the upper pitches due to loose rock and

poor protection. Within the highest vegetated area to the right of the obvious pine trees, scramble up to a prominent white block to the right of the obvious drainage/gully (the start of *Unfinished Symphony*). **Pitch 1** (5.9): From the top of the block, climb a thin crack up to large, loose, white blocks and belay. 80'. **Pitch 2** (5.10): Follow the obvious cracks left, then up, then left again, to the top of the crack systems. Belay on a ledge to the left, toward the *Unfinished Symphony* chimney. 150'. **Descent:** Either traverse left into *Unfinished Symphony* and rappel (two ropes may be needed) or continue up the loose, scary arête directly above the first two pitches past at least one more belay anchor.

26. **Unfinished Symphony** (5.11) FA: Ross Hardwick, Joe Herbst, Andre Langenbacher; Fall 1978. You'll be singing the blues if you don't like wide cracks! Bring lots of large gear and two ropes. Start on the right side of a nose about 100 yards right of three obvious pine trees and at the highest point of the vegetated hillside. This is directly below a gully leading to a prominent chimney system. **Pitch 1** (5.9): Climb the drainage/gully past numerous ledges to a belay below the obvious chimney/corner. 140'. **Pitch 2** (5.8 PG): Move right into the corner, then follow this past a bulge to a large sloping ledge. 90'. **Pitch 3** (5.9): Worm up a chimney to an alcove (5.8), then continue up the nasty off-width above to a belay stance on the right wall. 90'. **Pitch 4** (5.8): Follow the corner/crack/off-width to a belay in an alcove under a huge roof. 90'. **Pitch 5** (5.11): Three bolts lead up the central, overhanging crack (crux) to a hand crack, which is followed to the top. 120'. **Descent:** Rappel the route with two ropes.

27. **Strawberry Shubert** (5.10 X) FA (Pitches 1–4): The Uriostes; FA (Pitch 5): Bob Conz, Nick Nordblom; 1980s. The prominent crack system just left of *Unfinished Symphony* has been climbed for six pitches and has red bolt hangers on it. The first five pitches are 5.10-. The last pitch is 5.10 X. At the top of the sixth pitch, traverse into *Unfinished Symphony* and rappel with two ropes.

*28. **Breakaway** (5.10+ PG13) FA: Danny Meyers, Mike Ward; Summer 1991. Once you've done the route, you'll know where the name came from! Don't do this route if the rock is at all wet; you may destroy a classic line. This outstanding route climbs the very prominent black waterstreak to the left of *Unfinished Symphony*. Bring lots of quickdraws and two ropes for the rappel. Start on the right side of a white pillar at a small, sandy cave about 100' down and left of *Unfinished Symphony*. **Pitch 1** (5.8): Climb easy cracks on the right side of the pillar past a few ledges. Follow 4 bolts up and right on good varnished rock (a bit contrived) to a belay at two vertical cracks at the base of the steep wall with the waterstreak. Bring medium Friends for the belay, which is about 10' left of 2 bolts on the left side of a prominent chimney. The crux is by the second bolt. 150'.

Breakaway (5.10+): Mike Ward about to place a bolt on the first ascent. WARD COLLECTION

Pitch 2 (5.10+): Climb up and left (scary) to the first bolt on the pitch (you can also come in from the left), then face-climb up the steep wall past a total of 11 bolts to a belay station. 140'. **Descent:** Rappel the route with two ropes.

The next routes are on the right side of a small amphitheater and directly behind two prominent pine trees. The routes climb the smooth, varnished wall that is left of a nose and a huge, left-facing flake/corner.

Breakaway Area

29. **Earth Juice** (5.10+ PG13) FA: Kurt Reider, Chris Robbins, Augie Klein; circa 1979. A route to get your juices flowing. Start right of the large pine trees below a huge, left-facing corner. **Pitch 1** (5.10+ PG13): Scramble up blocks toward the gaping, left-facing flake/chimney, then follow bolts up a varnished face to a crack. Follow the crack to a bolt, then move left to a belay station. 150'. **Pitch 2** (5.10+ PG 13): Go up a steep corner to a bolt, downclimb, then head up and left on a blunt prow to a belay stance below a white ceiling. 140'. **Descent:** Rappel with two ropes.

*30. **Kisses Don't Lie** (5.12-) FA: Greg Mayer; October 1994. This route was attempted long ago and was rebolted and finished by Mayer. Bring several small TCUs, a #8 Stopper, and a few slings for the second pitch. **Pitch 1** (5.12a): Climb the face between *Amazing Grace* and *Earth Juice* past ten bolts to an anchor. **Pitch 2** (5.11+): Continue straight up, climbing to the top of a corner. Traverse a bit right, then up past a ceiling to a belay anchor. **Descent:** Rappel the route with two ropes. (Not shown.)

*31. **Amazing Grace** (5.9 PG) FA: Danny Meyers; rope solo, 1985. Another great pitch that involves sustained climbing. Carry gear to a #3.5 Friend and a few long slings. Begin behind the leftmost pine, 30' left of *Earth Juice*. Scramble up to a ledge with a bolt, then climb past 2 more bolts. Move right at the third bolt to the base of the obvious left-facing flake corner. Follow the corner up and left to an anchor. Rappel with two ropes.

32. **Grape Nuts** (5.10c PG13) FA: Rick Dennison, Randy Faulk, Alex Malfatto; August 1991. This route looks scarier than it actually is, although it is run-out. Rope up on a ledge 15' left of the first bolt on *Amazing Grace*. Follow 6 bolts up to the anchor on *Amazing Grace*. Rappel 100' to the ground. (Not shown.)

33. **Swing Shift** (5.10) FA: Mark Moore, Joe Herbst; Spring 1977. Start about 100' left of *Grape Nuts*, on the left side (toward the road) of a huge recess. This route starts up a right-leaning ramp, then climbs the prominent crack system leading to clean, light-colored corners near the top of the wall. It is seven pitches long with the crux on the fifth pitch.

34. **Greased Lightning** (5.10 PG13) FA: Nick Nordblom, Randy Marsh; 1989. Just left of *Swing Shift* is a rounded prow with a thin crack shaped like a lightning bolt. Climb this right-leaning crack system to a ledge that is just right of the top of the crack. Rappel from an anchor with two ropes.

SMEARS FOR FEARS AREA

The next routes are just above wash level and directly across from the right (east) end of Sunnyside Crag. Approach by following the trail in from the Icebox Canyon parking area for about 15 minutes, then turn left and follow a

small drainage down into the main wash (about 30 yards). Cross the main wash and scramble up through a short, bushy section to reach the ledge on which the routes start. The routes are at the right (west) edge of a large amphitheater that is clearly visible from the parking area. The routes are one pitch in length and are described from right (up canyon) to left (toward the road).

35. **Romeo Charlie** (5.10-) FA: Sal Mamusia, Robert Finlay; 1989. The farthest right route. Start on a ledge about 100' right of *Rojo* at a right-leaning crack that is just right of a mossy section of cliff. Climb the right-leaning

crack, then up the face along a rounded arête that divides brown and black rock. Pull over a bulge and angle slightly up right to a fixed anchor on a mossy slab. Rappel with two ropes. (Not shown.)

36. **Rojo** (5.11+ PG13) FA: Paul Van Betten, Sal Mamusia, Mike Ward; 1989. Rope up on a wide, flat ledge below a smooth, varnished face. A prominent, right-facing corner marks the left edge of this face. Climb a right-leaning crack/corner to its top, then face-climb to a shallow, right-facing corner. Climb the corner (bolt) and the smooth face above (2 bolts) to a bolted anchor. Rap with two ropes.

*37. **Smears for Fears** (5.11 PG13) FA: Sal Mamusia, Mike Ward, Robert Finlay, Paul Van Betten; 1989. A classic 1-pitch route, but not for the meek! Start 10' left of *Rojo* and 15' right of a prominent right-facing corner. The left side of the corner forms a jutting prow. Climb a shallow, right-leaning dihedral to a bolt 20' up, then go up the face past 2 more bolts to an overlap. Pull over this and continue past 2 more bolts to the top (scary!). Rappel from the anchor with dual ropes.

38. **Lebanese JoJo** (5.9+) FA: Sal Mamusia, Bob Conz, "Frodo" Lybarger, Mike Ward, Paul Van Betten; 1990. Good rock on this one, but the line is rather weird. Start about 75' left of *Smears for Fears* at a loose, right-facing corner below the left edge of a roof. Climb up to a pine tree, then traverse out right above the roof to a belay at a thin crack system. Climb the most obvious line up the varnished face above (see variation), then rappel with two ropes. **Variation:** The other three vertical crack systems on the face have been climbed. They are all of the same general difficulty.

BRIDGE MOUNTAIN

This is the mountain that separates Icebox and Pine Creek canyons. Numerous routes have been done on the Icebox Canyon side, but information was available for only one route. To approach this route, you'll either need to somehow climb the Frigid Air Buttress, then wander up through The Maze to the base of the arête, or come up from the back side of the ridge via Rocky Gap Road. Obviously, this is a big undertaking.

The approach described here begins on the Rocky Gap Road on the back of the ridge. Park at the Bridge Mountain trailhead on Rocky Gap Road. Hike in on the trail toward Bridge Mountain. The trail climbs to the top of the escarpment, then follows the ridgeline south for about 0.75 mile. The trail then drops down to the east/northeast, eventually fading on a rocky, red-colored slope above the head of Pine Creek Canyon. Look for small rock cairns marking the trail as it continues northeast to a rock bridge that connects to Bridge Mountain and separates the upper reaches of Icebox and Pine Creek Canyons.

Approach the prominent crack in the southwest corner of the mountain and look for black spray paint markings showing the trail up the crack. Ascend past the natural arch until just above the Hidden Forest. Traverse around to the north end of the forest and descend the drainage. A fourth-class descent takes you to the head of a short waterfall above a large pine tree. Traverse east on a small ledge for about 50 feet and you're at the base of the climb. For more detailed information on the hiking trail part of the approach, see *Hiking Las Vegas* by Branch Whitney. Allow 2 to 3 hours for the approach.

39. **The Northeast Arête** (5.6) FA: Sal Mamusia, Richard Harrison; 1982. This route climbs a major feature of the Red Rocks escarpment—a crack system up the northeast arête of Bridge Mountain. Plan on going light and moving fast. **Pitch 1** (5.6): Ascend a crack in the arête past a small roof about 30' above the belay ledge. Continue up the crack until it ends. Belay on a large, sloping ledge. 130'. **Pitch 2** (5.6): Step right into a crack, which begins above the sloping ledge. Follow this crack past a small pine tree, staying in the leftmost crack as you pass it. Belay on a tiny ledge at the base of a flaring chimney. 140'. **Pitch 3** (5.5): Go up the flaring chimney to a ledge. Step right into another flaring chimney and go up to a nice, large belay ledge. 160'. **Pitch 4** (5.3): Continue up the lower-angle crack to a large ledge in front of a roof. 160'. **Pitch 5:** Scramble left and up around the roof, then ascend third-class rock up to the summit plateau. **Descent:** Look for a ramp sloping down to the southwest on the western side of the summit plateau. This ramp should be marked by cairns and will take you to the south end of the Hidden Forest. Return to your vehicle by reversing the approach from the Hidden Forest.

FRIGID AIR BUTTRESS

Numerous shady routes have been done in the large amphitheater between *Smears for Fears* and The Necromancer. This wall is on the left (south) side of the canyon, roughly across from the right (east) end of Sunnyside Crags. From the road, follow the main trail until you are even with the obvious orange roofs to the right (north) of the trail (just before you reach the right edge of Sunnyside Crag). Turn left (south) and go down a small drainage into the main wash (about 30 yards). Cross the main wash and go up and right toward the obvious, huge amphitheater. Routes are described from right (up canyon) to left (toward the road and The Necromancer).

40. **Frigid Air Buttress** (5.9+) FA: Larry Hamilton, Joe Herbst; March 1976. Rope up at a prominent black flake system about 150 yards left of *Lebanese JoJo*. Carry a good selection of gear, including large cams and two ropes. **Pitch 1** (5.7): Climb the right side of a large black flake to its top. Move left and climb a thin crack to a ledge. 175'. **Pitch 2** (5.8): Move left from the belay, then climb up to a ledge with trees. Step right (watch for rope drag) and climb left-facing corners to another ledge. 160'. **Pitch 3:** Move left from the belay and wander up the cliff to a large ledge. 100'. **Pitch 4** (5.2): Climb an easy chimney above the ledge. 80'. **Pitch 5** (5.9-):

ICEBOX CANYON
FRIGID AIR BUTTRESS (5.9+)

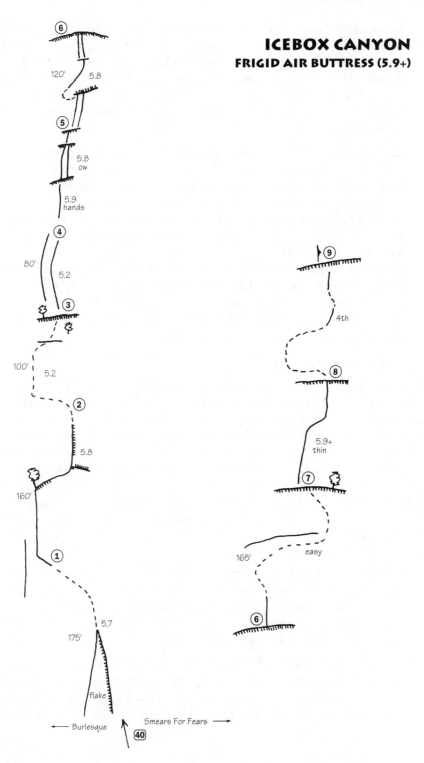

Climb a steep hand crack (5.9-), then continue up an off-width (5.8). **Pitch 6 (5.8)**: Climb a chimney, exit left via a hand-traverse, then worm up another chimney to a ledge. 120'. **Pitch 7 (5.4)**: Climb a corner, then wander up on easy rock to the base of a steep wall. 165'. **Pitch 8 (5.9+)**: Jam up the thin, varnished crack to the top of the headwall. **Pitch 9 (fourth-class)**: Wander up fourth-class terrain to the top. **Descent**: Rappel *Burlesque* with two ropes.

41. **Burlesque** (5.9) FA: Joe Herbst, Tom Kaufman; May 1979. Bring a standard rack, including several of the largest cams. This route begins near the back of the huge amphitheater on the right (northwest) side of the prominent waterfall. On the right side of a mossy slab is a chimney leading to a bushy ledge. Scramble up this chimney to the ledge (150'; third class). **Pitch 1 (5.7)**: Climb up and right from the bushy ledge to another ledge with a tree. 80'. **Pitch 2 (5.8+)**: Climb up into a prominent left-facing corner with a hand crack. Climb the corner until it is possible to move left on a ledge to the base of a flake. 160'. **Pitch 3 (5.9)**: Climb the left side of the flake past a bolt. Squirm up the narrow chimney, then up the corner above to a ledge. 160'. **Pitch 4**: Climb broken rock to a belay at a tree. **Descent**: Rappel the route with two ropes.

THE NECROMANCER

This dark, squat formation is on the left (south) side of the canyon and is clearly visible from the parking area. The formation is on the left side of a large amphitheater, and the routes lead to a huge terrace at the top of the formation. From the road, follow the main trail until you are even with the obvious orange roofs to the right (north) of the trail (just before you reach the right edge of Sunnyside Crag). Turn left (south) and go down a small drainage into the main wash (about 30 yards). Cross the main wash and follow a vague trail about 150 yards up the opposite hillside to a prominent, dark brown buttress. Again, this buttress forms the left side of an amphitheater that is clearly visible from the road. Routes are described from right to left (west to east), beginning at an obvious crack system near the right margin of the buttress.

*42. **Fold-Out** (5.8) FA: Tom Kaufman, Joe Herbst; March 1976. This climbs the rightmost crack system on the buttress. Bring a normal rack and two ropes if you plan on rappelling. Excellent rock and good protection will get you to an anchor on a ledge about 140' up. If you do go to the top of the buttress, walk off left (toward the road).

*43. **Sensuous Mortician** (5.9) FA: Nick Nordblom, Jon Martinet; Spring 1979. This route is one of the best moderate routes at Red Rocks. Begin about 20' left of the *Fold-Out* crack at the next crack line. Climb the obvious crack to its top, then move right to a black streak. Wander up the black

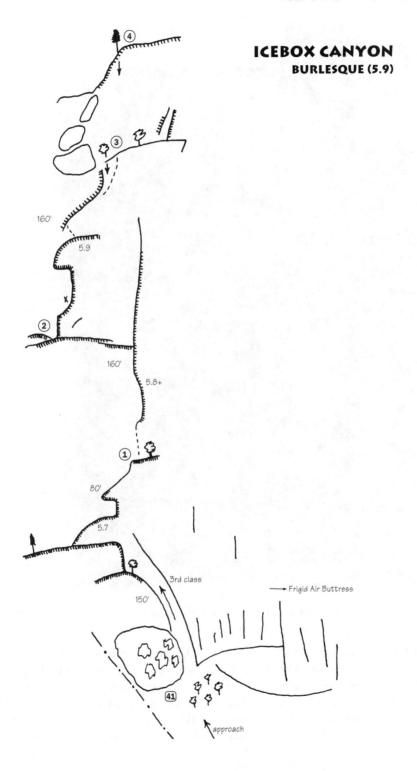

ICEBOX CANYON
BURLESQUE (5.9)

The
Necromancer Area

To Road

face to a ceiling, move left, then climb up to a 2-bolt belay. Bring lots of small gear and two ropes for the rappel.

44. **Black Magic Panties** (5.10- R) FA: Nick Nordblom, Jenni Stone, Danny Rider; 1988. Great climbing, but rather scary. Carry gear up to 3", plus a bunch of long slings. This route starts about midway between *Sensuous Mortician* and *Hop Route*. Wander up the face to a fixed piton about 30' up. Continue weaving up the wall following the obvious weaknesses to a bolt about 100' up. Move up and left past another bolt to an obvious

crack splitting the roof. Climb the crack through the roof and belay just above at horizontal cracks (#1.5 to #3 Friends for the anchor). Either traverse down and right to the anchor on *Sensuous Mortician* or go left and join *Hop Route*.

45. **Hop Route** (5.7+) FA: Dave Hop, Joe and Betsy Herbst; March 1975. The first pitch is very good, the rest a bit less interesting. Start about 10' left of *Black Magic Panties* at an obvious crack. **Pitch 1** (5.7): Climb a hand crack that is 15' right of a white, right-facing corner (see variation). Follow the crack as it veers left into the corner, then up that past a couple of chockstones to a belay ledge on the left. 100'. **Pitches 2 and 3:** Continue up the easy cracks to the top of the buttress. **Variation** (5.7+): You can climb the corner directly. It's a bit harder than the hand crack. **Descent:** Walk off left (toward the road).

The next routes are located above The Necromancer. Not much is known about these climbs.

46. **Crawford's Corner** (5.10) FA: Jay Smith, Paul Crawford; 1987. This 3-pitch route climbs a prominent, yellow, left-facing corner system that is located above The Necromancer.

47. **Unknown** (5.10+ R) FA: Jay Smith, Nick Nordblom; circa 1988. This route is to the right of *Crawford's Corner*. It is reportedly 2 to 3 pitches long and has some loose rock on it. (Not shown.)

48. **Unknown** (5.10?) FA: Danny Meyers; circa 1988. To the right of the last climb is a black, slabby face between two corners. This route ascends the face and has some bolts on it.

49. **Unknown** (5.11?) FA: Paul Van Betten, Jay Smith; circa 1989. To the right of the last three routes is a red tower. This route ascends the tower and is supposed to be of good quality

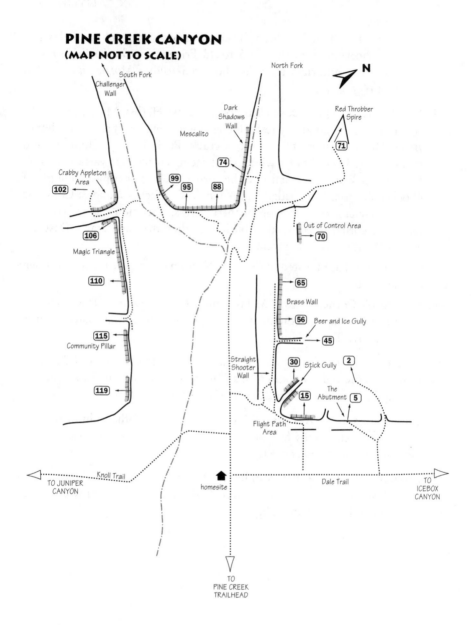

PINE CREEK CANYON
(MAP NOT TO SCALE)

N

South Fork

North Fork

Challenger Wall

Dark Shadows Wall

Red Throbber Spire

Mescalito

71

Crabby Appleton Area

99

74

102

95

88

106

Out of Control Area

70

Magic Triangle

110

65

Brass Wall

56

Beer and Ice Gully

115

45

Community Pillar

Straight Shooter Wall

30

Stick Gully

2

119

15

The Abutment

5

Flight Path Area

Knoll Trail

TO JUNIPER CANYON

homesite

Dale Trail

TO ICEBOX CANYON

TO PINE CREEK TRAILHEAD

PINE CREEK CANYON

Many fine routes are located in this beautiful canyon. To reach the trailhead, drive 10.3 miles along the scenic loop road. The parking lot is signed and lies just off the road on your right. There are outhouses at the parking lot, and the trail is well maintained until the Pine Creek drainage splits.

From the parking lot, follow the obvious trail past the Fire Ecology Trail and an old homestead into the canyon proper (about a 15-minute walk). Ahead, the canyon is split into north and south drainages by a pyramid-shaped formation called Mescalito. The first routes described in this chapter are on the right (north) side of the canyon well before it is split by Mescalito. These routes are on Bridge Mountain, which separates Icebox Canyon from Pine Creek. Routes are described from right to left (counterclockwise) in the canyon, moving across Mescalito onto the south wall of Pine Creek.

BRIDGE MOUNTAIN
EAST FACE
Numerous routes have been done on Bridge Mountain, but only a handful are described here. Most of the routes receive at least morning sun. The first routes

BRIDGE MOUNTAIN

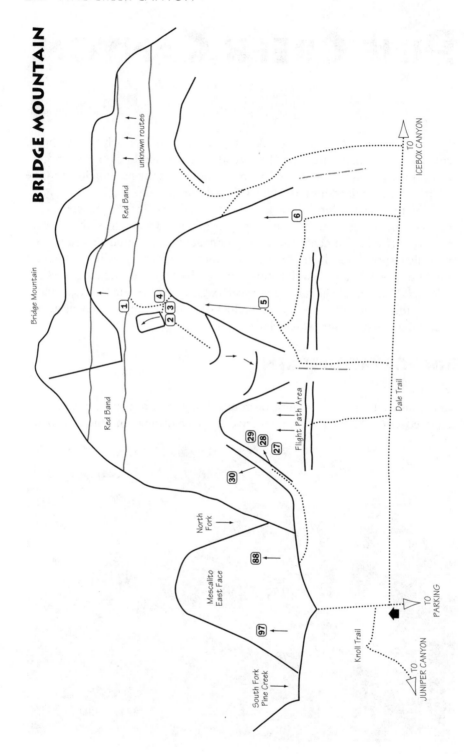

Bridge Mountain

Red Band

unknown routes

Red Band

North Fork

Mescalito East Face

South Fork Pine Creek

Flight Path Area

Dale Trail

Knoll Trail

TO ICEBOX CANYON

TO PARKING

TO JUNIPER CANYON

Bridge Mountain Overview

Bridge Mountain

Fear and Loathing

To Pine Creek Canyon

Gem Stone

The Abutment

Flight Path Area

Brass Wall

To Icebox Canyon

Dale Trail

described in this section are located on the upper left portion of the east face. To approach these routes, walk cross-country from the Pine Creek parking area, aiming for a prominent gully running up the center of the east face. It takes 10 minutes to walk to the Dale Trail, which contours along the base of the escarpment. Head up a dirt ridge to the right (north) of a drainage, going past a huge red boulder. Angle left into the prominent gully and scramble up this for several hundred yards. It should take you about 35 minutes to reach the base of a bushy gully that angles up and left (southwest) behind a huge white triangle of rock. Thrash up this gully to an obvious, narrow saddle that is behind the apex of the triangle. Scramble down the other side of the saddle to a point where the approaches to the different routes diverge.

To descend from these routes, you may go down the obvious gully below *Gemstone*. This gully is recognized by its smile-shaped ledges. The upper smile has a prominent red boulder on it that is visible from the parking area. A number of rappels take you to flat ground. Rappel from a small pine tree down on a ledge to the south of the prominent red boulder (150 feet). From the base of the first rappel, do another rappel from a bushy ledge down to easy terrain (50 feet). After scrambling down the gully some distance, do another rappel from a pine tree on the right side of the gully (40 feet). You may need to do a very short rappel over an overhang formed by a boulder. A final rappel from either a pine tree or a bush leads down a chimney (this is the route *Human Chockstones*) and get you to terra firma (50 feet).

1. **Fear and Loathing** (5.10) FA: Richard Harrison, Nick Nordblom; 1982.
   As the story goes, the two prominent corners high up on the east face of

Bridge Mountain had been climbed years ago. One corner was named *Fear*; the other, *Loathing*. In 1982, Harrison and Nordblom finally braved the 90-minute approach, only to find that the left corner (which was stuffed full of loose, refrigerator-sized blocks) didn't even reach the ground! They climbed the right-hand, right-facing corner system, which became the original *Fear and Loathing* of Red Rocks. From the saddle mentioned in the approach description, scramble up through cliff bands to the base of a dark, red-and-brown section of cliff. Bring lots of large cams for this 3-pitch route. There are no fixed anchors or protection on the route. **Pitch 1** (5.10 R): Climb the face up to the base of the prominent, right-facing corner. **Pitch 2** (5.9): Climb the corner. **Pitch 3** (5.10-): Climb the corner and belay atop a block. 75'. **Descent:** Downclimb somewhere nearby and do one rappel to get back to your pack.

Note: Numerous routes have been done on the large, red-and-white, horizontally banded cliff to the right of *Fear and Loathing*. I hope to include these routes in the next edition.

*2. **Gemstone** (5.10 PG13) FA: Nick Nordblom, Jenni Stone; 1985. Down and left of *Fear and Loathing* is a dark brown face with a prominent, left-arching crack. From the saddle mentioned in the approach description, go down and left through bushes to reach this obvious route. Bring triples of #.75–#3 cams for this fine route. **Pitch 1** (5.10): Climb the prominent crack, which is generally thin-hands. A block and fixed nut are installed for the belay. 140'. **Pitch 2** (5.10 PG13): From the belay, climb up and over a wide section of crack into a subsidiary crack. This crack also curves up and left. Climb up above this smaller crack to a white, right-facing flake. Follow weaknesses a bit up and right, then go up the face above. 140'. **Descent:** Do some rappels down a gully to the right of the route to get back to your packs.

3. **Bauble** (5.10+ TR) FA: Todd Swain, Jake Burkey; January 1999. Start at a varnished, left-facing corner 30' right of the *Gemstone* crack. Climb the corner to a ledge about 50' up. There are 2 fixed nuts for an anchor at the top of the corner. The route could be led with RP nuts and/or a knifeblade piton.

4. **Costume Jewelry** (5.3) FA: Todd Swain; solo, January 1999. About 40' down and right of the last route is a right-facing corner that goes up through honeycombed rock. Climb this corner to the top of the last route. (Not shown.)

The next route is located on the front of the huge white triangle of rock mentioned in the approach description to *Fear and Loathing*. It is basically in front of *Fear and Loathing*.

To approach this route, walk cross-country from the Pine Creek parking area, aiming for a prominent gully running up the left-center of the east face

(the descent gully from the *Gemstone*). It takes about 10 minutes to walk to the Dale Trail, which contours along the base of the escarpment. Cross the trail and head up a dirt ridge on the left of a drainage, going past a house-sized brown boulder. Angle left along the base of the mountain above this boulder (and above a red cliff band) for about 150 yards. Scramble up through several short, white cliff bands to reach a bushy, right-trending ramp. Follow this ramp upward for about 100 yards. The start of this route is about 75 feet left (south) of the base of a 100-foot-high white pillar that leans against the cliff. This pillar is visible from the parking area and is located slightly left of center on the huge white triangle of rock. Several small ribs of rock run parallel to the base of the cliff and form small chasms here also.

5. **Tri-Burro Bridge** (5.10) FA: Todd Swain, Jake Burkey, Reina Downing; February 1999. The approach to this sunny route takes about 45 minutes from the Pine Creek parking area. Bring wires, TCUs, and extra cams up to a #4 Camalot. **Pitch 1** (5.6): Climb a crack system on the right side of a brown and white huecoed face to a pine tree (or see variation). 130'. **Pitch 2** (third class): Scramble across a bushy area to the base of a varnished chimney. Scamper up the chimney to a flat ledge atop the huge block that forms the chimney. 100'. **Pitch 3** (5.8): Climb a shallow, right-facing corner above the belay anchor to a ceiling. Go around the left side of the ceiling into a left-facing corner, which is followed to a large ledge. 80'. **Pitch 4** (5.8): Climb an obvious left-facing corner just above a cave. The corner turns into an off-width at its top. Climb a varnished finger crack above, exiting left to a belay anchor. 90'. **Pitch 5** (5.10): Climb up and left past a bolt to reach the base of a crack/corner. Go up the crack, which becomes a prominent, brown dihedral. This dihedral is clearly visible from the old homesite in Pine Creek Canyon. Belay near the top of the dihedral from a bolt and fixed nut. 130'. **Variation** (5.10-): The brown-and-white, huecoed face to the left of the crack has been toproped. There are anchors on a large flat ledge at the top of the face. **Descent:** Rappel the route.

The next routes are located at the base of Bridge Mountain, just to the left (south) of the approach gully to *Fear and Loathing*. The cliff is about 100 yards directly uphill of a house-sized brown boulder and is brown in color.

THE ABUTMENT

This cliff is in the sun most of the day and has a relatively short approach. It is recognizable from the Pine Creek parking area by its square shape and chocolate color. Routes are described from right (north) to left (south). To descend from all of these routes, walk about 50 yards right (north), then follow a gully back down to the pine tree at the base of *Robin Trowel*. (No topo.)

6. **Robin Trowel** (5.7) FA: Unknown; 1980s. Start near the right side of the crag at a big pine tree. Climb a right-curving dihedral/flake to the top. Bring medium-to-large cams.

7. **Bridge of Sighs** (5.9) FA: Unknown; 1980s. Better than it looks. Bring wires, TCUs, and cams up to a #4 Camalot. Start just left of the pine tree at the right side of the cliff. Climb past large blocks in a chimney to a right-facing flake/corner, which is followed to the summit.

8. **Men Are from Mars, Women Are from Venice** (5.10+? PG) FA: Unknown. This route looks rather sporty. Bring lots of small wires and RPs. Rope up

BRIDGE MOUNTAIN
TRI-BURRO BRIDGE (5.10)

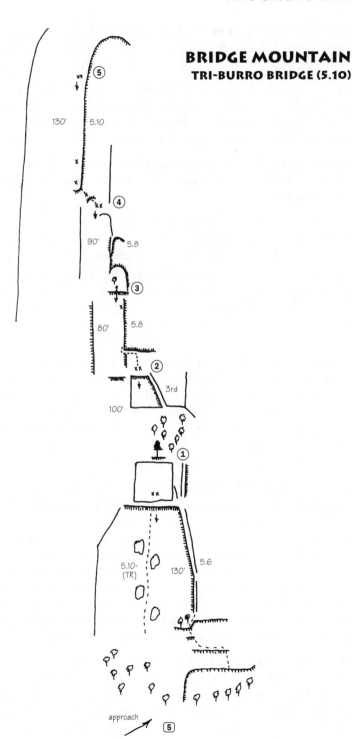

about 30' left of the pine tree near the middle of the varnished face. Climb up to a rotten ledge, then pull a ceiling at a vertical seam. Go up and slightly right, eventually reaching a bolt and the top.

9. **Crazy Girls** (5.10- PG13) FA: Dave Wonderly, Warren Egbert; circa 1988. A very good face route if you are a solid leader. Carry small stoppers and RPs to supplement the bolts on the route. Start on the left side of the main face about 20' right of a dihedral. Climb the varnished face past 3 bolts.

10. **Skewback** (5.10- TR) FA: Unknown; 1980s. Start atop a white pillar of rock that is at the base of a dihedral. Climb the dihedral past a ceiling (crux) to the top.

11. **Pier-Less** (5.10) FA: Unknown; 1980s. A good, steep crack climb. Bring some TCUs and cams up to at least a #4 Camalot. Starting atop the same white pillar as the last route, climb the prominent, leftmost vertical crack.

The next routes are located about 200 yards to the left (south) of The Abutment and just right of the *Gemstone* descent gully on a black, varnished cliff. They are best approached via the Pine Creek and Dale Trails (as for the routes on Flight Path). Routes are described from right (north) to left (south toward Flight Path).

12. **Cantilever Corner** (5.8+) FA: Unknown; 1998. This route is tucked into a recess about 100' right of a large pine tree at the base of the *Gemstone* descent gully. There is a large white flake just to the left of this route, which is visible from the parking area. The climb ascends a very nice varnished corner that faces south. Start on top of a 30-foot-high pedestal at the base of the corner. Climb the left-facing corner past a ceiling to an anchor about 75' up. Bring wires, TCUs, and cams up to a #4.

13. **Spanning the Gap** (5.9) FA: Todd and Donette Swain; May 1999. Rope up in the middle of the black face, about 50' right of a large pine tree and 50' left of the last route. Bring wires, TCUs, and cams to #3. **Pitch 1** (5.9): Pull a pink bulge into a varnished, left-facing corner. Follow the corner to a ledge, then go up a short, varnished flake to a ceiling. Climb a short section of imperfect rock past 2 bolts and a ceiling to a ledge. Continue up and slightly right on varnished plates to a belay anchor in a left-facing corner. 130'. **Pitch 2** (5.8): Go up and right from the belay, around the right side of a white bulge, then back up and left to an anchor just below the top of the wall. 90'. **Descent:** Rappel the route with two ropes.

14. **Human Chockstones** (5.6) FA: Unknown; 1970s. At the base of the *Gemstone* descent gully is a water-worn chimney that leads to a pine tree. By climbing this chimney, you can access the middle reaches of the gully and/or the tops of the last few routes. Climb up a short flake on the right side of the gully, then traverse left across a pink slab to reach the base of the

chimney. Worm your way up the chimney past a pinch (crux) to a ledge with bushes on it. Rappel with one rope.

The following routes are located about 100 yards left (south) of the *Gemstone* descent gully.

15. **Flight Path** (5.8+) FA: Tom Beck, Steve Haase; Spring 1999. There were several projects in this area at press time. This route climbs a pretty, varnished face past 3 bolts and some gear placements to an anchor 120' up. It is just right of a right-facing chimney. A second pitch is in the works.

16. **Clyde Crashcup** (5.10- ?) FA: Unknown. Climb the right-facing chimney just left of *Flight Path* to an anchor.

The following routes are located about 200 yards left (south) of the *Gemstone* descent gully and just right of another prominent gully that forms the right edge of Pine Creek Canyon.

FLIGHT PATH AREA

This crag was rediscovered in 1998 and has since become quite popular. The routes get morning sun and require about 30 minutes of hiking to reach.

To approach this cliff, follow the Pine Creek Trail to the old homesite in Pine Creek Canyon. Go right (north) on the Dale Trail along the front of Bridge Mountain for several hundred yards. You eventually find a side trail that leads left (toward the mountain). This trail is marked with cairns and leads up through the red cliff band to the base of this area. Routes are described from right (north) to left (south).

17. **Radio Free Kansas** (5.7+) FA: Teresa Krolak, Tom Beck; January 1999. Rope up about 35' right of a huge, right-facing dihedral. This is on the right side of a block and below a left-leaning crack. Climb the varnished crack until it ends. Continue up the face above past 3 bolts to a communal anchor. Bring gear up to a #2 Friend.

18. **Common Bond of Circumstance** (5.9+) FA: Steve Haase, Tom Beck; Spring 1999. Climb the face about 10' left of the last route and 15' right of a crack past six bolts. This route merges with the last climb near the top.

19. **Belief in Proportion to the Evidence** (5.10-) FA: Tom Beck, Teresa Krolak, Jules George; Spring 1999. Climb the face about 5' left of the last route and 10' right of a vertical crack. Go up past 5 bolts, staying left after the fifth bolt.

20. **Ignore the Man behind the Screen** (5.6) FA: Unknown; circa 1970. About 10' left of the last face climb and just right of a huge corner is an obvious, vertical crack. Climb the crack to a big ledge. Bring large cams for protection. Rappel from the communal anchor with at least a 60-meter rope.

21. **Sex in the Scrub Oak** (5.7 PG) FA: Unknown; circa 1970. In the center of the formation is a huge, light-colored corner that faces right (northeast). Climb the corner to its top, then go up and right to a ledge with an obvious pine tree. Rappel from the communal anchor with at least a 60-meter rope.

22. **They Call the Wind #!&%** (5.8) FA: Todd Swain, Teresa Krolak; February 1999. Just left of the huge corner described under the last route is a white arête. This route climbs the arête and face past 5 bolts to a ledge.

Rappel the route with two ropes. Bring wires, TCUs, and Friends up to #2.

The next routes are located about 100 feet to the left (toward Pine Creek Canyon).

23. **A Simple Expediency** (5.9-) FRA: Tom Beck, Steve House; December 1998. A good route. Bring wires and Friends up to #3.5. Rope up about 30' right of a huge, right-facing corner and below an obvious finger crack. Go up and right to a vertical crack on the right side of the face. Follow the crack past two bulges to a smooth section of black rock. Face-climb up along the thin crack (crux) to easier rock and a communal anchor.

24. **Car Talk** (5.9 PG) FRA: Todd Swain, Jake Burkey; January 1999. Climb the initial finger crack on *Doin' the Good Drive* then veer right at a triangular ceiling and go up a short dihedral. Continue straight up the black face past several pockets to the communal anchor. Rappel with one rope.

25. **Doin' the Good Drive** (5.9) FRA: Tom Beck, Steve House; December 1998. A great route. Bring wires, TCUs, and #2.5–4 Friends. Same start as the last two routes, about 30' right of a huge corner. Climb the obvious, vertical finger crack to a ledge (or see variation). Continue straight up through two bulges to a lower-angled black face. Traverse right to the communal anchor on the ledge above. Rappel with one rope. **Variation:** You can avoid the initial crack by climbing the face just left.

26. **Commuted Sentence** (5.9+) FRA: Todd Swain, Jake Burkey; January 1999. Not as gnarly as it looks. Carry TCUs and a double set of cams up to #4. Climb the huge right-facing corner to a ledge with a pine tree. Rappel from a ledge at the top of the corner.

STICK GULLY

Just left of Flight Path (toward Pine Creek Canyon) is a gully running up and right. This gully separates Pine Creek Canyon from the East Face of Bridge Mountain and is recognizable by two prominent white buttresses on its right side. To approach the gully, follow the Pine Creek Trail past the old homestead, then take a climber's trail that branches off to the right (north). This trail ascends the hillside and skirts the right (east) end of a red cliffband that runs horizontally below the main canyon wall. This is the same approach as for Straight Shooter Wall. Once above the red band, angle up and right (northeast) for several hundred yards to the mouth of Stick Gully. As you ascend the gully, stay on the right (north) side. The routes included in this guide are described as they are encountered going up the gully. The approach time to these routes is about 45 minutes. (No topo.)

27. **Stickball** (5.9) FA: Todd and Donette Swain; March 1999. About 300 yards up the gully are two obvious cracks that go through a bulge about

30' off the ground. These cracks form an alcove and have boulders at their base. Just right of this alcove is a varnished arête. Starting atop a boulder (or see variation), climb the arête along a small, right-facing corner. Above the corner, follow weaknesses to an anchor about 100' up. **Variation** (5.10 TR): Start 15' right at the base of a varnished right-facing corner. Climb to the top of the corner, then angle up and left across a steep face to join the regular route.

28. **Stick Right** (5.9) FA: Richard Harrison, Paul Van Betten, Sal Mamusia, Nick Nordblom; 1982. Bring gear up to a #4 Camalot. Rope up 5' left of *Stickball*, below the right-hand of two obvious cracks. Climb a varnished, left-facing corner past an overhang. Continue up the corner, which eventually becomes right-facing. Rappel from the same anchor as *Stickball*.

29. **Stick Left** (5.10) FA: Richard Harrison, Paul Van Betten, Sal Mamusia, Nick Nordblom; 1982. Carry at least three #3 Camalots, plus a set of cams up to #4. Begin 20' left of *Stick Right* at the base of a right-facing corner. Climb the crack/corner past an overhanging section (crux). Continue up the corner to a belay anchor that is about 100' up.

30. **Nature Is Fun** (5.9+) FA: Sal Mamusia, Richard Harrison, Nick Nordblom; 1983. On the left wall of the gully, directly across from *Stick Right* and *Stick Left*, is a tall white-and-black wall. This route apparently climbs a long, flared off-width somewhere in that area.

31. **The Elephant Penis** (5.10- R) FA: Richard Harrison, Paul Van Betten, Sal Mamusia, Nick Nordblom; 1983. Farther up the gully is a tower attached to the left wall (guess what it looks like). This 4-pitch route supposedly starts as face-climbing and ends on the left side of the tower. There is no pitch easier than 5.8 and you have to do multiple rappels to get down.

STRAIGHT SHOOTER WALL

As you enter the Pine Creek drainage, a short, red cliffband appears on the right. The Beer and Ice Gully is the obvious, huge cleft in the right wall of the canyon, and Straight Shooter Wall encompasses the climbs on the right side of this gully. To approach Straight Shooter Wall and Beer and Ice Gully, head off the trail by the homestead and skirt the right (east) end of the red cliffband. You can also hike directly up to Beer and Ice Gully, but this entails a bit of dicey soloing through the center of the red band. A well-beaten path runs along the base of the canyon wall in this area, which gets sun all day. The routes are described from right (east) to left (up canyon). The routes described here are located about 400' right of Beer and Ice Gully on a smooth, black face. Allow about 20 minutes for the approach.

32. **The Lazy Fireman** (5.11a) FA: Cameron Robbins, Randy Marsh; Spring 1991. At the right end of a smooth, black face is a boulder/prow that

Pine Creek Canyon
(North Side)

Out of Control Area

To The Mescalito

Brass Wall

Straight Shooter Wall

The Red Band

protrudes from the cliff. On the left (west) face is a short, overhanging dihedral with 2 bolts. Continue up the face above (contrived) past 2 more bolts to a chain anchor. You may want to bring a #3 Friend or equivalent to place between the second and third bolts. (Not shown.)

33. **Sidewinder** (5.11a) FA (TR): Unknown; 1980s. FA (lead): Rick Dennison, Daryl Ellis; April 1991. Better than it first appears; it's quite technical. Start 20' left of the last route and just right of a striking finger crack up the smooth, black wall. Climb the slippery face past 6 bolts, following small flakes and seams to a shared rappel anchor.

*34. **Straight Shooter** (5.9+) FA: Joe Herbst; circa 1975. Climb the perfect, smooth, finger crack splitting the black face to a communal anchor 50' up. Bring wires, TCUs, and Friends up to #3.

35. **Slabba Dabba Do** (5.11b PG13) FA (TR): Unknown. FA (lead): Mike Tupper; Winter 1985. It's dicey getting to the first bolt, scary and cruxy above the third bolt. Begin about 10' left of *Straight Shooter* and smear up the glassy face past 3 bolts with homemade hangers to the ledge 50' up. You can set up a directional at the top of the pitch using the $\frac{1}{4}$" bolt and a #0 TCU.

36. **Forget Me Knot** (5.11) FA (TR): Unknown. FA (lead): Mike Tupper; Winter 1985. Shades of Lynn Hill, Ken Nichols, and other good climbers who have forgotten to tie into the climbing rope properly! Start at a thin, vertical seam 20' left of *Straight Shooter*. Climb the seam to a bolt, then up a left-facing flake directly above a 3/8" bolt to a ledge (5.10+; possible belay directional here using the $\frac{1}{4}$" bolt and a #0 TCU). Continue up the right-leaning crack (*Bird Crack*) on the upper wall to a rap anchor (5.11-). *Bird Crack* was first climbed by Paul Van Betten and originally done as a second pitch to *Straight Shooter*.

BEER AND ICE GULLY

Beer and Ice Gully is an obvious, huge cleft in the right wall of the canyon. As you enter the Pine Creek drainage, a short, red cliffband appears on the right. To approach Beer and Ice Gully, head off the trail by the homestead and skirt the right (east) end of the red cliff band. You can also hike directly up to Beer and Ice Gully itself, but this entails a bit of dicey soloing through the center of the red band. Approach time is about 20 minutes.

37. **Orange Clonus** (5.10+) FA: Tom Kaufman, Joe Herbst; April 1977. Bring a huge rack, including at least triples of #1.5–3.5 cams. Rope up at the mouth of the Beer and Ice Gully on the right (east) side. **Pitch 1** (5.9+): Scramble up to the base of a dark, right-facing corner (variation exists). Climb the corner then move right and up another corner to a ledge. **Pitch 2** (5.5 X): Climb an easy face and belay on a ledge at the base of a chimney. **Pitch 3** (fourth class): Go up and right in chimneys and wide cracks. **Pitch 4** (third class): Continue up and right on a bushy terrace to reach the base of a white, left-facing corner. **Pitch 5** (5.8+): Climb the white corner to a belay stance below a finger crack. **Pitch 6** (5.10+): Jam up the finger crack to a ledge. Continue up the overhanging crack to a belay stance below a roof. **Pitch 7** (5.10-): Move right and climb a right-facing corner with a hand crack to a belay ledge. **Variation** (5.10+): Climb directly up a corner on the edge of the gully past several bolts. **Descent**: Go left on a ledge above the gully. Three 80-foot rappels and some downclimbing should get you back to the base of the climb.

38. **Too Pumped to Pose** (5.12 TR) FA: Paul Van Betten; 1987. As you enter the Beer and Ice Gully proper, there are a few obvious features on the right wall. This, the rightmost route, goes up a line of huecos and is toproped off the *Twenty-nine Posers* tree.

39. **Posby** (5.12 TR) FA: Paul Van Betten; 1987. This toprope route climbs huecos and holes just right of *Twenty-nine Posers* and left of the last route.

40. **Twenty-nine Posers** (5.11+) FA: Paul Van Betten, Bob Yoho; 1987. This route climbs a flake (Friends) to an overhanging, huecoed face. Power up

PINE CREEK CANYON
ORANGE CLONUS (5.10+)

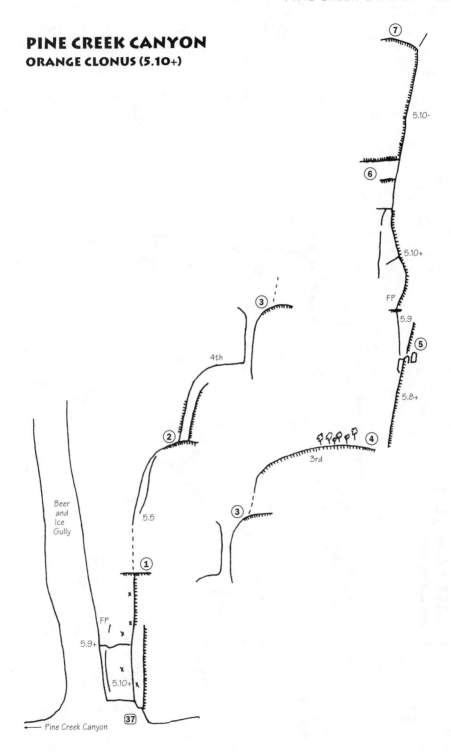

PINE CREEK CANYON
BEER AND ICE GULLY

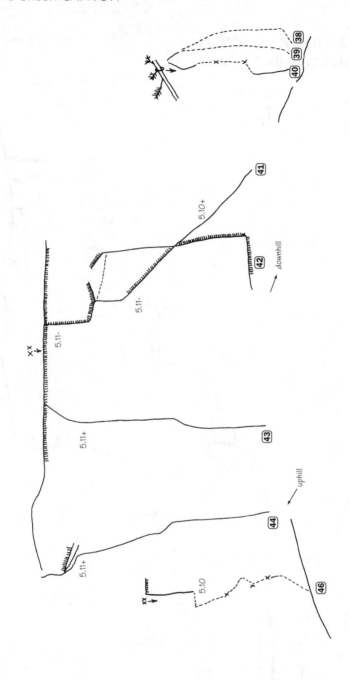

the face past 2 bolts and a blind #1.5 Friend placement to a tree. Rappel off the tree back to the ground (or toprope the last two routes).

41. **Moisture Brau** (5.11-) FA: Paul Van Betten, Bob Conz; 1988. Start at a left-slanting hand crack. Meet *This Bud's for You*, then go straight up a hand-and-fist crack to its top. Traverse left under roofs and finish up the top corner of *This Bud's for You*.

*42. **This Bud's for You** (5.11-) FA: Paul Van Betten, Bob Conz; 1988. An excellent route. Start 100 yards uphill from the last route at a left-facing, left-leaning book with a hand-and-finger crack in its back. Climb the corner to a 2-bolt belay station on a ledge. 130'.

43. **Corona Crack** (5.11+) FA: Paul Van Betten, Sal Mamusia, Bob Conz; Winter 1988. Begin 50' left of *This Bud's for You* at a curving, flaring finger crack. Bring an assortment of gear for this one. This route shares the belay with *This Bud's for You*.

44. **Stout Roof** (5.10+) FA: Mike Ward, Paul Van Betten, Bob Yoho; Winter 1987. An acquired taste. Climb a crack through an obvious roof to a ledge.

*45. **Terminal Velocity** (5.13-) FA: Mike Tupper, Greg Mayer; March 1989 (after a year of working on it!). A big undertaking, but a must for the true crack master. Allow about 45 minutes for the approach. Bring gear up to a #3 Friend, including a full set of TCUs, and Sliders or Lowe Balls. Scramble up Beer and Ice Gully to its end. **Pitch 1** (5.9): Scramble up a chimney/gully for 20', then exit onto the left wall. Climb the face and crack above to a 1-bolt belay. 160'. **Pitch 2** (5.11+): Exit right from the belay onto a vertical wall and crank up the flake (similar to Yosemite's *Wheat Thin* flake; bolts) to its top. Jog left and climb up a shallow dihedral to a 2-bolt belay. 60'. **Pitch 3** (5.11): Traverse 15' straight right over the lip of a small roof (exposed). Enter a right-facing dihedral and follow this to another 2-bolt belay. 70'. **Pitch 4** (5.13-): Climb a small dihedral for 30' (5.12-), then exit left to the base of a striking, thin-finger crack. Punch up the crack to a 2-bolt belay. 60'. **Pitch 5** (5.11+): Stem up a slightly overhanging corner past 2 bolts to a finger crack in the corner. Continue upward for another 50' to the top of the crack. Exit left across a slab to a 2-bolt belay. 65'. **Descent:** Rappel with two ropes as follows. From pitch 5 to pitch 4; from pitch 4 to pitch 3; from pitch 3 straight down 150' to a ledge with bolts; and finally 150' to ground.

46. **Chilly Ones** (5.10+ R/X) FA: Paul Van Betten, Sal Mamusia; 1988. Start directly across the gully from *This Bud's for You* on the left wall of the gully. Climb past 3 bolts to a hand-and-fist crack that leads to a ledge. Rappel with two ropes.

PINE CREEK CANYON
TERMINAL VELOCITY (5.13-)

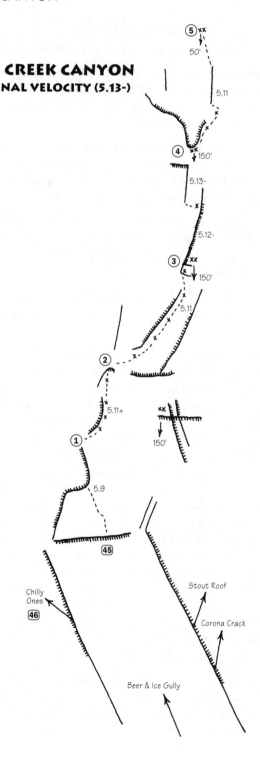

BRASS WALL

This is the section of cliff to the left (west) of Beer and Ice Gully, which is the obvious, huge cleft in the right wall of the canyon. As you enter the Pine Creek drainage, a short, red cliffband appears on the right. To approach Beer and Ice Gully, head off the trail by the homestead and skirt the right (east) end of the red cliffband. You can also hike directly up to Beer and Ice Gully itself, but this entails a bit of dicey soloing through the center of the red band. Allow about 25 minutes for the approach. Routes are described from right to left.

47. **The Bus Stops Here** (5.8?) FA: Unknown; circa 1980. This route climbs the right (east) side of a huge, black, pyramid-shaped flake that sits at the left edge of Beer and Ice Gully. Start in the bushy gully and climb the right-facing corner/chimney to a ledge just below the top of the flake. Rappel 140' from an anchor.

48. **Simpatico** (5.10-) FA: Jay Smith, Jo Bently, Jenni Stone; circa 1980. Begin in the bushy gully 10' left and around the corner from the last route. Climb to a ledge 15' up, then follow a nice, right-facing flake/corner up and right to the arête. Follow the arête and face to a ledge near the top of the huge flake. Rappel with two ropes.

49. **One Stop in Tonopah** (5.10?) FA: Paul Crawford; circa 1980. Begin 40' left at the right edge of bushes and below a 25-foot-high white flake. Climb the right edge of the flake to a bolt. Climb past two ledges then go up and right on dark varnish to finish in a short crack/corner that leads to the arête. Follow the last routes to the top of the huge flake, then rappel with two ropes.

50. **Go Greyhound** (5.11- R/X) FA: Paul Crawford; circa 1980. Same start as the last route, but climb the left side of the white flake. Step left across a pink scar then climb a thin, right-facing flake to a stance. Climb another, more prominent right-facing flake until it ends. Climb up the face past 2 bolts. Escape right to the arête by a bush, or persevere straight up to a ledge and the anchor. Rappel with two ropes.

*51. **Varnishing Point** (5.8+) FA: Joe Herbst; circa 1979. Start 30' left of the last route and 10' left of an oak tree, below an obvious crack that leads to the right side of a bushy ledge that is 70' up. Bring gear to a #4 Camalot and two ropes. **Pitch 1** (5.5): Climb the crack and huecos, stepping left to reach the bushy ledge. Belay in a cave. 70'. **Pitch 2** (5.8+): Climb the obvious, leftmost, left-facing corner past a ceiling (crux) to the top of the huge varnished flake. 70'. **Descent:** Rappel with two ropes.

52. **Serious Business** (5.10+?) FA: Unknown; circa 1982. Start on the bushy ledge at the top of the first pitch of *Varnishing Point*. Work your way up a thin, vertical seam to reach an obvious dihedral. Follow this up to an anchor.

PINE CREEK CANYON
BRASS WALL

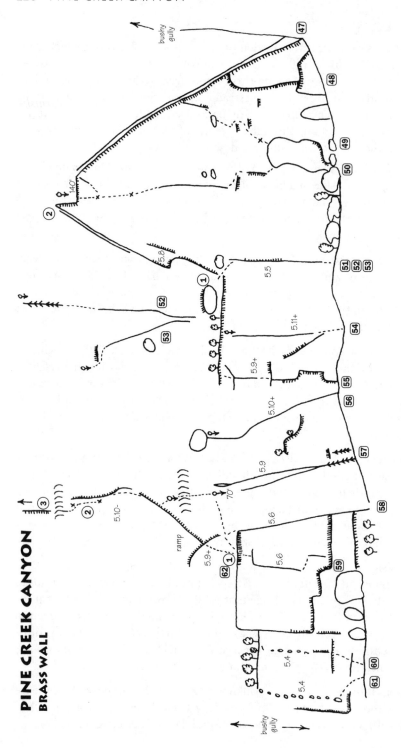

53. **No Laughing Matter** (5.10-) FA: Greg Child, Randal Grandstaff; 1979. Start 70' above the ground on the bushy ledge mentioned in the last route description and climb the most obvious, slightly left-leaning crack system to a rappel anchor.

54. **Fungus Folks** (5.11+) FA: Unknown; circa 1982. Start 50' left of *Varnishing Point* under the center of the bushy ledge that is 70' up. Climb the thin, vertical seam up the varnished face to the bushy ledge.

55. **Bush Pilots** (5.9+) FA: Randy Marsh, Paul Van Betten; circa 1984. Begin at a right-facing corner 20' left of the last climb. Climb the corner to a prominent ceiling, then follow the crack above to the left end of the bushy ledge.

56. **Mushroom People** (5.10+) FA: Dave Diegelman, Randal Grandstaff, Greg Child; 1979. Start about 15' left of the last route, directly below the left edge of a bushy ledge about 70' up. Climb an obvious, left-angling seam up slippery, black rock to a rap anchor just below a huge hueco. Two ropes are needed for the rappel.

*57. **Topless Twins** (5.9) FA: Randal Grandstaff, Wendell "The Dean" Broussard; 1980. Rope up below a series of short dihedrals leading to thin, parallel, black cracks 50' left of *Mushroom People*. Climb a dihedral and the right-hand crack to a rappel station 70' up, then zip back to the ground with one rope. You'll need a good selection of wires and TCUs for this route.

58. **Heavy Spider Karma** (5.6) FA: Unknown; circa 1980. Worthwhile. Start 10' to the left of the last route, at the base of a prominent hand crack leading to a ledge. Traverse right from the ledge to the *Topless Twins* anchor or continue up *Raptor*.

59. **Snivler** (5.5 R) FA: Unknown; circa 1980. A good route. Rope up 20' left of *Heavy Spider Karma* at a boulder below a ceiling. Step right off the boulder then go straight up a crack to a ledge. Step left and climb a series of pockets up the varnished face to a ledge. Step right and climb a short face to the big ledge. Traverse right to the *Topless Twins* anchor or continue up *Raptor*.

60. **Zen and the Art of Web Spinning** (5.4) FA: Unknown; circa 1980. Start 30' left of the last route on the left side of large boulders below a low-angle, Swiss-cheese face and 8' left of an obvious, left-facing corner. Climb the left-facing corner and Swiss-cheese rock to a tree-covered ledge.

61. **Arachnoworld** (5.4) FA: Unknown; circa 1980. Climb the easy, huecoed face 20' left of *Zen and the Art of Web Spinning* (and near the arête) to the tree ledge.

62. **Raptor** (5.10- R) FA: Nick Nordblom, Randy Marsh; 1990. This 4-pitch route starts atop the block climbed by the last four routes, making it actually a 5-pitch route. It is just right of a large gully. Bring a good selection of gear, including two 1" TCUs. **Pitch 1** (5.4–5.6): Climb one of the last four routes to the top of the block. **Pitch 2** (5.10-): Face-climb up to a ramp, which is followed up and right to a left-facing corner. Climb past 1 bolt to a belay stance. **Pitch 3** (5.10-): Climb up past a bolt and a bulge to a belay in a right-facing corner. **Pitch 4** (5.9): Climb the corner, then continue up the face to another right-facing corner and a belay. **Pitch 5** (5.10-): Climb the corner above the belay, then go up left past a bolt to the top. **Descent:** Go west and descend the gully as for the *Sea of Holes*, doing three rappels.

Note: At least three routes have been done between the gully and *The Black Hole*, but information was lacking at press time.

63. **The Black Hole** (5.8) FA: Jay Smith; 1980. This is supposed to be good. Start at a chimney a bit to the left of a vegetated gully. Climb up the chimney a bit, then up a shallow corner to a 2-bolt rappel anchor. 110'.

*64. **Sea of Holes** (5.10 R) FA: Nick Nordblom, Jay Smith (Pitch 1, 1980; Pitches 2 and 3, Fall 1988.) This route climbs *The Black Hole*, then continues up for 2 more pitches. Same start as *The Black Hole*. **Pitch 1** (5.8): Starting out of a chimney, climb a shallow corner to a 2-bolt belay. 110'. **Pitch 2** (5.10 R): Traverse out left using numerous huecos, then up through a roof at a crack on its left side. Friends in huecos for pro. One-bolt belay on arête. 160'. **Pitch 3** (5.10-): Go straight up the black face to a crack in a bulge. Continue up the face to a belay on the shoulder of the buttress. 165'. **Descent:** You'll find a rap station in the gully to descend in three rappels.

65. **Ripcord** (5.12- R) FA: Jay Smith, Nick Nordblom; 1989. This route starts at an arête to the left of *The Black Hole*. **Pitch 1** (5.12-): Make desperate moves up the arête past a bolt (crux), then continue up to a bolted belay. **Pitch 2** (5.10+ R): Move out left and climb up to a bolted belay at a ledge. **Pitch 3** (5.11): Go up past a couple of bolts to a belay at the base of a left-facing corner. **Pitch 4** (5.11): Climb the left-facing corner. **Descent:** Rappel down the gully as for *Sea of Holes* in 3 rappels.

66. **Brass Balls** (5.10) FA: Don Burroughs, Gary Fike; Winter 1997/98. Start to the left of *Ripcord* near a gully. Bring a good selection of gear and two ropes for rappelling. **Pitch 1** (5.10): Face-climb past a bolt, turn a roof, then follow a shallow corner into a wide crack. Belay on a ledge. **Pitch 2** (5.9): Climb a chimney for 20' (5.9), then follow a corner to an alcove (5.8). Climb a crack up a corner/gully to a belay. **Pitch 3** (5.8+): Climb a corner/gully past an off-width section. **Pitch 4** (5.10-): Undercling a roof. **Descent:** Rappel the route using two ropes. (No topo.)

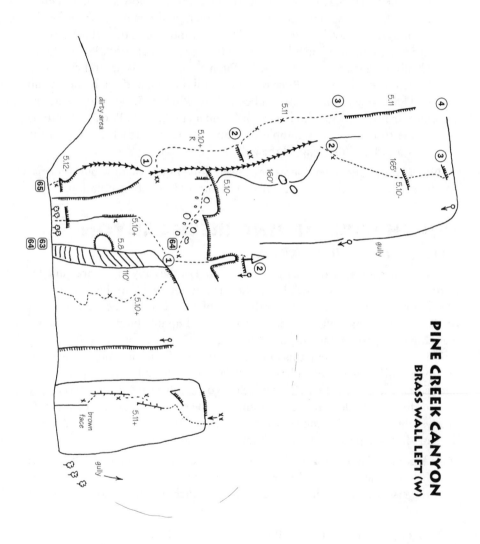

PINE CREEK CANYON
BRASS WALL LEFT (W)

67. **Spectrum** (5.11- PG) FA: Jay Smith, Randal Grandstaff; circa 1989. This climb is supposed to be quite good but a bit scary. Bring a full rack plus extra #2–#4 cams. Start about 100 yards to the left of *Ripcord* below a prominent right-facing corner. Above this corner is another obvious corner that arches to the right. **Pitch 1** (5.9): Climb a chimney to reach the prominent right-facing corner. Belay in the corner below a roof. 95'. **Pitch 2** (5.10): Traverse right under the roof, then go down a bit (scary for the second) to a belay. 70'. **Pitch 3** (5.7 R): Continue right, then climb a right-facing corner. Belay on a ledge at the base of a corner. 100'. **Pitch 4** (5.9): Climb a right-facing corner. 130'. **Pitch 5** (5.7 R): Go up and right to a belay under a roof. 95'. **Pitch 6** (5.11-): Pull the roof at a crack, then go up and left along a thin crack to a belay. 120'. **Pitch 7** (5.7+): Wander up the face to a belay. 150'. **Pitch 8** (5.7): Climb a crack. 150'. **Pitch 9:** Continue to the top. **Descent:** Scramble way up and right to reach the top of the Beer and Ice Gully. Rappel the gully.

Note: Numerous other routes have been done in the vicinity, but information is sketchy. The topo for this area has some additional information.

NORTH FORK OF PINE CREEK CANYON
OUT OF CONTROL AREA

The next few routes are on the right (north) wall of the canyon but are quite far from the last routes described. From the parking lot, walk up the trail toward Mescalito, then take the right (north) fork of Pine Creek. The trail becomes braided at this point, but the best route is to head uphill about 100 feet (above the red band of rock), then head left (west), contouring along the hillside on a trail. Roughly 350 yards up this drainage and past about three huge pine trees, the lowest cliff band on the right is split by a low-angle gully. Head up this gully until you are above the first cliffband, then go right (toward the road) on ledge systems for about 100 yards. You should now be even with the front (east) face of Mescalito. The following routes are described from left to right and are in the sun all day. Approach time is about 30 minutes.

68. **American Ninja** (5.10) FA: Paul Van Betten, Robert Finlay; 1986. Start below a clean, short, dihedral in an alcove that is about 50' above the traverse ledge. Climb the corner to rap anchors on the low-angle face above.

*69. **Out of Control** (5.10) FA: Randal Grandstaff, Dave Anderson; 1978. Begin about 150' up and right of *American Ninja* at the base of a long, straight, hand crack in a smooth, white wall. The crack is about 15' left of a huge dihedral. A sustained route; bring lots of hand-size gear and two ropes to rappel. Follow the crack past a roof to a rap station.

PINE CREEK CANYON
SPECTRUM (5.11- PG)

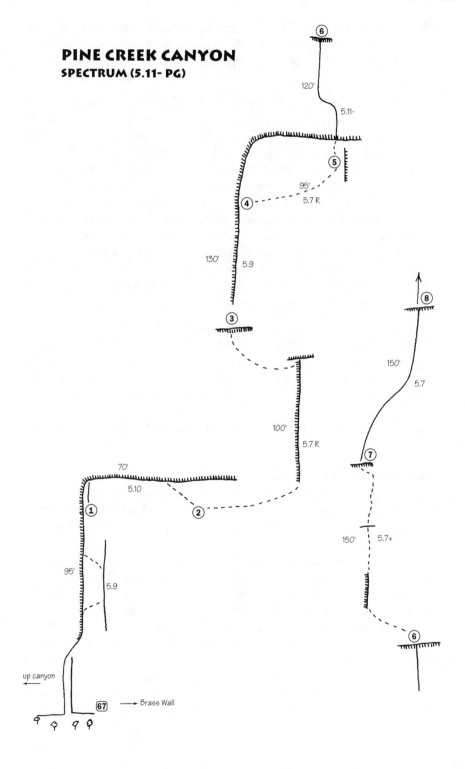

6

120'

5.11-

5

95'
5.7 R

4

130'   5.9

3

100'

5.7 R

70'

5.10

1

2

95'

5.9

8

150'

5.7

7

150'   5.7+

6

up canyon

67   → Brass Wall

70. **Remote Control** (5.9) FA: Dave Anderson, Randal Grandstaff; 1978. Rope up 15' right of *Out of Control* at the base of a huge corner. Climb the left-facing dihedral with a smooth, huge, right wall for 165' to a rappel anchor.

71. **Red Throbber Spire** (5.9+ R) FA: Bryan Kay, Dave Polari; February 1993. This route climbs a prominent, red-tipped spire that sits across the canyon from Dark Shadows Wall. To approach this formation, follow the Pine Creek Trail into the canyon until it forks. Take the right fork (as for *Dark Shadows* and *Out of Control*). Scramble up a long, third-class gully that generally heads up and left from near the base of *American Ninja*. Plan on taking several hours to get to the base of the route. Bring two ropes for the descent. **Pitch 1** (5.9+ R): Follow a dihedral up to a ledge. 160'. **Pitch 2** (5.8): Move the belay around a boulder on a ledge. 50'. **Pitch 3** (5.8 R): Climb up from the ledge past 1 bolt to a small notch. 140'. **Pitch 4** (5.7): Follow the exposed arête to the summit by gaining a small dihedral. 120'. **Descent:** Rappel to a notch, then down into a bowl. Reverse the approach gully, or rappel straight down a gully below the spire (three more rappels).

72. **A Rope, a Rubber Chicken, and a Vibrator** (5.10-) FA: George Watson, Norman Boles; circa 1990. This route is supposedly about 2.5 miles up the right (north) fork of Pine Creek Canyon on the right (north) wall of the canyon. **Pitch 1** (5.6): Climb up huecos to the right of a right-facing corner. **Pitch 2** (5.10-): Climb a right-facing corner past a ceiling to a big ledge. **Pitch 3** (5.6): Climb a crack (or see variation) past a bush to the summit. 60'. **Variation** (5.7): Ascend a feature to the left of the crack. (No topo.)

DARK SHADOWS WALL

The next routes are located on the north face of Mescalito, the pyramid-shaped formation splitting the canyon into two drainages. The rock is of excellent quality, rivaling the best in Black Velvet Canyon. Bring two ropes to get off all of these shady routes.

From the Pine Creek parking lot, follow the trail into Pine Creek Canyon, going past the Fire Ecology Trail and an old homesite. When the canyon forks, take the right (north) fork. The trail becomes a bit braided at this point. The best route is to head uphill on the right (north) side of the canyon for about 100 feet (above the red band of rock), then head left (west), contouring along the hillside on a relatively level trail. Follow the trail up canyon for about 600 yards, keeping well above the drainage bottom. Continue up-canyon until you are even with the farthest large pine trees in the drainage. You should now be able to clearly see the varnished north face of Mescalito. Pine Creek runs along the base of the wall here, and the surrounding vegetation is surprisingly lush and varied.

Red Throbber Spire

The climbs described next are all located on this varnished section of cliff and are described from right to left (down canyon). You may need to head down to the drainage bottom from the trail to see the pools noted in the route descriptions. Total approach time is about 30 minutes.

73. **Slot Machine** (5.10 PG) FA: Bob Conz, Sal Mamusia; July 1990. Those with small fingers will be rewarded on this worthwhile pitch. Start as for *Dark Shadows* atop a flat boulder at the right edge of the pool at the base of the cliff. Bring small RPs and gear up to a #3 Friend. Climb easily past

PINE CREEK CANYON
DARK SHADOWS AREA

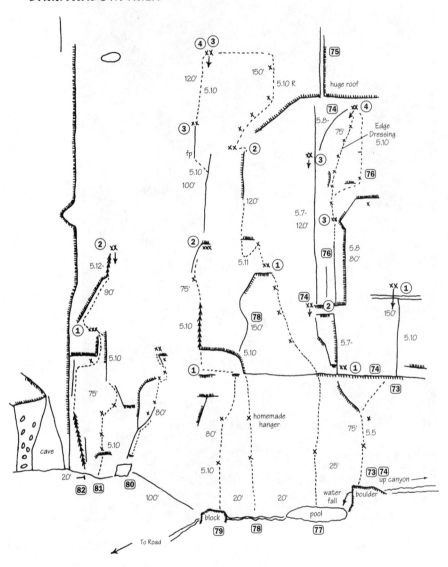

2 bolts to the base of a left-leaning ramp (as for *Dark Shadows*). Continue straight up a thin seam in a steep, varnished wall, passing 1 bolt to the anchor. Rappel with two ropes. 150'.

*74. **Dark Shadows** (5.8-) FA: Lots of different folks; 1973. One of the best 5.8 routes at Red Rocks and a popular soap opera in its time. The climb goes to the top of Mescalito, but only the first four pitches are described here. Bring a variety of gear and be prepared to have fun. Start on a flat boulder atop a small waterfall at the right edge of a pool and below a huge, black dihedral system capped by a giant roof. Good belay ledges on each pitch. **Pitch 1** (5.5 PG13): Face-climb up and right past 2 bolts to a left-leaning ramp that leads to the base of a varnished corner. Two-bolt belay anchor. 75'. **Pitch 2** (5.7-): Climb the clean, varnished, right-facing corner above, moving left to a belay ledge and an anchor. (Pitches 1 and 2 may be combined.) 75'. **Pitch 3** (5.7-): Stem up the beautiful dihedral to a ledge with two different belay anchors. 120'. **Pitch 4** (5.8-): Climb the right-curving crack in the right wall to another anchor belay under the giant roof. 75'. **Descent:** Three rappels using two ropes to get down.

75. **Heart of Darkness** (5.11) FA: Richard Harrison, John Long, Lynn Hill; Spring 1981. From the anchor at the top of the last pitch described on *Dark Shadows*, it's possible to climb out left through the giant roof, using an old bolt and manky fixed pegs for pro. The route continues up, but the section described is the most worthy of repeating.

76. **Chasing Shadows** (5.8+ PG13) FA: Randy Marsh, Pier Locatelli; Summer 1990. Good climbing on this one. Bring gear to a #4 Camalot for the second pitch of the route. The second pitch was originally done with only the silver bolt! **Pitch 1** (5.7-): Climb *Dark Shadows* to the belay at the base of the huge corner (this can be done in one or two pitches). 150'. **Pitch 2** (5.8+): From the *Dark Shadows* belay, move back right to the right-hand (and widest) of two vertical crack systems. Follow this past a wide section to a 2-bolt belay. 80'. **Pitch 3** (5.8+ PG13): Continue straight up the vague arête past a couple of bolts with black hangers, then move out right above a ceiling to a bolt with a silver hanger (variation exists). Wander up and slightly right along the arête (wires, TCUs, small Friends) to the belay on *Dark Shadows* below the huge *Heart of Darkness* roof. 120'. **Variation /Edge Dressing** (5.10 PG): FA: Randy Marsh, Pier Locatelli, Brett Fishman; November 1993. Move up left to a bolt, then up past 6 more bolts to the belay on *Dark Shadows* below the right edge of the huge *Heart of Darkness* roof. Bring a #3 Friend to supplement the bolts. **Descent:** Do three rappels using two ropes, as per *Dark Shadows*.

77. **Sandstone Sandwich** (5.10c PG13) FA: Bob Conz, George Smith, Jim Lybarger; July 1990. Don't bite off more than you can chew! A wonderful

bolted face-climb between the first pitches of *Dark Shadows* and *Excellent Adventure*. Rappel with two ropes from the first belay on *Excellent Adventure*, or continue up that route. Bring #1 and #1.5 Friends.

*78. **Excellent Adventure** (5.11 R) FA: Mike Tupper, Greg Mayer; Fall 1989. Perhaps the best route on the wall. Really scary on the last pitch for both the leader and follower. Start 20' right of *Risky Business* and 25' left of *Dark Shadows* at the left edge of the deeper pool at the base of the cliff. **Pitch 1** (5.10): Climb to the right end of the arching ceiling on *Risky Business*, passing 2 bolts with homemade hangers en route. Follow the arching ceiling left for 15', then pull the ceiling. Intimidating climbing leads left to a crack system. Follow this up and slightly right past an overhang to a belay stance with bolts. 150'. **Pitch 2** (5.11): Go up from the belay, then make tricky moves down and left (bolts). Climb up the right side of a vague arête, stepping back out left to a belay anchor. 120'. **Pitch 3** (5.10) R: Get ready! Follow bolts up and right along the lip of the giant roof, then straight up. Eventually, you can angle back left to the final rap station on *Risky Business* and rappel the route. Whew!

79. **Risky Business** (5.10+ PG) FA: Mike Tupper, Greg Mayer; Summer 1985. Certainly as good as the movie, maybe better! Begin 20' left of the last route and 100' right of *Parental Guidance* where the stream runs along the base of the cliff and directly in front of some large blocks. **Pitch 1** (5.10): Up a short, left-facing flake, then face-climb past 2 bolts. Move slightly right to a flake (scary) then easily up left (or see variation) to a belay at the left end of an arching ceiling. 80'. **Pitch 2** (5.10): Follow the shallow dihedral above the left edge of the ceiling, then continue along a seam to a belay station under a small ceiling. 75'. **Pitch 3** (5.10): Step left and climb to a bolt. Head back right to a crack, which is climbed until you can go left to a corner with a fixed piton. The bolted belay is above. 100'. **Pitch 4** (5.10+): Continue up the varnished wall above past numerous bolts to another rap station. 120'. **Variation** (5.11+): It's possible to undercling the arching ceiling (but who'd want to?). **Descent:** Rappel with two ropes.

80. **Short Circuit** (5.11 PG) FA: Mike Ward, Nick Nordblom; July 1992. A very sustained and sporty pitch. Unless you have a lot of talent and a cool head, you may short out! Bring a couple of tiny TCUs, a large stopper, and a couple of long slings. Start atop a boulder 20' right of *Parental Guidance* and climb a shallow, right-leaning flake/corner past a fixed peg and 2 bolts to a ledge. Step right, then make very hard moves past another bolt to a short corner and the belay anchor. Rappel with one rope.

81. **Parental Guidance** (5.12- PG13) FA: Mike Tupper, Greg Mayer; Winter 1988. The first pitch is worth doing by itself. Bring numerous small Friends,

TCUs, and wires for the first pitch. Start about 100' left of *Risky Business* and 8' right of *Lethal Weapon* at a small block leaning against the cliff. **Pitch 1** (5.10): Climb the face to an overlap 15' up (bolt), then continue past 2 more bolts to a stance (bolt). Angle up left to an obvious, vertical flake. At the top of the flake, step left to a communal belay. 75'. **Pitch 2** (5.12-): Face-climb past bolts to a right-leaning flake/crack, and pull past this into a shallow dihedral. 90'. **Descent:** Rap the route.

82. **Lethal Weapon** (5.12) FA: Mike Tupper, Greg Mayer; Fall 1989. The left (east) margin of this wall is defined by a huge, right-facing chimney/corner system, the bottom of which forms a cave (this chimney/corner system is *Negro Blanco*). Start 20' right of the cave in a cleared area that is below several small corners and a huge flake/chimney system. Climb the easy, bigger dihedral to the base of a gaping chimney, then angle right up a corner to a roof. Traverse right under the roof (bolt) and follow a flake to a belay station.

MESCALITO, EAST FACE

The next routes generally face the Pine Creek parking area and are described from right to left (north fork to south fork). The routes receive limited sunshine, depending on the season. Approach as for *Dark Shadows* on the main Pine Creek Trail. Approach time is about 25 minutes.

83. **Negro Blanco** (5.10+) FA: Lynn Hill, John Long, Richard Harrison; Spring 1981. This route climbs a huge, right-facing flake/corner system that forms the left margin of the varnished Dark Shadows Wall. Bring a good selection of gear. Start at the base of the chimney/flake system in a right-facing corner. **Pitch 1** (5.10): Climb the corner past a flare. Move left to a belay at the base of a flaring crack. **Pitch 2** (5.8): Follow a crack straight up to a belay stance atop a white flake. **Pitch 3:** Climb the flake, then face-climb to a belay stance on the right. **Pitch 4:** Move left back into the corner and follow it to the top. Continue up the face to a belay stance. **Pitch 5** (5.9): Climb the face above the belay to an obvious crack. Belay in the crack at the end of the pitch. **Pitch 6:** Follow the crack to a right-leaning ramp. Go up this ramp to join *Heart of Darkness* and other routes to the summit of Mescalito.

84. **Flakes of Wrath** (5.10+ R/X) FA: Nick Nordblom, Kevin Lowell; 1990. This 4-pitch route starts to the left of *Negro Blanco*. Bring two ropes to rappel. Not much is known about this route, except that it keeps to the right of *Centerfold*. **Pitch 1** (5.8 R): Face-climb up steep black rock to an anchor consisting of a nut and a piton. **Pitch 2** (5.8+): Continue up the steep black face to an anchor on a ledge. **Pitch 3** (5.10 R): Angle up and left on plates to a white slab. Belay at the base of a left-facing corner at a bolt and peg. **Pitch 4** (5.10+ R/X): Go up and left along the crack/corner

PINE CREEK CANYON
E. FACE MESCALITO RIGHT SIDE

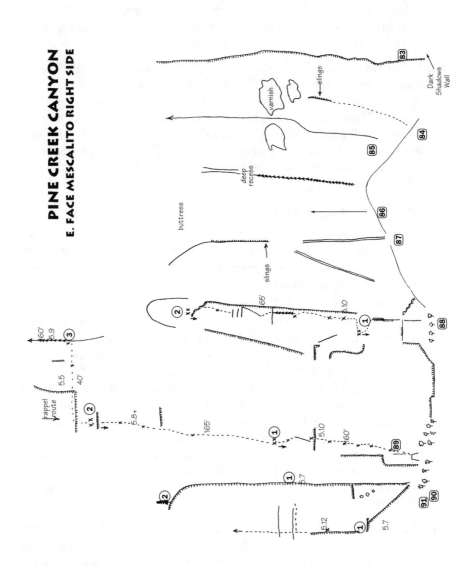

onto the face (scary) to a bolt and pin belay anchor. **Descent:** Do 4 rappels with two ropes.

85. **Centerfold** (5.10) FA: Scott Woodruff, Joe Herbst, Larry Hamilton; April 1977. Reportedly not a great route. This route climbs the center of the huge, white face to the left of *Negro Blanco*. The route goes up obvious white cracks and flakes to the top of a prominent tower. From the top of the tower, continue to the summit of Mescalito, utilizing obvious cracks.

86. **Bloodline** (5.11- PG) FA: Guys from Colorado; 1980s. I have been unable to definitively locate this route. It is reportedly about 100' up and left of *Negro Blanco* near the height of land and below a huge recess (the recess is *Deep Space*, 5.9 and is described in the Urioste guide). Do an easy pitch up to a ledge, then climb a splitter finger crack through a bulge to a 2-bolt belay.

87. **Ride the Tiger** (5.9) FA: Nick Nordblom, Randal Grandstaff; 1982. Start about 100' up and left of *Negro Blanco* at the top of a dirt cone. The route climbs a buttress between two ugly-looking chimney systems. **Pitch 1** (5.6): Climb a broken face through black plates at the base of a big buttress. **Pitch 2** (5.7): Continue up the plated face, which gets a little steeper. **Pitch 3** (5.9): Layback up a flake resembling the one on Yosemite's *Wheat Thin*. Belay on a ramp at the top of the flake. **Pitch 4** (5.9 R): Angle left around the arête onto a face which is climbed to the top of the feature. **Descent:** There are no fixed anchors, but you may be able to traverse left to reach *Y2K* and rappel that route.

88. **The Next Century** (5.10 PG) FA (Pitch 1): Unknown. FA (Pitch 2): Todd Swain, Paul Ross; November 1998. The combined age of the first ascent party was 100. Good climbing on both pitches. Bring wires, TCUs, and cams to #3. Start at a dihedral about 50' down and left from the top of the dirt cone (below *Deep Space* and *Bloodline*). The left side of this dihedral has a low overhang that parallels the ground. **Pitch 1** (5.7): Climb an obvious crack system 10' right of the corner to a ledge. Continue up another crack in a small, varnished corner. When the corner ends, exit left and climb up the face to an anchor. 100'. **Pitch 2** (5.10): Move right from the belay to the arête. Make hard moves up the varnished face past 2 bolts, then continue up along the arête to a shallow dihedral. Tricky moves up the corner (bolt) lead to bigger holds. A final bolt protects moves onto the belay ledge. 165'. **Descent:** Rappel with two ropes.

To get to the next few routes you have to scramble up through some small cliffbands and dense oak bushes to reach the base of the cliff.

*89. **Y2K** (5.10) FA (Pitch 1): Unknown; 1997 or earlier. FA (Pitches 2–4): Todd Swain, Paul Ross; November 1998. A great route. Most of the route is 5.8 climbing and, by using a small amount of aid, the hard moves can be avoided. Bring RPs, wires, TCUs, and cams to #3. This climb is located about 20' right of a prominent, varnished dihedral. The climb starts atop a boulder that is at the base of a 40-foot high, pink dihedral capped by a roof. **Pitch 1** (5.10): Face-climb along vertical seams that are just right of a corner, past about 5 bolts to a ceiling. Pull the ceiling (bolt; 5.10, easily aided), then climb a fantastic varnished crack and face past 1 more bolt to an anchor. 160'. **Pitch 2** (5.8+): Wander up the varnished face past 3 bolts and numerous gear placements. Belay on a ledge with an anchor. 165'. **Pitch 3** (5.5): Climb 10' up onto a big ledge, then traverse straight right past 1 bolt to a belay in a varnished corner. 1 bolt and traditional gear make up the belay. 40'. **Pitch 4** (5.9): Climb the beautiful, varnished dihedral to a ledge. Step left on the ledge and climb easy rock to a belay anchor on a higher ledge. Many tiny wires needed near the top of the corner. 160'. **Descent:** Rappel with two ropes as follows. From Pitch 4's anchor down the yellow face to Pitch 2's anchor (145'). From Pitch 2's anchor to Pitch 1's anchor (160'). From Pitch 1's anchor to the ground (160').

90. **Pauligk Pillar** (5.7+) FA: Mr. and Mrs. Roland Pauligk, Randal Grandstaff; 1981. Guess what Australian Roland Pauligk invented? Bring a good assortment of gear, including RPs. Begin below an obvious, varnished dihedral 20' left of the last route. There is a pine tree visible from the Pine Creek Trail at the top of the dihedral. **Pitch 1:** Climb the corner to a belay from slings. **Pitch 2:** Continue up the corner to its top. **Descent:** Rappel the route with two ropes.

91. **Welcome to Red Rocks** (5.12) FA: Sal Mamusia, Paul Van Betten; 1986. Difficult climbing on this one. Start just left of the base of the *Pauligk Pillar* dihedral at a left-leaning ramp system with bushes on it. **Pitch 1** (5.7): Climb the left-leaning ramp to a belay at the base of a very clean, right-facing corner. 100'. **Pitch 2** (5.12): Stem, lieback, and do whatever else it takes to get up the 40-foot corner (1 bolt and small wires for protection; or see variation). From the top of the corner, continue up the face and rappel *Pauligk Pillar*. **Variation** (5.11): It is possible to avoid the crux section of the corner by traversing out a horizontal crack, moving up, then following another horizontal crack back into the corner. This makes the section easier.

The next routes are located on the left (south) side of a huge pillar leaning against the middle of the east face of the Mescalito. Approach these routes as for *Cat in the Hat*, taking the South (left) Fork of Pine Creek, then wandering up the dirt slope below the east face.

92. **$C_{11}H_{17}NO_3$** (5.5) FA: Bob Logerquist, John Williamson; April 1971. One or both of these guys had to have been a chemist to know the formula for mescaline (a.k.a. peyote). This route climbs the better-looking of the crack/chimney systems immediately left of the huge pillar leaning against the

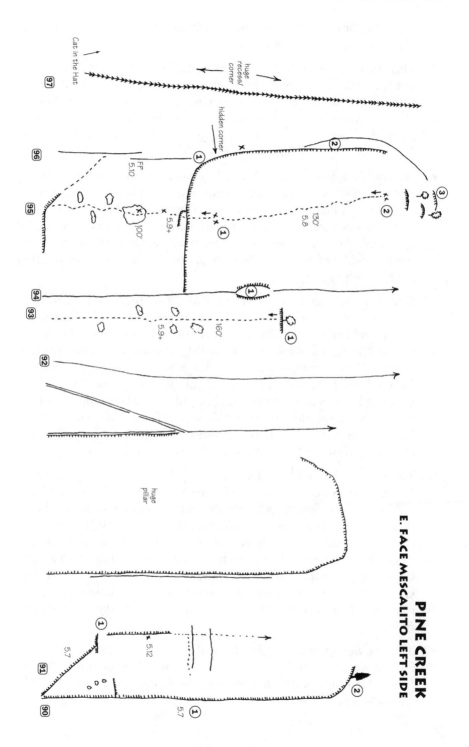

Cat in the Hat

97

huge
recess/
corner

hidden corner

96

FP
5.10

1

2

95

3

2

13.0'
5.8

1

100'

5.9+

94

1

93

1

16.0'

5.9+

92

huge
pillar

PINE CREEK
E. FACE MESCALITO LEFT SIDE

1

5.7

5.12

91

2

90

1

5.7

middle of the east face. You should eventually be able to reach *Cat in the Hat* and rappel that route with two ropes.

93. **This Ain't No Disco** (5.9+ PG) FA: Randal Grandstaff, Randy Marsh; 1982. On the left side of the huge pillar leaning against the middle of the east face are several crack/gully systems. This 1-pitch route climbs the black, hueco-covered face between two of these crack systems. A rappel anchor is about 160' up on a bushy ledge just right of the *When a Stranger Calls* crack. Rappel with two ropes.

94. **When a Stranger Calls** (5.8) FA: Randal Grandstaff, Steve Anderson; Spring 1981. A good-looking, moderate, crack line. Bring large gear. Start about 50' left of the huge pillar leaning against the middle of the east face. The route follows a prominent crack system that has a recess in it about 150' up. Climb the crack system for about three pitches until you reach the south shoulder of Mescalito. You should be able to rappel down *Cat in the Hat* with two ropes.

95. **Pine Nuts** (5.9+ PG) FA: Chris Gill, Paul Ross, Todd Swain; December 1998. Paul Ross worked with natural food guru Euel Gibbons at Hurricane Island Outward Bound School in the 1970s. Bring wires, TCUs, and up to a #3.5 Friend. Rack up on a nice ledge just left of a prominent crack system (*When a Stranger Calls*). This ledge is directly below a roof about 70' up. **Pitch 1** (5.9+ PG): Climb the gray face past natural gear placements and 2 bolts to a large ceiling about 70' up. Pull the ceiling at a flake (crux), then climb the varnished face to an anchor. 100'. **Pitch 2** (5.8): Climb straight up the beautiful varnished face above the belay to an anchor. 130'. **Descent:** Rappel the route with two ropes.

96. **The Walker Spur** (5.10 PG) FA: John Long, Lynn Hill, Richard Harrison; Spring 1981. A challenging route for the 5.10 leader. Bring a good selection of gear and two ropes for the descent. Start in the same location as *Pine Nuts,* on a nice ledge below a ceiling about 70' up. **Pitch 1:** Move out left from the ledge and climb the gray face to a thin, vertical crack. Climb this (5.10) to a hanging corner at the left side of the ceiling. **Pitch 2** (5.9): Climb the corner (bolt) and crack above to a belay near the arête. **Pitch 3:** Continue up the crack onto a face and belay on a yellow ledge on the south shoulder of Mescalito. **Descent:** Rappel *Cat in the Hat* with two ropes.

97. **The Cookie Monster** (5.7) FA: Joe and Betsy Herbst; 1970s. This route ascends the huge corner/recess near the left (south) shoulder of the east face of Mescalito. After a few pitches, you should merge with *Cat in the Hat,* which can be used as a descent.

98. **Pauline's Pentacle** (5.10- R) FA: Randal Grandstaff, Randy Marsh, Pauline Schroeder; 1982. Start below a section of good-looking, chocolate-colored varnish left of *The Cookie Monster*. Three pitches of face-climbing lead to the south (left) shoulder of the Mescalito. There is reportedly some loose rock on the first pitch. Rappel *Cat in the Hat* with two ropes. (No topo.)

SOUTH FORK OF PINE CREEK CANYON

MESCALITO, SOUTH FACE

From the Pine Creek parking lot, follow the trail into Pine Creek Canyon, going past the Fire Ecology Trail and an old homesite. When the canyon forks, take the left (south) drainage for about 75 yards, then follow a trail on the right (Mescalito) side of the creekbed. Continue on this vague trail around the toe of the south buttress, keeping well above the drainage bottom and passing numerous crack systems (some of the routes listed above). A well-worn trail up a talus slope brings you to the base of this sunny route. Total approach time is about 30 minutes.

*99. **Cat in the Hat** (5.6+) FA: Bruce Eisener, Joanne Urioste; April 1976. A wonderful, moderate route that can be done during colder weather. Carry a good selection of gear, including long slings and two ropes for rappelling. This route is located on the south side of the Mescalito, the pyramid-shaped formation splitting Pine Creek Canyon. Start at a crack system that is 75' left of a prominent chimney. Directly uphill from the start of the climb is a bushy gully that leads to steep, broken, brown rock. **Pitch 1** (5.5): Climb an obvious, slightly left-slanting crack past numerous huecos, moving right to a ledge with a small bush and slings around a horn. 90'. Climb the left-slanting fist crack above to another ledge, then continue up the corner/chimney directly above to belay on a sloping terrace. 150'. **Pitch 2** (5.5): From the right-center portion of the terrace, climb a steep, black wall to a ledge. Step left and follow a left-facing corner to a ledge with a tree (many rappel slings on the tree). 60'. **Pitch 3** (5.6): A great pitch. From the first ledge above the rappel tree, climb the black face just left of a left-facing corner along a thin crack. Move left just below a white ceiling and follow a finger crack up the wall to a ledge. Belay on the highest ledge at slings around a block. 110'. **Pitch 4** (5.3): Step down and traverse around right to a series of blocky ledges with slings. This pitch can be combined with Pitch 5. 50'. **Pitch 5** (5.6+): Climb the beautiful crack up the center of the black wall. When it ends in the white rock, angle right around a corner to a bolt, then up the crack above to the top (2-bolt belay). 100'. **Descent:** Rappel with two ropes as follows. First do a 110-foot rappel to the block atop pitch 3. Follow this with another 110-foot rappel to tree. Then do a 60-foot rappel to a terrace. Next scramble down the terrace to bolts on a ledge. Last, a 130-foot rappel from bolts gets you to the ground.

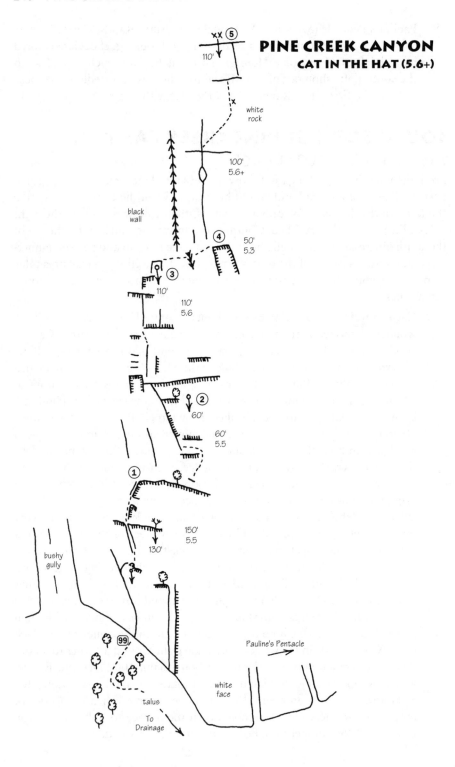

PINE CREEK CANYON
CAT IN THE HAT (5.6+)

xx ⑤
110'

white
rock

100'
5.6+

black
wall

④ 50'
5.3

③
110'

110'
5.6

② 60'

60'
5.5

①

150'
5.5

130'

bushy
gully

Pauline's Pentacle

⑨⑨

white
face

talus

To
Drainage

The next two routes are about 150 yards up and left of *Cat in the Hat.*

100. **OB Button** (5.10-) FA: Paul Obenheim; 1982. The left-hand of the two routes mentioned above. Climb a crack through a roof, then continue upward for a total of two pitches. Rappel.

101. **OB Fist** (5.10-) FA: Nick Nordblom, Paul Van Betten; 1982. Climb the right-hand line, which is a fist crack through a roof.

Note: Farther up this fork of the canyon is the Challenger Wall, which is supposed to have many good quality hard routes.

CRABBY APPLETON AREA

The next three routes are on a large diamond-shaped face that sits up high on the south side of the canyon. The routes are in the shade most of the day. From the Pine Creek parking lot, follow the trail into Pine Creek Canyon, going past the Fire Ecology Trail and an old homesite. When the canyon forks, take the left (south) drainage for about 400 yards until a prominent gully leading up left is seen on the left (south) wall of the canyon. Scramble up the gully (fourth- and easy fifth-class), staying on its right edge, to a small cave. Exit the cave through a hole in its top. Continue up the gully for another 50' or so to a big ledge. This approach takes about 90 minutes and is not for the weak of heart.

*102. **Crabby Appleton** (5.9+ PG) FA: Richard Harrison, Wendell Broussard, Paul Van Betten; 1982. This is supposed to be a good route. **Pitch 1** (5.3): Traverse right about 80' to the base of an obvious crack system. 80'. **Pitch 2** (5.7): Follow the crack, angling right to a big dish with 1 bolt. 120'. **Pitch 3** (5.8): Exit left out of the dish, then follow the crack past an overlap to a ledge with a pin and bolt. 120'. **Pitch 4** (5.5): Climb a left-facing arch for 20' (or see Variation 1), step right, then climb a beautiful black face to a huge ledge under a headwall. 100'. **Pitch 5** (5.9+): Walk right on a ledge for 20' (or see Variation 2). Climb straight up a crack over a bulge (crux). Continue upward, eventually belaying in a crack. 130'. **Variation 1** (5.9): Continue up the corner. **Variation 2** (5.5): Escape left. **Descent:** Walk off to the right (west) to the top of an obvious ramp, which is then followed back down toward the road and the base of the route.

103. **Tom Terrific** (5.10- PG) FA: Richard Harrison, Wendell Broussard; 1985. Don't get whipped into a frenzy on this one. Carry wires, TCUs, and Friends up to #4. Start to the right of *Crabby Appleton* on the descent ramp. **Pitch 1** (5.10-): Pull over a bulge (crux), then straight up the face toward the bottom of a right-facing arch. Belay in a dish with 1 bolt. 100'. **Pitch 2** (5.7): Continue straight up the face to the base of the arch (big Friends needed for the anchor). 110'. **Pitch 3** (5.9+): Step left around

PINE CREEK CANYON
CRABBY APPLETON AREA

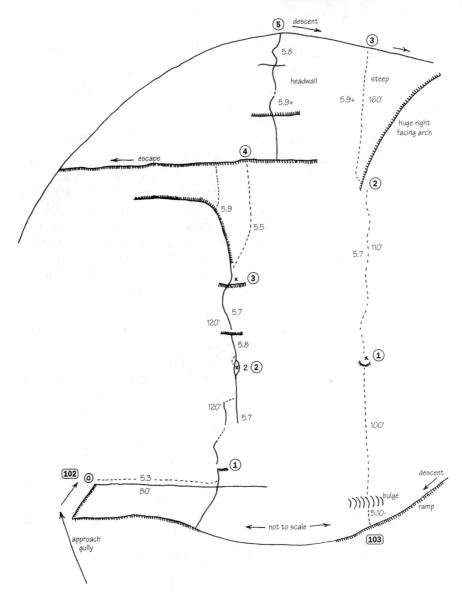

the arch, then angle left up the face to the top. 160'. **Descent:** Walk off to the right (west) to the top of an obvious ramp, which is then followed back down toward the road and the base of the route.

104. **Creepshow** (5.10 X) FA: Robert Finlay, Richard Harrison; circa 1985. Climb the face to the right of *Tom Terrific*, along some black waterstreaks. (No topo.)

105. **The Whitehouse Effect** (5.10+) FA: Dave Wonderly, Warren Egbert; 1988. These guys did a 2-pitch route somewhere up here (this may be the same route as *Creepshow*). **Pitch 1:** Climb a crack past a hole to a bolted belay. **Pitch 2** (5.10+): The second pitch is protected by about 4 bolts and goes through some bulges. **Descent:** Walk down and right, then down the ramp to the base of the route. (No topo.)

MAGIC TRIANGLE AREA

The next routes are located to the left (east) of the *Crabby Appleton* approach gully on the south wall of the canyon. All of the routes are east (toward the road) of the front face on Mescalito. From the Pine Creek parking lot, follow the trail into Pine Creek Canyon, going past the Fire Ecology Trail and an old homesite. When the canyon forks, take the left (south) drainage for about 300 yards until you encounter a red slab on your left. A huge boulder with several large pines is about 75 yards upstream. From here, you can see the obvious, left-leaning *Crabby Appleton* gully and other features. Routes are described from right to left, moving toward the mouth of the canyon. (No topo.)

106. **Lunar Escape** (5.11-) FA: Dave Wonderly, Warren Egbert; 1988. Start in the *Crabby Appleton* gully, about 50' right of an arête. **Pitch 1** (5.10-): Climb a steep, black face to a bolted belay stance. **Pitch 2** (5.10): Traverse right, then wander up the face past about 7 bolts to a bolt anchor. **Pitch 3** (5.11-): Climb up to a steep headwall with bolts, which is climbed to the top of the buttress. **Descent:** Rappel *Edge of the Sun* with two ropes.

*107. **Edge of the Sun** (5.10+) FA: Dave Wonderly, Warren Egbert; 1988. This is supposed to be a very good route. Start at the base of the *Crabby Appleton* gully, just right of an arête. Bring two ropes to rappel. **Pitch 1** (5.10-): Climb the face to a ledge on the prow. **Pitch 2** (5.9+): Climb the face on the left of the arête past bolts to a bolted belay below a ceiling. **Pitch 3** (5.10+): Go up and left under the ceiling onto a steep white face, then up waterstreaks (bolts). **Descent:** Rappel the route with two ropes.

108. **Clone Babies** (5.10+) FA: Paul Crawford, Richard Harrison; 1983. Start about 75 yards to the left of the *Crabby Appleton* gully. Climb overhanging, twin cracks, then go up and left to the top of a pillar (160'). Rappel with two ropes.

109. **Midnight Oil** (5.11-) FA: Richard Harrison, Paul Crawford, Randy Marsh, Nick Nordblom; 1983. Harrison was pictured on the first ascent of this route in the first edition of the guide. Bring two ropes and a good-sized rack. This climb begins below a huge, black triangle of rock (*The Magic Triangle*, which is described in the Urioste guide) about 150 yards to the left of the *Crabby Appleton* gully. Climb a dihedral with a hand crack, then face-climb up along a seam (crux). Mantle a couple of sloping ledges into a corner, which is followed past a bolt to a rappel anchor. 165'.

*110. **Small Purchase** (5.10) FA: Joe Herbst; 1970s. This is an outstanding 1-pitch climb on the south wall of the canyon. Bring gear to a #4 Camalot, plus extra TCUs in the smaller sizes. From the red slab described in the approach, you can see this climb. It's a 100-foot-high pillar with a left-leaning dihedral on its right (west) side. It sits between two obvious gullies that run up the entire cliff. From the wash, follow any of the numerous social trails about 300 yards up to the base of the climb. Start at an alcove that is about 40' right (west) of a prominent, rectangular block/pinnacle. Climb the classic, right-facing corner to a 3-bolt belay atop the pillar. With a 165' rope, you can just reach a ledge, then scramble down the initial 20' of the climb.

111. **Five and Dime** (5.10+) FA: Unknown; before March 1994. Climb the knife-edged arête 15' left of *Small Purchase* past at least 6 bolts. Rappel with a 165' rope as for *Small Purchase*.

112. **Dukes of Hazard** (5.9?) FA: Randal Grandstaff, Shelby Shelton; circa 1983. Climb the front of a pillar just right (west) of the *Cartwright Corner/Chocolate Flakes* gully.

The next two routes climb obvious, varnished dihedrals that sit midway up the left side of a huge gully. The gully is about 100 feet left of *Small Purchase* and is clearly visible from the approach trail and the old homesite.

113. **Chocolate Flakes** (5.10+) FA: Robert Finlay, Tom Ebanoff; 1985. FFA: Paul Van Betten, Nick Nordblom; 1985. Start at the base of the gully at a nice, flat area surrounded by lush vegetation. **Pitch 1** (5.8): Climb up the dirty chimney system to a big ledge on the left side, below a wide crack in a corner. 130'. **Pitch 2** (5.9 PG): Climb the crack in the corner to a ledge, then go up another wide crack to a large ledge. **Pitch 3** (5.10+): Climb the right-hand of two dihedrals to a ledge. **Pitch 4** (5.10-): Continue up the corner to its top. **Pitch 5**: Scramble to the top. **Descent**: Go right (up canyon) to the *Crabby Appleton* descent ramp, which is followed back down toward the road.

PINE CREEK CANYON
CARTWRIGHT CORNER/
CHOCOLATE FLAKES

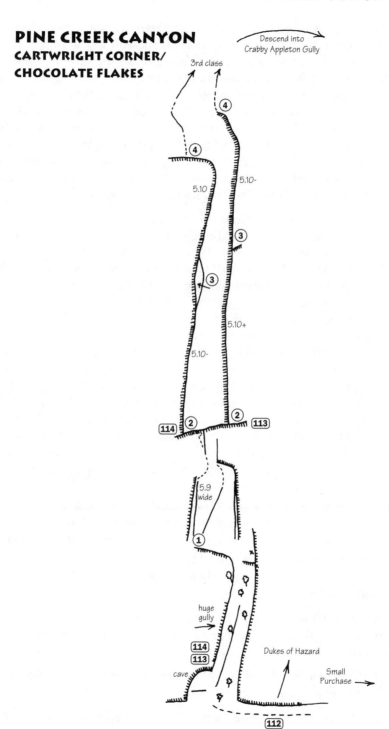

Descend into
Crabby Appleton Gully

3rd class

④

④

5.10

5.10-

③

③

5.10+

5.10-

114 ②

② 113

5.9
wide

①

huge
gully

114
113

Dukes of Hazard

Small
Purchase →

cave

112

114. **Cartwright Corner** (5.10) FA: Richard Harrison, Nick Nordblom, Paul Van Betten, Wendell Broussard; 1985. Supposedly a great route if you can get past the first two pitches. Start as for *Chocolate Flakes* at the base of the gully at a nice, flat area surrounded by lush vegetation. **Pitch 1** (5.8): Climb up the dirty chimney system to a big ledge on the left side, below a wide crack in a corner. 130'. **Pitch 2** (5.9 PG): Climb the wide crack in the corner to a ledge, then go up another wide crack to a large ledge. **Pitch 3** (5.10-): Climb the left-hand of two dihedrals to a belay in a pod. **Pitch 4** (5.10): Continue up the corner to a ledge at its top. **Pitch 5**: Scramble to the top. **Descent:** Go right (up canyon) to the *Crabby Appleton* descent ramp, which is followed back down toward the road.

115. **Community Pillar** (5.9) FA: Joe Herbst, Tom Kaufman; March 1976. This route is supposed to be good. Bring gear up to a #5 Camalot. Start at a 10-foot-wide chimney that is to the left (east) of the *Cartwright Corner/Chocolate Flakes* gully. **Pitch 1** (5.9): Climb the obvious chimney up to a huge chockstone. Either tunnel through a hole (tight) or go left under the chockstone. Belay on a ledge above. 140'. **Pitch 2** (fourth-class): Continue up easy terrain to the base of steeper rock. 100'. **Pitch 3** (5.6): Climb a chimney, then tunnel through a hole to a belay. 80'. **Pitch 4** (5.8): Climb the off-width crack on the right (or see Variation 1) then tunnel through another hole to a belay ledge. 130'. **Pitch 5** (5.8): Go up a crack and belay in a cave. 100', 5.7. **Pitch 6**: Climb the chimney (or see Variation 2) to a ledge. 120'. **Pitch 7** (fourth-class): Wander up to another ledge. 140'. **Pitch 8** (5.6 PG): Scramble to the top. 200'. **Variation 1** (5.9): Climb the crack on the left. **Variation 2:** Climb the crack on the outside of the chimney. **Descent:** Rappel from a pine tree, then continue down the *Chocolate Flakes/ Cartwright Corner* gully or continue up from the pine tree until you can descend by *Crabby Appleton*.

The next four routes are located near the mouth of Pine Creek Canyon at a large, pink corner. These routes are best approached from the Knoll Trail, that runs along the base of the escarpment between Pine Creek and Oak Creek Canyons. (No topo.)

116. **Cold Blue Steel** (5.10) FA: Greg Mayer; 1988. This route climbs the right arête of the pink corner past 5 bolts and some gear placements to a communal anchor.

117. **Dependent Variable** (5.12) FA: Mike Tupper; 1988. Stem and lieback up the pink corner past 4 bolts and some gear placements to the communal anchor.

118. **Without a Paddle** (5.11d) FA: Mike Tupper; 1988. Climb the left arête of the corner past 8 bolts to the communal belay anchor.

119. **Dog Police** (5.10) FA: Unknown; 1980s. Rope up at a striking crack system to the left of the pink corner. Climb a superb crack up the center of a white face. Rappel with two ropes.

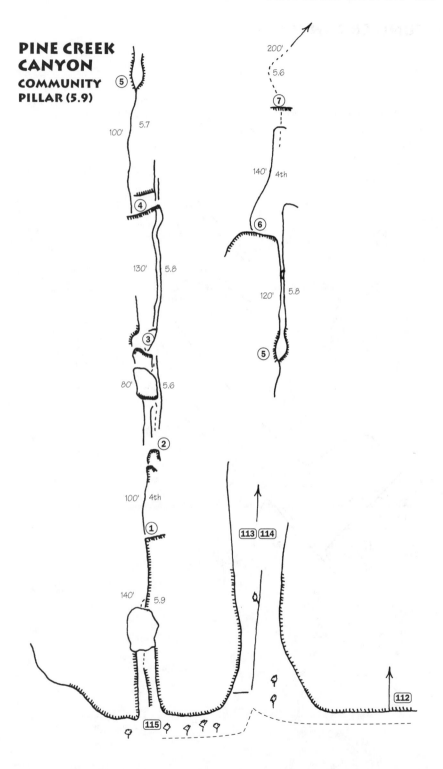

PINE CREEK CANYON
COMMUNITY PILLAR (5.9)

JUNIPER CANYON

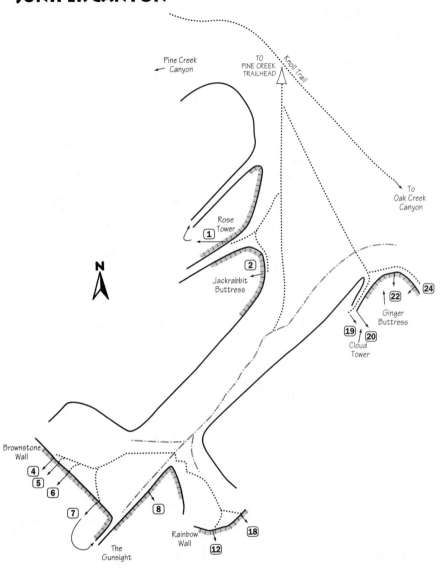

JUNIPER CANYON

It is probably best to approach Juniper Canyon by parking at the Pine Creek parking area, located 10.3 miles along the scenic loop road. A spur road leads off the loop road to access Oak Creek Canyon and this may also be used to access Juniper Canyon. From the Pine Creek parking area, follow the well-marked Pine Creek Canyon Trail past the old homesite, then take the Knoll Trail that runs south in front of the escarpment. Various social trails also lead directly across the desert from the Fire Ecology Trail to Juniper Canyon. Once you enter Juniper Canyon, follow the main drainage to avoid dense scrub oak. The selected climbs are scattered throughout the canyon—each route has its own detailed description to find its start. Routes are described from right to left (north to south).

ROSE TOWER

Rose Tower is a separate formation from the right (north) wall of Juniper Canyon. The top of the formation is light pink in color, hence the name.

From the Pine Creek parking area, follow the Pine Creek Canyon Trail down the hill and past the Fire Ecology Trail and old homestead. Turn left off the Pine Creek Trail onto the marked hiking trail that runs south along the base of the escarpment (the Knoll Trail). This trail crosses the Pine Creek drainage, then angles up a red hillside to flat ground. Follow this trail south to a point just before the mouth of Juniper Canyon. Head up right along a climber's trail into a tree-filled gully to the left (west) of Rose Tower. This approach takes about 45 minutes.

1. **Olive Oil** (5.7 PG) FA: Jorge and Joanne Urioste, John Williamson; February 1978. A slick route. Bring large gear to protect the last two pitches. Scramble about 200 yards up the tree-filled gully to the base of the route, which is in the sun all day. Start the climb at the base of a left-leaning chimney/corner with an obvious tree about 150' up. The base of the chimney/corner forms somewhat of a cave. **Pitch 1** (5.7 PG): Climb up the left-leaning ramp just left of the ugly chimney/corner to a tree and ledge (rap anchors here). 150'. **Pitch 2** (5.7): Slither up a short chimney, then up the obvious finger-and-hand crack about 15' right of a large, right-facing corner. Belay in the crack when you run out of rope. 150'. **Pitch 3** (5.6): Continue up the crack and face, eventually moving left into the right-facing corner. Belay on a large ledge just left of the corner. 120'. **Pitch 4** (5.5): Traverse right about 20' and follow the central crack. At the end of the pitch, move right into the left-facing corner and belay. 150'. **Pitch 5** (5.4): Continue up the corner for 30' to a huge ledge on the right. Walk about 25' to the right. 55'. **Pitch 6** (5.7 PG): Angle up right across the face into the huge dihedral above. Continue up this until you've run out of rope. 150'. **Pitch 7** (5.6): Continue up the corner to the top. 150'. **Descent:** Scramble about 150' up slabs, then walk to the top of Rose Tower. Walk left (west) to a notch, then drop down right (north) into the gully. A typically bushy but easy descent to the valley floor follows.

Note: Numerous routes have been done on the varnished wall across from the start of *Olive Oil*, but information is lacking.

JACKRABBIT BUTTRESS

Jackrabbit Buttress is located just left of Rose Tower toward the main portion of Juniper Canyon. When viewed from the Pine Creek parking area, Jackrabbit Buttress forms what appears to be the right skyline of Juniper Canyon.

From the Pine Creek parking area, follow the Pine Creek Canyon Trail down the hill and past the Fire Ecology Trail and old homestead. Turn left off the Pine Creek Trail onto the marked Knoll Trail, which runs south along the base of the

JUNIPER CANYON
ROSE TOWER
OLIVE OIL (5.7 PG)

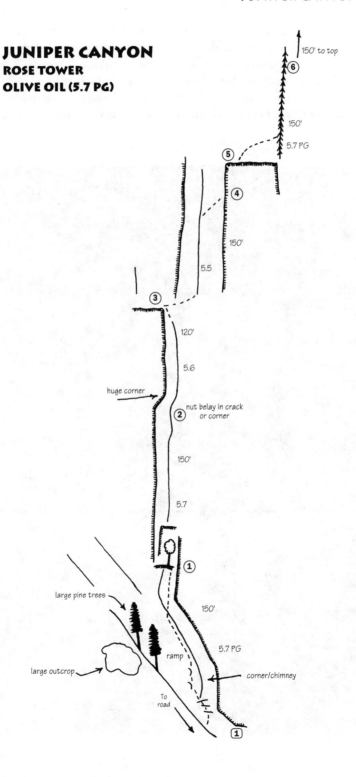

150' to top

⑥

150'

5.7 PG

⑤

④

150'

5.5

③

120'

5.6

huge corner

nut belay in crack
or corner

②

150'

5.7

①

large pine trees

150'

5.7 PG

ramp

corner/chimney

large outcrop

To
road

①

escarpment. This trail crosses the Pine Creek drainage, then angles up a red hillside to flat ground. Follow this trail south to a point just before the mouth of Juniper Canyon. Head up right along a climber's trail, aiming for a tree-filled gully to the left (west) of Rose Tower (a separate formation from the right/ north wall of Juniper Canyon). At the mouth of the gully, head left (south) along the base of the cliff for about 200 yards. This approach takes about 45 minutes.

*2. **Geronimo** (5.7) FA: Bill and Michelle Cramer; May 1992. This route should become very popular—it is of good quality. Bring wires, TCUs, and cams up to #4. Carry two ropes and some extra sling or rope material for the descent. The route starts in a brush-filled gully below an obvious dogleg crack and is in the sun all day. **Pitch 1** (5.7): Climb the dogleg crack to a large ledge with boulders. 155'. **Pitch 2** (5.6): Move to the left side of the ledge and climb a thin crack, which leads to a ledge (optional belay here). Climb the face above the big ledge to one of a couple of belay stances. 150'. **Pitch 3** (5.3): Continue up onto a big terrace, then move left to the base of a black face. Belay from bushes on the terrace. 50'. **Pitch 4** (5.7): Climb the black face, aiming for a dihedral near the skyline. Belay on the skyline at a small stance (cams). 150'. **Pitch 5** (5.6): Step up and right from the belay onto a sloping shelf (exposed). Climb the lower-angle face to the summit. 90'. **Descent:** Rappel as follows: From a bolt anchor on the summit, rappel straight down a dark wall to the highest point of the bushy terrace atop pitch 3 (165'). Scramble down on the terrace to the top of a gully. This gully should be just right (north) of where you came up onto the bushy terrace. About 10' down the gully is a large chockstone with slings around it. Rappel with one rope down the gully/chimney to another chockstone. Be careful not to lose your rope in the crack! Rappel with one rope from the second chockstone down to a ledge with a tree. Rappel from the tree to the ground, making sure that your ropes will pull.

BROWNSTONE WALL

The large, brown wall at the very rear of Juniper Canyon is called Brownstone Wall. On the left (south) side of the wall is The Gunsight, which provides a nontechnical way to enter or exit the top of the canyon. The approach to Brownstone Wall from Pine Creek parking area takes about 1.5 hours.

From the Pine Creek parking area, follow the Pine Creek Canyon Trail down the hill and past the Fire Ecology Trail and old homestead. Turn left off the Pine Creek Trail onto the marked Knoll Trail, which runs south along the base of the escarpment. This trail crosses the Pine Creek drainage, then angles up a red hillside to flat ground. Follow this trail south until you are close to the Juniper Canyon drainage. Hike up the drainage until a large, white lump of rock with a pine tree on its left side splits the canyon. The Rainbow Wall is up on the left and Brownstone Wall is visible about 100 yards right of the white lump, just right of a lone pine tree. Go through bushes below and right of the white lump (cairn), then up an open talus slope. Follow easy slabs up and right to reach the base of Brownstone Wall.

3. **High Anxiety** (5.10) FA: Joanne and Jorge Urioste; May 1978. This climb ascends the large, left-facing corner system to the right (north) of *The Nightcrawler*. This feature is just left of a huge cleft in the right side of Brownstone Wall. Bring gear up to a #5 Camalot. Start below and to the

JUNIPER CANYON
JACKRABBIT BUTTRESS
GERONIMO (5.7)

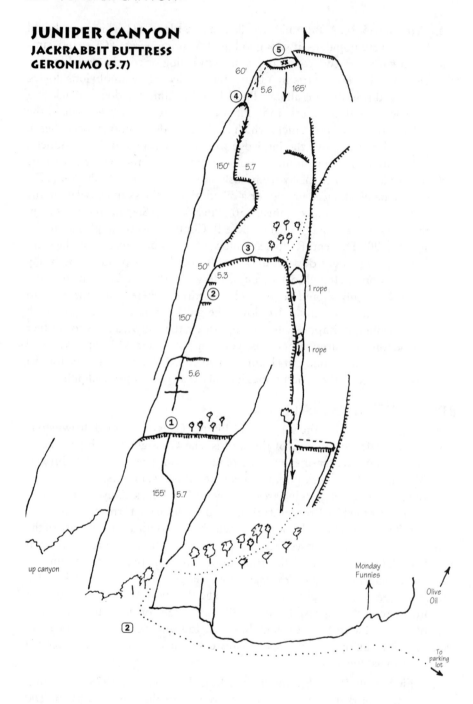

5
XX
60'
5.6   165'
4
150'   5.7
3
50'
5.3
2
1 rope
1 rope
5.6
1
155'   5.7

up canyon

Monday
Funnies

Olive
Oil

To
parking
lot

2

JUNIPER CANYON
BROWNSTONE WALL

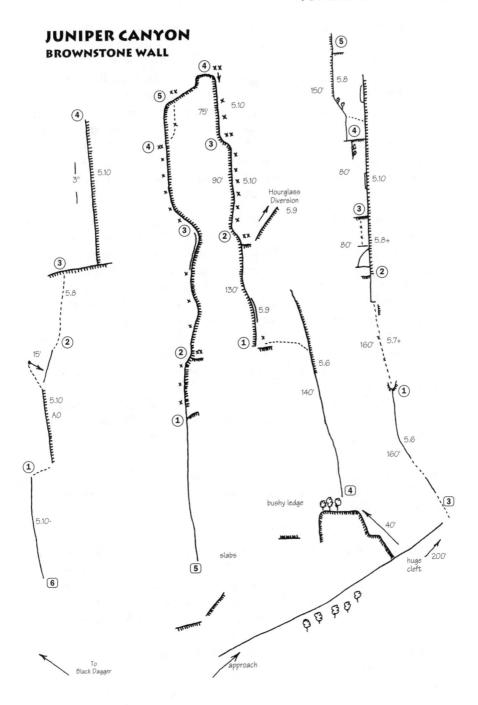

④

3" 5.10

③

5.8

15' ②

5.10
AO

①

5.10-

⑥

④ xx

⑤ xx

75' 5.10

④

③

90' 5.10

Hourglass
Diversion
5.9

③

② xx

130'

① 5.9

② xx

①

⑤ slabs

⑤

150' 5.8

④

80' 5.10

③

80' 5.8+

②

160' 5.7+

①

5.6

160'

③

5.6

140'

④

bushy ledge

huge
cleft

40' 200'

To
Black Dagger

approach

right (north) of the prominent left-facing corner system. **Pitch 1** (5.6): Climb up and left on a light-colored face. Belay in a lower-angle area. 160'. **Pitch 2** (5.7+): Go up and slightly left along cracks and the face to the base of the huge left-facing corner system. 160'. **Pitch 3** (5.8+): Start up a flake left of the main corner, then go up past 2 bolts to a ledge. 80'. **Pitch 4** (5.10): Fret and worry your way up the corner to a belay ledge. 80'. **Pitch 5** (5.8): Go up the corner, then move left into another corner system. Follow that corner system to a belay ledge. 150'. **Pitch 6** (5.7+): Continue up along obvious features. **Descent:** Go left (south) from the top of the route and go down the Gunsight (the notch between the Brownstone Wall and the Rainbow Wall).

*4. **The Nightcrawler** (5.10) FA: Jorge and Joanne Urioste; April 1978. Don't be lured onto this route without a large Friend or two and two ropes for rappelling. Begin on a bushy ledge about 40' above the ground and 200' left of an obvious break in Brownstone Wall. The route takes the large, right-facing corner system formed by a huge flake leaning against the wall. This portion of the wall is in the sun most of the day, but the corner pitches will be shaded. **Pitch 1** (5.6): Follow easy cracks up and slightly left for 140', then traverse about 10' left to a bolt belay. 165'. **Pitch 2** (5.9): Climb the huge, right-facing corner system up to a bolted belay stance, worming up a chimney en route. 130'. **Pitch 3** (5.10): Stem and lieback up the amazing corner, passing 6 bolts to a bolt anchor. 90'. **Pitch 4** (5.10): Continue up the corner past 2 bolts and more liebacking to the top of the giant, hourglass-shaped flake. Bolt belay. 75'. **Descent:** Do four rappels using two ropes (watch out for stuck ropes in the crack just below the third anchor).

5. **Time's Up** (5.11+) FA: The Uriostes; 1985. This 5-pitch route climbs the left side of the huge hourglass-shaped flake leaning against the wall (*The Nightcrawler* climbs the right side). Not much is known about the route other than what is shown on the topo.

6. **Bad Guys Approaching** (5.10+ A0) FA: Paul Van Betten, Robert Finlay, Nick Nordblom; 1989. This 4-pitch route climbs the next major corner system to the left of *Time's Up*. Bring lots of 3-inch pieces to protect the fourth pitch. **Pitch 1** (5.10-): Climb a crack system. **Pitch 2** (5.10 A0): Move right, then climb a left-facing corner to its top. Pendulum about 15' to the right then climb up to a belay. **Pitch 3** (5.8): Climb up to a big ledge. **Pitch 4** (5.10+): Move right and climb the huge, left-facing corner to its top. **Descent:** Rappel?

*7. **The Black Dagger** (5.7+ PG) FA: Joe Herbst, Rick Wheeler; 1977. A sharp route. This route is located on the left (south) side of Brownstone Wall. Bring large gear for Pitch 3. The route is in the sun most of the day during the spring and summer. The white lump of rock mentioned in the approach

JUNIPER CANYON
BROWNSTONE WALL
THE BLACK DAGGER (5.7+ PG)

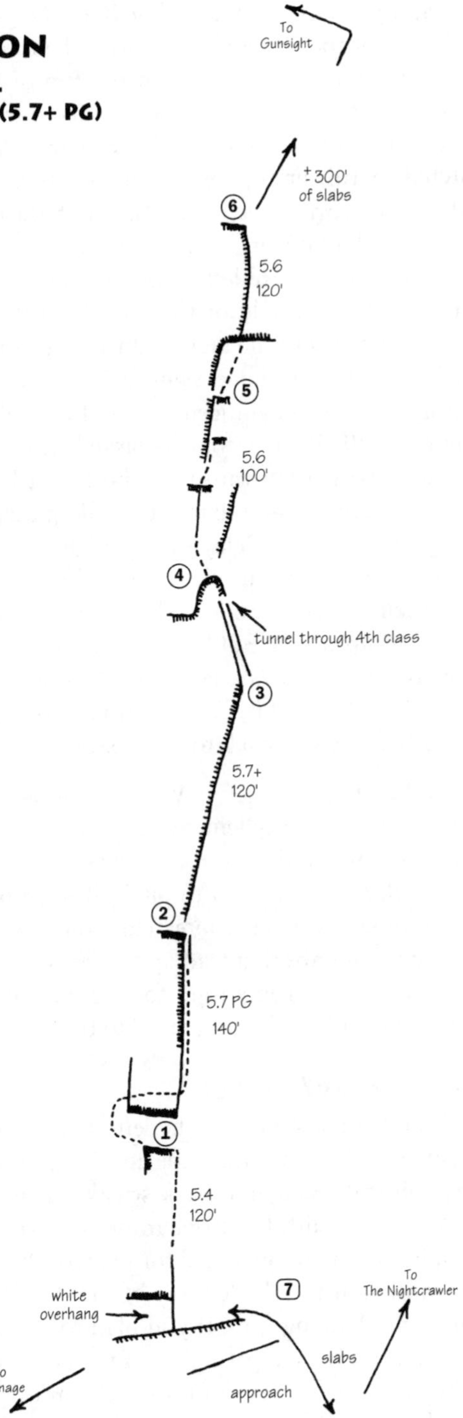

To
Gunsight

± 300'
of slabs

6

5.6
120'

5

5.6
100'

4

tunnel through 4th class

3

5.7+
120'

2

5.7 PG
140'

1

5.4
120'

white
overhang

7

To
The Nightcrawler

slabs

To
Drainage

approach

description obscures most of *The Black Dagger*. Go through bushes below and right of the white lump (cairn), then up an open talus slope. Follow easy slabs up and left to reach the top of the lump from its right side. Traverse left (south) across more slabs to the obvious right-facing corner system near the left edge of Brownstone Wall. Start at an easy-looking crack/dihedral just right of a white overhang. This is directly below a huge right-facing corner. **Pitch 1** (5.4): Climb the crack and easy face to a belay atop a block that is just below a prominent white roof. 120'. **Pitch 2** (5.7 PG): An airy traverse left from the block starts the pitch. Climb up to a crack on the left side of the roof (scary), then traverse back right on varnished plates to the main right-facing corner system. Continue up this to a ledge below the huge, right-facing corner. 140'. **Pitch 3** (5.7+): Lieback and stem up the magnificent corner for a full pitch. Belay at the base of a chimney. 120'. **Pitch 4** (fourth-class): Wiggle up the very easy and aesthetic chimney, exiting left through a hole to a huge ledge. 80'. **Pitch 5** (5.6): From the top of the pillar, climb the plated face to a low-angle, right-facing crack/corner. Belay on the highest ledge, just below a roof. 100'. **Pitch 6** (5.6): Climb up the face to the roof, then pull over this into the right-facing corner. Follow the corner to a large ledge. 120'. **Descent:** Scramble up about 300' of very easy cracks and slabs to the top of Brownstone Wall. Walk left (south) along the top of the formation to the notch (The Gunsight). A very straightforward but bushy descent down the gully takes you back to your pack.

8. **Paiute Pillar** (5.9 PG) FA: Vincent Poirier, Andrew Fulton; April 1998. This supposedly excellent route climbs the right (northeast) shoulder of The Rainbow Wall. The route crosses an old Urioste route named *Bird Hunter Buttress* on the fifth pitch. Bring a 60-meter rope and a good selection of gear for this route. This route apparently starts to the right of the approach slabs that lead up to *The Rainbow Wall* proper at a band of red rock. See the route topo for more details. To descend, go southwest and downclimb to slabs that lead to the Gunsight at the top of the canyon.

THE RAINBOW WALL

The Rainbow Wall sits high on the left (south) side of Juniper Canyon and is clearly visible from the Calico Hills and Sandstone Quarry areas. It is characterized by colorful green and black streaks, as well as huge red arches on the right portion of the cliff. Only one route is thoroughly described (the only one I've done), but topos are included for most of the other recorded routes on the wall. The wall is in the shade most of the day and takes 3 to 4 hours to approach if you're hauling gear. If you plan to spend the night on the wall, you need to obtain a bivouac permit from the BLM visitor center. Depending on where you park (Pine Creek or Oak Creek parking areas on the loop road or at the old Oak Creek Campground), you'll need to hike to the mouth of Juniper

JUNIPER CANYON
PAIUTE PILLAR (5.9 PG)

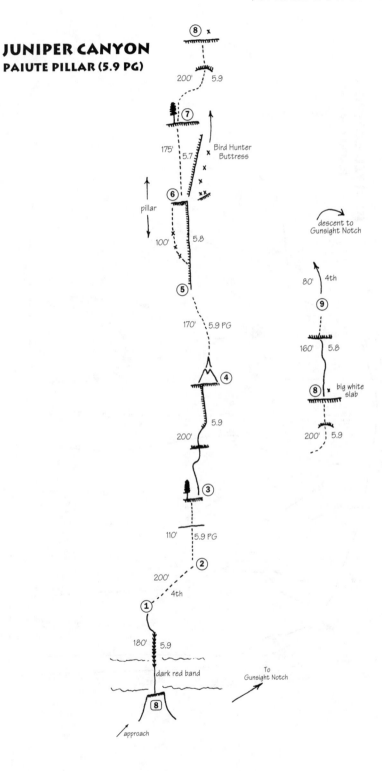

8 x

200'   5.9

175'   5.7   Bird Hunter
               Buttress

        x

pillar   x
                x x

6
                x
100'   x
        x   5.8
        x

5

170'   5.9 PG

descent to
Gunsight Notch

4   80'   4th

        5.9   9

200'   160'   5.8

3   8   x   big white
                                 slab
110'   5.9 PG
                       200'   5.9
200'

2

4th

1

180'   5.9

dark red band   To
                             Gunsight Notch

8

approach

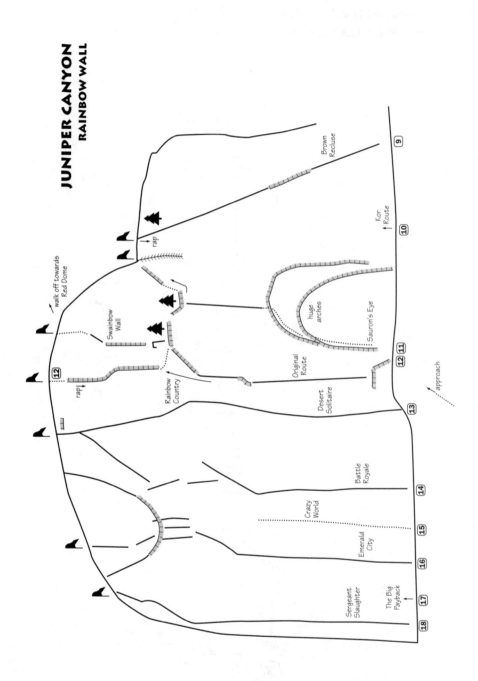

JUNIPER CANYON
RAINBOW WALL

Brown Recluse

walk off towards Red Dome

rap

Swainbow Wall

Rainbow Country

rap

Kor Route

Original Route

huge arches

Sauron's Eye

Desert Solitaire

approach

Battle Royale

Crazy World

Emerald City

Sergeant Slaughter

The Big Payback

9 10 11 12 13 14 15 16 17 18

Canyon. Follow the Juniper Creek drainage upstream to a big, white lump of rock that divides the drainage in two. Climb slabs up left (south) for about 600 lung-searing yards to the base of the wall. Routes are listed from right (west) to left (toward the road).

9. **Brown Recluse** (5.11) FA: Roxanna Brock, Brian McCray; June 1998. This 9-pitch free route goes up near the right side of the Rainbow Wall. It is primarily face-climbing with a few awkward cracks. Bring wires (extra of the smaller sizes), TCUs (doubles on the smaller sizes), a set of cams up to a #3, and two ropes for the descent.

10. **The Kor Route** (5.? A?) FA: Layton Kor, Allison Sheets; 1989. Supposedly, Kor and Sheets did a route somewhere on the wall to the right of the huge, red arches.

11. **Sauron's Eye** (5.10+ R A4) FA: Brian McCray and partners; February 1999. This route required several attempts, including one that resulted in a serious accident. Bring the following rack to supplement the 6 bolts and 3 rivets on the climb: Triple TCUs (#00–4), double cams (#2–3.5), single cams (#4–6), many small to medium nuts, several large stoppers, one set of Ballnuts, many hooks (including a large one), double cam hooks, Beaks (11), RURPs (3), knifeblades (17), and Lost Arrows (6). Rappel *Brown Recluse.*

*12. **Original Route** (5.9 A2 or 5.12) FA: Joe Herbst, Larry Hamilton; April 1973. FFA: Leo Henson; April 1994. This route can be done in a day, but the view of the Las Vegas lights from the bivouac ledge can't be beat! In 1993, the route had a number of bolts added to it during the first free ascent. Many of these bolts were subsequently removed. See *Onsight Magazine* (issue 2) for an account of the first free ascent. Bring a set of Friends, a #4 Camalot, a set of TCUs, one set of wires, a set of RPs, and lots of slings. The route starts at an obvious dihedral system roughly 100' left of the prominent red arches on the right side of the wall. **Pitch 1** (5.6): Start left of a pine tree and wander up the face to a belay ledge. 75'. **Pitch 2** (5.7 A2 or 5.12-): Free climb up, then free or aid a blank section of dihedral (bolts). Continue up to a bolted belay anchor. 75'. **Pitch 3** (5.8 A2 or 5.11+): Lieback a wide crack (5.8), then free or aid up the corner to a sloping ledge. 75'. **Pitch 4** (5.9 A2 or 5.11): Free and/or aid up the dihedral past a ledge to belay stance above a wide crack. 85'. **Pitch 5** (5.7 A1 or 5.11): Climb a loose flake, then aid and/or free up around a ceiling. Belay off bolts in the dihedral above. 110'. **Pitch 6** (5.4 A1 or 5.11): Continue up the dihedral past bushes to an easy chimney (see Variation 1) and climb this chimney to a ledge with small trees and bolts. 100'. (Note: This is the lower left edge of Faith Ledge, a long, multitiered ledge that provides an adequate bivouac spot at its upper end, at the mouth of The Bat Cave. There is room for two to sit, but if you bring hammocks, better

JUNIPER CANYON
RAINBOW WALL
BROWN RECLUSE (5.11)

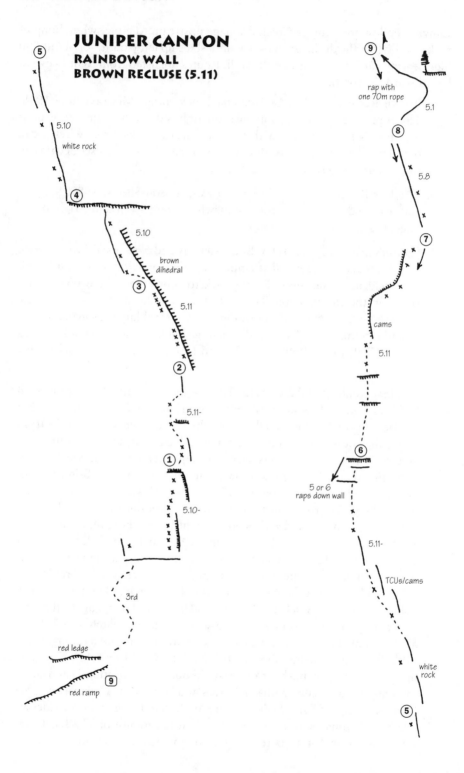

5

5.10
white rock

4

5.10

brown
dihedral

3

5.11

2

5.11-

1

5.10-

3rd

red ledge

9

red ramp

9

rap with
one 70m rope

5.1

8

5.8

7

cams

5.11

6

5 or 6
raps down wall

5.11-

TCUs/cams

white
rock

5

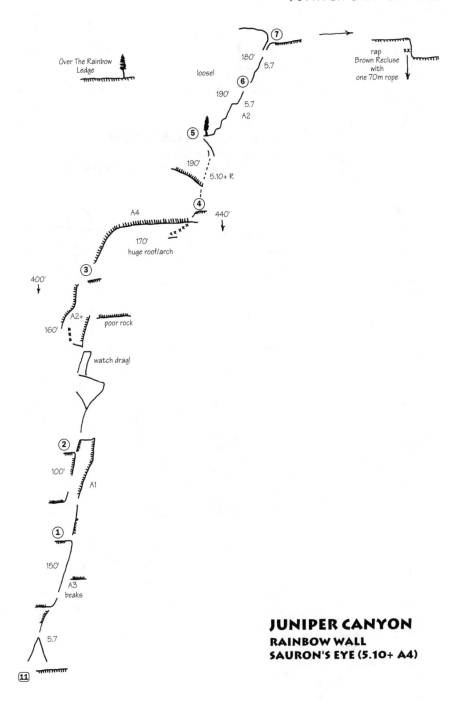

rap
Brown Recluse
with
one 70m rope

7

180'   5.7

loose!

6

190'   5.7
              A2

5

190'

5.10+ R

Over The Rainbow
Ledge

4

A4   440'

170'
huge roof/arch

3

400'

A2+   poor rock

160'

watch drag!

2

100'

A1

1

150'

A3
beaks

5.7

11

JUNIPER CANYON
RAINBOW WALL
SAURON'S EYE (5.10+ A4)

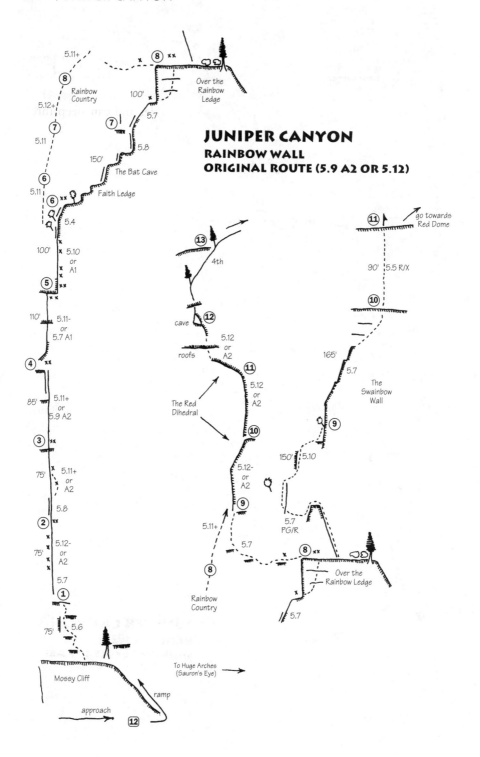

JUNIPER CANYON
RAINBOW WALL
ORIGINAL ROUTE (5.9 A2 OR 5.12)

accommodations can be had. **Pitch 7** (5.8): Follow broken ledges up right, then climb a left-facing corner to a stance just left of a chimney. 150'. **Pitch 8** (5.7): Struggle up the short chimney to a ledge (bolt), then traverse around right and climb an easy but dirty face to a long, flat ledge with a huge pine tree on its right end. Belay from bolts. 100'. (Note: This is Over the Rainbow Ledge. It is about 75' long, 7' wide, and can sleep three people comfortably. This is the bivouac ledge to shoot for—the view is great!) **Pitch 9** (5.7): From the left end of the ledge (see Variation 2), traverse left (occasionally with tension) on ledges past a bolt, then face-climb up to the base of the Red Dihedral and a bolt belay. **Pitch 10** (A2 or 5.12-): Aid or free up the huge, left-facing corner to an anchor. **Pitch 11** (A2 or 5.12): Continue up the arching corner past bolts to a bolted belay. **Pitch 12** (A2 or 5.12): Negotiate the summit roofs to belay in a cave, or if the rope drag isn't bad, continue up to a tree just below the top of the wall. **Pitch 13** (fourth-class): Scramble to the top.

Variation 1/Rainbow Country (5.12+) FA: Dan McQuade; December 1996. This is reportedly a more direct and aesthetic line up the middle part of the *Original Route*. This variation avoids parts of pitches 6 through 9 and comes into the bottom of the Red Dihedral. The pitch ratings of the variation are 5.11b, 5.11c, 5.12d, and 5.11d.

Variation 2/The Swainbow Wall (5.10 PG13): FRA: Jeff Rickerl, Mark Hoffman, Todd Swain; June 1992. This provides a direct finish to the *Original Route*. **Pitch 9** (5.10 PG): From the center of Over the Rainbow Ledge, climb a shallow, left-leaning dihedral to a pedestal. Traverse down and left to the arête (no pro), then up a low-angled face to an obvious, right-facing flake. Climb the flake, angle right into the big, left-facing corner, then up this past a ledge to a hanging belay from a tree (nuts and Friends). 150'. **Pitch 10** (5.7): Follow the corner past numerous ledges, then step around right. Angle up and right across a face to a belay on a sloping ledge in white rock. This is a difficult belay anchor to set up; you'll need lots of TCUs and Friends. 165'. **Pitch 11** (5.5 R/X): Climb the scary vertical face above the belay to the summit. Good training for the Eiger! 90'.

Descent: You should be able to rappel the route with two ropes. If not, walk south about 300 yards toward the red domes behind The Rainbow Wall, which are at the rim of Oak Creek Canyon. From the top of the red domes, angle slightly southwest down a ridge with rock outcrops. Curve around left (south) onto white rock and follow the ridge and slabs down left to the top of the Oak Creek drainage. It should take about 30 to 40 minutes from the summit of The Rainbow Wall to the top of Oak Creek Canyon. Follow the drainage down and east (toward the road) past numerous waterholes. You eventually exit the drainage on its right (south) bank and follow a trail and the old road back to your vehicle. If you parked on the spur road, you exit left (north) from the drainage and head toward the road. Not only is this descent quicker than going back down Juniper Canyon, you're much more likely to encounter water in Oak Creek to soak in!

13. **Desert Solitaire** (5.9 A3+) FA: Nick Nordblom; roped solo, Spring 1989. This route climbs the first major crack system to the left of the *Original Route*. Bring knifeblades (9); Lost Arrows (8); small angles (3); double sets of TCUs, Friends, and wires; one set each of RPs and HBs; hooks (including a bathook); one small copperhead; one Crack Tack; one birdbeak; and several rivet hangers. There were a total of 40 holes drilled on the route: 14 belay bolts, 18 rivets, and 8 for pro.

14. **Battle Royale** (5.9 A2) FA: Richard Harrison, Nick Nordblom, Wendell Broussard; Spring 1983. Climbs a broken, right-facing corner through the obvious black waterstreaks. Not recommended.

15. **Crazy World** (5.7 A4) FA: Bart Groendycke, Todd Alston; May 1992. One of the hardest aid routes on the wall at present. This climb doesn't go to the top of the cliff and has fixed rappel stations. The route climbs just left of the prominent black waterstreaks on the wall. The first ascent party recommends fixing three ropes and sleeping at the base of the route. Gear list: short thin knifeblades (7), RURPs (15), Lost Arrows (5), hooks (2), one Fish hook, 3/8" bolt hangers (3), #1 copperheads (25), #2 copperheads (30), #3 copperheads (20), #4 copperheads (10), extra 3/8" copperheads (25) for ladders, three sets of RPs, two sets of stoppers, three sets of TCUs, two #1 Camalots, and one each #2 to #4 Camalots.

Climber on *Crazy World* (5.7 A4).
GROENDYCKE COLLECTION

16. **Emerald City** (5.10 A2) FA: Randal Grandstaff, John Thacker; Spring 1983. The route climbs a series of

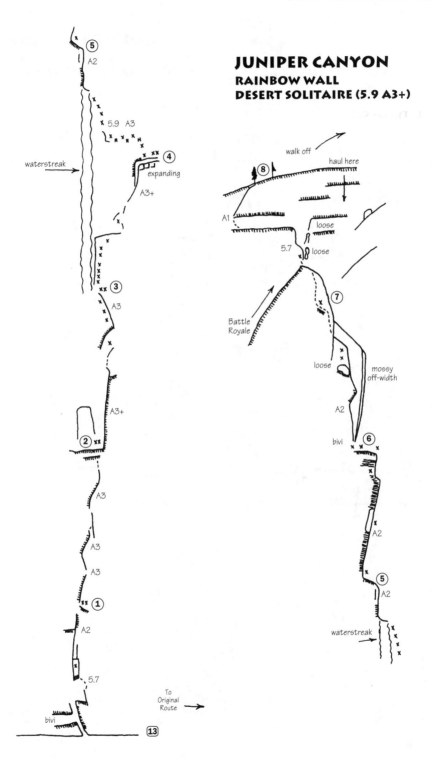

JUNIPER CANYON
RAINBOW WALL
DESERT SOLITAIRE (5.9 A3+)

⑤ A2

5.9 A3

waterstreak

④ expanding

A3+

③

A3

A3+

② xx

A3

A3

A3

① xx

A2

5.7

bivi

To Original Route →

⑬

walk off

⑧ haul here

A1

loose

5.7 loose

⑦

Battle Royale

loose mossy off-width

A2

bivi ⑥

A2

⑤ A2

waterstreak

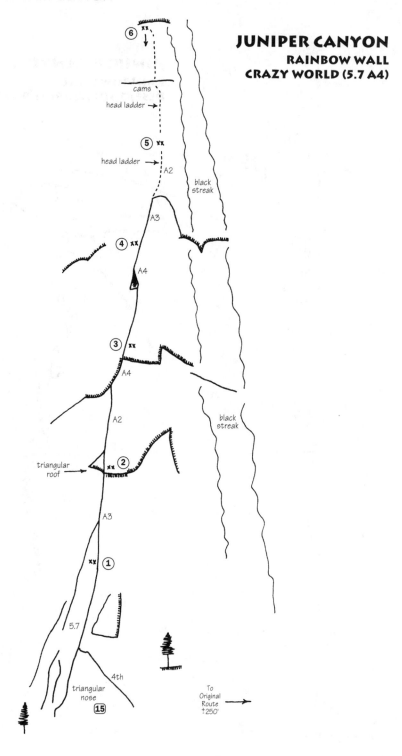

JUNIPER CANYON
RAINBOW WALL
CRAZY WORLD (5.7 A4)

JUNIPER CANYON
RAINBOW WALL
EMERALD CITY (5.10 A2)

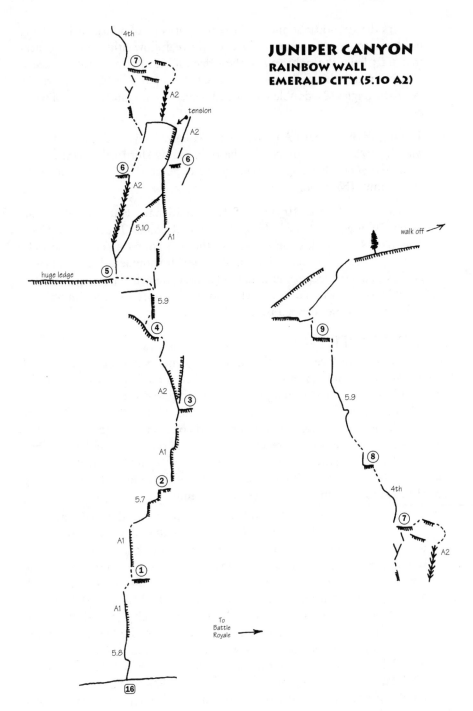

corners that trend right and lead to the right edge of a large ledge. A big black waterstreak comes off this ledge. Above, follow either of two corners that start from the right end of the ledge and lead to a shattered recess. Climb through this to the top. Gear needed: knifeblades (4), Lost Arrows (4), baby angles (2), double sets of TCUs and Friends, and one set of wires and RPs.

17. **The Big Payback** (5.10 A3) FA: Kevin Daniels, Tony Sartin, Dave Evans; March 1998. This route climbs the right-facing slot to the right of *Sergeant Slaughter*, then continues up right along right-leaning weaknesses to the summit. (No topo.)

18. **Sergeant Slaughter** (5.10 A3 or 5.12) FA: Richard Harrison, Paul Van Betten; Winter 1984. FFA: Brian McCray, Roxanna Brock; May 1998. The first ascent of this route was also the first winter ascent of the wall. Follow the corner systems that parallel the left shoulder of the wall for 6 pitches to a large ledge. Climb behind a large, detached pillar, gaining the shoulder of the wall. Follow cracks and corners up, aiming for an obvious right-facing corner capped by a roof.

CLOUD TOWER

The next routes are located on Cloud Tower, which sits near the mouth of Juniper Canyon. Cloud Tower has a distinctive red summit and is located at the top of a prominent, right-leaning ramp. The ramp and the tower are clearly visible from the Pine Creek parking area on the left (south) side of Juniper Canyon. These routes generally face north and consequently receive very little sun. It takes about an hour to reach the top of the ramp from either the Pine Creek or Oak Creek parking areas. If you approach from Oak Creek, contour along the base of the mountain to reach the base of the ramp rather than trying to angle up across the hillside to intersect the ramp.

*19. **Cloud Tower** (5.11+) FA: Paul Van Betten, Richard Harrison, Nick Nordblom; Spring 1983. Called *The Astroman* of Red Rocks by some; the final pitch is one of the very best in the area. Bring a good selection of wires, extra TCUs, a full set of cams, and two ropes. Start about 200' down from the top of the ramp and 100' right of *Crimson Chrysalis*. **Pitch 1** (5.8): Climb a left-facing corner to a belay. 150'. **Pitch 2** (5.8): Continue up the corner and belay on a bushy ledge. 100'. **Pitch 3** (5.10-): Power up the beautiful straight-in hand crack. 150'. **Pitch 4** (5.11+): Stem up the right-facing, right-leaning corner with a tips crack in its back to a ledge with 2 bolts and a loose block. Bring lots of TCUs for this crux pitch. 120'. **Pitch 5** (5.10): Pull over a roof, then up a hand-and-fist crack in the middle of a face to a belay ledge. 140'. **Pitch 6** (5.10+): Struggle up a scary off-width to the top of the tower. 60'. **Pitch 7** (5.11+): Climb the incredible right-facing corner with a hand-and-finger crack in its back. The crux

JUNIPER CANYON
RAINBOW WALL
SERGEANT SLAUGHTER
(5.10 A3 OR 5.12)

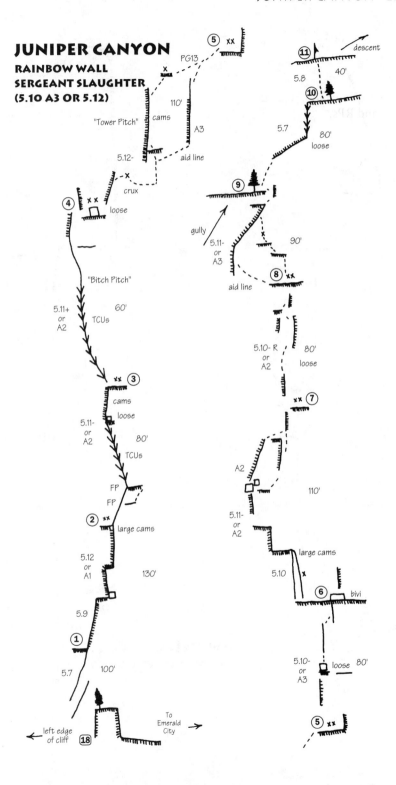

PG13

110'

"Tower Pitch"

cams

A3

5.12-

aid line

crux

④ loose

"Bitch Pitch"

5.11+
or
A2

60'

TCUs

③

cams

loose

5.11-
or
A2

80'

TCUs

FP

FP

② large cams

5.12
or
A1

130'

5.9

①

5.7   100'

left edge
of cliff   ⑱

To
Emerald
City →

⑤ xx

descent →

⑪

5.8   40'

⑩

5.7

80'
loose

⑨

gully

5.11-
or
A3

aid line

90'

⑧ xx

5.10- R
or
A2

80'
loose

xx ⑦

A2

110'

5.11-
or
A2

large cams

5.10

⑥   bivi

5.10-
or
A3

loose   80'

⑤ xx

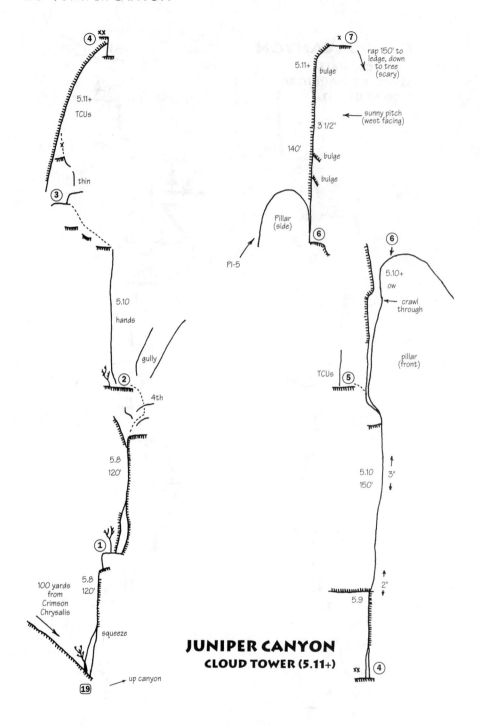

JUNIPER CANYON
CLOUD TOWER (5.11+)

is at the top of the pitch, reaching the bolts. 160'. **Descent:** Rappel straight down (not down the route), keeping right of the tower. It'll be a bit dicey to reach a couple of the anchors even with 60-meter ropes.

*20. Crimson Chrysalis (5.8+) FA: Jorge and Joanne Urioste; October 1979. A superb route that requires some crack climbing skills and stamina. Bring two ropes and a good selection of bigger gear. Start about 100' downhill (west and up canyon) from the top of the prominent approach ramp. **Pitch 1** (5.7): Climb the obvious crack and right-facing corner to a belay anchor. 125'. **Pitch 2** (5.8-): Continue up the crack/corner past 4 bolts to another anchor in a recess. 90'. **Pitch 3** (5.8+): Jam up the same fissure past 3 bolts and a steep section to a hanging belay from bolts. 60'. **Pitch 4** (5.8): Worm up a chimney (bolt), then follow lower-angle thin cracks through two bulges to a belay ledge. 90'. **Pitch 5** (5.8+): Climb a finger-and-hand crack past 1 bolt to a belay station at a small, good ledge. 90'. **Pitch 6** (5.6): Go up left past 2 bolts, then up and right past 3 more bolts to the anchor. 90'. **Pitch 7** (5.6+): Nine bolts will get you to the belay, which is 25' into the red rock. 110'. **Pitch 8** (5.7): Climb up 25' to a ramp (bolt), traverse straight right, then climb up left along a ramp. Climb the chocolate-colored face past 3 more bolts to the belay. 75'. **Pitch 9** (5.8): Climb up and right on a plated wall past 4 bolts and a ceiling to the shoulder of the tower. 80'. **Descent:** Rappel with two ropes, being careful not to get the ropes stuck in the crack.

21. Hook, Climb, and Whimper (5.10- R) FA: Bruce Lella, Mike Carr; March 1989. This route climbs the face to the left of the first 4 pitches of *Crimson Chrysalis*. Bring wires, TCUs, extra cams up to #2.5, and two ropes. **Pitch 1** (5.8): Climb the face and discontinuous cracks past 2 bolts to an anchor. **Pitch 2** (5.9): Climb a crack and corner system above the belay to its top (5.8). Move up and left to a belay. **Pitch 3** (5.10-): Go up and right past 3 bolts to a ledge (crux). Angle up and left from the ledge (5.9 R) past a bolt to the belay anchor. **Pitch 4** (5.8 R): Wander up the face above the belay to a bolt, then traverse straight right past another bolt to the fourth belay on *Crimson Chrysalis*. **Descent:** Rappel *Crimson Chrysalis* with two ropes.

GINGER BUTTRESS

The next routes are located several hundred yards to the left (southeast) of the Cloud Tower ramp on the right edge of Rainbow Mountain (the peak that separates Juniper and Oak Creek canyons). A very prominent black waterstreak can be seen leading down light-colored rock from an obvious ledge in this area. *Power Failure* ascends this waterstreak, which is also the descent route for *Ginger Cracks*. Like Cloud Tower, these routes may be approached from either the Pine Creek or Oak Creek parking areas on the loop road. From the base of the

JUNIPER CANYON
CRIMSON CHRYSALIS (5.8+)
(NOT ALL BOLTS SHOWN)

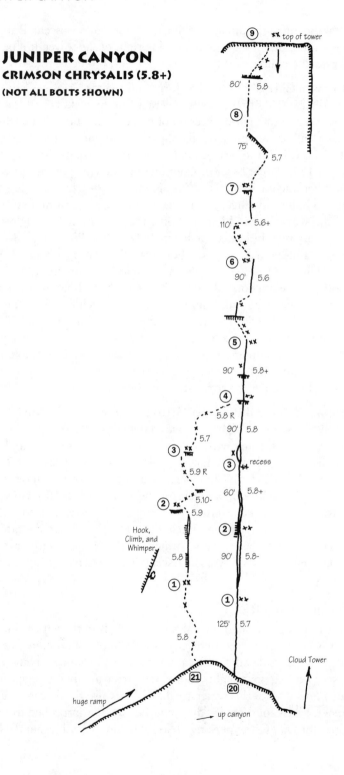

Cloud Tower ramp, head up and left (south) toward the obvious buttress. It takes a bit over an hour to reach the bases of these sunny routes.

22. **Ginger Cracks** (5.9) FA: Mark Moore, Lars Holbeck; 1977. This popular climb follows a prominent crack system to the right of the black waterstreak and a curving chimney system. Bring wires, TCUs, a full set of cams with extra of the smaller sizes, and two ropes. **Pitch 1** (5.7): Climb a crack to a ledge with a tree (5.7). Step right and climb up a bit, then move left and climb past an alcove to the top of a flake. 130'. **Pitch 2** (5.8): Step down and right from the flake to a crack. Climb the crack past a chimney and overhang (5.8), then continue up an obvious crack to a ledge at the base of a right-facing corner. 150'. **Pitch 3** (5.7): Climb the right-facing corner and belay above a bush. 80'. **Pitch 4** (5.9): Move up and right into a crack, which is followed up to a bolt. Continue up the crack to a belay. 150'. **Pitch 5** (5.8): Wander up the face on less-than-perfect rock to the higher of two ledges. 160'. **Pitch 6** (fourth class): Climb a corner to another ledge, then step left and climb up, keeping left of a bushy gully. Belay on a ledge at the base of a left-facing corner. 130'. **Pitch 7** (5.6): Climb the short left-facing corner to its top. Move right and continue up the larger, left-facing corner to the summit. 110'. **Descent:** Do one rappel to the south and scramble down to the top of the obvious black waterstreak. Do three

Rainbow Mountain

Ginger Buttress

Cloud Tower

Cloud Tower/ Ginger Buttress Area

Original Route Rainbow Wall

24

20

approach

22

To Brownstone and Rainbow Walls

JUNIPER CANYON
GINGER BUTTRESS
GINGER CRACKS (5.9)

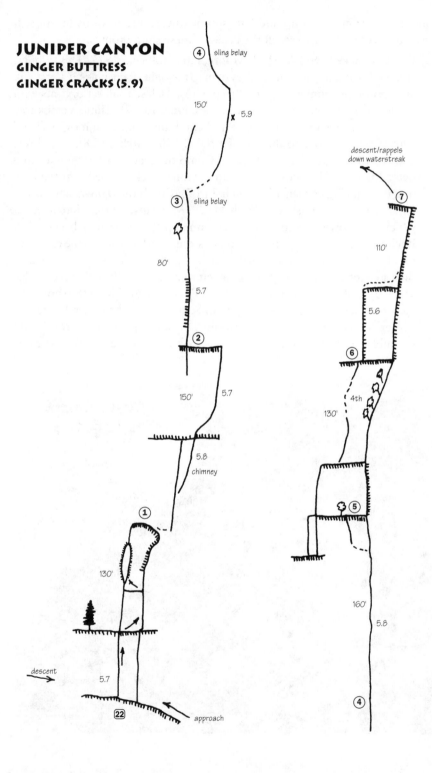

④ sling belay

150'

x 5.9

descent/rappels
down waterstreak

⑦

③ sling belay

110'

80'

5.7

5.6

②

⑥

150' 5.7

4th

130'

5.8
chimney

①

🌲🌺 ⑤

130'

🌲

160'

5.8

descent

5.7

④

㉒

approach

double-rope rappels down the waterstreak (the general line of *Power Failure*).

23. **Unimpeachable Groping** (5.10+) FA: Michael Clifford, Jorge Urioste; November 1998 to April 1999. The route requires about 15 quickdraws and a small nut or TCU to protect some easy ground. The approach is the same as for *Ginger Cracks*. Continue uphill from the start of *Ginger Cracks* along the east face of Rainbow Mountain toward the obvious black waterstreak (the descent for *Ginger Cracks* and the approximate line of *Power Failure*). About 200 yards uphill at the base of the wall is a flat area with a 50-foot-tall pine tree. The route begins by climbing the tree until the first bolt can be used. The route is steep, and all 6 pitches are about 5.10. At the end of the third pitch is a huge ledge where you can untie. The crux is the sustained nature of the route and a roof problem getting off the huge ledge to start Pitch 4. **Descent:** Rappel the route. (No topo.)

*24. **Power Failure** (5.10) FA (Pitch 1): Bill Hotz. FA (Pitch 2): Joanne and Jorge Urioste. FA (Pitch 3): Kevin Campbell, Joanne and Jorge Urioste, Teresa Krolak, Bill Hotz. This is supposed to be a very good route. Bring wires, TCUs, cams up to #2.5, and two ropes. Start at the bottom of the *Ginger Cracks* rappel route about 50' right of the prominent waterstreak. **Pitch 1** (5.8+): Climb up and right past about 6 bolts to an anchor on a ledge. 80'. **Pitch 2** (5.10): Go straight up the smooth white face past about 6 bolts to an anchor. 120'. **Pitch 3** (5.9): Ascend a crack in a corner to the large ledge at the top of the waterstreak. 140'. **Descent:** Rappel with two ropes. (No topo.)

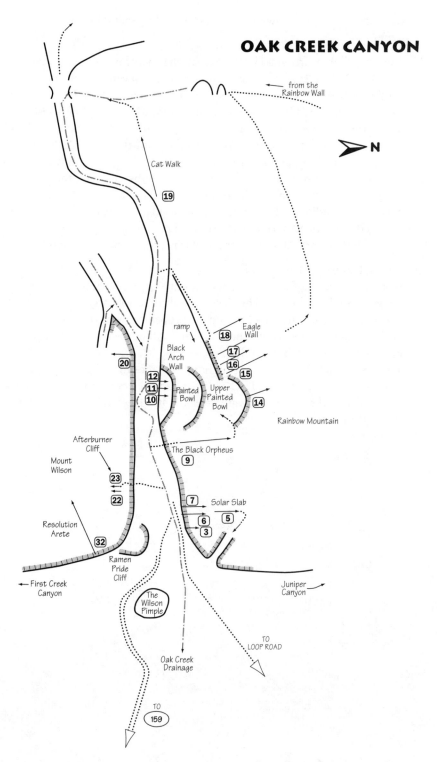

OAK CREEK CANYON

Cat Walk

19

from the
Rainbow Wall

N

ramp

Eagle
Wall

18

17

16

15

Black
Arch
Wall

20

12

11

10

Painted
Bowl

Upper
Painted
Bowl

14

Rainbow Mountain

Afterburner
Cliff

The Black Orpheus

9

Mount
Wilson

23

22

7

Solar Slab

6

5

Resolution
Arete

32

3

← First Creek
Canyon

Ramen
Pride
Cliff

Juniper
Canyon

The
Wilson
Pimple

TO
LOOP ROAD

Oak Creek
Drainage

TO
159

OAK CREEK CANYON

This canyon is on a par with Black Velvet, harboring some of the best routes at Red Rocks; however, the approaches are generally much longer than Black Velvet. Routes are described from right (north) to left (south) starting at the Solar Slab Area and ending on Mount Wilson.

There are two ways to approach the climbs in Oak Creek Canyon. 1) Start at the Oak Creek Canyon parking area, which is located at the end of a spur road leading off the scenic loop road. While this trailhead and adjoining trail provide a faster approach than the old Oak Creek Road, the opening and closing times of the loop road may prove problematic for those attempting the longer routes. From the parking area it is about a 30-minute hike to the mouth of the canyon. 2) It is also possible to walk the old Oak Creek Road, which begins at the old Oak Creek Campground. The old campground is located 1.4 miles south (toward Blue Diamond) on Nevada 159 from the exit of the scenic

Mount Wilson
& Oak Creek Canyon

Mount Wilson

First Creek Canyon

Rainbow Mountain

Rainbow Buttress

loop road. From the old campground, walk 1.5 miles along the obvious road-bed to the mouth of the canyon.

Both approaches go by the huge dirt mound situated at the canyon mouth. The mound is called Wilson Pimple. These trails then drop into the main Oak Creek drainage, which is followed some distance up-canyon.

SOLAR SLAB AREA

On the far right (north) side of the canyon is a huge, obvious gully running about 500 feet up the cliff to the base of a white face. The gully is *Solar Slab Gully* and the white face above is *Solar Slab*. About 200 feet to the right (to-ward the road) of the gully is a large pinnacle with a huge boulder on the summit. This is *The Friar*. To the left of *Solar Slab Gully* is a huge, varnished right-facing corner. This is the line of *Beulah's Book*. These routes are in the sun and take about 45 minutes to approach from the Oak Creek Canyon parking area on the loop road.

From the Wilson Pimple, follow the old roadbed and/or a trail up toward the canyon until the trail drops into the streambed. Walk up the streambed about 150 yards, then follow a trail 200 yards up to the base of the routes. The trail ascends the hillside about 75 yards left (west) of the red rock band in the hillside.

*1. **Red Zinger** (5.10+) FA: Joe Herbst; 1970s. This route is a classic. Bring a bunch of medium-sized cams and some muscle. About 200' right (east) of *The Friar* pinnacle is an alcove that faces up-canyon (west). This alcove is on the right (north) side of the canyon a few hundred yards from the mouth. *Red Zinger* climbs a striking crack in a small, left-facing corner in this area. The route is not visible from below, but once you're near the base of *Solar Slab Gully*, you can't miss it. **Pitch 1** (5.10+): Climb the crack and corner to a ledge with an anchor. **Pitch 2** (5.10+): Continue up the crack, then traverse left under a ceiling to a right-facing corner. Follow this corner up to an anchor. **Descent:** Rappel.

Note: The corner just left of *Red Zinger* is supposed to be 5.9.

2. **The Friar** (5.9+ PG) FA: Joe Herbst, Tom Kaufman, Steve Allen; April 1977. The first pitch of this route is excellent and a good way to round out a day. This route climbs the front (south) face of a 250' pillar that is to the right of *Solar Slab Gully*. A trail leads over from the gully to the base of the route. Rope up below a varnished dihedral that begins about 10' off the ground. **Pitch 1** (5.7): Climb up onto a ledge at the base of a corner, then climb the varnished dihedral to an obvious ledge. 100'. **Pitch 2** (5.7): From the lower of two ledges (see Variations 1 and 2), move right and climb an obvious crack system to another ledge with an anchor. 90'. **Pitch 3** (5.6 R): From the highest ledge, climb up the face along vertical seams to

the base of the summit boulder. Go left (west) past an anchor to a large ledge between the boulder and the main canyon wall. 90'. **Pitch 4** (5.9 PG): Starting on the overhanging west arête of the boulder, climb up and right (scary), then up to the top. 40'. **Variation 1:** From the higher of the two ledges, you can walk off left (toward *Solar Slab Gully*). This can also be used to toprope the first pitch. **Variation 2** (5.7 PG): From the higher ledge, climb straight up the scary face, keeping about 20' left of the normal

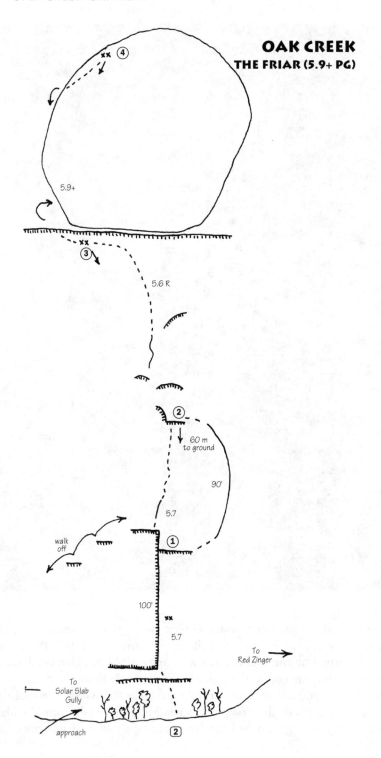

OAK CREEK
THE FRIAR (5.9+ PG)

xx ④

5.9+

xx
③

5.6 R

②
60 m
to ground

90'

5.7

walk
off

①

100'

xx

5.7

To
Red Zinger

To
Solar Slab
Gully

approach

②

Pitch 2 crack. **Descent:** Rappel with one rope as follows: Rappel from an anchor atop the summit boulder. Then rappel from the anchor just under the summit boulder to the anchor atop Pitch 2. And finally, with a 60-meter rope, you can just barely make it from the anchor atop Pitch 2 to a ledge just above the ground. If you have a shorter rope, rappel to the top of Pitch 1, then walk off.

3. **Horndogger Select** (5.8+ PG13) FA: David Pollari, Shawn Pereto; February 1993. FFA: David Pollari, Brian Kaye, Mark ?; February 1993. This route climbs features between *The Friar* and *Solar Slab Gully* to the large terrace. It then follows a discontinuous line of cracks and corners to the right of *Sunflower* (a 5.9 route described in the Urioste guide). Bring a standard rack with cams up to a #4. Start below an obvious crack about 100' right of the base of *Solar Slab Gully*. **Pitch 1** (5.8+): Climb the obvious crack until just below a large overhang. Move right past intermittent cracks and horns to a short white headwall with spots and nubbins. Climb the headwall (5.8+) and belay in the first dark hueco directly above. 165'. **Pitch 2** (5.8): Climb straight up a line of easy huecos to an overhanging bulge about 85' above the belay. Exit left via a left-trending crack (5.8), then continue up to a belay on the first very large ledge. **Pitch 3** (fourth-class): Traverse left over the top of a gully/chimney to a belay at the base of a right-trending fist crack. **Pitch 4** (5.7): Jam up the fist crack (5.7) to ledges below *Solar Slab*. 150'. **Pitch 5** (5.6 R): Climb a short cliff between large ledges (or see Variation) to gain the upper ledge. **Pitch 6:** Ascend discontinuous cracks for about 60' to enter a dark, left-facing corner. Climb to a belay at the top of the corner. 180'. **Pitch 7** (5.8 PG): Go up and right on a steep face past 2 bolts. Continue slightly right to reach a crack, which is followed to an area of dark jugs. 150'. **Pitch 8** (5.7 PG13): Pull past an overhang on scary horns to reach a shallow ledge. Follow this ledge left, moving up to place gear, then down to the ledge again to proceed safely. Continue left until a crack is reached. Belay in the crack. 150'. **Pitch 9** (5.4): Climb the crack and easy corner system. 165'. **Pitch 10** (5.4): Continue up easy terrain to the top. 165'. **Variation** (third-class): You can avoid the short cliff by traversing around it. **Descent:** Either go down the *Solar Slab* descent gully or use the *Solar Slab* rappel route. (No topo.)

*4. **Solar Slab Gully** (5.3) FA: Unknown; 1970s. A great excursion for the novice climber. Most climbers use this as an approach to *Solar Slab* or *Sunflower* (a 5.9 route described in the Urioste guidebook). The route can be rappelled with one rope, and all of the anchors are fixed. The crux section is a short waterfall (usually dry) near the top. Start at the base of an obvious gully about 100' right of a prominent, right-facing corner system (*Beulah's Book*) and 200' left of a freestanding pillar (*The Friar*). **Pitch 1** (5.1): Start at the right-hand chimney, near a small oak tree. Climb

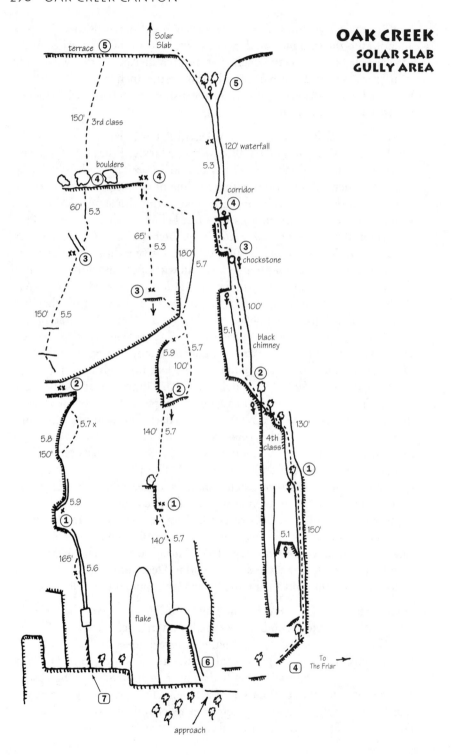

OAK CREEK
SOLAR SLAB
GULLY AREA

Solar Slab

terrace ⑤

⑤

150' 3rd class

120' waterfall

5.3

boulders

⑤

corridor

60' 5.3

④ ④

④

65'

5.3

③ chockstone

180'

5.7

③

100'

③

5.1

black chimney

150' 5.5

②

②

5.9 5.7

②

100'

130'

5.7 x

140' 5.7

4th class

5.8

150'

①

①

5.9

①

5.1

150'

①

165' 5.6

140' 5.7

flake

⑥

⑦

④ To The Friar

approach

straight up a varnished 8- to 12-inch-wide crack, passing ledges at 40' and 80', to yet another ledge with a tree and fixed piton. 150'. **Pitch 2** (fourth-class): From the anchor, scramble up the bush-filled gully, then angle up left along ledges past a gnarled oak tree with rappel slings (80'). Continue up to a huge alcove at the base of a dark, water-worn chimney. 130'. **Pitch 3** (5.1): Climb straight up the black gully/corner and belay on a ledge to the left, just above a chockstone with numerous slings around it. About 60' up the pitch, you pass a rappel anchor made from a natural thread. 100'. **Pitch 4** (third-class): A short and easy chimney leads to a tree in a corridor. 40'. **Pitch 5** (5.3): Walk up the corridor, then ascend a 20-foot waterfall (5.3) to a bolt and piton. Scramble up the gully to the huge terrace. 120'. **Descent:** Rappel the route.

*5. **Solar Slab** (5.6 PG) FA: Joe Herbst, Tom Kaufman, Larry Hamilton; January 1975. If you do this one in the summer, it would be best named "Sizzle Slab." This is a long route, so start early and move fast. Bring a good assortment of gear. This route is on the white face above *Solar Slab Gully*, so the approach entails climbing up to about 5.3 in difficulty. It is an enjoyable excursion for the novice climber. The gully is about 500' long and the most difficult section is near the top. There are fixed anchors up the gully because it is a standard descent route. The gully ends on a large terrace below the white *Solar Slab* and takes roughly 90 minutes for most parties to climb. **Pitch 1** (5.5): Begin on the terrace about 100' up and left from the top of *Solar Slab Gully*. This terrace is below a white slab and an obvious hand crack that doesn't reach the terrace. Climb the slabby face to varnished plates left of the crack. Eventually step right into the crack and follow it to a belay ledge with a prominent bush. 165'. **Pitch 2** (5.5): Follow the left-leaning ramp/chimney, passing a ledge about 90' up (possible belay here). Continue up the corner above, to belay on a ledge with a dead tree. 165'. **Pitch 3** (5.6): Traverse right 15', then climb a finger-and-hand crack to a ledge. Traverse right 10' and follow a small, right-facing corner to a belay stance (#2.5 and #3 Friends and small wires). 130'. **Pitch 4** (5.6): Traverse 10' right and climb a left-facing flake/corner (tricky) to a ceiling. Step down and right to a belay ledge. 150'. **Pitch 5** (5.5): Climb the obvious hand crack directly above, belaying at a stance in the crack (if you have a 60-meter rope, you can combine this pitch with the next). 150'. **Pitch 6** (5.4): Continue up the crack, which becomes a right-facing corner. Belay at the pillar's top. 60'. **Pitch 7** (5.3): Angle right across a white face to an obvious low-angle crack. Climb the crack to a ledge, then move right 10' and climb a right-facing corner to a huge terrace. 150'. **Pitch 8:** Walk and scramble up easy slabs (or see variation) to the base of a varnished, left-leaning dihedral. 150'. **Pitch 9** (5.5): Climb the corner to the top. 100'. **Variation:** If time is short, you can avoid the final pitch by traversing right around the outside corner, then scrambling to the top.

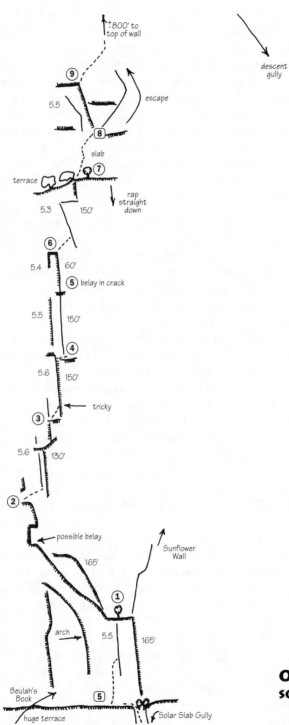

±800' to
top of wall

9

5.5

escape

8

slab

7

terrace

rap
straight
down

5.3   150'

6

5.4   60'

5   belay in crack

5.5   150'

4

5.6   150'

tricky

3

5.6   130'

2

possible belay

Sunflower
Wall

165'

1

arch   5.5   165'

Beulah's
Book

5

huge terrace

Solar Slab Gully

descent
gully

OAK CREEK
SOLAR SLAB (5.6 PG)

Descent: There are several options. 1) The climb has bolted rap stations (set up for two 50-meter ropes) starting about three-fourths of the way up Pitch 7. The rap line goes straight down the face (not down the route), so you won't be able to see the rap stations as you climb. The last two pitches do not have bolted rap stations. If you wish to top out, either downclimb Pitch 8 and Pitch 9, or scramble back left to the top of Pitch 7 via the variation. 2) Walk about 800' up easy slabs to the bright, red rock. Head right (east) and enter a huge gully system. Do two or three rappels depending on your downclimbing ability. The descent can be done unroped, if you can solo down 5.6. In winter, the gully may contain ice and snow because it is in the shade all day. The bottom of the descent gully is about 400' right (east) of the base of *Solar Slab Gully*. 3) For another alternative descent, head down left (west) at the red rock and down into the Painted Bowl (as for *The Black Orpheus*).

*6. **Johnny Vegas** (5.7) FA: Harrison Shull, Tom Cecil, Dave Cox, Todd Hewitt; November 1994. This sunny route has become very popular and rightly so. Bring wires, TCUs, cams up to #3, and two ropes. Start atop a white pillar 25' left of *Solar Slab Gully*. This pillar is just right of a 60-foot-high white flake leaning against the cliff. Scramble up to a stance just below the summit boulder of the pillar and rope up. **Pitch 1** (5.7): Climb the vertical crack system that is 10' left of a dihedral. Follow the crack to its top, then angle up and left across varnished plates. Belay at an anchor at the base of an obvious right-facing corner. 130'. **Pitch 2** (5.7): Climb the varnished right-facing corner above the belay to its top. Go up and slightly right to reach a vertical varnished crack. Continue straight up the face from the top of the crack to a belay anchor on a sloping ledge. 140'. **Pitch 3** (5.7): From the belay, go up and right (see Variation 1) onto obvious varnished plates near the arête. Climb the arête past the right side of a huge roof, then angle back out left above the roof (see Variation 2) to a ledge and an anchor. 100'. **Pitch 4** (5.3): Climb the easy face to another anchor at the edge of the huge terrace. 65'. **Variation 1** (5.9): The original route went up the right-facing corner above the belay, then traversed right to the arête. Watch out for rope drag! **Variation 2** (5.7): Instead of angling back out left above the roof, follow the obvious right-leaning crack. You eventually exit left onto the face and up to the anchor atop Pitch 4. 180'. **Descent:** Rappel the route with two ropes.

*7. **Beulah's Book** (5.9-) FA: Randal Grandstaff, Dave Anderson; 1979. One of the early chapters of this book deals with off-widths. Bring lots of gear up to a #4 Camalot. For fast parties, it's possible to combine this route (or *Johnny Vegas*) with *Solar Slab* to give nearly 1,500' of great climbing. Start 100' left of *Solar Slab Gully* at a series of dihedrals. This climb begins at the dihedral with a large, jammed block about 20' up and an oak tree growing out of the corner's base. **Pitch 1** (5.6): Climb the dihedral past the jammed block (possible belay), then climb the narrow face just left of the chimney past a bolt. Step back right into the chimney and follow it to a ledge. 165'. **Pitch 2** (5.9-): Continue up the corner/chimney system, passing a flaring bomb bay section (bolt, #4 Camalot) to the base of an obvious layback corner. Power up the 5.8+ corner (or see Variation) to a ceiling, then step left to a belay ledge in white rock. 150'. **Pitch 3** (5.5): Wander up the white face, angling slightly right to eventually belay at some left-leaning cracks. 150'. **Pitch 4** (5.3): A short, easy pitch leads up to a huge ledge with large boulders on it. 60'. **Pitch 5** (third-class): Scramble up slabs to the huge terrace where *Solar Slab* starts. 150'. **Variation** (5.7 X): It is possible to climb the face to the right of the corner. **Descent:** Either descend *Johnny Vegas* (two ropes needed) or *Solar Slab Gully* (one rope needed).

8. **Bossa Nova** (5.11) FA: Merlin Larsen, Jim Munson; 1996. The bossa nova is a form of music from Brazil. I know more about that type of music than I do this route! Start about 30' right of *The Black Orpheus*. **Pitch 1** (5.11): Climb a big flake into a dihedral/chimney. Go up and left into an obvious dihedral with a thin finger crack. Belay on a sloping ledge. 150'. **Pitch 2:** Walk right around a fin. Pull onto a sloping shelf (being tall supposedly helps), then go up a right-facing flake (good nut). Climb past an overhang, mantling on holds at the lip. Continue up the face to a right-facing corner made up of stacked blocks. 110'. **Pitch 3** (5.9): Go up and right for about 15', then move back left through an overhang. Climb a plated face above to a big ledge (Pitch 4 or 5 on *The Black Orpheus*). **Descent:** Unknown. (No topo.)

*9. **The Black Orpheus** (5.9+) FA: Joanne and Jorge Urioste; April 1979. A long route with a short crux. The route is named after a 1959 movie that was based on a Greek legend. This route is in the sun most of the day and the approach takes about 1 hour. From The Wilson Pimple, follow the old roadbed and/or a trail toward the canyon until the trail drops into the streambed. Walk up the streambed as it weaves back and forth across the canyon, then go 200 yards past a buttress that comes down to wash level on the right (north) side of the drainage. A steeper, brown wall is on the left side of the canyon at this point, and it is another 350 yards to the fork in the Oak Creek drainage (if you reach that, you've gone too far). Scramble up brown slabs on the right side of the canyon, aiming for an obvious, left-facing corner system with a prominent V-notch in it. The corner starts about 600' above the streambed. The upper part of the approach is over steeper ground, but it's easy. Start in the first left-facing corner that is right of a large, white, recessed wall at the bottom of a huge, brown buttress. Above, a giant, brown, right-facing corner marks the top of the route. The

OAK CREEK
THE BLACK ORPHEUS (5.9+)

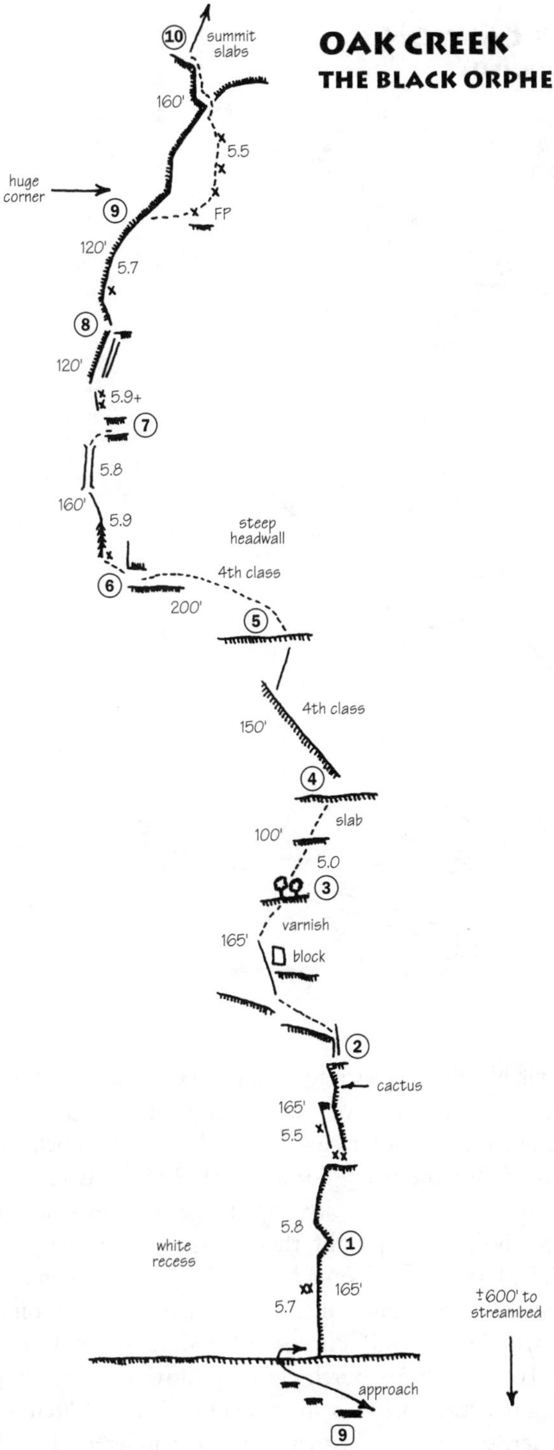

10 summit slabs

160'

5.5
X
FP

huge corner →

9

120'

5.7
X

8

120'

X 5.9+
7

5.8

160'

5.9
X

steep headwall

4th class

6

200'

5

4th class

150'

4

100' slab

5.0

3

varnish

165'

block

2

← cactus

165'

5.5
X
XX

5.8

1

white recess

XX 165'

5.7

±600' to streambed

approach

9

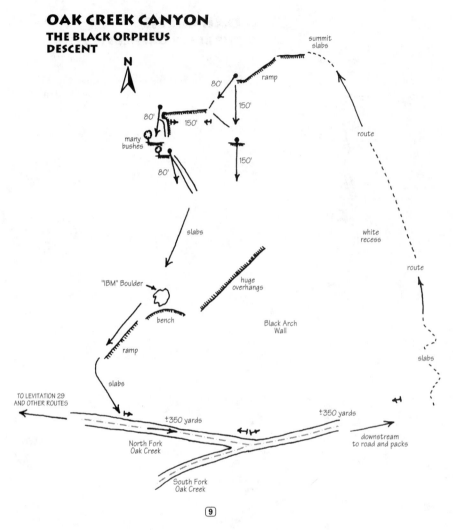

OAK CREEK CANYON
THE BLACK ORPHEUS
DESCENT

N

summit slabs

ramp

80'

150'

80'

150'

many bushes

150'

80'

route

slabs

white recess

route

"IBM" Boulder

huge overhangs

bench

ramp

Black Arch Wall

slabs

slabs

TO LEVITATION 29 AND OTHER ROUTES

±350 yards

±350 yards

downstream to road and packs

North Fork Oak Creek

South Fork Oak Creek

9

brown corner is visible from the vicinity of the old Oak Creek Campground, while the rest of the route is hidden until you're in the canyon. **Pitch 1** (5.7): Climb the left-facing corner past 2 bolts 100' up to a belay in the V-notch (small Friends for the belay). 165'. **Pitch 2** (5.8): Continue up the corner (5.8), then climb past 2 bolts on a ledge to a left-leaning crack. Climb past 1 more bolt and step right, then go up a corner to a large ledge. 165'. **Pitch 3** (5.5): Diagonal left on a huge ledge for 75', then up vertical and left-leaning cracks to a stance just above varnished rock on the edge of lower-angled white rock. 165'. **Pitch 4** (5.0): Scamper up the easy white face to a ledge. 100'. **Pitch 5** (fourth-class): Follow a left-leaning crack/ ramp to a sloping platform below a steep headwall. 150'. **Pitch 6** (fourth-class): Angle left across a smooth, brown slab. Belay under a small triangular ceiling at the very left end of the ledges (Friends for the belay). 200'. **Pitch 7** (5.9): Make an exposed traverse left for 20' to a shallow dihedral (bolt). Climb the dihedral and chimney, then exit right to a belay ledge (nuts and large Friends). 160'. **Pitch 8** (5.9+): Scramble up ledges, then climb a short, steep, thin crack (5.9+, 2 bolts) to a corner. Jam up beautiful cracks to the second ledge above. 120'. **Pitch 9** (5.7): Lieback up the huge dihedral past 1 bolt, then traverse right 35' to a belay anchor (bolt and drilled piton). 120'. **Pitch 10** (5.5+): Climb up the loose pink face past bolts to the dihedral, then exit left out of that into another corner. Follow this to easy summit slabs. 160'. **Descent:** If you have your gear with you, it's probably best to descend the gully to the right (east) of the buttress, as for *Solar Slab*. This can be done without a rope if you are good at downclimbing, and a few rappels can be done if you aren't. In winter, the gully may contain ice and snow because it is in the shade all day. If you left your gear at the streambed below the climb, contour left (west) along ledges in the summit slabs, then go down a ramp. Do an 80' rappel (bolt and fixed wire) to a ledge, then walk right (west) 150' to the end of the ledge. Another 80'rappel (thread and fixed nuts) down a chimney leads to a ledge with lots of vegetation. Yet another 80'rappel will put you in the lower section of the Painted Bowl (there are other ways to get here, including a route using two 150' rappels directly down from the first anchor). From the base of the rappels, head down white slabs toward an obvious bench with a large boulder (looks like an IBM Selectric typewriter ball). From the boulder, head right (west) down a low-angle ramp to the streambed. You should now be about 700 yards upstream from your gear and 350 yards above the fork in Oak Creek Canyon. Head downstream to your packs and the road.

BLACK ARCH WALL

This section of the cliff is located just before Oak Creek Canyon forks into north and south drainages. It is on the right (north) side of the canyon and is characterized by a huge (you guessed it) black arch. Not much is known about these routes, except that they are supposed to be sunny and of high quality.

10. **Tuscarora** (5.12+) FA: Tom Cecil, Tom Barnes, John "The Gambler" Rosholt; circa 1995. This 4-pitch route is named after a Native American tribe that was known for its use of hemp. The route is somewhere to the right of *There and Back Again*. Bring gear up to 3" with extra of the finger sizes. Pitch 3 goes over a roof (5.11) and Pitch 4 climbs a very difficult finger crack (5.12+). Rappel the route with two ropes.

11. **There and Back Again** (5.8) FA: Jim Boone, Ellen Dempsey; February 1980. On the right side of Black Arch Wall is a white recess. This route

OAK CREEK CANYON
BLACK ARCH WALL MAP

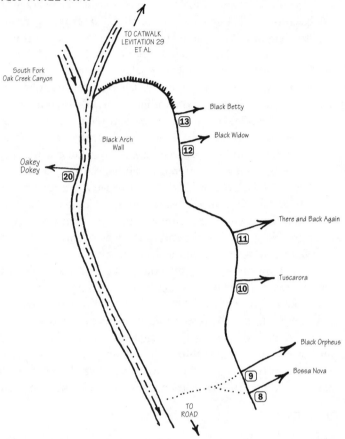

starts about 150' to the right of the recess, at a huge block that leans against the cliff. Scramble up slabs to reach the base of the block. **Pitch 1** (5.5): Climb the center of the huge block to its top. 165'. **Pitch 2** (5.7): Follow obvious features to the top of a tower. 160'. **Pitch 3** (5.8): Climb up and left on a face, then angle back right to a dihedral. Follow the dihedral to the top of another tower. 120'. **Pitch 4** (5.8): On the left side of the ledge is a face with a thin vertical crack. Climb the crack to its top, then go up a corner. Belay on a large ledge to the left of the corner. 80'. **Pitch 5** (5.8): Climb a steep corner, exiting left to easier terrain. 80'. **Pitch 6** (fourth-class): Scramble left into Painted Bowl. **Descent:** Rappel as follows: From a pine tree in Painted Bowl to a bushy ledge (two ropes). From the bushy ledge down to a ledge about 30' above the ground (two ropes); from the ledge to the ground (one rope).

OAK CREEK CANYON
TUSCARORA (5.12+)

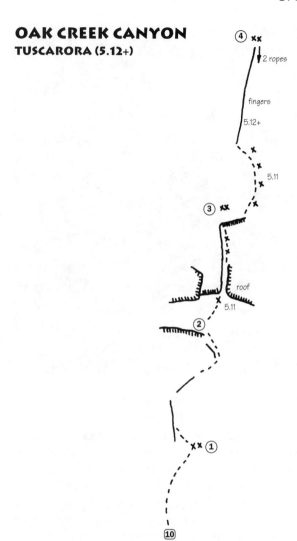

12. **Black Widow** (5.11) FA: Tom Cecil; circa 1995. This climb is to the left of *Tuscarora* near the left (up-canyon) side of the wall. **Pitch 1:** Climb double cracks past 6 bolts. **Pitch 2:** Go over a roof to the top. **Descent:** Unknown. (No topo.)

13. **Black Betty** (5.10) FA: Tom Cecil; circa 1995. Somewhere to the left of *Black Widow* is a finger crack. The route is supposed to be two pitches long and has fixed anchors. (No topo.)

EAGLE WALL AREA
This sunny wall sits high up on the right (north) side of Oak Creek Canyon and is best viewed from around the First Creek trailhead. Take the north fork of

Eagle Wall

Walk off

Painted Bowl

Eagle

15

18

16

17

Huge ramp

Up canyon to Catwalk, etc.

Oak Creek Canyon, then follow a huge ramp up and right (northeast) to the bases of the routes. Total approach time is about 2 hours.

*14. **Chicken Lips** (5.10-) FA: Jorge and Joanne Urioste; April 1980. This route begins in Upper Painted Bowl, which sits high above the Oak Creek Canyon floor. There are several ways to reach the base of the route. You can climb *Solar Slab* or *The Black Orpheus*, or approach as for *Rainbow Buttress*. The route begins several hundred yards to the right (toward the road) of *Rainbow Buttress* near the center of Upper Painted Bowl. To the right (east) of the start of the climb is a large recess capped by a roof. The descent route from *The Black Orpheus* passes close to the start of this route. Bring a full rack. **Pitch 1** (5.10-): Face-climb up a water-polished slab to the base of a right-facing corner. 100'. **Pitch 2** (5.10-): Climb the right-facing corner, then go right out around a point of rock and back up left to a belay. 110'. **Pitch 3** (5.8): Climb the obvious, right-facing corner for about 60'. Swing out left onto the arête and go up this to a belay stance. 130'. **Pitch 4** (5.10-): Climb the face just left of the arête to a large ledge with a tree. 150'. **Pitch 5** (5.9): Lieback up a right-facing corner past 4 bolts to a belay. 120'. **Pitch 6** (5.8): Climb a chimney past a ceiling to a belay stance in a recess. 130'. **Pitch 7** (5.6): Continue up the chimney system to the summit. 120'. **Descent:** Either go east (toward the road) and

OAK CREEK CANYON
CHICKEN LIPS
(5.10-)

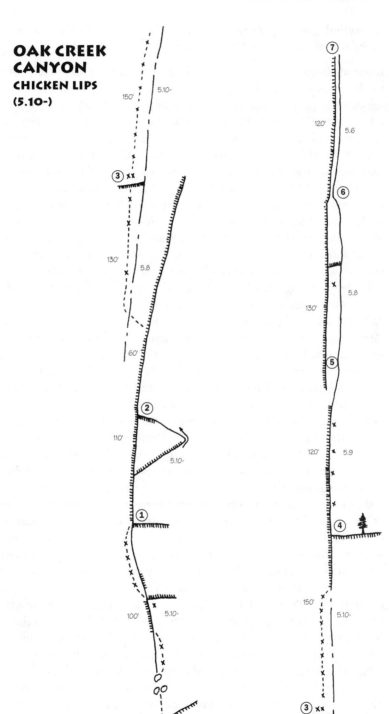

150'   5.10-

③ xx

130'   5.8

60'

②
110'   5.10-

①
100'   5.10-

⑭

⑦

120'   5.6

⑥

130'   5.8

⑤

120'   5.9

④

150'   5.10-

③ xx

downclimb and rappel toward the top of *The Black Orpheus*, or go west to the top of Oak Creek Canyon (as for *Rainbow Buttress*).

*15. **Rainbow Buttress** (5.8 PG) FA: Joe Herbst; 1970s. A great route, but with the long approach and descent, you'll need to move fast! Bring a good selection of gear for the belays as well as the climbing (including extra #3.5 and #4 Friends for Pitch 6). From The Wilson Pimple, follow the old roadbed and/or trail toward the canyon until the trail drops into the streambed. Hike up Oak Creek Canyon for about 1 hour until it splits. Continue up the right (north) fork until a huge, slabby ramp leads back up right toward the huge cliffband on the right. It is probably best to leave your pack here. Follow the ramp up (east; some cairns) for about 15 minutes to the base of the route. Start at the very top of the huge approach ramp about 400' uphill from *Levitation 29* and left (west) of Upper Painted Bowl. **Pitch 1** (5.4): Climb a shallow, varnished, left-facing corner that leads to a wider section of crack. Angle right across the white face to a belay ledge. Bring friends for the belay. 80'. **Pitch 2** (5.8): A good pitch. Climb the corner to a huge ledge (5.6), then continue up the left-facing corner to a big ledge with a bush. Nuts and the bush form the belay. 100'. **Pitch 3** (5.7): Swim up the off-width above (5.7), then up a corner system to a chimney. Exit right out of an alcove onto the face, then up the main, right-facing corner system to a belay ledge that is 20' below a bush. TCUs for the belay. 110'. **Pitch 4** (5.5): Climb the corner system past a ledge with bushes to a chimney, which leads to the top of The Black Tower. Slings around the summit of the tower and a #3 Friend form the belay. (Note: *Ringtail*, a 5.10 described in the Urioste guidebook, climbs the left side of the tower and terminates at this point.) 90'. **Pitch 5** (5.6): Step across from the top of the tower to a crack, then traverse 15' right to a right-facing corner. Climb this for about 40', then traverse 40' right across a slab to the base of an obvious left-facing corner. Belay in the corner (#3.5 and #4 Friends) at a point about 30' above a huge pedestal. 110'. **Pitch 6** (5.8 PG): Climb the obvious left-facing corner past a scary stemming section, a fist crack, and numerous bushes in a chimney. Belay above on a large ledge. 150'. **Pitch 7** (5.5): Continue up the easy, loose, and low-angle crack/chimney system to a huge, sloping ledge with a pine tree. Belay from the tree. 100'. **Pitch 8** (5.5 X): Climb the lower-angle face to the left of a left-facing corner, angling up and left to a ledge. Wander up and right to a belay on a terrace 50' below the summit. 140'. **Descent:** Scramble about 100 yards up toward the canyon rim, then contour left (west). Aim for ramps that lead toward a large, red pinnacle at the right edge of a red blob on the canyon rim. Go around the right (north) side of the pinnacle and blob, then follow a trail down along the canyon rim to the top of the Oak Creek drainage. This should take about 30 minutes. Follow the drainage down and east (toward the road) past numerous waterholes to the base of the approach ramp, a huge pine and your packs. From the top of the route, it should take about 1 hour to reach your pack at the base of the ramp.

*16. **Levitation 29** (5.11 PG) FA: Jorge and Joanne Urioste, Bill Bradley; April 1981. FFA: Lynn Hill, John Long, Joanne Urioste; May 1981. Considered by many to be the best route at Red Rocks. The climb is on a section of cliff that gets sun all day and is visible from the road. Bring lots of quickdraws and the usual assortment of wires, TCUs, and Friends up to #3. From The Wilson Pimple, follow the old roadbed and/or trail toward the canyon until the trail drops into the streambed. Hike up Oak Creek Canyon for about 1 hour until it splits. Continue up the right (north) fork, until a huge, slabby ramp leads back up right toward the huge cliffband on the right. Follow the ramp (some cairns) to the base of the route, which is about 400' down from the ramp's top and about 200' right of a huge, black pillar where some varnished cracks lead to a giant roof about 100' up. **Pitch 1** (5.10): Climb thin, varnished cracks past 4 bolts to an anchor. 80'. **Pitch 2** (5.11): Move right, then go up to the roof. Fire this (bolts) and belay up and left from bolts. 80'. **Pitch 3** (5.8): Climb a crack for 75', then angle up right past bolts to a bolted belay at a stance. 115'. **Pitch 4** (5.10): Follow a crack up the face past 7 bolts to an anchor just below a steeper section of the wall. 140'. **Pitch 5** (5.11): The pumpfest. Follow the obvious crack and 13 bolts to a bolt anchor. 90'. **Pitch 6** (5.10): Climb seams up left past 5 bolts to the fixed belay. 70'. **Pitch 7** (5.10+): Pussyfoot up and left along a white, rounded seam to a depression. A bit of power liebacking gets you up the right edge of the depression and to the safety of the belay anchors. 100'. **Pitch 8** (5.9): Go up and right to a thin crack. When it ends, go left to a belay on a slab. 100'. **Pitch 9** (5.8): Climb up and right along corners and cracks to a right-slanting, right-facing corner. Belay from 2 bolts, after clipping 7 on the pitch. 100'. **Pitch 10** (fourth-class): Some fourth-class climbing leads to the top of the wall. **Descent:** Many people rappel with two ropes after the seventh pitch. If you elect to hike down, walk left (west) along the top of the wall, curving around left (south) onto white rock. Follow the ridge and slabs down left to the top of the Oak Creek drainage. It should take about 30 minutes from the summit to the top of Oak Creek Canyon. Follow the drainage down and east (toward the road) past numerous waterholes.

*17. **Eagle Dance** (5.10- A0) FA: Jorge and Joanne Urioste; March 1980. This route and the formation are named for the likeness of a huge eagle (flying west) formed by desert varnish in the center of the wall. This climb goes through the eagle's neck, and *Levitation 29* goes through the tail. The climb is on a section of cliff that gets sun all day and is visible from the road. Bring lots of quickdraws, lightweight aiders (or long slings), and the

OAK CREEK CANYON
EAGLE WALL
LEVITATION 29 AREA

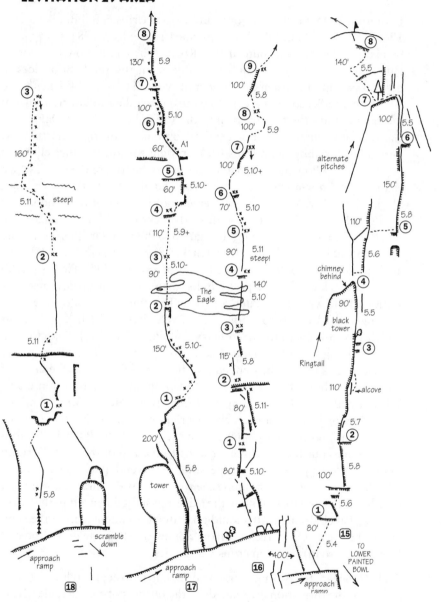

usual assortment of wires, TCUs, and Friends up to #2.5. From The Wilson Pimple, follow the old roadbed and/or a trail toward the canyon until the trail drops into the streambed. Hike up Oak Creek Canyon for about 1 hour until it splits. Continue up the right (north) fork until a huge, slabby ramp leads back up right toward the huge cliffband on the right. Follow the ramp (some cairns) to the base of the route. Start at a shallow, varnished dihedral about 50' right of a huge, black pillar that rests against the cliff. This is about 450' down from the very top of the approach ramp. **Pitch 1** (5.8): Climb the dihedral and crack above to a belay ledge with bolts. This ledge is about 30' above the top of the black pillar. 200'. **Pitch 2** (5.10-): Move right and climb past 2 bolts (use long slings); follow a seam up left past 8 more bolts (and a possible belay) to a belay stance atop a block at bolts. 150'. **Pitch 3** (5.10-): Fly straight up the white face, passing through the eagle's neck and 13 bolts. Belay at a stance with a bolted anchor. 90'. **Pitch 4** (5.9): Nine more bolts lead up to a bolt belay on a sloping ledge. 110'. **Pitch 5** (5.10-): Move up right past 1 bolt to a ledge at the base of a short, left-facing corner. Climb up loose flakes and a right-facing corner (bolt) to a stance with bolts. 60'. **Pitch 6** (5.8 A0): Follow a thin crack up to a bulge, then thrash and dangle out the bulge (8 bolts) to a crack and the belay anchor. 60'. **Pitch 7** (5.10): Follow the corner/groove and 7 bolts to the next anchor (on a ledge). 100'. **Pitch 8** (5.9): Go up and left in a corner past 4 bolts to a ledge. 130'. **Pitch 9**: Scamper up a corner to the top. **Descent:** There are two options. Rappel the route with two ropes from the top of Pitch 7, or, walk left (west) along the top of the wall, curving around left (south) onto white rock and follow the ridge and slabs down left to the top of the Oak Creek drainage. It should take about 30 minutes from the summit to the top of Oak Creek Canyon. Follow the drainage down and east (toward the road) past numerous waterholes. You eventually exit the drainage on its right (south) bank and follow a trail and the old road back to your vehicle. If you parked on the spur road, exit left (north) out of the drainage to return to your car.

*18. **Dances with Beagles** (5.11) FA: Jeff Rhoades, Todd Swain; Spring 1993. Bring gear up to a #1.5 Friend, at least 17 quickdraws(!), and two ropes for the rappel. From The Wilson Pimple, follow the old roadbed and/or trail toward the canyon until the trail drops into the streambed. Hike up Oak Creek Canyon for about 1 hour until it splits. Continue up the right (north) fork until a huge, slabby ramp leads back up right toward the huge cliffband on the right. Follow the ramp (some cairns) to the base of the route. Start about 300' left (west) of *Eagle Dance* at a point 40' left of a 50-foot-high pillar. This is just right of a huge, varnished, left-facing corner. **Pitch 1** (5.8): Climb an easy, varnished dihedral to a steep seam/crack. Follow the seam/crack past 2 bolts then continue up and slightly left along the fissure to its end. Go up and right to a ledge with an anchor. 140'. **Pitch 2** (5.11): Follow a flake above the belay to a thin, left-leaning seam in very smooth rock. Climb the seam and ceiling above (bolt) to an easier face. Move up and right (bolt) to a thin, varnished crack, which is followed to a 2-bolt belay stance. 130'. **Pitch 3** (5.11): Follow 17 bolts up the steep face above, belaying at a 2-bolt stance. 160'. **Descent:** Rappel the route using two ropes.

UPPER OAK CREEK CANYON

The upper reaches of Oak Creek Canyon are beautiful. There are large pine trees, slickrock, and pools of water. One route is described in this area. It ascends the right wall of the canyon along a very prominent, left-leaning crack system.

19. **Catwalk** (5.6+ PG) FA: Margo Young, Joe Frani; February 1975. A good introduction to the longer routes at Red Rocks. The climbing isn't always aesthetic, but the location is great. From The Wilson Pimple, follow the old roadbed and/or trail toward the canyon until the trail drops into the streambed. Hike up Oak Creek for about 1 hour until you reach the point where the canyon splits. Take the right (north) fork and follow this to the rear of the canyon. The route climbs an obvious, left-leaning crack system that passes through two very prominent black waterstreaks. Beyond the bottom couple of pitches, there is no easy way to retreat from the route. Total approach time is about 2.5 hours. The route is in the sun most of the day. Start at the base of the waterstreaks above several large pine trees in the northern Oak Creek drainage. Scramble up slabs as far as you dare, angling to the right of the rightmost waterstreak. **Pitch 1:** Continue up right via roped climbing (if needed) to a belay on a ledge about 400' above the pine trees and at the base of the left-leaning crack system. A huge roof is about 80' above. **Pitch 2** (5.4 R): This is the first of the technical pitches. Follow the left-leaning crack past numerous huecos to a belay ledge just below the roof. 80'. **Pitch 3** (5.6): Continue up the crack past the left side of the roof. Follow the crack to a belay in a pothole just left of the rightmost black streak. 130'. **Pitch 4** (5.6): Climb the crack to a right-facing corner with scrub oak. Stretch the rope if you can to a belay on a spacious ledge (above the bushes) on the left. 165'. **Pitch 5** (5.5): Continue up the crack into a huge, right-facing corner. Follow this past numerous ledges to a belay below a right-facing chimney/corner on the left. 150'. **Pitch 6** (5.6): Climb the chimney, exiting left at its top. Belay on the highest of three ledges on the left. **Pitch 7** (5.6+): The best pitch on the route. Pussyfoot up the steep, black, finger-and-hand crack above. As the angle eases, move right to a belay ledge. 150'. **Pitch 8** (5.3): Scamper up an easy face to pine trees and the summit. 60'. **Descent:** Head down left (west) into the obvious

OAK CREEK CANYON
CATWALK (5.6+ PG)

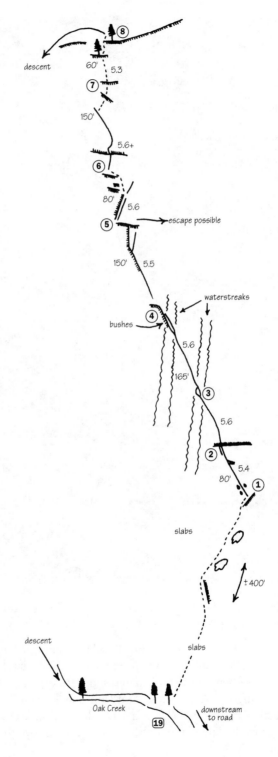

descent

60'   5.3

150'

5.6+

80'   5.6

escape possible

150'   5.5

waterstreaks

bushes

5.6

165'

5.6

5.4

80'

slabs

±400'

descent

slabs

Oak Creek

19

downstream
to road

drainage and follow the upper part of Oak Creek downstream. The descent is very easy. You'll be back at your pack in less than 15 minutes!

20. **Oakey Dokey** (5.10 PG) FA: Bob Harrington, Alan Bartlett, Bill St. Jean; 1978. This route is on the prominent north-facing buttress that overlooks the confluence of the north and south forks of Oak Creek Canyon (across the canyon and just upstream from Black Arch Wall). The most striking feature of this buttress is a large, left-facing arch. The route climbs the face to the left of the arch, meeting it at its top. Bring RPs, wires, TCUs,

and cams to #4. To reach the start of the route, third-class up and left, roughly 100' left of the big arch. **Pitch 1** (5.9): Go up and right to the bottom of a left-facing corner capped by a roof. Lieback up the corner, then exit the corner before the roof. Go up and right to a ledge. Belay near the right end of the ledge. **Pitch 2** (5.10 PG): Climb to a ledge at the bottom of a left-facing, inverted-staircase flake. **Pitch 3** (5.9): Face-climb to the left of the inverted flake and up into a large left-facing corner. **Pitch 4**: Easy climbing leads to the top. **Descent**: Go west into the south fork of Oak Creek. (Note: At least one route has been done to the left of the buttress, but no more is known.)

MOUNT WILSON

AFTERBURNER CLIFF

This 160-foot-high wall faces north and is roughly across from *Johnny Vegas* on the left (south) side of the canyon. The cliff is black on the upper section and lighter colored near the bottom. It is about 300 yards uphill from the canyon floor and requires some third-class scrambling to reach. Routes are described from left (east) to right (up canyon).

21. **Finger Fandango** (5.11-) FA: Paul Van Betten, Jay Smith, Paul Obenheim; 1984. Climb a right-facing corner to a fixed peg, then up a fingertip crack. Rappel with two ropes.

22. **Afterburner** (5.12-) FA: Paul Van Betten, Sal Mamusia; 1984. Start about 30' right of the last route. Ascend a thin finger crack with a fixed pin near the bottom of the crack.

*23. **Eliminator Crack** (5.11+) FA: Paul Van Betten, Randy Marsh; 1984. This is supposedly the best pure finger crack at Red Rocks. Begin 30' right of *Afterburner* and climb a straight-in finger crack. Near the top, angle right for 40' to a belay anchor with fixed wires. Rappel with two ropes.

24. **Deguello** (5.10-) FA: Sal Mamusia, Danny Meyers, Paul Van Betten, Brad Stewart; 1984. Don't lose your head on this one! Climb the right-slanting hand crack to a ramp. Scramble off to the right.

25. **'34 Ford with Flames** (5.10+) FA: Mike Ward, Bob Yoho; 1985. Down and right of the last routes is a right-leaning thin crack in perfect white and brown rock. You'll need RPs and small Friends to protect the route.

RAMEN PRIDE CLIFF

This dark brown cliff is supposedly on the very left edge of a gully leading up to a subsidiary peak of Mount Wilson. The crag reportedly faces east and sits very low on the hillside. Routes are described from left to right (east to west).

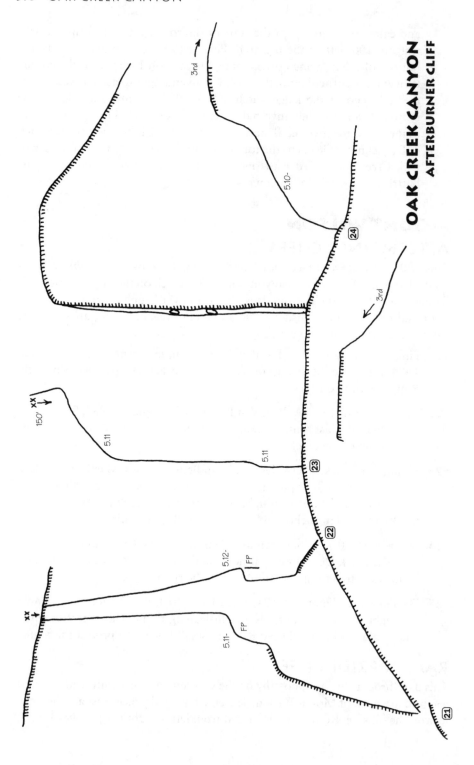

OAK CREEK CANYON
AFTERBURNER CLIFF

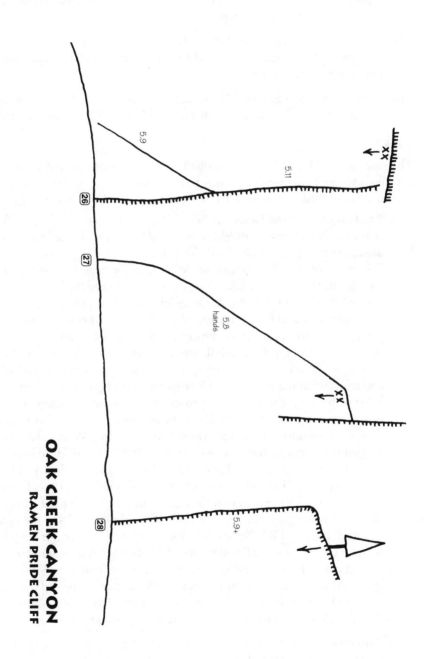

OAK CREEK CANYON
RAMEN PRIDE CLIFF

26. **Ramen Pride** (5.11) FA: Paul Van Betten, Sal Mamusia; 1983. Climb a right-leaning hand crack (5.9) to a left-facing corner, which is stemmed to the top. Rappel with two ropes.

27. **Zippy** (5.8) FA: Paul Van Betten, Sal Mamusia; 1983. Start about 20' right of the last route. Climb a right-leaning hand crack to an anchor in a left-facing corner. Rappel.

28. **Stemtation** (5.9+) FA: Sal Mamusia, Paul Van Betten; 1983. Begin about 30' right of *Zippy*. Climb the left-facing corner to a pine tree on a ledge.

EAST FACE

The east face of Mount Wilson is probably the largest cliff at Red Rocks. It is very featured and contains numerous buttresses and towers. Only a few long routes are described on this massive wall, none of which I've done (yet).

29. **The Gift of the Wind Gods** (5.10+) FA: Patrick Putnam, Michael Clifford, Joanne Urioste; Summer 1996. From the old Oak Creek Campground, walk along the rough and rocky Oak Creek Road to its end (about 1.5 miles). Follow the old roadbed around the left side of the huge dirt mound blocking the canyon (the hill is called The Wilson Pimple and the large cliff above on the left is Mount Wilson). Angle up left (southwest) toward Mount Wilson, aiming for a gully to the right of a hanging gully/waterfall. Go up the White Rot Gully (fourth-class). Proceed beyond the left (south) turn to *Resolution Arête* and continue uphill (west). In several hundred yards, the terrain flattens and becomes surprisingly lush. Continue until you can look up and left toward the wall and see a large ponderosa pine tree. Go up to the ledge with the pine tree. Total approach time is about 2.5 hours. The start of this route is to the right of *Woodrow* and just left of another relatively new route (no information was available at press time). **Pitch 1** (5.8): Go up and left through a groove to an anchor. 90'. **Pitch 2** (5.10): Head back right past a bolt to a crack. 120'. **Pitch 3** (5.8): Go straight up. **Pitch 4** (5.8): Go straight up. **Pitch 5** (5.10): This pitch rates 5.10. **Pitch 6** (5.10+): The route veers right at a set of anchors at the top of Pitch 5 or Pitch 6. At that point, the newer route goes left. Go right and follow about 8 bolts to the bottom of a huge groove. 130'. **Pitches 7–9** (5.8): Continue for 2 or 3 more pitches to easier terrain (possible bivouac here). 140'. Getting to the summit is tricky. Go left a few hundred yards, then up a weakness that allows third-class travel. After two or three short pitches, it's 10 minutes of walking to the summit. **Descent:** It's probably best to go down First Creek Canyon, although a descent down Oak Creek Canyon is possible. (No topo.)

30. **Woodrow** (5.10- R) FA: Richard Harrison, John Long; Spring 1981. This route climbs the right of two left-leaning gashes on the right side of the Aeolian Wall. The *Aeolian Wall—Original Route* starts up the left of the two leaning gashes and joins this climb at about the tenth pitch.

*31. Aeolian Wall—Original Route (5.9 A3+) FA: Joe Herbst, Larry Hamilton; March 1975. This big route goes up the center of the face to the right (west) of the *Resolution Arête*. It climbs the left of two left-slanting gashes on the wall. A left-facing corner leads up to the gash. Carry a full rack, including the following pitons: 2 baby angles, 1 angle, 6 Lost Arrows, 4 knifeblades, and 2 Bugaboos. This route has been done in 11 hours from car to car!

OAK CREEK CANYON
AEOLIAN WALL,
ORIGINAL ROUTE (5.9 A3+)

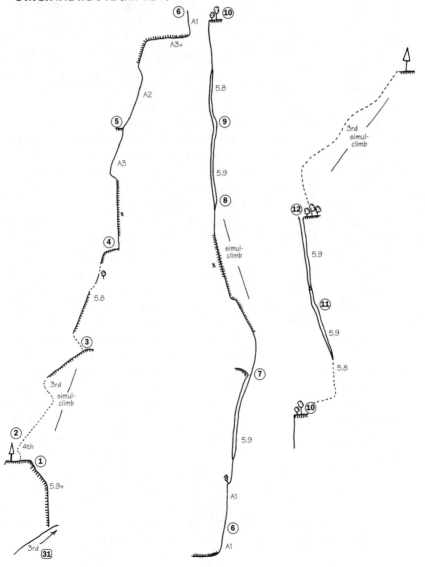

*32. Resolution Arête (5.11+ or 5.10 A1) FA: Phil Broscovak, Geoffrey Conley; January 1981. FFA: Paul Van Betten, Richard Harrison; 1984. Plan on going fast and light, as it's supposedly very difficult to haul gear. The route itself has been done in as little as 6 hours! Crucial holds have supposedly broken off at the crux roof, potentially making it a bit harder to free-climb. Bring wires, TCUs, a double set of cams to #4, and lots of slings to cut down on rope drag. There are almost no fixed anchors on the route. The climb ascends cracks in the right center of a huge, pyramid-shaped buttress, then climbs an obvious, pillared buttress that starts just right of a huge, tree-covered ledge that dominates the middle of the east face (Sherwood Forest). From the old Oak Creek Campground, walk along the rough and rocky Oak Creek Road to its end (about 1.5 miles). Follow the old roadbed around the left side of the huge dirt mound blocking the canyon (The Wilson Pimple). Angle up left (southwest) toward Mount Wilson, aiming for a gully to the right of a hanging gully/waterfall. Scramble up the White Rot Gully (cairns; fourth-class) past a big, obvious tree on the left. Continue up a fin and the gully for quite a while to reach a ledge with a big tree (possible bivouac here). Downclimb from the tree, then go left about 50' to a chimney that is formed by a huge pillar and the cliff. It will take about 1.5 hours to reach the base of the route. **Pitch 1** (5.9 PG): Go left in the chimney, then climb a crack through a ceiling to a dubious bolt. **Pitch 2** (5.8): Climb a crack to the top of a red pillar. **Pitch 3** (5.9+): On the right side of the pillar, climb a very thin corner. Belay in a chimney. 160'. **Pitch 4** (5.8): Continue up and left to the top of the next pillar. 80'. **Pitch 5** (5.7+ R): Climb the white face above, aiming for a point just right of the top of the triangular buttress. **Pitch 6** (third-class): Head down and left through a notch behind the buttress, passing a couple of cracks to a steep, loose corner. 300'. **Pitch 7** (5.10): Climb the obvious right-facing corner with loose blocks to a bulging 4" crack (see Variations 1 and 2). Climb the crack through the bulge (5.10) and belay about 30' above on a ledge. 130'. **Pitch 8** (5.9 PG): Climb a left-facing corner to a belay stance under a large roof. 80'. **Pitch 9** (5.11+ or 5.9 A0): Either free or aid the roof at a 1–1.5" crack. Continue up for about 60', doing some 5.9 face-climbing en route to the belay stance. **Pitch 10** (5.10): A good pitch. Climb up a corner (the first 30' is hard), then move left to a huge ledge on the left side of a prow. A belay bolt and possible bivouac here. 100'. (Note: Historically, people have rappelled 100' down to the Sherwood Forest ledge from here to bivouac. Supposedly, there's some type of shelter there to protect you from the elements.) **Pitch 11** (5.8): Head up a left-leaning ramp, then continue up the face when the ramp ends. Belay on a ledge at the base of a steep face. (Note: If you go right/west through a notch, there's supposed to be an excellent bivouac ledge.) **Pitch 12** (5.8): Climb a short, steep face then up easier rock to a belay on a ledge with a block that's at

OAK CREEK CANYON
RESOLUTION ARETE (5.11+ OR 5.10 A1)

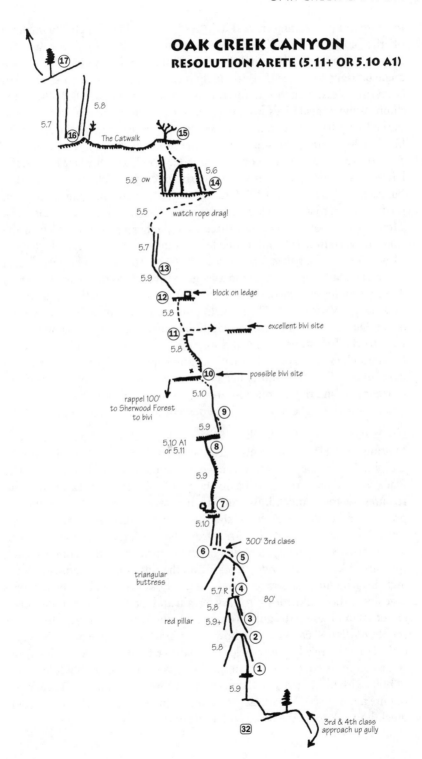

17

5.8

5.7

16   The Catwalk   15

5.8 ow   5.6
14

5.5   watch rope drag!

5.7

13
5.9

12   block on ledge
5.8

11   excellent bivi site
5.8

x   10   possible bivi site
5.10

rappel 100'
to Sherwood Forest   9
to bivi   5.9

5.10 A1   8
or 5.11

5.9

7
5.10

300' 3rd class
6   5

triangular
buttress   5.7 R   4
5.8   80'
red pillar   5.9+   3

2
5.8

1

5.9

32   3rd & 4th class
approach up gully

the base of a left-leaning crack. **Pitch 13** (5.9): A brilliant pitch. Downclimb off the block, then climb up the left-leaning crack through a headwall. Belay in a chimney. 110'. **Pitch 14** (5.7): Slither up the chimney (5.7), then angle up right on a face (5.3) to the right side of a blocky, two-tiered pillar. Belay in recess. Watch out for rope drag on this pitch. 100'. **Pitch 15:** There are several choices from here. Face-climb up a wide crack to the top of the first pillar (see Variation 3). Make steep face moves to the top of the block. Move left to the south end of the block. Climb a steep crack up a 50-foot wall to a dead tree on a good ledge. **Pitch 16** (third class): Shuffle left across a ledge past a left-facing corner/recess to a chimney/crack that bulges (see Variation 4). 120'. **Pitch 17** (5.7): Jam up a bulging crack, then go up and left to a large, sloping ledge with a big tree. **Pitches 18–20** (5.2): Move around left, then climb three easy pitches up to the notch in the summit. **Variation 1:** Climb to the left through white rock (may be loose). Move right to the belay. **Variation 2** (5.10+?): Traverse right past a bush to a recess. Stem up the recess to a ledge. Move left to the belay. **Variation 3** (5.8): On the left side of the blocky pillar is an off-width that leads to the same ledge. **Variation 4:** The first chimney you encounter (by a dead tree) is 5.8. **Descent:** A number of possibilities exist, of which this is one. Walk west to the limestone (about 0.5 mile), then go down a gully to a tree-filled notch (a large, red pillar with a van-shaped block on top marks this particular gully). Descend either gully from here (the right one requires four rappels and the left one requires two short rappels and lots of fourth- and easy fifth-class climbing). Total descent time is about 3 hours.

*33. **Inti Watana** (5.10) FA: Michael Clifford, Jorge Urioste, Sam Pratt, Nick Nolting, Bill Holtz, Steve Rhodes; Summer 1997. This route name is Quechuan, a native Bolivian language of Jorge's homeland. It means "The Place from Which You Can Lasso the Sun." The climb is 12 pitches and requires 12 to 14 quickdraws and a small standard rack. Follow the approach for *Resolution Arête* to the top of White Rot Gully. Scramble up toward the base of *Resolution Arête* from the top of the gully, then go south up a narrow side gully (you would normally turn left at this point to reach the start of *Resolution Arête*). Looking up the side gully you can see a seemingly insurmountable garage-sized boulder choking the gully. A hidden passage under the boulder leads to easy terrain and the base of the route (this is about 10 minutes up the gully from the *Resolution Arête* approach). As for the *Resolution Arête*, knowing how to get into the White Rot Gully is crucial. (Sorry I can't be more helpful. I haven't been there yet.) This route begins on moss-covered rock but quickly gets better. There should be a line of bolts with black hangers that marks the route. Some pitches are easy and require a few pieces of natural protection. Others are 5.10 and require only quickdraws. Rappel the route with two ropes. (No topo.)

WILLY'S COULOIR

This gully provides access to Sherwood Forest, the huge tree-covered ledge in the middle of Mount Wilson's east face. This gully starts above the end of the old Oak Creek Road (near the Wilson Pimple) and diagonals up and left (southeast). The following routes are supposed to be on the left (northeast, toward the road) side of the gully.

34. **Otters Are People Too** (5.8) FA: Unknown; circa 1996. Climb a right-leaning crack system for two pitches to a terrace. **Pitch 1** (5.8): Starting atop a pillar, climb the right-leaning crack past a wide section to a ledge. **Pitch 2** (5.7): Follow the crack system up to a terrace. Walk right and rappel with two ropes from the top of *Slick Willy*.

OAK CREEK CANYON
MOUNT WILSON
WILLY'S COULOIR

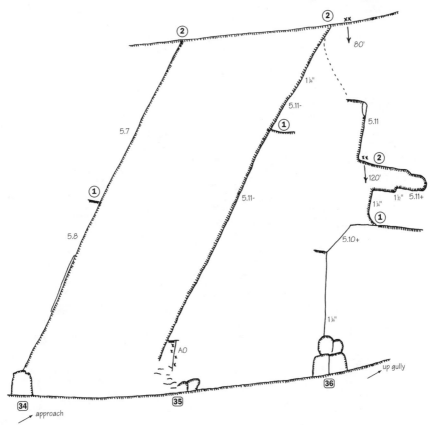

35. **Slick Willy** (5.11- A0) FA: Unknown; circa 1996. Bring at least five #1.5 and #2 Friends. The crack size is continuous. This route starts below a bolt ladder to the right (uphill) of the last route. The route is two pitches and ends at a rappel anchor on a terrace. **Pitch 1** (5.11- A0): Aid up a short bolt ladder, then climb the right-leaning crack system to a belay ledge. **Pitch 2** (5.11-): Continue up the crack system to the terrace. Rappel with two ropes.

36. **Free Willy** (5.11+) FA: Unknown; circa 1996. Carry extra #1.5–2.5 Friends. Start atop boulders to the right (uphill) of the last route and below a vertical crack. **Pitch 1** (5.10+): Climb a vertical finger crack, then angle up and right to a ledge. **Pitch 2** (5.11+): Follow a flake system up and right (crux), then back left to a belay stance. **Pitch 3** (5.11): Climb a right-facing corner, then angle up and left to join *Slick Willy* to the top. Rappel with two ropes.

FIRST CREEK CANYON

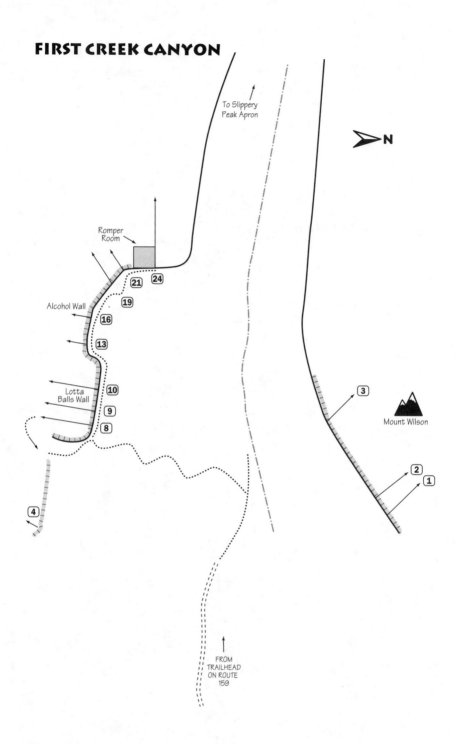

To Slippery
Peak Apron

N

Romper
Room

Alcohol Wall

Lotta
Balls Wall

Mount Wilson

21
24
19
16
13
10
9
8
4
3
2
1

FROM
TRAILHEAD
ON ROUTE
159

320

FIRST CREEK CANYON

Lots of rock here, but only a few routes are included in this guide. Park at the First Creek trailhead, which is 0.7 mile south of Oak Creek on Nevada 159. Follow the old road toward the canyon (west). When the trail forks, take the Upper Trail (left), then the left fork when this trail splits again. Stay on the left (south) side of the drainage to the mouth of the canyon.

MOUNT WILSON

Several generally sunny routes are included on the southeast side of Mount Wilson. Routes are described from right (north) to left (into First Creek Canyon). These big climbs require fast movement (or liberal use of headlamps!). From near the mouth of First Creek Canyon, angle up and right in obvious gullies to reach the bases of the first two routes.

1. **Lady Wilson's Cleavage** (5.9) FA: Joe Herbst, Jorge and Joanne Urioste; March 1977. This route climbs a single crack system for about 700' and is supposed to be of very good quality. The climbing is sustained and consists mostly of wide cracks. The route climbs the wall to the left of the left

First Creek
Overview

Mount Wilson

Slippery
Peak

Romper
Room

Lotta Balls
Wall

FIRST CREEK CANYON
MOUNT WILSON
LADY WILSON'S CLEAVAGE (5.9)

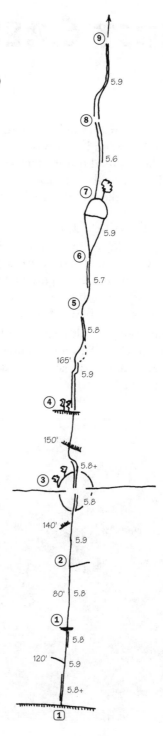

edge of Sherwood Forest (the huge tree-covered ledge about halfway up the east face of Mount Wilson). **Pitch 1** (5.9): Climb the crack past two off-width sections to a ledge. 120'. **Pitch 2** (5.8): Continue up the crack to a belay in an alcove. 80'. **Pitch 3** (5.9): Climb the crack to a belay at some trees. A horizontal crack intersects the vertical crack system at this point. 140'. **Pitch 4** (5.8+): Go up the chimney/off-width crack past a bulge to a belay at some trees. 150'. **Pitch 5** (5.9): Ascend a chimney and off-width. 165'. **Pitch 6** (5.7): Go slightly right to a gully. Climb the left side of the gully to a belay in a chimney. **Pitch 7** (5.9): Stem and lieback up the chimney (on early ascents, climbers could use a tree). **Pitch 8** (5.6): Climb a bushy crack and chimney to the base of a chimney. **Pitch 9:** Climb the chimney and off-width to the top. **Descent:** Hike west (toward the limestone and setting sun), then go north down a gully to the bottom of Oak Creek Canyon. This gully involves a few rappels and downclimbing.

2. **Son of Wilson** (5.10-) FA: Pat Brennan, Steve Untch; April 1990. This route begins on the left (south) side of the cirque left of *Lady Wilson's Cleavage*. The fifth pitch is supposed to be of great quality. Presumably you descend as for *Lady Wilson's Cleavage*.

3. **Dirtbagger's Compensation** (5.10-) FA: Shawn Pereto, Dave Pollari; February 1993. This route climbs a prominent spire on the south ridge of Mount Wilson. The spire is located near the mouth of First Creek Canyon and faces south across the drainage toward *Lotta Balls*. Approach on the First Creek Trail until below the spire, which is characterized by several large water trough systems in the center of the spire. Once below the spire, scramble up a large talus cone to the right (east) of the spire and cut through lower cliffs via brushy gullies on a steep trail. When you reach the large ledges (brush again), work your way about 250 yards to the left to a point directly below the spire. At one point you have to drop down a short gully to a ledge. Start below a small pinnacle that has a chimney/gully behind it. Bring wires, TCUs, and cams up to #4. **Pitch 1** (5.8): Climb a crack/corner to a belay in a chimney. **Pitch 2** (5.10-): Go up a right-facing corner. **Pitch 3** (third-class): Scramble up to a ledge. **Pitch 4** (5.8): Climb cracks and a corner to a large ledge. **Pitch 5:** Traverse right on an easy ledge past a blank section of rock to a black face. **Pitch 6** (5.8): Climb a face past a few bolts (5.8), then move right and follow a crack (5.6) to a belay. **Pitch 7** (5.8): Continue up discontinuous cracks and jugs to a belay on horns and gear. 150'. **Pitch 8** (5.6 R): Climb up and right on a face to ledges below the summit. 140'. **Pitch 9** (fourth class): Easy climbing leads to the summit of the spire. **Descent:** Rappel the route with two ropes. Bring lots of slings and extra hardware to beef up the anchors.

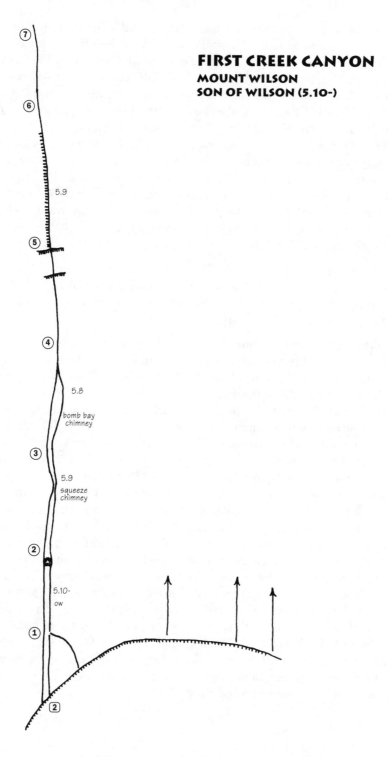

FIRST CREEK CANYON
MOUNT WILSON
SON OF WILSON (5.10-)

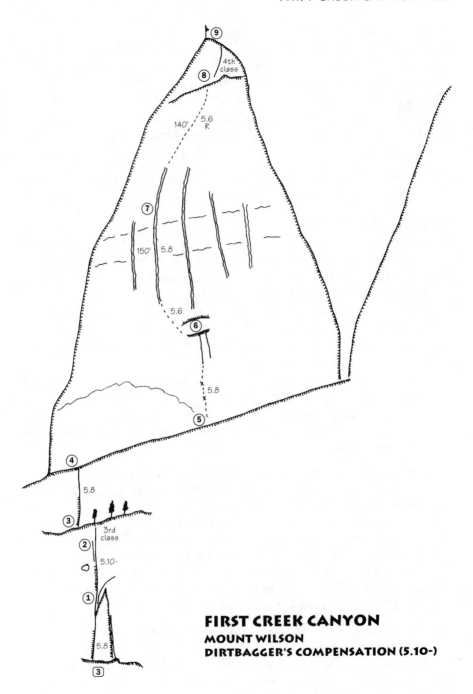

FIRST CREEK CANYON
MOUNT WILSON
DIRTBAGGER'S COMPENSATION (5.10-)

INDECISION PEAK

The mountain that separates First Creek and Sandstone canyons is named Indecision Peak. On the northeast corner of the peak (the southeast edge of First Creek Canyon) are numerous lines. Two good crack climbs are located on a white section of rock above a pink outcrop.

4. **Lucky Nuts** (5.9) FA: Randal Grandstaff, Dave Anderson; April 1977. Climb a flaring crack to the top of a buttress. Bring gear up to a #4 cam. To descend, go east (toward the road), then do a rappel from a tree.

5. **Mudterm** (5.9) FA: Joe Herbst; 1976. Despite its name, this is a good route. Jam up a crack/corner system about 10' right of *Lucky Nuts*.

LOTTA BALLS WALL

All of the routes included in this section are on the left (south) wall of the canyon several hundred yards to the west (right) of the last climbs. Lotta Balls Wall is the first large buttress that protrudes into the canyon. Its profile is visible from the parking area, and it is recognizable by its dark bottom and white top. Follow the trail into the canyon, then scramble about 150 yards uphill to the base of the buttress. The approach takes about 45 minutes and is primarily flat. These routes are generally shady. Routes are described from left (toward the road) to right (west).

6. **Power to Waste** (5.8) FA: Matt and Mark Hermann, Derek Willmott, Mandy Kellner; May 1995. This route climbs the front of the huge fin that forms the left (east) edge of the Lotta Balls Wall. Bring wires and TCUs to supplement the 6 bolts on the first pitch. A second pitch may have been done.

7. **Trihardral** (5.8); FA: Joe and Betsy Herbst, Jorge and Joanne Urioste, Randal Grandstaff; December 1976. This line climbs the huge, right-facing corner system in the left center of Lotta Balls Wall. **Pitch 1** (5.7): Climb cracks and the corner to a belay ledge. 140'. **Pitch 2** (5.8): Continue up the huge right-facing corner to a ledge. Watch out for loose blocks. 150'. **Pitch 3** (5.5): Climb the corner to the top of the huge fin. 155'. **Pitch 4** (fourth-class): Easy rock leads to the top of the wall. 100'. **Descent:** Go down a gully to the left (east) of the buttress. Do two short rappels and some scrambling to get back to the base of the route.

*8. **Lotta Balls** (5.8 PG) FA: Betsy and Joe Herbst, Randal Grandstaff, Tom Kaufman; March 1977. This route is named for the surrealistic rock formations on the second pitch, not for an inordinate amount of courage needed. Start 50' right of a gigantic boulder at the northeast corner of Lotta Balls Wall and 10' right of an oak tree growing out of the cliff. **Pitch 1** (5.6): Climb a series of stacked blocks, then move right to a notch in a ceiling about 20' up. Pull through the ceiling into a left-facing corner, then

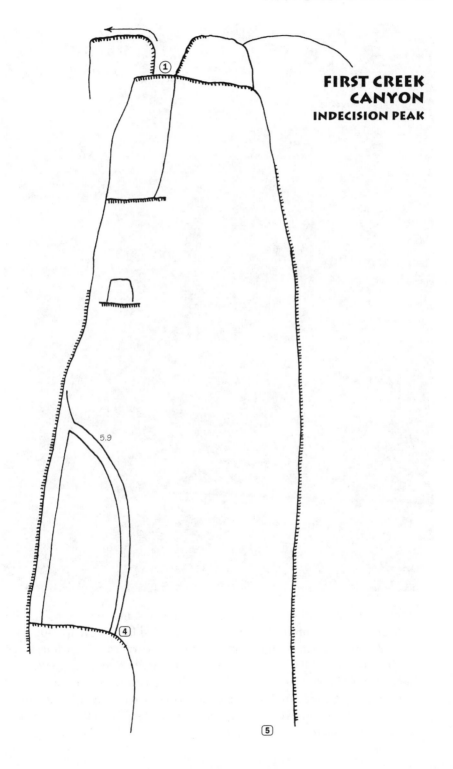

**FIRST CREEK
CANYON**
INDECISION PEAK

follow a huge white flake up right to a belay stance with 2 bolts. 100'
Pitch 2 (5.8): Climb the famous marble-studded face above for 40', passing 2 bolts. Continue up an easy right-facing corner to a spacious ledge.
150'. **Pitch 3** (5.5): Continue up the easy corner to a roof 75' above, then
step left and follow an obvious crack. Move left at the end of the pitch to
a belay ledge with a tree. 165'. **Descent:** Go down a gully to the left (east)
of the buttress. Do two short rappels and some scrambling to get back to
the base of the route.

9. **Bruja's Brew** (5.9 PG) FA: Todd Swain, Debbie Brenchley; December 1991. This will cure a powerful thirst! Start below a left-facing corner capped by a roof 8' right of *Lotta Balls*. **Pitch 1** (5.9): Climb up the corner and crack to the roof, then traverse right to the nose. Continue straight up the face past 1 bolt, then angle right to a ledge. Go up the obvious crack above for about 10', then swing out right on knobs. Climb up a left-facing corner to a belay stance with 1 bolt and nut placements. 135'. **Pitch 2** (5.6): Shoot straight up the varnished face above to belay about 35' below the center of the roof looming above. 150'. **Pitch 3** (5.6): Move up to the center of the roof, then angle out left on a ramp system. Belay above in the white rock at a crack. 150'. **Pitch 4:** Continue up the easy white rock to the top of the buttress. 140'. **Descent:** Go down a gully to the left (east) of the buttress. Do two short rappels and some scrambling to get back to the base of the route.

10. **Black Magic** (5.8 PG) FA: Jorge and Joanne Urioste; April 1978. Bring your rabbit's foot for the intimidating first pitch. Begin 40' right of *Lotta Balls*, atop a boulder and just left of a left-facing corner.. **Pitch 1** (5.8): Climb a flake and the varnished face above past 2 bolts. At the second bolt, traverse right, then up an obvious thin crack. Continue up the crack and varnished face above past 1 more bolt to a belay stance (natural thread, nuts). 150'. **Pitch 2** (5.6): Continue straight up the brown face to a belay in a crack about 35' below the right center of the roof. 140'. **Pitch 3** (5.8): Climb up to the roof, then traverse out right to the nose and a bolt. Move straight up easier white rock to a belay stance in a crack with bushes growing out of it. 140'. **Pitch 4:** Scamper up easy white rock to the top. 140'. **Descent:** Go down a gully to the left (east) of the buttress. Do two short rappels and some scrambling to get back to the base of the route.

11. **Kick in the Balls** (5.8) FA: Josh Thompson, Brian ?; circa 1996. Directly above Lotta Balls Wall is a varnished buttress with a prominent crack system. From the top of Lotta Balls Wall, scramble up third-class gullies then traverse to the base of the crack system. Bring a good selection of cams, including several of the largest sizes. **Pitch 1** (5.8): Climb the crack, which goes from fingers to off-width. Belay from an anchor on the side of the crack. 160'. **Pitch 2** (5.8): Continue up the widening crack, which becomes a chimney (you may want Big Bros for this pitch). 120'. **Descent:** Downclimb and rappel the gully to the west, then join the regular Lotta Balls Wall descent route.

ALCOHOL WALL

This wall plays host to a number of excellent 1-pitch routes, all of which are in the shade all day. Bring two 165-foot ropes for the rappel. From the base of *Lotta Balls*, walk right (west) along a ledge system and go under the boulder

FIRST CREEK CANYON
LOTTA BALLS WALL/ALCOHOL WALL

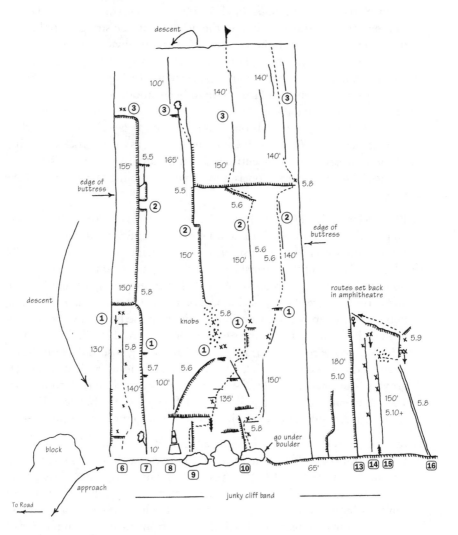

that *Black Magic* starts on. Follow the ledge system for 50 feet to the base of a huge, right-facing corner. Just right is the start of *Gin Ricky*.

12. **Straight Shot** (5.11+ PG) FA: Paul Van Betten; 1983. Stem, lieback, and power up the short, right-facing corner at the left edge of Alcohol Wall. The top of this corner turns into a big flake.

13. **Gin Ricky** (5.10) FA: Richard Harrison, Paul Crawford, Paul Van Betten, Sal Mamusia, Paul "Obi" Obenheim; 1983. Bring lots of gear from wires to a #4 Friend. Begin below a long, right-facing corner 65' right of *Black Magic*. Follow the corner to shaky rappel anchors 180' up.

*14. **Rob Roy** (5.10- PG) FA: Richard Harrison, Paul Crawford, Paul Van Betten, Sal Mamusia, Paul Obenheim; 1983. A bit sporty, but excellent. Bring wires and camming units up to #2.5. Start 10' right of *Gin Ricky* below a left-facing corner system. Climb the face past a bolt, then follow the corner past 2 more bolts to the rappel anchors. 150'.

15. **Mai Tai** (5.10+ R) FA: Richard Harrison, Paul Van Betten, Paul Obenheim, Sal Mamusia; 1983. A stiff drink—beware! Begin 12' right at a short dihedral capped by a ceiling. Ascend the dihedral to gain the obvious left-facing corner. Follow this past 3 bolts. At the third bolt, traverse right past a plethora of knobs to a 2-bolt anchor in the large, left-facing corner of the *Friendship Route*. 150'.

16. **Friendship Route** (5.9) FA: Joe Herbst and friends; Fall 1988. Better than it first appears. Bring large gear for the initial wide crack and an attentive belayer for the crux bulge above. Start about 30' right of *Mai Tai* and below an obvious left-leaning corner with a wide crack at the right edge of the wall. Swim up the crack to a ledge (5.8), then climb the steep corner/bulge above past several bolts to a terrace. Belay from a bush and medium-sized Friends. **Descent:** Walk up and left on the terrace to the rappel anchor on *Gin Ricky* and rappel with two ropes.

ROMPER ROOM AREA

Numerous moderate routes are located roughly 100 feet to the right (up canyon) of the Alcohol Wall. Most of the routes listed are one-pitch and have anchors for rappelling. Approach via the ledge system that runs under Lotta Balls Wall and Alcohol Wall. (No topo.)

17. **Guise and Gals** (5.4) FA: Kimi Harrison, Leslie Appling (NOLS staff); April 1992. About 60' right of the *Friendship Route* and around an outside corner is a water-polished dihedral rising from behind a cabin-sized boulder. Climb the dihedral, then move slightly left into a left-facing corner with a bush. Continue up the corner until you can step left to a 2-bolt rappel anchor. A 75' rappel gets you back to the ground.

18. **Girls and Buoys** (5.5 PG) FA: Kimi Harrison, Leslie Appling (NOLS staff); April 1992. Start 20' right of the last route, on the opposite side of the cabin-sized boulder at a series of three corners. Climb the leftmost corner for 40' to a ledge, then step left and climb the right-hand of two corners (or see Variation) to a 2-bolt rappel anchor. Carry up to a #3 Friend and rappel with one rope. **Variation** (5.4): Move a bit farther left and climb the left-hand dihedral to the anchor. This can also be reached by starting up the previous route.

*19. **Kindergarten Cop** (5.7+) FA: Donette and Todd Swain; September 1994. One of the better routes in this area. Bring small Tri-Cams, TCUs, Friends to #4 (for placements in pockets), and some long slings. Rope up atop a boulder that sits below a triangular ceiling 30' right of *Girls and Buoys*. Climb through the ceiling at a notch, then go up the varnished and white face past 4 bolts and gear placements to a communal anchor. Rappel with two ropes. 130'.

20. **Magic Mirror** (5.5) FRA: Todd and Donette Swain; September 1994. Carry a good selection of gear for this one. Begin 20' right of the last route, at an obvious left-facing corner that has a varnished right wall. Climb past three ledges, then up the corner to a communal belay. Rappel with two ropes.

21. **Buzz, Buzz** (5.4) FA: Leslie Appling, Kimi Harrison (NOLS staff); April 1992. Medium-sized Friends/Camalots needed. Gear up 50' right of the last route, on the opposite side of a bushy area where a sentry box stands below a dihedral. This dihedral is 30' from a bushy chimney that forms the left margin of an obvious varnished face visible from the parking area. Squirm up the sentry box/chimney, then up the dihedral to a 2-bolt rappel anchor. Rappel with one rope.

22. **Doobie Dance** (5.6?) FA: Unknown; late 1970s. Not much is known about this obvious line. Start 40' right of the last route, at the left side of the obvious varnished face visible from the parking area. Climb the crack past a bush to a ledge below a big ceiling. Rappel with one rope.

23. **Romper Room** (5.7+) FA: Unknown; late 1970s. This one looks harder than it actually is. Bring wires, TCUs, and Friends up to #3.5. Watch out for loose flakes in the crack. Climb the crack/flake system in the center of the varnished wall to a bolt anchor just below a ledge. Rappel with one rope (it just barely reaches).

24. **Algae on Parade** (5.7) FA: Jon Martinet, Jeff Gordon; 1978. Bring a good selection of big gear for this route. Start at a left-facing corner at the right edge of the obvious varnished wall. Climb the corner in three or so pitches to the top of the buttress. Walk off left, going over the top of *Lotta Balls*, then descend as for *Lotta Balls* down a gully (a couple of short rappels are needed).

Note: At least six more 1-pitch moderate routes have supposedly been done to the right of *Algae on Parade*. Some can apparently be toproped by going up an easy gully.

25. **Rising Moons** (5.5 PG) FA: Jono McKinney and friends; circa 1990. Supposedly a good beginner route. It's located several hundred feet to the right (up canyon) of *Algae on Parade*. Bring a standard rack and two ropes for rappelling. **Pitch 1:** Climb a classic chimney to a ledge, then continue up to a belay at the base of a corner. 150'. **Pitch 2:** Climb the corner and varnished face to its right to a belay stance with bolts. 140'.

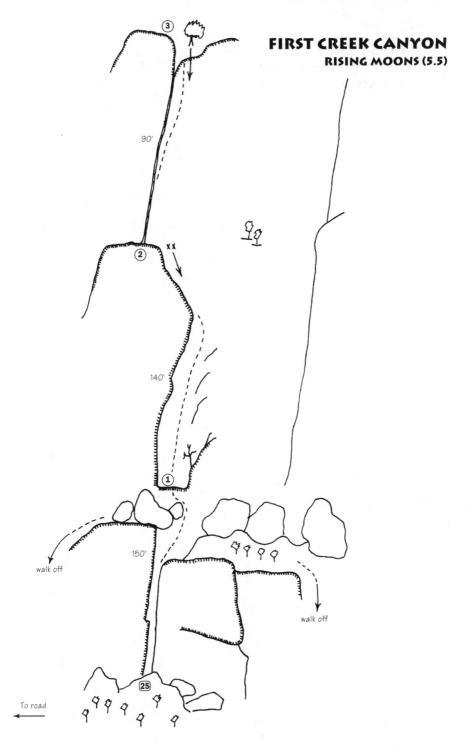

FIRST CREEK CANYON
RISING MOONS (5.5)

3

90'

2   X X

140'

1

150'

walk off

walk off

25

To road

FIRST CREEK CANYON
SLIPPERY PEAK APRON
THE RED AND THE BLACK (5.7)

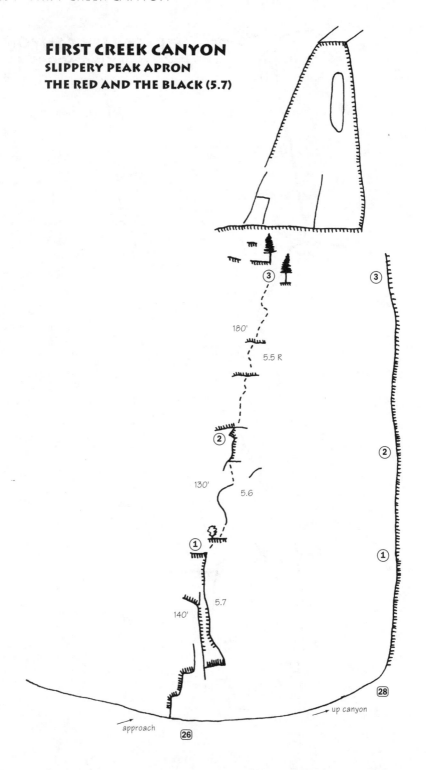

180'

5.5 R

130'

5.6

140'

5.7

approach

26

up canyon

28

Pitch 3: Go up along a varnished crack to a ledge. 90'. **Descent:** Rappel as follows: From atop Pitch 3 to Pitch 2's anchor (90'); from Pitch 2's anchor to a ledge near the top of the chimney (150'). Scramble down to the base of the route.

SLIPPERY PEAK APRON

Slippery Peak is located at the rear of First Creek Canyon and is recognizable by its pointed shape. The slabs below the peak are referred to as Slippery Peak Apron. It takes about 90 minutes to reach the base of the apron from the First Creek trailhead.

26. **The Red and the Black** (5.7) FA: Jon Martinet, Jeff and Scott Gordon; 1978. This route supposedly climbs the center of Slippery Peak Apron. **Pitch 1** (5.7): Climb up past a bolt to a belay at a bush. 140'. **Pitch 2** (5.6): Continue up. 130'. **Pitch 3** (5.5 R): Climb to the top. 180'. **Descent:** Rappel *Advance Romance* or (maybe) *Real Domestic Chickens*.

27. **Real Domestic Chickens** (5.10) FA: Rick Dennison, Mark Fredrick, Dan Cox; Spring 1994. Another route that reportedly climbs the middle of the Slippery Peak Apron. It is unknown which side of the last route this climb is located on. Bring small gear to supplement the bolts. **Pitch 1** (5.10): Climb past 6 bolts to an anchor. 140'. **Pitch 2** (5.8+): Continue up past 4 bolts. 140'. **Descent:** Presumably you rappel the route. (Not shown.)

28. **Advance Romance** (5.6) FA: John Martinet, Scott Gordon; 1978. Climb a left-facing corner near the right margin of the apron. This route is supposedly three pitches long. Rappel the climb.

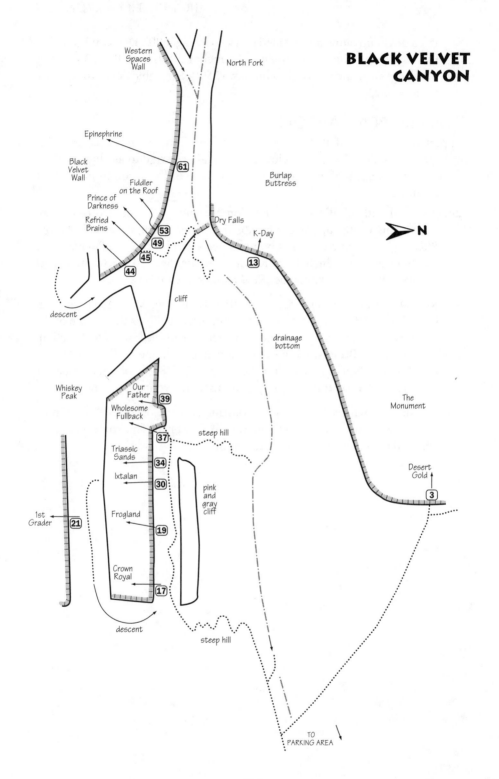

BLACK VELVET
CANYON

Western
Spaces
Wall

North Fork

Epinephrine

Black
Velvet
Wall

61

Burlap
Buttress

N

Fiddler
on the Roof

Prince of
Darkness

Refried
Brains

53

49

45

44

Dry Falls

K-Day

13

cliff

descent

drainage
bottom

Whiskey
Peak

Our
Father

39

The
Monument

Wholesome
Fullback

37

steep hill

Triassic
Sands

34

Ixtalan

30

pink
and
gray
cliff

1st
Grader

21

Frogland

19

Desert
Gold

3

Crown
Royal

17

descent

steep hill

TO
PARKING AREA

BLACK VELVET CANYON

Black Velvet Canyon is home to the most famous and classic routes at Red Rocks. The approach hike isn't too long (compared to some of the other canyons) and is actually quite enjoyable. To reach the trailhead, you must drive west on Nevada 160 for 4.6 miles (from the intersection with Nevada 159) to a dirt road. If you reach mile marker 16, you have gone too far. The dirt road is not marked by a sign, so keep your eyes open!

Turn right (north) at a cattle guard and follow the dirt road 1.9 miles to the third dirt road on the left. Make this left turn, drive another 0.5 mile to a T-intersection, then turn right and drive 0.3 mile to the parking areas at the end of the road. To get here, you'll be driving on rough dirt roads, but there is no need

for a special type of vehicle. To continue beyond the normal parking areas (to which there is no real benefit), you'll need four-wheel-drive.

As of press time, there was a distinct parking area at the end of the passable road, and the BLM did not allow camping here. There is no water, trash pickup, or bathrooms, so please do your part to keep this area clean and unpolluted. Again, if we don't police ourselves, there could be major repercussions!

THE MONUMENT

The following routes are located just outside the mouth of the canyon, to the right (north) on a formation named The Monument. As you look at the mountainside to the right of the canyon, you see a large, red band of rock below the brown sandstone. The following routes are above the left (south) end of the widest portion of red rock and climb a thin yellow stripe of rock capped by a roof. The light-colored roof is *Desert Reality* and is visible from the parking area. Many other climbs have been done in the area, but only the following routes are described in this edition.

From the parking area, walk straight across the desert toward a steep drainage that leads up to the climbs. The approach takes about 45 minutes. The routes are sunny. (No topo.)

*1. **Desert Crack** (5.12+) FA: Paul Van Betten, Sal Mamusia; April 1987. The short but very difficult finger crack leading up to the huge roof of *Desert Reality*.

*2. **Desert Reality** (5.11) FA: Paul Van Betten, Richard Harrison; February 1984. The obvious crack out the huge, light-colored roof. This was originally approached from the left via aid (2 bolts).

*3. **Desert Gold** (5.13-) FA: Stefan Glowacz, Paul Van Betten; May 1987. The link-up of the two routes listed above.

4. **Violent Stems** (5.12-) FA: Paul Van Betten; February 1987. Climb a left-facing dihedral below *Desert Reality*.

5. **Clipper** (5.11-) FA: Paul Van Betten, Mike Ward; February 1987. Climb a right-facing dihedral below *Desert Reality*.

6. **Scumby** (5.8) FA: Mike Ward, Paul Van Betten; February 1987. Ascend a right-leaning hand crack below a roof.

7. **Seduction Line** (5.11) FA: Unknown; circa 1988. This route starts about 300 yards right (north) of *Desert Reality*. Climb a small, right-facing corner with a $^1/_2$-inch crack in its back to an anchor about 80' up. Bring lots of thin gear.

8. **No Name** (5.10) FA: Unknown; circa 1988. Named for a famous seafood restaurant near Boston. About 100 yards right (north) of *Seduction Line* is a hand crack. Climb the crack to an anchor.

Desert Reality (5.11): Paul Van Betten and Mike Ward on the 5.11 crack. KURT MAUER PHOTO

9. **Chinese Handcuffs** (5.11+) FA: Unknown; circa 1988. About 200 yards to the right of *No Name* is a striking, left-leaning crack. Climb a shallow corner to double cracks. Above, follow a left-leaning thin crack past 1 bolt to an anchor.

10. **Lizard Locks** (5.11) FA: Unknown; circa 1988. Rope up about 75' right of the last route (roughly 650 yards right of *Desert Reality*) at a shallow, left-facing corner. Climb the corner to an anchor 50' up. Bring wires and Friends up to #2.

11. **All the Right Moves** (5.10) FA: Unknown; circa 1988. This route is supposed to be scary if you're short. Start 5' right of *Lizard Locks* and end at the same belay. Bring RPs and small wires.

12. **Cornucopia** (5.10- PG13); FA: Mark Moore and partner; circa 1976. On the right side of The Monument is a huge, rectangular, white scar. Just right of this scar is a gully (the line of *Blue Diamond Sanction* (5.8+), which is described in the Urioste guidebook). *Cornucopia* begins to the right of the gully, below a series of thin cracks. Bring RPs, TCUs, and cams up to a #5. Since the descent comes down far from the base of the route, plan on going light from the car, or carrying your pack up the route. **Pitch 1** (5.8): Scamper up some ledges, then climb a crack up to the base of a left-facing chimney. 150'. **Pitch 2** (5.10-): Climb the chimney to a ledge. Go up the steep cracks and face above to a belay ledge. 150'. **Pitch 3** (5.7): Go up the crack and face above to a belay ledge. 150'. **Pitch 4** (fourth-class): Scramble up and left along ledges to the edge of the huge gully. 50'. **Pitch 5** (5.10-): Face-climb up a varnished wall to a crack in a corner. Belay above a wide crack on a ledge with a tree. 150'. **Pitch 6** (third-class): Scramble about 300 feet up to the top. **Descent:** From the summit, go west, then south (toward the mouth of Black Velvet Canyon) down a gully. Some short rappels may be required depending on your down climbing skills.

BURLAP BUTTRESS

This generally sunny buttress is across the canyon from the Black Velvet Wall. Approach this formation by following the road for about 300 yards from the parking area, then take a trail that branches off right where the road makes a hard left turn. Hike this trail toward the canyon for about 0.5 mile, until it forks. Take the right fork and drop down into the drainage. Follow the rocky creekbed upstream for about 600 yards until the drainage is blocked by a cliff/waterfall. Routes are described from right (northeast) to left (up canyon).

13. **K-Day** (5.12) FA: Paul Van Betten, Jay Smith; 1990. This route starts above some boulders on the right side of the wall. Climb a brown face just left of a curving crack, past 1 bolt to a left-leaning corner. Lieback up the corner past 3 bolts (crux) to an anchor. 140'. Rappel with two ropes.

BLACK VELVET CANYON
THE MONUMENT
CORNUCOPIA (5.10-)

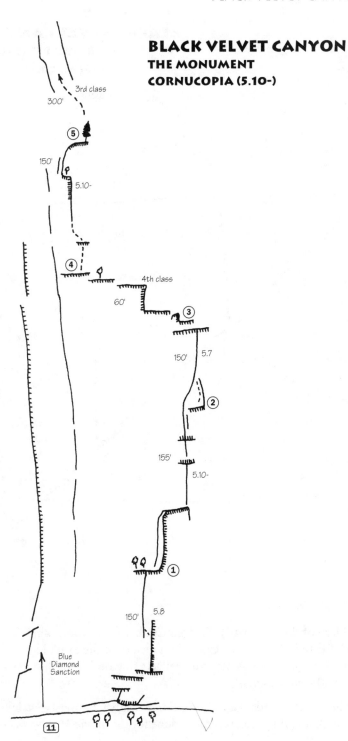

3rd class
300'

⑤

150'

5.10-

④

4th class

60'

③

150' 5.7

②

155'

5.10-

①

150' 5.8

Blue
Diamond
Sanction

⑪

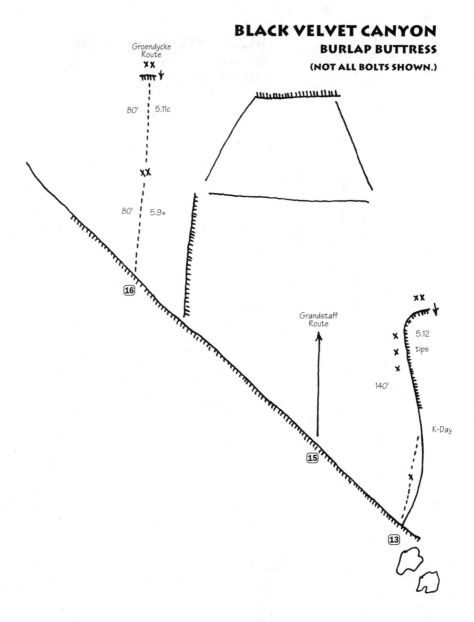

BLACK VELVET CANYON
BURLAP BUTTRESS
(NOT ALL BOLTS SHOWN.)

Groendycke
Route

80'   5.11c

80'   5.9+

Grandstaff
Route

5.12
tips

140'

K-Day

14. **Children of the Sun** (5.10) FA: Tom Cecil, Tony Barnes, John "The Gambler" Rosholt; November 1994. I am unsure of the exact location of this route. It is described as being on the left side of Burlap Buttress and just left of a broken arch.

15. **Unknown** FA: Randal Grandstaff, Randy Marsh; Spring 1991. Like *Integrity of Desire*, this first ascent was done for the movie *Moving over Stone*.

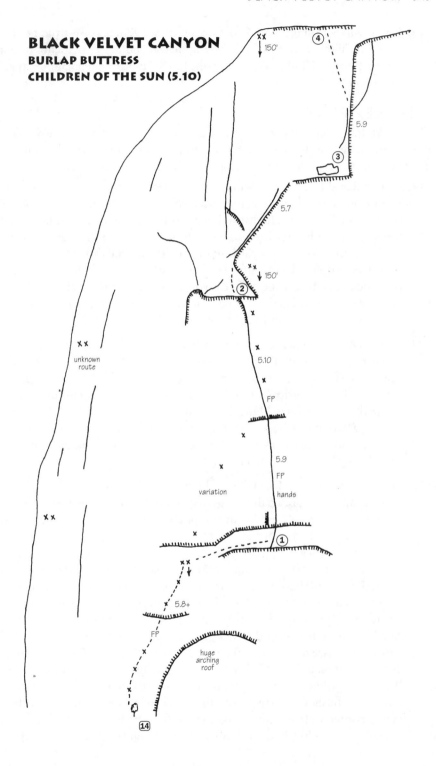

BLACK VELVET CANYON
BURLAP BUTTRESS
CHILDREN OF THE SUN (5.10)

16. **Unknown** (5.11c) FA: Bart Groendycke; circa 1993. Start just right of the waterfall. **Pitch 1** (5.9): Climb past numerous bolts to an anchor about 80' up. **Pitch 2** (5.11c): Continue up the face to another anchor. 80'. Rappel the route.

WHISKEY PEAK

The next routes described are on the left (south) side of the canyon on Whiskey Peak. Routes are described from left (east) to right (up canyon). Each climb has its own approach and descent descriptions. These routes are generally shady.

17. **Crown Royal** (5.8) FA: Unknown; 1980s. Follow the roadbed about 300 yards from the parking area, then take a trail that branches off right where the road makes a hard left turn. Hike this trail for about 0.5 mile until it forks. Take the left trail (the right fork drops down a hill into the main drainage) for another 200 yards until you are on a red dirt ridge. Follow a trail steeply uphill, heading for the left (east) edge of an obvious red and pink rock band below the main canyon wall. The route is a bit right of the dirt ridge mentioned in the approach and about 200' left (east) of *Frogland*. The route is five pitches long and involves some chimneying.

18. **Rain Dance** (5.10+) FA: Dave Wonderly, Don Wilson; Spring 1990. An excellent pitch to round out the day—just watch out for those dark clouds! The route can by toproped after doing the first pitch of *Frogland*. Bring wires, TCUs, and Friends to #2.5. Rope up as for *Frogland*, on a ledge above the main terrace. Make sporty face moves up the wall 20' left of the *Frogland* corner to a bolt. Continue up thin, right-facing flakes to a ledge. Step left and climb left-facing flakes to a ledge. Rappel from the middle of three bushy ledges with two ropes.

*19. **Frogland** (5.8-) FA: Mike Gilbert, Joanne and Jorge Urioste; May 1978. The sustained nature of the route may keep you hopping! Bring a good selection of gear because all of the pitches are long and wander a bit. Follow the roadbed about 300 yards from the parking area, then take a trail that branches off right where the road makes a hard left turn. Hike this trail for about 0.5 mile, until it forks. Take the left trail (the right fork drops down a hill into the main drainage) for another 200 yards until you are on a red dirt ridge. Follow a faint trail steeply uphill, headed for the left (east) edge of an obvious red and pink rock band below the main canyon wall. Once atop the rock band, contour right (west) about 200 yards to the base of the route. The approach takes about 30 minutes. Start at a clearing on a ledge 100' right (west) of a huge, white section of cliff. Between the white section of rock and this route are numerous crack systems filled with bushes and trees. The first pitch of this route ascends a left-facing corner system with a large, white flake at its base. **Pitch 1** (5.7): Scramble atop a block, then climb a left-facing dihedral past 3 bolts to an

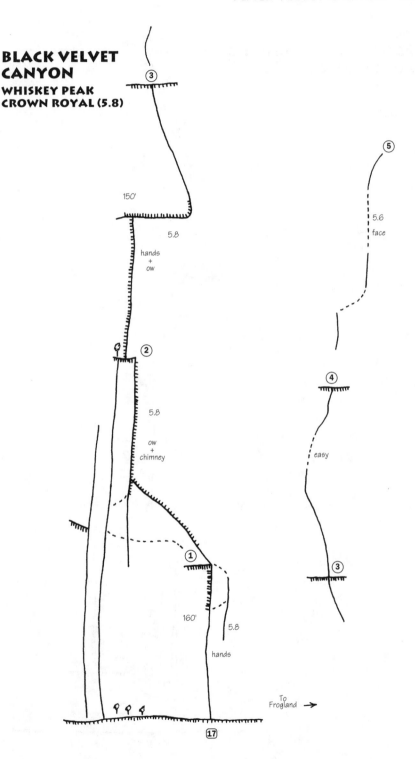

**BLACK VELVET
CANYON**
**WHISKEY PEAK
CROWN ROYAL (5.8)**

③

150'

5.8

hands
+
ow

②

5.8

ow
+
chimney

①

160'

5.8

hands

⑰

⑤

5.6
face

④

easy

③

To
Frogland →

BLACK VELVET CANYON
FROGLAND (5.8-)

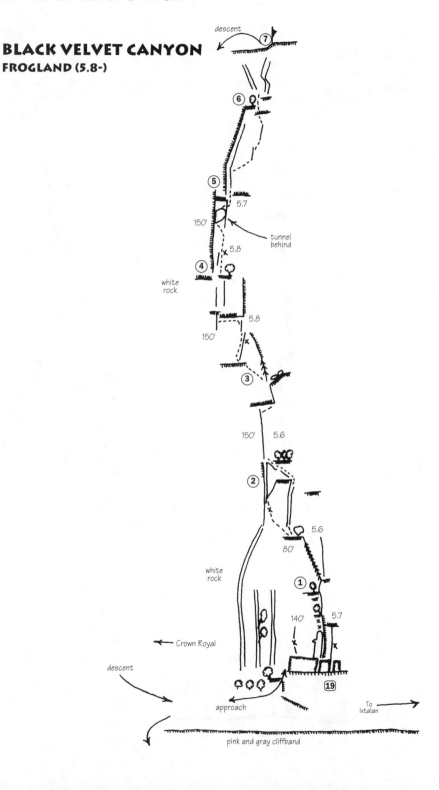

descent

7

6

5

5.7

150'

tunnel
behind

5.8

4

white
rock

5.8

150'

3

150'   5.6

2

5.6

80'

white
rock

1

140'   5.7

Crown Royal

descent

19

approach

To
Ixtalan

pink and gray cliffband

Frogland Area

obvious sapling. Continue up to the highest ledge with oak bushes on it. 140'. **Pitch 2** (5.6): Climb a beautiful low-angled dihedral above to a ledge (80'). Continue straight up the chimney/flake (or see Variation) to another ledge just below a prominent, bushy ledge. 150'. **Pitch 3** (5.6): Pull a small ceiling, then angle left under the bushy ledge to the main dihedral. Follow this to a bulge, then move right and up to a belay stance in a varnished, left-leaning corner. 150'. **Pitch 4** (5.8-): Angle left across the varnished face to a ledge. Climb the low-angle white dihedral to a bolt, then continue up 8' to a ceiling. Finger-traverse straight left to the arête, then up a thin crack to a stance. Continue up the face and shallow dihedrals above to a stance at a bush. 150'. **Pitch 5** (5.8-): Face-climb up white rock to a bolt, then angle up left into a chimney with a huge chockstone jammed in it. Tunnel easily underneath the chockstone, then step right above it and pull past a white bulge to belay in the easy chimney above. 150'. **Pitch 6** (5.6 PG): Scamper up the chimney a bit, then angle right out on the face. Follow thin cracks up to a ceiling and move back left to the corner and a bushy ledge. 120'. **Pitch 7** (fourth class): Scramble up any of the easy routes to the top of the buttress. 100'. **Variation:** The original route traversed left to a corner, then went up that to rejoin the line described here. **Descent:** From the top of the buttress, head left (east) down a gully toward the road. There are three gullies leading down; take the rightmost (southern) one, then contour back around to the base of the route. This is very simple and surprisingly quick.

There are also two excellent routes on the right wall of the descent gully about 200 yards from the top of *Frogland*. (Not shown.)

20. **Back to Basics** (5.7) FA: Wendell Broussard, Ed Prochaska; July 1992. Start below an obvious, right-facing corner and make difficult moves (using a boulder) into the corner. Rappel with two ropes from a 2-bolt anchor.

21. **First Grader** (5.6) FA: Wendell Broussard, Ed Prochaska; July 1992. Begin 15' right of *Back to Basics* and climb a beautiful finger crack to face-climbing and the bolt anchor.

The following routes are to the right of *Frogland*.

22. **As the Toad Turns** (5.10+) FA: Nick Nordblom, Jenni Stone, Jay Smith; 1989. Same start as *Frogland,* on a ledge 100' right (west) of a huge, white section of cliff. **Pitch 1** (5.10+): Climb to the top of the initial flake on *Frogland*, then move right into a shallow corner. Go up the corner past a bolt (crux), then right onto the face. Wander up black rock past another bolt to a stance on the arête. 150'. **Pitch 2** (5.9): Go straight up the narrow, black face, eventually moving left into *Frogland*. 90'. **Descent:** Either finish up *Frogland* or rappel with two ropes. (No topo.)

23. **Romance Is a Heart Breakin' Affair** (5.10-) FA: Nick Nordblom, Richard Harrison, Brad Ball; circa 1989. Begin immediately right of *Frogland*. Climb a crack in the arête, passing through a large hole. Go up and right to ledges (150'). Rappel from slings. (No topo.)

24. **Kenny Laguna** (5.10+) FA: Richard Harrison, Paul Crawford, Paul Van Betten, Sal Mamusia; 1983. Begin about 180' right of *Frogland* atop large blocks that are under a huge roof and about 25' above the ground. **Pitch 1** (5.10+): Climb a short dihedral under the center of the roof, then follow an obvious break out right through the roof. Climb up to a ledge below a

BLACK VELVET CANYON
IXTALAN AREA

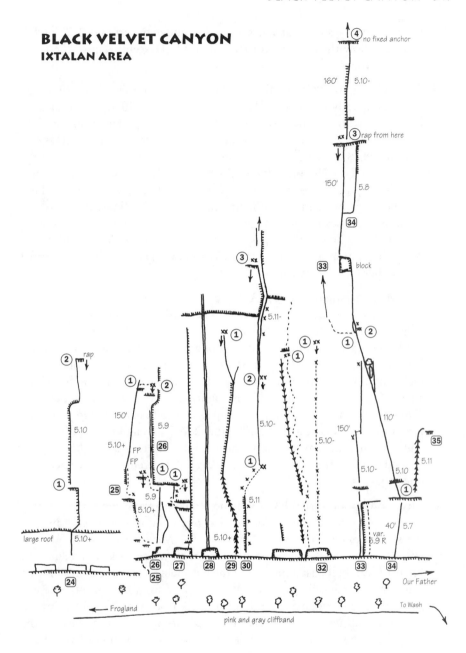

④ no fixed anchor

160'   5.10-

xx ③ rap from here

150'   5.8

34

③ xx

5.11-

33   block

x ①

xx ①
①

② xx

② xx

① xx
①

①

② rap

① xx   ②

① xx   ②

150'   5.9   26

5.10+   FP
FP

① ①

25

5.9
5.10+

5.10+

5.10

①

large roof   5.10+

5.10-

5.10-

5.11

5.11

110'

150'

5.10-

5.10-   5.10

① 35
5.11

①

40'   5.7
var.
5.9 R

24   25   26   27   28   29 30   32   33   34

Our Father

← Frogland

To Wash →

pink and gray cliffband

huge dihedral system that starts about 75' above the ground. 75'. **Pitch 2** (5.10): Follow the obvious corner system up. **Descent:** Rappel the route with two ropes.

25. **Perplexity** (5.10+ PG) FA: Todd and Donette Swain; October 1994. Well worth doing. About 60' right of *Kenny Laguna* (and 240' right of *Frogland*) is a recess with a brown, varnished dihedral 80' up. This is at the right (west) edge of a low roof. This route climbs the left wall of the recess and *The Misunderstanding* climbs the dihedral. Bring at least doubles of the smaller-sized TCUs, plus wires, Friends to #3, and some long slings. Scramble up past a couple of ledges, then step left to a cold shut. Climb past another shut and a right-facing flake to a ledge (bolt). Step left and climb weaknesses to the base of a right-facing corner. Climb the corner and shallow dihedral above past 2 fixed pegs to a ledge. Move right to the bolted belay atop the second pitch of *The Misunderstanding*. 150'. Rappel with either one or two ropes.

26. **The Misunderstanding** (5.9) FA: Dave Anderson, Randal Grandstaff; Fall 1975. This route offers two pitches of surprisingly good crack climbing. Begin 60' right of *Kenny Laguna* and 60' left of the *Mazatlan* corner, at a recess. This recess is at the right edge of a large roof and directly below a brown, varnished dihedral that starts 80' up. Bring a full set of Friends, including at least two extra of #3.5 and some long slings. **Pitch 1** (5.9): Scramble up ledges, then climb the right-hand crack/corner to a ceiling. Traverse left under the ceiling, then up to a 2-bolt belay anchor on a ledge left of the varnished dihedral. 80'. **Pitch 2** (5.9): Stem, lieback, off-width, and squirm your way up the varnished dihedral to a ledge. Move right around a ceiling then up to a 2-bolt belay. 80'. **Descent:** Rappel twice with one rope.

27. **Miss Conception** (5.10) FA: Todd and Donette Swain; June, 1995. Carry a good selection of Friends for the first pitch and lots of quickdraws for the second pitch. Rope up 15' right of *The Misunderstanding*, below a left-facing corner that leads to a ceiling with white rock on its left side. **Pitch 1** (5.9): Pull past a bulge into the left-facing corner, then up this to a stance below the ceiling. Move up left (bolt) onto a higher, rotten ledge, then go up and right past another bolt to a belay anchor. 75'. **Pitch 2** (5.10): Climb up along an arête into a right-facing corner, then up the steep face above to a belay anchor. Many bolts to clip and/or hang. 120'. **Descent:** Rappel with two ropes.

28. **Return to Forever** (5.10+) FA: Richard Harrison, Paul Crawford, Paul Van Betten, Sal Mamusia, Stanley Clarke; 1983. You'll be jazzed after doing this one. Bring two ropes and some *big* gear. Not much is known about this route, as you'll gather once you read the route description.

Start about 50' right of *The Misunderstanding* and 30' left of *Mazatlan* at some huge blocks. **Pitch 1** (5.10+): Climb the prominent off-width through the roof and belay above. **Pitch 2** (5.10): Continue up. **Pitch 3** (5.8): Continue up. **Descent:** Rappel the route.

*29. **Mazatlan** (5.10+) FA: Dave Anderson, Randal Grandstaff; 1978. A classic pitch. Bring a good selection of gear, as well as two ropes for the rappel. From the parking area, follow the roadbed toward the canyon for about 300 yards, then take a trail that branches off right when the road makes a hard left turn. Hike this trail for about 0.5 mile, until it forks. Take the right fork and drop down into the drainage. Follow the rocky creekbed up for about 300 yards, until you reach a trail leading steeply up left (south). Take this trail up, skirting the right (west) edge of a pink rock band below the main canyon wall. You should now be roughly below *Wholesome Fullback* and need to contour left (toward the road; east) about 100 yards to reach the base of this route. Start 300' right of *Frogland* at a clean, varnished dihedral that is 6' left of *Ixtalan* (the obvious off-width splitting a roof about 100' above the ground). Climb the corner/dihedral to a belay station under a ceiling. Supposedly a second pitch has been done, but no more is known. A two-rope rappel will get you down from the top of the first pitch.

*30. **Ixtalan** (5.11) FA: Jorge and Joanne Urioste, Dan "Spiderman" Goodwin; June 1981. Sharpen your off-width skills before trying this one! The bolts next to the off-width on Pitch 3 were placed on aid using a giant wooden Friend! To approach this route, follow the roadbed for about 300 yards from the parking area, then take a trail that branches off right where the road makes a hard left turn. Hike this trail toward the cliffs for about 0.5 mile, until it forks. Take the right fork and drop down into the drainage. Follow the rocky creekbed upstream for about 300 yards, until you reach a trail leading steeply up left (south). Take this trail up, skirting the right (west) edge of a pink rock band below the main canyon wall. You should now be roughly below *Wholesome Fullback* and will need to contour left (toward the road; east) about 100 yards to reach the base of this route. Approach time is roughly 30 minutes. Rope up directly below the obvious off-width crack splitting a roof about 100' above, and 6' right of a beautiful varnished dihedral. **Pitch 1** (5.11c): Power up a shallow right-facing corner past 4 bolts with red hangers, then angle right past 3 more bolts to a hanging belay at the base of *Ixtalan*'s crack. 70'. **Pitch 2** (5.10-): Lieback and jam up the widening crack to another hanging belay. 60'. **Pitch 3** (5.11): The longest 60-foot pitch you'll ever do! Struggle up the famous off-width, then lieback through the roof to a belay stance with bolts. 60'. **Descent:** Continue up the easy chimney above (not too interesting) or rappel the route.

31. **Matzoland** (5.12a) FA: Dan McQuade; Fall 1997. Start about 15' right of the start to *Ixtalan* below a small left-leaning corner. Climb the corner to the first belay on *Ixtalan*.

31a. **Cabo San Looseness** (5.10?) FA: Unknown; 1980. There is an old route that climbs the blunt arête between Ixtalan and Sand Felipe. A belay station is visible about 150' up under a small ceiling. No more is known about the route.

32. **Sand Felipe** (5.10- PG13) FA: N. Modelo, T. Caté; Fall 1994. Climb the face just left of *Sandblast* past 9 bolts to a chain anchor. Take care getting to the second bolt; there's groundfall potential. Rappel with two ropes.

33. **Sandblast** (5.10- R) FA: Joe Herbst, Larry Hamilton; May 1972. FFA: Paul Van Betten, Nick Nordblom; Fall 1987. The first pitch of this route climbs the original aid line of *Triassic Sands*. It then trends left and continues up for two pitches of additional climbing. Approach this somewhat loose climb by following the roadbed for about 300 yards from the parking area, then take a trail that branches off right where the road makes a hard left turn. Hike this trail toward the canyon for about 0.5 mile, until it forks. Take the right fork and drop down into the drainage. Follow the rocky creekbed up for about 300 yards, until you reach a trail leading steeply up left (south). Take this trail up, skirting the right (west) edge of a pink rock band below the main canyon wall. You should now be roughly below *Wholesome Fullback* and will need to contour left (toward the road; east) about 200' until below a striking finger-and-hand crack (the line of *Triassic Sands*). Begin at an obvious left-facing flake/corner with a wide crack in its back. **Pitch 1** (5.10-): Climb a left-facing chimney formed by a giant flake (or see Variation) to a ledge. Follow a thin, vertical crack system for about 50' to an old bolt. Move right to a wider crack and follow this up to join *Triassic Sands* and on to a stance with 2 bolts. 150'. **Pitch 2** (5.9+): Go left, then climb a thin seam and loose flakes to a belay. 120'. **Pitch 3** (5.7): A short, easy pitch up a wide crack leads to a ledge. 50'. **Variation** (5.9 R): Climb the arête on the right edge of the chimney. **Descent:** Rappel with two ropes.

*34. **Triassic Sands** (5.10) FA: Joe Herbst, Larry Hamilton; May 1972. FFA: Augie Klien, Tom Kaufman, Randal Grandstaff, Chris Robbins, Joe Herbst; Spring 1979. An old route, on even older rock! Bring numerous pieces to 3" for the second pitch. Many people rappel with two ropes from the top of the third pitch. If you continue above, there may be no fixed anchors for rappelling. Approach this route by following the roadbed for about 300 yards from the parking area, then take a trail that branches off right where the road makes a hard left turn. Hike this trail toward the canyon for about 0.5 mile, until it forks. Take the right fork and drop down into the drainage. Follow the rocky creekbed up for about 300 yards, until you reach a trail leading steeply up left (south). Take this trail up, skirting the right (west) edge of a pink rock band below the main canyon wall. You should now be roughly below *Wholesome Fullback* and will need to contour left (toward the road; east) about 200' until below a striking finger-and-hand crack. You'll be at the base of the climb about 30 minutes after leaving your car. Find the route 100' right of the prominent *Ixtalan* crack system and 20' right of a left-facing flake/corner. Start at a left-facing corner with a 3" inch crack. **Pitch 1** (5.7): Climb the left-facing corner to a ledge at the base of a striped dihedral. 40'. **Pitch 2** (5.10): Step left and jam the slightly left-leaning finger crack, past a ceiling, then continue up the hand-and-fist crack to a belay stance with 2 bolts. 100'. **Pitch 3** (5.8): Continue up the crack, past a block, then up one of two cracks to a good ledge with bolts. 160'. **Pitch 4** (5.10): Climb the right-facing corner to another ledge (no fixed anchors). 160'. **Pitches 5–6:** 2 easy pitches up a series of broken corners lead to the top of the buttress. **Descent:** Rappel from the top of the third pitch (two 150' rappels). Otherwise, from the top of the buttress, head left (east) down a gully toward the road. There are three gullies leading downward—take the rightmost (southern) one, then contour back around to the base of the route. This is very simple and surprisingly quick.

35. **Cole Essence** (5.11 PG) FA: Charles Cole, Randal Grandstaff; circa 1990. Climb the initial corner of *Triassic Sands* (5.7), then go up the striped dihedral directly above. At the top of the dihedral, exit right to a belay station on the arête. Either rappel or continue up *Archeoptryx*.

36. **Archeoptryx** (5.11 R) FA: Nick Nordblom, Lynn Robison; Fall 1988. Named for a fossilized bird-type thing of the Jurassic period (the age of dinosaurs). To approach this route, follow the roadbed for about 300 yards from the parking area, then take a trail that branches off right where the road makes a hard left turn. Hike this trail toward the cliffs for about 0.5 mile, until it forks. Take the right fork and drop down into the drainage. Follow the rocky creekbed upstream for about 300 yards, until you reach a trail leading steeply up left (south). Take this trail up, skirting the right (west) edge of a pink rock band below the main canyon wall. You should now be roughly below *Wholesome Fullback* and will need to contour left (toward the road; east) to reach the base of this route. This approach should take about 30 minutes. Start either atop *Cole Essence* or in the gully to the right of the prominent *Triassic Sands* crack. The route basically follows the arête above the *Cole Essence* dihedral for three pitches. **Pitch 1** (5.10- R): Angle out left from the gully and climb past bolts to a belay. **Pitch 2** (5.10-): Continue up the arête past more bolts to another belay. **Pitch 3** (5.11 R): Scary and difficult climbing up the arête leads to another belay. **Descent:** Rappel the route with two ropes.

37. **Wholesome Fullback** (5.10-) FA: Cal Folsom, Lars Holbeck; May 1975. An excellent route that can be done to round out your day. The route name was derived from the first ascent party's last names. Bring gear up to a #4 Friend, with emphasis on the 1" to 3" sizes. This route can be approached by following the roadbed for about 300 yards from the parking area, then taking a trail that branches off right where the road makes a hard left turn. Hike this trail toward the canyon for about 0.5 mile, until it forks. Take the right fork and drop down into the drainage. Follow the

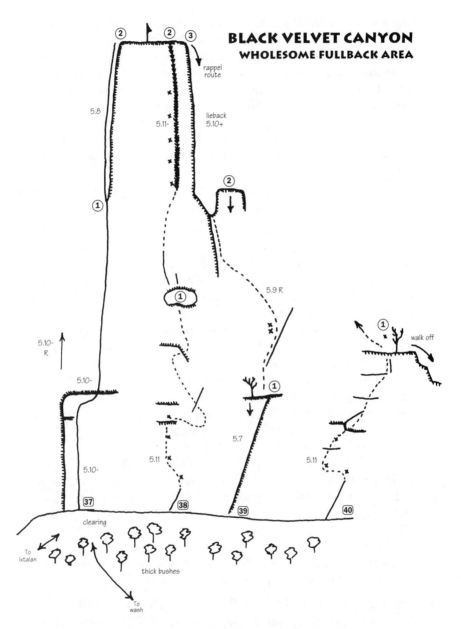

BLACK VELVET CANYON
WHOLESOME FULLBACK AREA

rocky creekbed upstream for about 300 yards, until you reach a trail leading steeply up left (south). Take this trail up, skirting the right (west) edge of a pink rock band below the main canyon wall. You should now be roughly below *Wholesome Fullback*, which climbs the left side of a prominent pillar that only goes partway up the cliff. The approach takes roughly half an hour. Begin 200' right of the *Triassic Sands* finger-and-hand crack, and about 10' right of a right-facing corner, below an obvious finger crack in a brown, varnished slab. **Pitch 1** (5.10-): Climb the slabby face to reach the crack, then follow this past a ledge to an overhang. Jog right (or see variation), then continue up the crack to a belay at the base of a chimney. 150'. **Pitch 2** (5.8): Follow the chimney to the top of the pillar. 100'. **Variation** (5.10- R): FA: Nick Nordblom, Teresa Krolak; circa 1998. At the point where *Wholesome Fullback* moves right, climb straight up the face for a full pitch. You eventually move back right to the top of the tower. **Descent:** Go down *Our Father* on the right (west) side of the pillar in three short rappels.

Note: A route has been done between *Wholesome Fullback* and *The Delicate Sound of Thunder,* but details are lacking.

*38. The Delicate Sound of Thunder (5.11 PG13) FA: Dave Wonderly, Marge Floyd, Dave Evans; November 1988. As awesome as it sounds! Not for the faint of heart. Your rack should include a bit of gear up to a #2 Friend. This route is best approached by following the road from the parking area for about 300 yards, then taking a trail that branches off right where the road makes a hard left turn. Hike this trail toward the canyon for about 0.5 mile, until it forks. Take the right fork and drop down into the drainage. Follow the rocky creekbed up for about 300 yards, until you reach a trail leading steeply up left (south). Take this trail up, skirting the right (west) edge of a pink rock band below the main canyon wall. You should now be roughly below *Wholesome Fullback*, which climbs the left side of a prominent pillar that only goes partway up the cliff. This approach should take about 30 minutes. Start about 50' right of *Wholesome Fullback* at a short, small, right-leaning corner. This left-facing corner is about 10' left of *Our Father*. **Pitch 1** (5.11 PG13): Wander up the face past 4 bolts, making difficult moves past the second bolt. Traverse right from the fourth bolt, making 5.10 moves way out. Climb up to a ceiling, then swing around right and up the face to an alcove (funky anchors, nothing good fixed). 140'. **Pitch 2** (5.11-): Climb a short crack above the alcove, then continue up the obvious arête past 5 bolts to the top of the pillar. Excellent positions! 100'. **Descent:** Rappel down *Our Father* on the right (west) side of the pillar in three short rappels (only one rope needed).

39. Our Father (5.10+ R) FA: Rick Wheeler, Joe Herbst, Randal Grandstaff, Vern Clevenger (of Tuolumne fame); Spring 1977. Say your prayers before leading the second pitch! Bring extra 2" to 3.5" gear. This route is best approached by following the road from the parking area for about 300 yards, then taking a trail that branches off right when the road makes a hard left turn. Hike this trail toward the canyon for about 0.5 mile, until it forks. Take the right fork and drop down into the drainage. Follow the rocky creekbed up for about 300 yards, until you reach a trail leading

Wholesome Fullback

steeply up left (south). Take this trail up, skirting the right (west) edge of a pink rock band below the main canyon wall. You should now be roughly below *Wholesome Fullback*, which climbs the right side of a prominent pillar that only goes partway up the canyon wall. This approach takes about 30 minutes. Begin 60' right of *Wholesome Fullback* at a right-leaning crack/corner and below a prominent, white, right-facing corner marking the right side of a pillar leaning against the main canyon wall. **Pitch 1** (5.7): A fun pitch in itself. Climb the right-leaning crack/corner to a belay ledge with a tree. 60'. **Pitch 2** (5.9 R): Climb up the face to double bolts, then angle left into the obvious right-facing corner. Belay above, atop a block (fixed anchor). 100'. **Pitch 3** (5.10+): Jam and lieback up the perfect right-facing corner above. 50'. **Descent:** Do three short rappels (only one rope needed) to get down.

40. **Tales from the Gripped** (5.11) FA: Todd Swain, Elaine Mathews (of *Vulgarian Digest* fame); November 1990. Don't worry, it's not that scary! Bring gear up to a #2.5 Friend and two ropes to rappel. Approach this route by following the roadbed for about 300 yards from the parking area, then take a trail that branches off right where the road makes a hard left turn. Hike this trail for about 0.5 mile, until it forks. Take the right fork and drop down into the drainage. Follow the rocky creekbed upstream for about 300 yards, until you reach a trail leading steeply up left (south). Take this trail up, skirting the right (west) edge of a pink rock band below the main canyon wall. You should now be roughly below *Our Father*, which climbs the right side of a prominent pillar that only goes partway up the canyon wall. It'll take about 30 minutes to reach the routes in this area. Start 20' right of *Our Father* at the next set of parallel, right-slanting cracks. **Pitch 1** (5.11): Climb the crack to its end (bolt), then move straight left to another bolt. Make difficult face moves up to a ceiling, passing a third bolt. Swing right around the ceiling and up to a belay ledge with a bolt and small tree. 60'. **Pitch 2** (5.10): Go left up a ramp, then climb the arête past 2 bolts (5.10). Move back right to a flake and a long, right-facing corner. Higher up the corner, follow bolts out right to a hanging belay. 130'. **Pitch 3** (5.11): Climb past 2 bolts to an overlap. Pull this (5.10), then angle left to a stance (bolt). Follow 2 more bolts up left toward a right-facing corner, then angle back right on sloping holds to a vertical seam. Climb up along this to a belay station. 90'. **Descent:** Rappel the two upper pitches with two ropes, then walk off west from the top of the first pitch.

41. **Only the Good Die Young** (5.11) FA: The Uriostes; 1984. This route climbs dihedral systems on the buttress to the right of the *Wholesome Fullback* buttress and across the gully from *Cutting Edge*. Jay Smith was pictured on the route in an old issue of *Rock & Ice* magazine. Unfortunately, I don't have a lot of info on the route. It has 4 pitches and they are supposedly rated 5.10+, 5.10, 5.11, and 5.7+. Apparently, the descent is down the gully to the right, between Whiskey Peak and Black Velvet Wall.

BLACK VELVET WALL

The next routes are on the Black Velvet Wall. This wall is separated from Whiskey Peak by a series of large gullies. These routes are described from left to right and are in the shade most of the day (all day in the winter).

BLACK VELVET CANYON
TALES FROM THE GRIPPED (5.11)

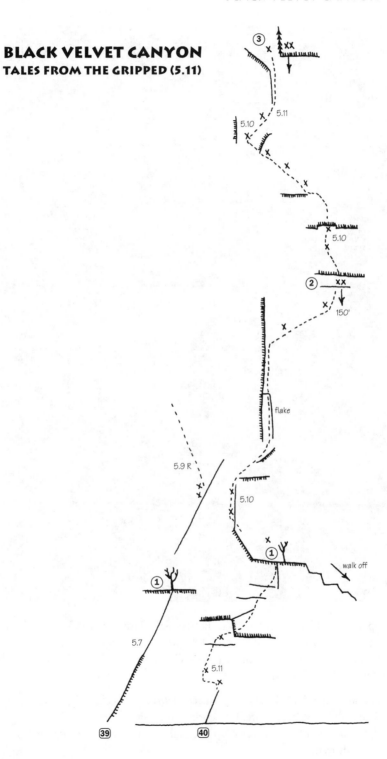

Black Velvet
Wall

up canyon

42. **Spark Plug** (5.10) FA: Paul Van Betten, Sal Mamusia; 1983. Start about 100 yards left of *Refried Brains* and 100' uphill from *Smooth as Silk*. Climb a very thin crack up a shallow corner (5.10). Continue straight up the corner to belay slings (150'). (Not shown.)

43. **Cutting Edge** (5.11) FA: Danny Meyers; 1987. An excellent 1-pitch route. Climb a very thin crack up a shallow corner (the initial corner of *Spark Plug*), step right and do a hand traverse up and right past bolts to a bolted belay (120'). (Not shown.)

44. **Smooth as Silk** (5.10+ PG13) FA: Jay Smith, Paul Crawford, Randal Grandstaff, Dave Diegleman; 1981. Bring small TCUs and wires. Approach this route by following the roadbed for about 300 yards from the parking area, then take a trail that branches off right where the road makes a hard left turn. Hike this trail toward the canyon for about 0.5 mile, until it forks. Take the right fork and drop down into the drainage. Follow the rocky creekbed upstream for about 600 yards until the drainage is blocked by a cliff/waterfall. Go left (southeast) into the bushes on a path, then scramble up the cliff on big ledges. Follow the trail up left about 100 yards to the base of the large, smooth wall. Continue up along the base of the wall for about another 200 yards, the last part of which lies in a large gully. Start just right of an obelisk leaning against the wall at a pair of right-leaning cracks. **Pitch 1** (5.10): Climb a corner/crack that goes right, then up leaning cracks on a smooth face to a belay anchor in an alcove. 140'. **Pitch 2** (5.10): Go up an obvious, big, flaring corner to anchors. 150'. **Descent:** Rappel with two ropes.

45. **Refried Brains** (5.9) FA: Joanne and Jorge Urioste, Stephanie Petrilak; November 1979. A good pun—the route is OK, too. Bring two ropes to rappel the route and large gear for the wide cracks. Approach this climb by following the road for about 300 yards from the parking area, then take a trail that branches off right where the road makes a hard left turn. Hike this trail toward the canyon for about 0.5 mile, until it forks. Take the right fork and drop down into the drainage. Follow the rocky creekbed upstream for about 600 yards until the drainage is blocked by a cliff/waterfall. Go left (southeast) into the bushes on a path, then scramble up the cliff on big ledges. Follow the trails up left about 100 yards to the base of the large, smooth wall. This section of cliff has some of the best routes in all of Red Rocks. *Refried Brains* is at the left margin of this wall and starts near the base of an obvious tree-filled gully leading up left (southeast). Plan on 30 minutes for the approach hike. Start about 160' right of *Smooth as Silk* and 40' left of a huge block leaning against the base of the crag. **Pitch 1** (5.8+): Climb a crack up and right past a bolt to reach an obvious crack. Follow this to a small left-facing corner. At the top of the corner, step left to a belay below a prominent, right-facing corner. 130'. **Pitch 2** (5.8+): Step left, then climb up via face, crack, and a right-facing corner (the last 20' of which becomes a chimney/slot). Stretch the rope to belay atop a pillar at the "tree-of-a-thousand-slings." 160'. **Pitch 3** (5.9): Traverse straight right on a shelf for 20' to a crack. Follow this up past a couple of off-width sections to a hanging belay in the crack. 145'. **Pitch 4** (5.9): Continue up the crack system to a small tree with slings. Wander up and left past blocks to an obvious bolted belay on the arête. 140'. **Pitch 5** (5.8): Face-climb up and left (keeping left of the arête), then straight up past 3 bolts. Turn a bulge on the left (bolt), then up and right to another

BLACK VELVET CANYON
REFRIED BRAINS (5.9)

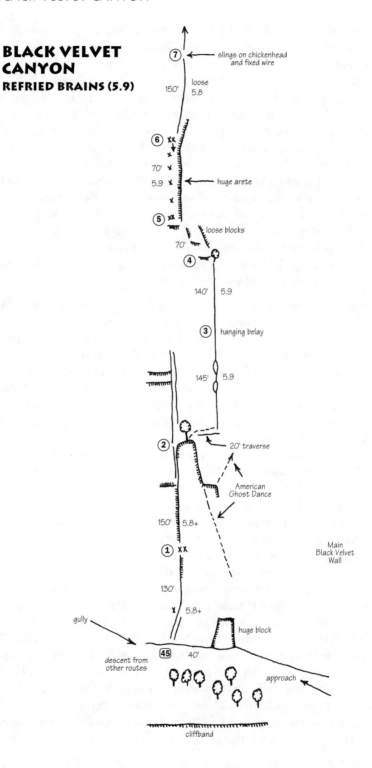

slings on chickenhead
and fixed wire

loose
5.8

150'

huge arete

loose blocks

70'

5.9

140'   5.9

hanging belay

145'   5.9

20' traverse

American
Ghost Dance

150'   5.8+

Main
Black Velvet
Wall

130'

5.8+

gully

huge block

descent from
other routes

40'

approach

cliffband

bolted belay. 60'. **Pitches 6–7 (5.8):** These are best avoided because the rock deteriorates, and there are poor fixed anchors atop Pitch 6. If you want to continue, follow cracks to the top of the pillar. **Descent:** Rappel the route with two ropes, at times using anchors other than those used for belays on the ascent.

46. **American Ghostdance** (5.12-) FA: Jordy Morgan, Kevin Fosburg; November 1988. The technical testpiece of the wall. Many people rappel after doing the first pitch. If you decide to do the whole route, bring wires, TCUs, and Friends up to # 2.5. Approach this route by following the road for about 300 yards from the parking area, then take a trail that branches off right where the road makes a hard left turn. Hike this trail toward the canyon for about 0.5 mile, until it forks. Take the right fork and drop down into the drainage. Follow the rocky creekbed upstream for about 600 yards until the drainage is blocked by a cliff/waterfall. Go left (southeast) into the bushes on a path, then scramble up the cliff on big ledges. Follow the trail up left about 100 yards to the base of the large, smooth wall. Approach time is about half an hour. Begin at a bush just uphill from *Sandstone Samurai* and below a bolt that leads to an obvious right finger-traverse below the varnished band. **Pitch 1 (5.12-):** Climb to a bolt, finger-traverse up right, and continue up past 4 bolts (many difficult moves). Move left (sidepulls) to a bolt, then make more hard moves to escape the varnished band. Continue up past 2 more bolts (sporty 5.10-) to the anchor. 130'. **Pitch 2 (5.10):** Climb past 4 bolts to a belay in a crack. 150'. **Pitch 3 (5.7):** A short pitch up a crack leads to a belay ledge at a right-facing corner. 20'. **Pitch 4 (5.10):** Clip 6 bolts (moving slightly left after the fifth bolt) to a bolted belay. 150'. **Pitch 5 (5.9):** Three bolts lead to a belay in a crack. 150'. **Pitch 6 (5.9):** Continue up the crack, then move out left and climb past 2 bolts to a right-facing corner/flake. Belay at a bolt at a corner. 100'. **Pitch 7 (5.10):** Climb up and slightly left past 2 bolts and a ceiling to a bolted belay on a ledge. 100'. **Pitch 8:** Fifth-class climbing and scrambling lead to the top. **Descent:** Go left (east; toward the road) until you can walk down to the notch between Whiskey Peak and Black Velvet Wall. Head down the gully between the formations to the base of the climb and your gear.

47. **Sandstone Samurai** (5.11- R/X) FA: Paul Van Betten, Nick Nordblom; Spring 1988. Leading this is akin to hara-kiri (or so you'll think if you're on the sharp end). Access this climb by following the roadbed for about 300 yards from the parking area, then take a trail that branches off right where the road makes a hard left turn. Hike this trail toward the canyon for about 0.5 mile, until it forks. Take the right fork and drop down into the drainage. Follow the rocky creekbed upstream for about 600 yards until the drainage is blocked by a cliff/waterfall. Go left (southeast) into

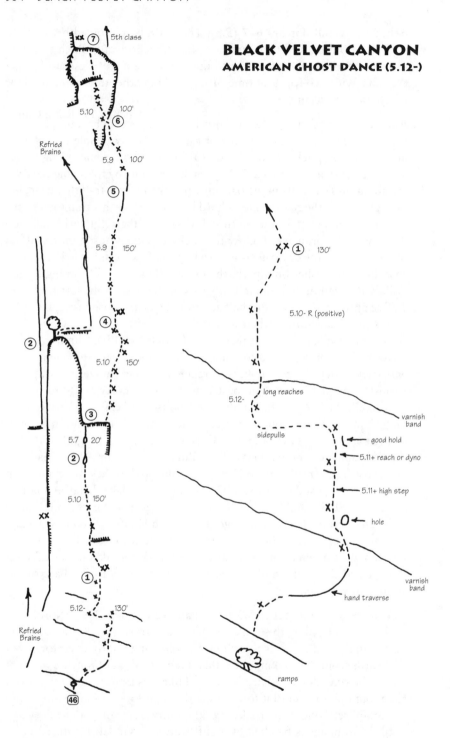

BLACK VELVET CANYON
AMERICAN GHOST DANCE (5.12-)

5th class

7

xx

6

5.10   100'

Refried
Brains

5.9   100'

5

5.9   150'

4

xx

5.10   150'

2

3

5.7   20'

2

5.10   150'

xx

1

5.12-   130'

Refried
Brains

46

1   130'

5.10- R (positive)

long reaches

5.12-

varnish
band

sidepulls

good hold

5.11+ reach or dyno

5.11+ high step

hole

varnish
band

hand traverse

ramps

the bushes on a path, then scramble up the cliff on big ledges. Follow the trail up left about 100 yards to the base of the large, smooth wall. You should be to the base of the route in about 30 minutes. Rope up at a smooth varnished face to the right of a low ceiling and left of a short pillar forming a left-facing corner. This is the same starting point as *Rock Warrior* and is 30' left of *The Prince Of Darkness*. **Pitch 1** (5.11- R/X): Climb 40' up white rock to a left-leaning white ramp (bolt). Traverse right on the white slab (or see variation), then diagonal up and left past 2 bolts to a smooth, varnished section. Make hard and scary moves straight up to another bolt and then the belay (2 bolts and wires). 140'. **Pitch 2** (5.10-X): Climb up to a short seam (TCU and wire), then continue up and slightly left (a couple of poor RPs may go in) to a bolt 50' above the belay. Head up and slightly right to the next belay anchor. 140'. **Pitch 3** (5.10- R): Wander straight up the face to a bolt anchor, placing some RPs for pro along the way. 150'. **Pitch 4** (5.10- R): Continue straight up, then angle right to a crack over a small roof. No bolts on the pitch, but a bolt and pin at the anchor. 150'. **Pitch 5** (5.11- R): Climb a small right-facing corner, then traverse up and left to the anchor. five bolts on the pitch. 150'. **Variation:** There are some newer bolts just left of this route with SMC hangers. I've been unable to determine if this is a totally separate route or merely variations. **Descent:** Rappel the route.

*48. **Rock Warrior** (5.10 R) FA: Richard Harrison, Jay Smith, Nick Nordblom; Fall 1983. A classic route, but **lots** scarier than *The Prince of Darkness*. Bring a selection of smaller-size gear, two ropes, and a cool head. Approach this route by following the roadbed for about 300 yards from the parking area, then take a trail that branches off right where the road makes a hard left turn. Hike this trail toward the canyon for about 0.5 mile, until it forks. Take the right fork and drop down into the drainage. Follow the rocky creekbed upstream for about 600 yards until the drainage is blocked by a cliff/waterfall. Go left (southeast) into the bushes on a path, then scramble up the cliff on big ledges. Follow the trail up left about 100 yards to the base of the large, smooth wall. This section of cliff has probably the best long routes in all of Red Rocks, including this one. It takes roughly 30 minutes to reach the route from your car. Rope up at a smooth, varnished face to the right of a low ceiling and left of a short pillar forming a left-facing corner. This is the same start as *Sandstone Samurai* and is 30' left of *Dream of Wild Turkeys* and *The Prince of Darkness*. **Pitch 1** (5.10- R): Climb 40' up and right on white rock (easy, but dangerous) to a slab. Clip a bolt, climb up, and traverse right until beneath the anchor. Climb up past 1 more bolt and make sporty moves to reach the belay. 150'. **Pitch 2** (5.10): Angle slightly left from the belay to a bolt, then wander straight up to another bolt by a shallow, left-facing corner. Make difficult moves up the arête of the corner to a seam, which is followed up and slightly right past a bit more fixed gear to the anchor. 150'. **Pitch 3** (5.10-R): Go slightly left from the belay, then up the face, past a little bit of fixed gear to a ceiling. Pull this and move up to a belay station. 150'. **Pitch 4** (5.9 R): Wander up the face to a 3-bolt belay at a corner (the first ascent party bivied here in hammocks). 150'. **Pitch 5** (5.9 R): Climb the corner, then up the face past a few bolts to another station. 150'. **Pitch 6** (5.10-R): Climb over a ceiling, then up along cracks and seams to a belay. 150'. **Descent:** Either continue up (5.8/5.9, then third class) or rappel with two ropes.

*49. The Prince of Darkness (5.10c) FA: The Uriostes, Bill Bradley, Mike Ward; Fall 1984. This route is impressive—not only for the positions you'll be in, but for the amount of effort needed to drill all the bolts you'll encounter (some say it's overbolted). Bring lots of quickdraws, a few medium-sized stoppers, butt bag (all the belays are hanging belays), and two ropes for the descent. The bolt hangers are painted black, as the route name might imply (ominous, eh?). Approach this route by following the road-bed for about 300 yards from the parking area, then take a trail that branches off right where the road makes a hard left turn. Hike this trail toward the canyon for about 0.5 mile, until it forks. Take the right fork and drop down into the drainage. Follow the rocky creekbed upstream for about 600 yards until the drainage is blocked by a cliff/waterfall. Go left (southeast) into the bushes on a path, then scramble up the cliff on big ledges. Follow the trail up left about 100 yards to the base of the large, smooth wall. This section of cliff has some of the best routes in all of Red Rocks. *The Prince of Darkness* follows the left edge of a prominent, black waterstreak in the center of the smooth wall. Approach time is about 30 minutes. Same start as *Dream of Wild Turkeys*, below the left end of an obvious, right-leaning crack 100' up and directly below a right-facing crack/corner about 40' up. **Pitch 1** (5.6): Scamper up easy rock to the base of a short, right-leaning crack/corner with a vertical crack leading straight up. Follow either feature up to a slab and a belay station with 3 bolts. 75'. **Pitch 2** (5.10b): Follow a crack/seam system up, then slightly right, passing 14 bolts to a 3-bolt belay station. 110'. **Pitch 3** (5.10a): Continue straight up the seam past 15 bolts to a 3-bolt belay. 130'. **Pitch 4** (5.9): Zip up along the crack past 13 bolts (at least 2 are missing hangers) to a 3-bolt belay. 125'. **Pitch 5** (5.9): Step left, then follow a crack past 8 bolts to a 3-bolt belay. 125'. **Pitch 6** (5.10c): Power up the smooth, varnished slab (crux) past 13 bolts to a large ledge and a 2-bolt belay (same belay as *Dream Of Wild Turkeys*). 100'. **Descent:** Rappel this route, *Yellow Brick Road*, or *Dream of Wild Turkeys* with two ropes.

*50. Dream of Wild Turkeys (5.10-) FA: The Uriostes; early 1980s. One of the earliest routes up this section of cliff. The name is a goof on a famous

BLACK VELVET CANYON
BLACK VELVET WALL
(NOT ALL BOLTS SHOWN.)

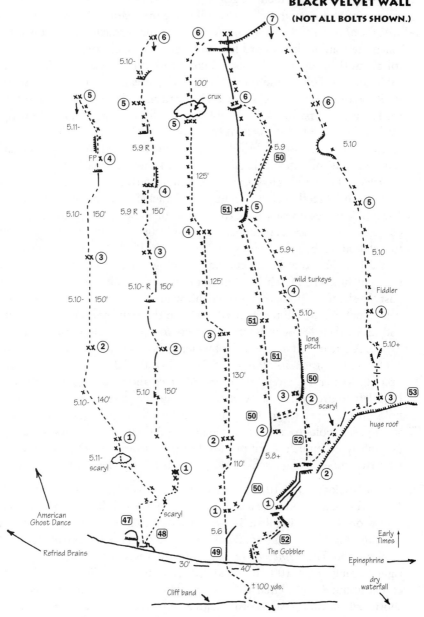

7

6   6   7

5.10-

5   5   6   6

100'   crux   6   5.10

5.11-   5

FP   4   5.9 R   5   5.9   50

5.10-   150'   5.9 R   4   150'   51   5   5

125'   4   5.9+   5.10

5.10-   150'   3   3   wild turkeys   Fiddler

5.10-   R   150'   125'   4   5.10-   4

XX   2   2   51   long   5.10+
5.10-   150'   pitch

130'   51   50   53
3   3   2   scary!   3

5.10-   140'   50   2   huge roof
2   2   52   2

1   1   1   5.8+   50

5.11-   scary!   2   110'   1

American   scary!   1
Ghost Dance   47   1   52   Early   Times

Refried Brains   48   5.6   49   The Gobbler   Epinephrine

30'   40'   dry
waterfall

±100 yds.

Cliff band

climb located on a sea cliff in Wales *(Dream of White Horses* on Wen Slab). Bring an assortment of gear up to a #3 Friend and two ropes to rap the route. Approach this climb by following the roadbed from the parking area for about 300 yards, then taking a trail that branches off to the right when the road makes a hard left turn. Hike this trail toward the canyon for about 0.5 mile, until it forks. Take the right fork and drop down into the drainage. Follow the rocky creekbed upstream for about 600 yards until the drainage is blocked by a cliff/waterfall. Go left (southeast) into the bushes on a path, then scramble up the cliff on big ledges. Follow the trail up left about 100 yards to the base of the large, smooth wall. This section of cliff has some of the best routes in all of Red Rocks. Give yourself about 30 minutes to reach the base of the wall. Same start as *The Prince of Darkness*, below the left end of an obvious right-leaning crack 100' up and directly below a right-facing crack/corner about 40' up. **Pitch 1 (5.6):** Scamper up easy rock to the base of a short, right-leaning crack/corner with a vertical crack leading straight up. Follow either feature up to a slab and a belay station with 3 bolts. 75'. **Pitch 2 (5.8+):** Angle right past a bolt into the prominent right-leaning crack and follow this to a belay anchor. 110'. **Pitch 3 (5.9):** Go up the crack a bit, then traverse right past 6 bolts to the base of a prominent, white flake/corner system and the belay anchors. 80'. **Pitch 4 (5.10-):** Climb the flake/corner system to its end (5.8), then face-climb left past bolts to a bolt anchor. 165'. **Pitch 5 (5.9+):** Angle up left across a slabby face (6 bolts) to a ledge at the base of a left-facing corner. 50'. **Pitch 6 (5.9):** Follow the left-facing corner/ramp up right to a crack. Go up the crack and face above (bolts), then traverse back left (more bolts) to a vertical crack in a waterstreak. Belay from 2 bolts on a scooped ledge. 140'. **Pitch 7 (5.9):** Climb the left-slanting crack/seam past 5 bolts to a spacious ledge with 2 bolts. 75'. **Pitches 8–12:** It's possible to continue up, but most folks rappel from here. **Descent:** Rappel with two ropes, using anchors on *Yellow Brick Road* and/or this route.

51. **Yellow Brick Road** (5.10) FA: The Uriostes, Mike Ward, Bill Bradley; Fall 1985. You don't need to be a wiz to know that the bolt hangers are painted yellow on this one. Really a 3-pitch variation to *Dream of Wild Turkeys*; the climbing is safe and enjoyable. Start at the base of *Dream of Wild Turkeys* and *The Prince of Darkness* below the left end of an obvious, right-leaning crack 100' above and directly below a right-facing crack/corner about 40' up. **Pitch 1 (5.6):** Scamper up easy rock to the base of a short, right-leaning crack/corner with a vertical crack leading straight up. Follow either feature up to a slab and a belay station with 3 bolts. 75'. **Pitch 2 (5.8+):** Angle right past a bolt into the prominent right-leaning crack and follow this to a belay anchor. 110'. **Pitch 3 (5.10b/c):** Continue straight up the crack and face above to a hanging belay from bolts. 120'.

Pitch 4 (5.10a/b): Follow 10 bolts up the face to rejoin *Dream of Wild Turkeys* at a belay station. 125'. **Pitch 5:** Ascend the left-facing flake to a bolt, then move left and up a crack/corner (2 more bolts) to a 2-bolt belay on a scooped ledge. **Descent:** Either continue up *Dream of Wild Turkeys* or rappel the route with two ropes.

52. **The Gobbler** (5.10-) FA: The Uriostes, Bill Bradley, Mike Ward; July 1980. A good way to round out the day or start *Dream of Wild Turkeys*. Make sure you have some long slings and gear up to 3". This route is best approached by following the road from the parking area for about 300 yards, then taking a trail that branches off right when the road makes a hard left turn. Hike this trail toward the canyon for about 0.5 mile, until it forks. Take the right fork and drop down into the drainage. Follow the rocky creekbed upstream for about 600 yards until the drainage is blocked by a cliff/waterfall. Go left (southeast) into the bushes on a path, then scramble up the cliff on big ledges. Follow the trail up left about 100 yards to the base of the large, smooth wall. It'll take about 30 minutes to reach the base of the route from the parking area. Start below a right-leaning gash about 60' up (rappel anchors are clearly visible) and 40' right of *Dream of Wild Turkeys*. This climb is at the left (east) end of a huge arch/ceiling at the base of Black Velvet Wall. **Pitch 1** (5.9): Climb easy white rock for 30' to a bolt in a depression. Go up left 10' to another bolt then up to a horizontal break. Move up right past 2 bolts, then finger-traverse up right to a left-leaning crack/corner. Follow this past a bolt to a ledge and belay station (watch out for rope drag). 110'. **Pitch 2** (5.10-): Jam up cracks just right of the right-leaning gash/chimney past 1 bolt to another anchor (5.9, possible belay here). Power up the steep face past more bolts to a belay on *Dream of Wild Turkeys* at the base of a white, left-facing flake/corner system. 130'. **Descent:** Either continue up *Dream of Wild Turkeys* or rappel the route. Watch out for ropes stuck in the cracks!

*53. **Fiddler on the Roof** (5.10+ PG13) FA: Dave Wonderly, Warren Egbert, Jennifer Richards; November 1990. Bring your prussiks! This exciting route starts at the second anchor on *The Gobbler* and traverses out right above the lip of the huge arch/ceiling. Rumor has it that 1 or 2 bolts have been added to the route, which could make it less sporty than the protection rating implies. Start below a right-leaning gash about 60' up (rappel anchors are clearly visible) and 40' right of *Dream of Wild Turkeys*. This climb is at the left (east) end of a huge arch/ceiling at the base of the Black Velvet Wall. **Pitch 1** (5.9): Climb easy white rock for 30' to a bolt in a depression. Go up left 10' to another bolt then up to a horizontal break. Move up right past 2 bolts, then finger-traverse up right to a left-leaning crack/corner. Follow this past a bolt to a ledge and belay station (watch out for rope drag). 110'. **Pitch 2** (5.9): Jam up cracks just right of the right-leaning gash/chimney past 1 bolt to another belay anchor. 60'. **Pitch 3:** Trend out right along the lip of the huge roof (don't fall!), passing 2 bolts and a few gear placements to a belay station. 165'. **Pitch 4** (5.10+): Climb pretty much straight up the spectacular face past 2 bolts to a bolted belay. 150'. **Pitch 5** (5.10): Continue up the magnificent varnished face, past 6 bolts and some traditional gear placements. Fixed anchor. 150'. **Pitch 6** (5.10): Follow 2 bolts up the face to a ledge (5.10), then continue up past 1 more bolt to the belay. 150'. **Pitch 7:** Two more bolts lead to Turkey Ledge. **Descent:** Rappel *Dream of Wild Turkeys* with two ropes.

54. **Early Times** (5.10-) FA: Unknown; circa 1980s. To the right of *The Gobbler* is a corner system that leads through the giant roof. Climb up to the roof, then traverse out along the corner to the lip. Belay and rappel from the anchor above.

55. **Johnny Come Lately** (5.10+?) FA: Unknown; circa 1980s. Climb the bolted face below and right of *Early Times*.

*56. **Sour Mash** (5.10-) FA: The Uriostes; July 1980. A primarily natural line up the wall just right of the huge arch mentioned in *Fiddler on the Roof* and *The Gobbler*. Carry a good selection of pro and two ropes. Access this climb by following the roadbed from the parking area for about 300 yards, then taking a trail that branches off to the right when the road makes a hard left turn. Hike this trail toward the canyon for about 0.5 mile, until it forks. Take the right fork and drop down into the drainage. Follow the rocky creekbed upstream for about 600 yards until the drainage is blocked by a cliff. Go left (southeast) into the bushes on a path, scramble up the cliff band as per the other routes, then go up to the base of the wall on one of the trails. Total approach time is about 30 minutes. Begin below the right end of the huge roof and just left of a large, white, pyramid-shaped buttress. The route ascends the right side of a brown triangle of rock about 60' up, then follows crack systems that keep right of the huge roof. Scramble 20' up to a ledge with a bush. **Pitch 1** (5.10-): Climb up a shallow, right-facing corner, then step right and go up a steeper lieback crack to a ledge with a bush. Climb the left-facing corner/crack above (this is the right side of the brown triangle) past bolts to the top of the triangle. Follow an easier, right-leaning crack/corner to a belay stance between two bushes. Large Friends are needed for the belay. 150'. **Pitch 2** (5.8): Move right from the belay to an arête, then up this past a bolt to the ceiling. Pull the first ceiling to a second bolt, then follow a crack up and right to a belay anchor (possible belay here). Continue up a crack past 2 bolts. Step left on a ledge to a bolt, then up 20' to another ledge with a bolted anchor. 150'. **Pitch 3** (5.7): Climb the center of three crack systems above to a hanging belay. 50'. **Pitch 4** (5.9): Follow the crack up and

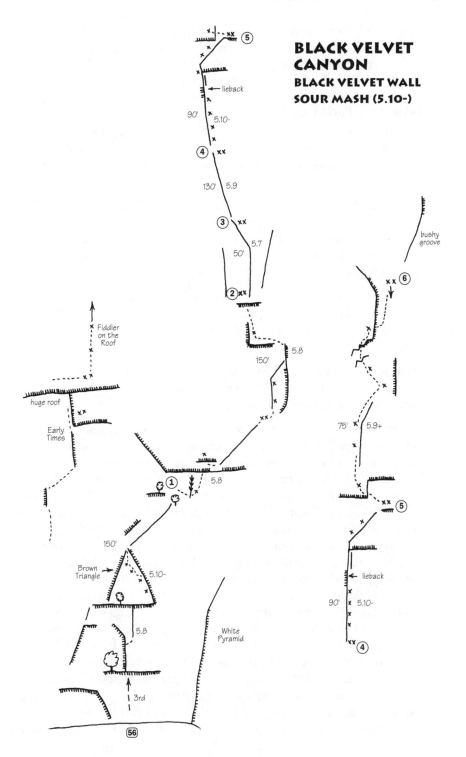

BLACK VELVET CANYON
BLACK VELVET WALL
SOUR MASH (5.10-)

lieback

90'   5.10-

130'   5.9

50'   5.7

bushy
groove

Fiddler
on the
Roof

huge roof

Early
Times

150'   5.8

75'   5.9+

5.8

150'

Brown
Triangle   5.10-

lieback

90'   5.10-

5.8   White
Pyramid

3rd

56

slightly left to a hanging belay. 130'. **Pitch 5** (5.10-): Continue up the obvious, slightly left-leaning seam/crack past bolts to a stance. Lieback a flake up a smooth section past a small ceiling, then angle up and right to a 2-bolt belay anchor below another light-colored ceiling. 90'. **Pitch 6** (5.9+): Step over the ceiling to a bolt. Face-climb along a crack past 2 bolts to a smooth section. Make difficult moves past bolts to a left-facing corner. Step right and up to a rappel anchor. 75'. **Descent:** Rappel with two ropes straight down to *Fiddler on the Roof*'s belay at the lip of the huge roof. Another wild rappel and a bit of downclimbing return you to the base of the route.

57. **My Little Pony** (5.11+) FA: Paul Van Betten, Richard Harrison, Shelby Shelton; Summer 1990. Not much is known about this route. It starts just left of the left side of the *Epinephrine* tower (a.k.a. The Black Tower) and goes out the left side of a giant scoop above. The route is seven pitches long and you can rappel with two ropes.

58. **Velveeta** (5.10+) FA: Richard Harrison, Wendell Broussard; Summer 1990. This route climbs out the right side of the scoop that is just left of the *Epinephrine* tower (a.k.a. The Black Tower). It is six or seven pitches long.

59. **Malicious Mischief** (5.10) FA: Joe Herbst, Stephanie Petrilak, Mike Gilbert; May 1978. This off-width route ascends the left side of the *Epinephrine* tower (a.k.a. The Black Tower).

60. **Chalk Is Cheap** (5.10+ R) FA Mike Ward, Mike Clifford, Eric Sutton; Fall 1989. Kind of like *The Prince of Darkness*, except the rock is bad and there are no bolts! Bring two ropes and a good selection of gear because there are no fixed anchors. Start 50' left of *Epinephrine*, at a left-slanting ramp on the lowest tier of the cliff. Scramble out left along the ramp, then up one of two cracks to the bushy ledge 60' up. Start on a small, high ledge beneath a left-facing corner that leads to a ceiling. **Pitch 1** (5.9 R): Climb the left-facing corner to the ceiling, step out right, and climb the scary face to a right-slanting corner that becomes a larger, left-facing corner. Belay amid blocks below an obvious crack in a dihedral 140'. **Pitch 2** (5.8): Climb the crack in the dihedral, then follow it up the left wall of a broken corner. Just before the crack ends, move around right to a stance below an obvious V slot (watch for rope drag). Climb the slot and continue up the easy corner to a belay atop a pillar. 120'. **Pitch 3** (5.10+ R): Climb the left edge of the steep brown wall (or see variation), moving out right to a fixed peg. Follow a vertical seam up to the center of a ceiling and pull through this. Angle slightly left up an easy ramp to a belay at a short, vertical crack. 140'. **Pitch 4** (5.10 R): Climb one of the two leftmost cracks up the buttress until you run out of rope. 150'. **Pitch 5** (5.6): An easy pitch

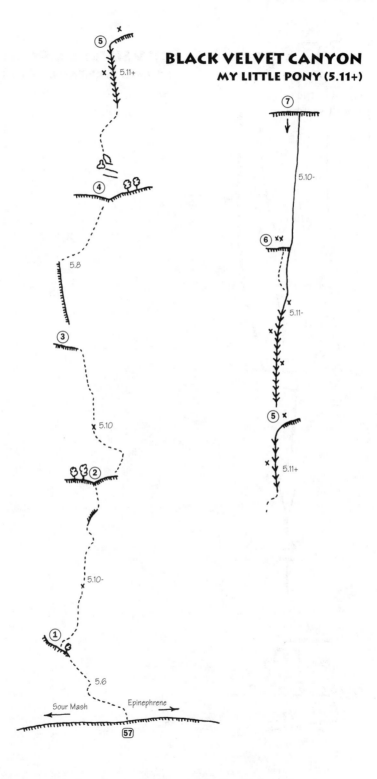

BLACK VELVET CANYON
MY LITTLE PONY (5.11+)

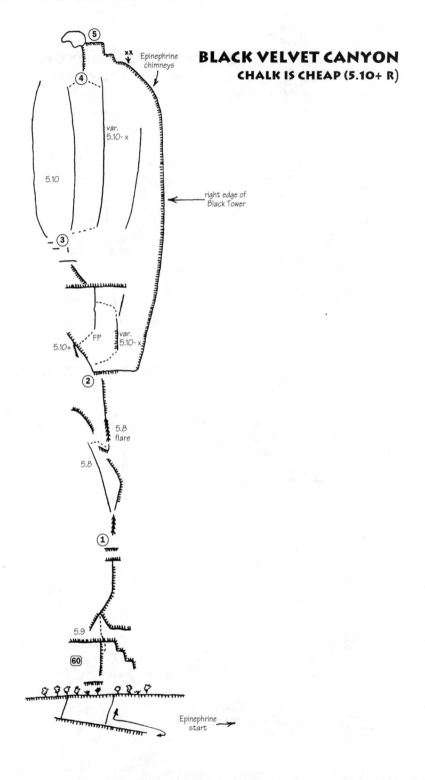

BLACK VELVET CANYON
CHALK IS CHEAP (5.10+ R)

Epinephrine
chimneys

var.
5.10- x

5.10

right edge of
Black Tower

FP   var.
5.10- x

5.10+

5.8
flare

5.8

5.9

60

Epinephrine
start

leads to the top of the tower. 40'. **Variation/Choss Is Cheaper** (5.10- X): FA: Bobby Knight, Todd Swain; April 1995. On Pitch 3, from the top of the pillar, go up and left a bit, then go out right on big holds to a vertical seam. Climb the seam to an obvious, right-facing flake/corner (this is about 10' right of the fixed peg). Follow the flake/corner to a good stance then angle up left to reach the vertical seam leading to the ceiling. Follow the regular route over the ceiling and up to the belay. 140'. On Pitch 4 (5.10-X), go up and left from the belay, then angle up right to reach the third crack system from the left edge of the tower. Follow this until it ends and belay. 150'. **Descent:** Rappel the *Epinephrine* chimneys.

*61. **Epinephrine** (5.9) FA: The Uriostes, Joe Herbst; August 1978. One of the best climbs I've done, but you'd better be solid on 5.9 chimneys! A long route with sustained climbing and lots of third-and-fourth-class scrambling to get off. The pitches are described as they were originally done, but it's entirely possible to combine pitches (especially above the top of the tower) to make the climb go faster. Approach this fine outing by following the roadbed from the parking area for about 300 yards, then taking a trail that branches off to the right when the road makes a hard left turn. Hike this trail toward the canyon for about 0.5 mile, until it forks. Take the right fork and drop down into the drainage. Follow the rocky creekbed upstream for about 600 yards until the drainage is blocked by a cliff/waterfall. Go left (southeast) into the bushes on a path, scramble up the cliff as for the other routes, then go right and down to the pebbly streambed. Approach time is about 40 minutes. *Epinephrine* is 60 yards up-canyon from the waterfall and starts below a gray face with 3 bolts (red hangers), which is 15' right of a right-slanting crack. If speed is a consideration, you can avoid the first pitch by starting 50' farther right and soloing up easy ledges (30' left of a yellow, left-facing corner, which is the line of *Texas Hold'em*). **Pitch 1** (5.8): Climb the gray face past 3 bolts to a bushy ledge. 60'. **Pitch 2** (5.7): From the left side of the ledge, follow the obvious features up and slightly left past 3 bolts to another vegetated ledge. 100'. **Pitch 3** (5.6): Climb an easy chimney and belay above at one of many trees. 150'. **Pitch 4:** Scramble up to the base of the chimneys, which are on the right side of the huge pillar (The Black Tower). **Pitch 5** (5.9): Struggle up the beautiful chimney to a belay station. 150'. **Pitch 6** (5.9): Continue up the chimney to another anchor (awesome positions). 75'. **Pitch 7** (5.9): Another pitch of wiggling and thrashing leads to the chimney section's top. 90'. **Pitch 8:** Scramble to the top of the tower. (Note: The top of the tower is quite spacious, leans inward, and is really the only place to bivy. Many folks climb to here, then rappel back down the route. The rappels down the chimney are set for two 60-meter ropes.) **Pitch 9** (5.7): Face-climb past 2 bolts to a belay. 75'. **Pitch 10** (5.7): Pull a ceiling, then go up to a bushy ledge. 75'. **Pitch 11** (5.6): Traverse right about 50',

BLACK VELVET CANYON
BLACK VELVET WALL
EPINEPHRINE (5.9)

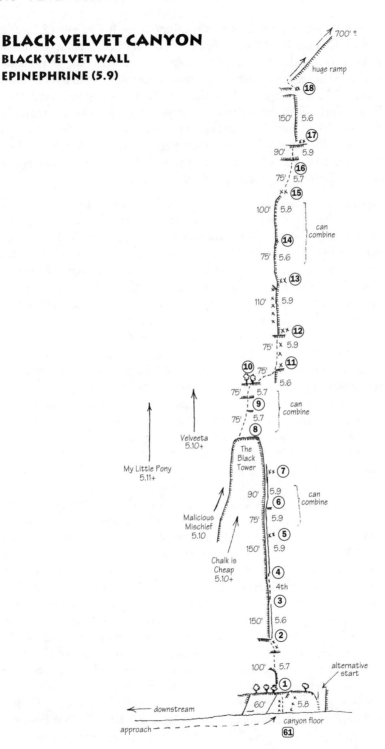

then climb up to a belay ledge with 1 bolt. 75'. **Pitch 12** (5.9): A bit of tricky face-climbing past 2 bolts leads to another belay ledge. 75'. **Pitch 13** (5.9): Climb the prominent dihedral past 5 bolts to a belay in an alcove. 110'. **Pitch 14** (5.6): Continue up the dihedral to belay on a ledge. 75'. **Pitch 15** (5.8): Upward! 100'. **Pitch 16** (5.7): More of the same. Belay under a roof. 75'. **Pitch 17** (5.9): Climb the roof on the right (exposed), then up to a belay anchor. 90'. **Pitch 18** (5.6): Up! Belay on a ledge to the left under a ceiling. Bolt anchor. 150'. **To the top:** Move left from the belay onto a huge, right-leaning ramp (many large ledges to organize on). Follow this ramp up right for about 700', passing numerous places where folks have had to bivy (some for the second time!). This involves fourth- and easy fifth-class climbing, sometimes with big air below. The last bit of the route follows bushy ledges around an amphitheater to the top of the wall. **Descent:** Walk up and left (south) to the highest summit (don't be lured down the first gully you come to), then follow the ridge down to the top of Whiskey Peak (you'll be heading down toward the parking area). From the top of Whiskey Peak, drop down into the left (northwest) gully and scramble down past *Refried Brains* and the other routes to your pack. To the right (southeast) is the fastest way to the car, if you have all of your gear with you. The whole descent takes roughly an hour (if you have something other than your tight climbing shoes with you!).

62. **Texas Hold'em** (5.11): FA: Unknown; circa 1990. This is a big route with sustained climbing. Bring two ropes and a double set of cams up to #4. Start about 80' right of *Epinephrine* at ledges leading to a left-facing corner.

63. **Lone Star** (5.10+) FA: Richard Harrison, Paul Crawford, Paul Van Betten, Paul Obenheim; April 1984. This route starts up *Yellow Rose of Texas* (described in the Urioste guide), then continues up the huge wall to the right. Begin to the right of *Epinephrine* at a left-facing chimney/corner that is about 75' left of a pool. Not much is known about this route, other than what is shown on the accompanying topo.

WESTERN SPACES WALL

Note: The next seven routes are much farther up the canyon. I haven't even eyeballed these climbs, but they are all supposed to be of high quality.

This shady wall is located in the south (left) side of the south (left) fork of upper Black Velvet Canyon. To reach the base of the routes you'll need to continue up canyon past *Epinephrine* until you arrive at a fork in the canyon. Go up the narrow left canyon (fourth class), eventually climbing slabs on the right side of the canyon to bypass a waterfall. The routes begin on a ledge system to the left (southeast) of the top of the waterfall. Most routes are descended via a rappel route on the right (west) side of the wall.

BLACK VELVET CANYON
BLACK VELVET WALL
TEXAS HOLD'EM (5.11)

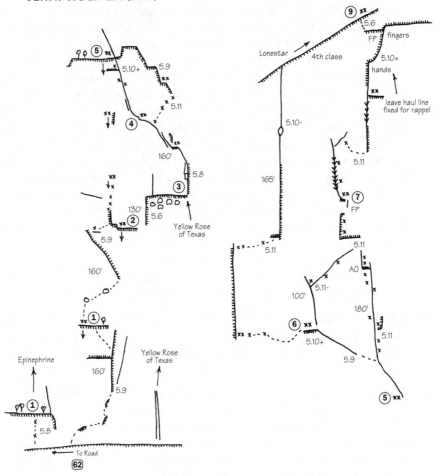

*64. **Sick for Toys** (5.10+) FA (**Pitches 1 and 2**) Unknown; FA (**Pitches 3 and 4**): Brad Stewart, Danny Meyers; November 1988. This is supposed to be a very high quality slab route. Bring RPs, wires, TCUs, cams up to #2.5, and two ropes.

65. **Tranquility Base** (5.10+) FA: Dave Wonderly, Warren Egbert; circa 1989. Bring a full rack and two ropes.

66. **Desert Solitude** (5.10+ PG) FA: Dave Wonderly, Warren Egbert; circa 1989. Bring wires, a double set of cams to #4, and two ropes.

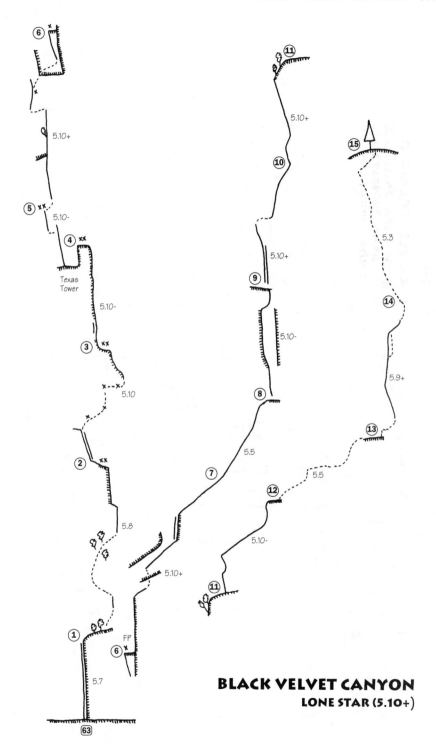

BLACK VELVET CANYON
LONE STAR (5.10+)

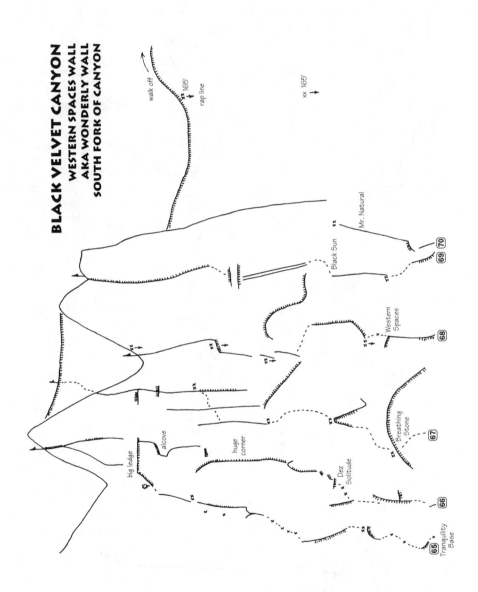

BLACK VELVET CANYON
WESTERN SPACES WALL
AKA WONDERLY WALL
SOUTH FORK OF CANYON

walk off

165'
rap line

xx 165'

Black Sun

Mr. Natural

70

69

Western
Spaces

68

Breathing
Stone

67

big ledge

alcove

huge
corner

Dez
Solitude

66

65 Tranquility
Base

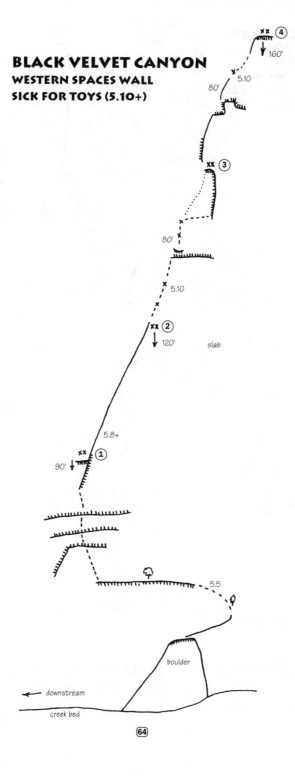

BLACK VELVET CANYON
WESTERN SPACES WALL
SICK FOR TOYS (5.10+)

160'

5.10

80'

③

80'

5.10

②
120'

slab

5.8+

①
90'

5.5

boulder

← downstream

creek bed

64

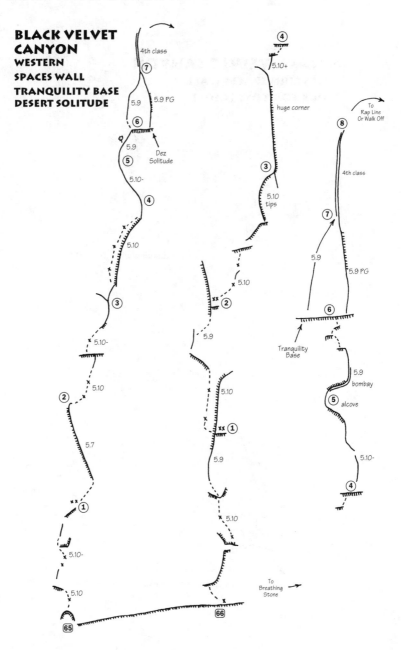

**BLACK VELVET
CANYON**
**WESTERN
SPACES WALL
TRANQUILITY BASE
DESERT SOLITUDE**

4th class

⑦

5.9   5.9 PG

⑥

5.9

⑤   Dez
Solitude

5.10-

④

5.10

③

5.10-

②   5.10

5.7

①

5.10-

5.10

㊅⑤

④   5.10+

huge corner

③

5.10
tips

②   5.10

5.9

①   5.10

5.9

5.10

5.10

To
Breathing
Stone

㊅⑥

To
Rap Line
Or Walk Off

⑧

4th class

⑦

5.9   5.9 PG

⑥

Tranquility
Base

5.9
bombay

⑤   alcove

5.10-

④

67. **The Breathing Stone** (5.11+) FA: Dave Wonderly, Dave Evans, Jennifer
Richards; November 1989 . Carry a full rack, including extra finger-sized
cams and two ropes.

*68. **Western Spaces** (5.11-) FA: Don Wilson, Dave Wonderly, Warren Egbert; March 1989. Rappel the route with two ropes.

69. **Black Sun** (5.10) FA: Warren Egbert, Dave Wonderly; circa 1989. Carry extra wires, extra TCUs, cams to #4, and two ropes.

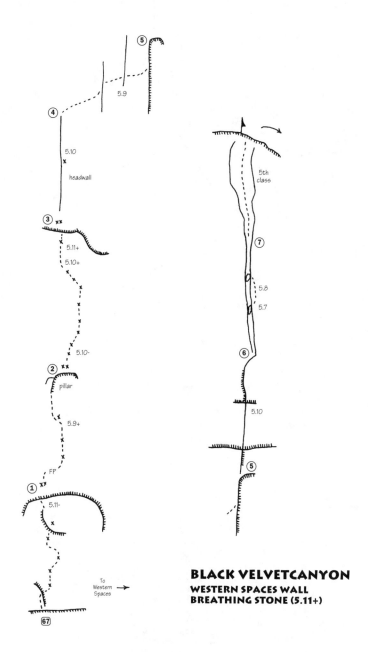

BLACK VELVETCANYON
WESTERN SPACES WALL
BREATHING STONE (5.11+)

BLACK VELVET CANYON
WESTERN SPACES WALL
WESTERN SPACES (5.11-)

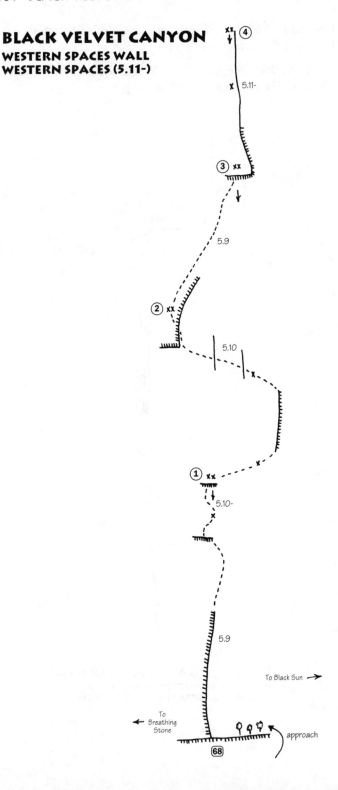

XX
4
5.11-
X

3 XX

5.9

2 XX

5.10

1 XX

5.10-
X

5.9

To Black Sun →

To
Breathing
Stone

approach

68

70. Mr. Natural of the Desert (5.10+) FA: Warren Egbert, Dave Wonderly; circa 1989. A 1-pitch route on the right side of the wall climbs a finger-to-hand crack.

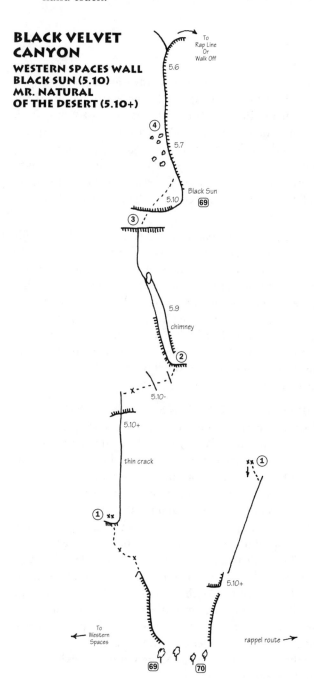

BLACK VELVET CANYON
WESTERN SPACES WALL
BLACK SUN (5.10)
MR. NATURAL
OF THE DESERT (5.10+)

To Rap Line Or Walk Off

5.6

④

5.7

Black Sun

5.10

⑥⑨

③

5.9

chimney

②

5.10-

5.10+

thin crack

① xx

xx ①

5.10+

① xx

To Western Spaces

rappel route →

⑥⑨ ⑦⓪

WINDY CANYON

Several good, sunny routes are located in and near Windy Canyon. This canyon is located about 1 mile north of Illusion Crags and is accessed via dirt roads between Black Velvet Canyon and Illusion Crags. The east face of Windy Peak is to the right (north) of the canyon mouth and left (south) of Mud Spring Canyon (the first canyon south of Black Velvet Canyon). The south face of Windy Peak is recognizable by a bushy ledge system that runs up the right (north) side of the approach gully at the base of the face. It takes about 90 minutes of hiking to reach the bases of these climbs. The climbs are described from right (east) to left (up canyon).

1. **Diet Delight** (5.8+) FA: Jorge and Joanne Urioste; February 1977. This fun, sunny route ascends the center of the east face. Start to the left (south) of a huge pillar/corner in the middle of the east face on a bushy ledge. **Pitch 1** (5.8+): Climb a thin crack, then move left to a belay. 165'. **Pitch 2** (5.8): Climb up and left along corners, then up a right-facing corner to a ledge with a scrub oak. 165't. **Pitch 3** (5.7): Go up and right (or see Variation) past a cave to the top. **Variation** (5.9-): To the left of the cave is a slightly left-leaning hand crack. **Descent:** Scramble up, then go down and left (south) in a gully. Depending on your routefinding and downclimbing abilities, you may need to do a short rappel.

2. **Ain't No Saint** (5.10) FA: Danny Rider, Luis Saca; Winter 1996/97. This route starts just left of *Saint Stephen* (described in the Urioste guidebook), near the middle of the south face of Windy Peak. Rope up in a low-angle gully at the base of a corner system that is shaped a bit like western Texas (if you haven't been to Hueco, you may be in trouble!). **Pitch 1** (5.8 PG): Climb up the corner and face until the corner veers left. Head up the face to the top of the corner system, then go up and left to a large ledge with a bush. **Pitch 2** (5.9): Head right up a ramp to a left-leaning crack/off-width. Climb the crack to its top. **Pitch 3** (5.10-): Follow bolts out right to another crack system. Climb this to the base of a corner that leads up to a small roof. **Pitch 4** (5.10-): Climb the corner and pull the roof. Stay in the crack and veer right when possible. Continue up the crack to a belay ledge below a hand crack. **Pitch 5** (5.10): Climb the crack/seam up through a ceiling with a corner (crux). Continue up to the roof. Step right when possible and continue up the face to a ledge with a pine tree. **Pitch 6** (5.7): Go up and left on slabs (this is the same as *Saint Stephen*). **Pitch 7** (5.2): Continue to the top. **Descent:** Walk off to the west.

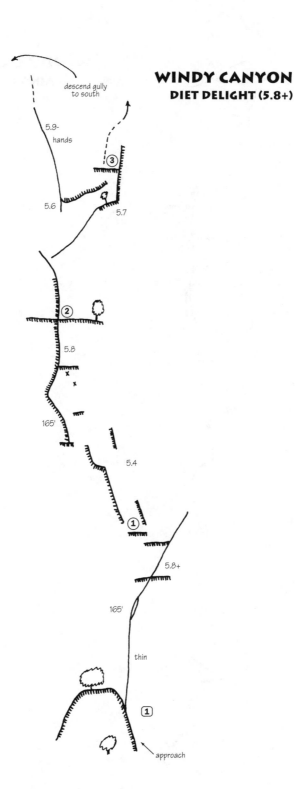

WINDY CANYON
DIET DELIGHT (5.8+)

descend gully
to south

5.9-
hands

5.6

③

5.7

②

5.8

x
x

165'

5.4

①

5.8+

165'

thin

1

approach

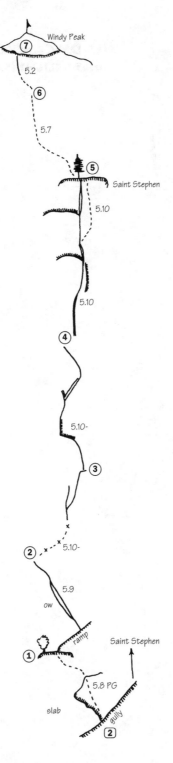

Windy Peak

⑦

5.2

⑥

5.7

⑤ Saint Stephen

5.10

5.10

④

5.10-

③

5.10-

②

5.9

ow

ramp

①   Saint Stephen

5.8 PG

slab   gully

②

WINDY CANYON
AIN'T NO SAINT

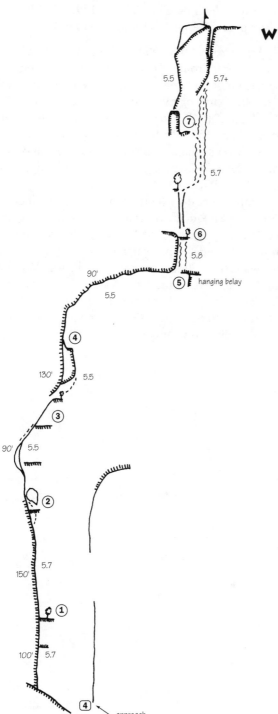

WINDY CANYON
JUBILANT SONG
(5.8)

5.5   5.7+

⑦

5.7

⑥

5.8

90' ⑤ hanging belay

5.5

④

130' 5.5

③

90' 5.5

②

5.7

150'

⑨ ①

100' 5.7

④ → approach

3. **Slabotomy** (5.9) FA: Danny Rider, Luis Saca; Winter 1996/97. Climb the face to the left of the first pitch of *Ain't No Saint*. (No topo.)

4. **Jubilant Song** (5.8) FA: Joe Herbst, Terry Schultz; December 1972. This is supposed to be a good, moderate route. This climb ascends a prominent crack system near the left (west) side of the south face of Windy Peak. **Pitch 1** (5.7): Climb the left-hand of two prominent cracks to a belay ledge with a tree. 100'. **Pitch 2** (5.7): Continue up the crack to a belay ledge with a large, brown flake. 150'. **Pitch 3** (5.5): Continue up the corner past a large ledge. Belay on a smaller ledge above. 90'. **Pitch 4** (5.5): Go up the corner past a ledge with cactus. Belay on a small ledge about 30' below the big roof. 130'. **Pitch 5** (5.5): Climb up to the roof and traverse right. To avoid rope drag, do a hanging belay in a small corner under the roof. 90'. **Pitch 6** (5.8): Pull the overhang and climb up a corner (see Variation 1) to a belay at a bush. 50'. **Pitch 7** (5.7): Go up a chimney to an oak tree, then move right and go up a waterstreak to a ledge. **Pitch 8** (5.7+): Continue up the waterstreak (see Variation 2) to the top. **Variation 1** (5.5): You can avoid the crux roof to the right. **Variation 2** (5.5): From the belay, go up and left by a black face to the top. **Descent:** Go to the top of Windy Peak, then southwest to the top of Windy Canyon. Go down the canyon past the base of the climb to your car.

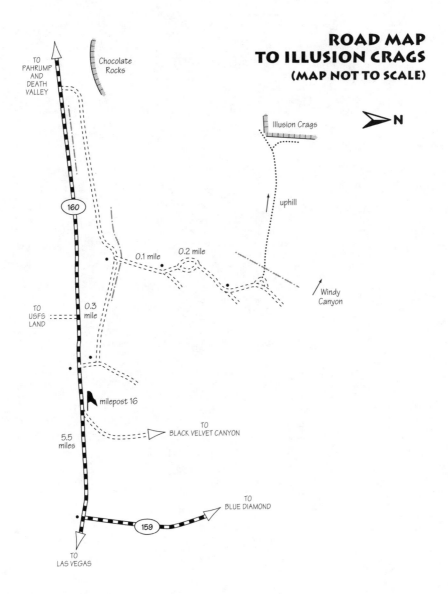

ROAD MAP
TO ILLUSION CRAGS
(MAP NOT TO SCALE)

Chocolate Rocks

TO PAHRUMP AND DEATH VALLEY

Illusion Crags

N

160

uphill

0.1 mile

0.2 mile

TO USFS LAND

0.3 mile

Windy Canyon

milepost 16

5.5 miles

TO BLACK VELVET CANYON

TO BLUE DIAMOND

159

TO LAS VEGAS

ILLUSION CRAGS

This cliff faces primarily northeast and has some very good varnished rock. Most routes are less than 150 feet high and have established rappel anchors. Despite the good quality rock and advances in bolting technology, it appears that this crag received very little traffic in the 1970s and 1980s. The Urioste guidebook listed ten climbs here, but I was unable to match the cliff photo and many of the brief descriptions with the features on the crag. The routes listed in this guide are the "best of the bunch" and should provide several days of enjoyable climbing for those who brave the 20-minute uphill approach.

To reach this cliff, drive west on Nevada 160 from the intersection with Nevada 159 for 5.5 miles (passing the turnoff for Black Velvet Canyon). Turn right (north) on a dirt road and parallel the main road for 0.3 mile. Turn right (north) at a wash and go to a fork in the road (0.1 mile). Bear left, pass a large dip, then bear left again (0.2 mile). Continue 100 yards to a parking spot. The cliff is clearly visible across a wash and up the hillside.

LEFT SIDE

The first routes described are on the far left (southwest) side of the formation overlooking a drainage that is clearly visible on the approach. These routes face southeast and are much more broken than the main wall. These 1-pitch climbs are described from right to left (north to south) as you approach up the ridge to the cliff. (No topo.)

1. **Changelings** (5.6 PG) FA: Donette and Todd Swain; April 1994. The first three climbs are on a low-angle, pyramid formation that has a jutting block several hundred feet above it. Climb the shattered right arête of the formation, starting 40' right of an alcove. Rappel from a natural thread on the ledge 75' up.

2. **Chameleon Pinnacle** (5.4) FA: Bill Lowman, Joe and Betsy Herbst, Matt McMackin, Nanouk Borche, Howard Booth; February 1973. This route is shown in the Urioste guide as going to the top of the cliff—only the first pitch is described here. Begin 40' left of the last route at an alcove with two junky-looking cracks above. Move out right from the alcove onto a low-angle, plated face and climb this to a belay 75 feet up. Rappel from the communal anchor.

ILLUSION CRAGS

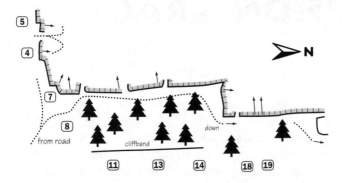

3. **Morph Out!** (5.7) FA: Donette and Todd Swain; April 1994. For Power Rangers only. Starting in the alcove shared with *Chameleon Pinnacle*, swim up the junky-looking, left-facing corner/crack to the belay.

4. **Mirage** (5.7) FA: Betsy and Joe Herbst, Joanne Urioste; Fall 1976. Who would have thought a casino would be named for this climb? Begin 150' left of the last two routes, on a separate cliff that has cleaner, smoother rock. Climb a crack system that is 15' right of the cleanest, most obvious right-facing corner (*Arm Forces*). At the top, go right (east) then descend down the gully separating the two crags.

5. **Arm Forces** (5.9) FA: Joe Herbst, Nanouk Borche; February 1973. Rope up 15' left of *Mirage* and about 165' left of *Chameleon Pinnacle* at an obvious right-facing corner. Climb the clean corner past three ceilings. Walk off right as for the other routes on this formation.

6. **French Bulges** (5.7) FA: Nanouk Borche, Joe Herbst; February 1973. Begin at a pine tree 20' left of the last route. Climb the smaller, right-facing corner to a bushy ledge. Walk off right and descend the gully separating the cliffs.

MAIN CLIFF

The next climbs are on the larger, steeper, main wall. These climbs face east and are described from left to right (south to north) as you approach up the ridge to the crag.

7. **Smoke and Mirrors** (5.9 R) FA: Todd Swain; November 1993. This route climbs a shallow corner system at the left edge of the main cliff. It is around the left side of an arête and just left of a pine tree. Follow the corner to join *David Copperhead* to the belay ledge. Rappel from fixed anchors with one rope.

8. **David Copperhead** (5.8+) FA: Todd Swain, Bobby Knight; November 1993. Start at an obvious wide crack that is just right of a prominent pine tree and just right of the main cliff's left edge. Begin in the wide crack and traverse 15' left on a horizontal crack to the obvious arête (or see Variation). Follow the edge past a short, vertical crack and a small overhang to the belay ledge. Rappel from anchors with one rope. **Variation** (5.10): Start 15' left and climb up the overhanging face to the end of the traverse.

9. **Who, Deany?** (5.8) FA: Joe Herbst; early 1970s. Climb the obvious clean, wide crack that is near the left edge of the main cliff and just right of a prominent pine tree. Rappel with one rope from 2 cold shuts on a ledge.

10. **First Lady of Magic** (5.9) FA: Todd and Donette Swain; November 1993. Protection is better than it appears from the ground. Rope up 5' right of the *Who, Deany?* crack at a left-facing corner that curves left to form an arch. Climb the corner for 15', then step right over the arch/corner onto the face. Climb up to a bolt, then up and slightly right to a small ledge. Continue straight up to an obvious crack, which is followed to a belay ledge with 2 cold shuts. Bring gear up to a #2.5 Friend and two ropes for the rappel.

11. **Deez Guys** (5.8+) FA: Todd Swain, Bobby Knight; November 1993. Begin 30' right of the *Who, Deany?* crack, at a small clearing that is just left of an ugly crack system. Wander up the varnished face aiming for a shallow, right-facing flake/corner 40' up. Continue up the face along a thin, vertical crack to a belay on a large ledge. Bring a double set of TCUs, extra wires, and gear to a #3 Friend. Rappel with two ropes.

12. **Con Jurors** (5.7) FA: Raleigh Collins, Brandt Allen; October 1994. Start 90' right of the last route and 40' left of a pine tree that is just right of an ugly chimney. Scramble 20' up to a ledge, then move left to a right-leaning crack that is just right of an ugly crack system. Follow the crack up and right to a shaky belay anchor. Rappel with one rope back to the ledge.

13. **Sore Sirs** (5.8 PG13) FA: Bobby Knight, Todd Swain; November 1993. Follow the previous route to a ledge 20' up, then climb straight up the varnished face toward a prominent chimney near the top of the cliff. Rappel from a poorly-bolted belay just left of the chimney. With one rope, you can get down to the ledge that is 20' off the ground.

*14. **Spell Me** (5.11 PG) FA: Bobby Knight, Todd Swain; November 1993. You may want some help leading this excellent route. Bring RPs, TCUs, and a #2.5 Friend. Begin at the left edge of a short, south-facing buttress 140' right of *Sore Sirs*. Climb an easy, left-leaning crack to a small ledge, then follow a difficult, vertical seam and 3 bolts to the top. Rappel with one rope from slings around a block.

15. **Illusions of Grandstaff** (5.11 TR) FA: Todd Swain, Bobby Knight; November 1993. Same start as *Spell Me* at a left-leaning crack. Climb the steep face along obvious left-facing flakes. Continue straight up (a bit contrived), keeping left of prominent bushes.

16. **Petit Deceit** (5.8) FA: Bobby Knight, Todd Swain; November 1993. Begin as for the last two routes, on a bushy ledge below a short, south-facing buttress. Climb the obvious left-facing corner to a stance, then continue up the face, keeping right of two prominent bushes. Continue straight up the final varnished wall above a left-leaning crack to a huge ledge. Rappel with one rope from slings around a block.

17. **Shell Game** (5.9) FA: Todd and Donette Swain, Bobby Knight; April 1994. Begin 100' down and right of the last three routes, where a pine tree marks the left edge of a varnished wall. Carry gear to 4" and lots of slings to reduce rope drag (and/or use double ropes). Climb up the center of a varnished pillar past horizontal cracks and a vertical seam to a ledge (5.9). This pillar forms the left edge of an alcove capped by a ceiling. Move right from the top of the pillar and climb a crack out the roof (as on *Magician's Hat*). Above the roof, move back left toward the arête. Follow 3 bolts up the steep wall (5.9) to a shallow dihedral. Climb the dihedral to a belay ledge in an alcove. Traverse 20' right and rappel from the communal anchor on *False Perception* with two ropes.

18. **Magician's Hat** (5.9) FA: Joe Herbst, Bo Hansson; 1970s. Bring lots of large gear and some long slings. Rope up 5' right of a pine tree, at a point below an alcove with two cracks leading through a roof. Climb the left crack past the roof (*Shell Game* joins this route briefly at the roof) to a belay ledge in an alcove 120' up. Traverse 20' right and rappel from the communal anchor on *False Perception* with two ropes.

*19. **Slight of Hand** (5.9) FA: Joe Herbst; early 1970s. This classic route may have been listed as *Skinny Mini* or *Sweet Little Whore* in the Urioste guidebook. Climb the obvious crack system 150' down and right from *Spell Me*. It starts as a beautiful finger crack then jogs left and widens. If done in one pitch, you'll need to bring lots of extra gear up to 4". Rappel with two ropes from cold shuts atop *False Perception*.

*20. **False Perception** (5.10+ PG13) FA: Todd and Donette Swain; November 1993. Perhaps the best route on the crag. Bring TCUs and wires for the upper crack. Begin below a line of bolts 10' right of *Slight of Hand*. Follow bolts up the chocolate-colored varnish, finishing in a spectacular, thin crack. Rap from a cold shut anchor with two ropes.

OTHER AREAS

If you tire of Red Rocks, or the weather is uncooperative, there are other climbing areas fairly close to Las Vegas. This section is not meant to be a guide to these areas but simply a source of other climbing options.

BLACK CANYON OF THE COLORADO

Numerous short, pocketed routes have been done about 0.5 mile upstream of Hoover Dam. These climbs are on the east (Arizona) side of the canyon and must be approached by boat. The routes currently range in difficulty from 5.7 to 5.11+. Quickdraws and small gear needed.

CHRISTMAS TREE PASS

This surreal area is located within Lake Mead National Recreation Area, a unit of the National Park Service. The rock is quartz monzonite (like Joshua Tree), but of a fairly coarse and poor quality. Numerous routes have been done at all grades, the majority being bolt-protected slabs. The large, domed formations are fairly close to the road and face a variety of directions. See *Summit* (October 1976) and *Climbing* (no. 94).

CLARK MOUNTAIN

Described by some as America's best crag, this area is about an hour south of Sin City in Mojave National Preserve (a National Park Service site). The climbing area is on the California side of the state line and on the northwest side of Interstate 15. There is a guidebook available; also see *Climbing* (no. 177).

CRAWDAD CANYON (A.K.A. VEYO-POOL)

A private climbing "park" located 17 miles north of Saint George, Utah on Utah Highway 18. Numerous sport climbs and a huge swimming pool make this a perfect family spot.

KEYHOLE CANYON

This small area has a wealth of Native American rock art (petroglyphs) and a few good climbs. The rock is a fine-grained quartz monzonite (like the better rock at Joshua Tree), with the longest route being about half a rope-length. While the climbing is limited, the rock art and canyon itself make a trip worthwhile.

MAP TO CHRISTMAS TREE PASS
(MAP NOT TO SCALE)

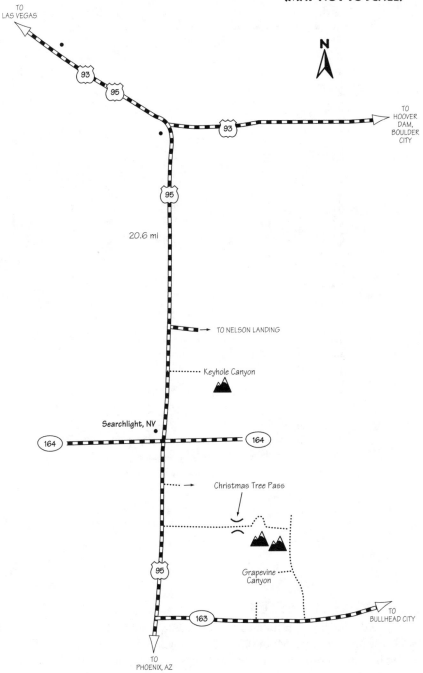

TO
LAS VEGAS

N

TO
HOOVER
DAM,
BOULDER
CITY

93

95

93

95

20.6 mi

TO NELSON LANDING

Keyhole Canyon

Searchlight, NV

164

164

Christmas Tree Pass

Grapevine
Canyon

95

163

TO
BULLHEAD CITY

TO
PHOENIX, AZ

MAP TO KEYHOLE CANYON
(MAP NOT TO SCALE)

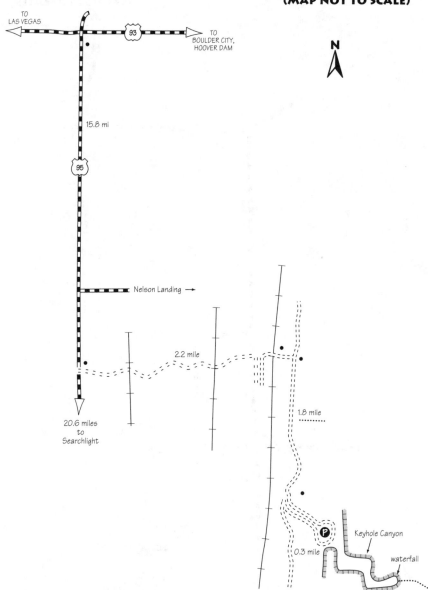

LAS VEGAS LIMESTONE

At least a dozen different limestone areas are located within the Las Vegas valley. These include Lone Mountain, The Gun Club, and Trenchtown. These areas are in a guidebook available at Las Vegas climbing shops. Articles can found in *Climbing* (nos. 161 and 177), *Allez* (no. 3), and *Rock & Ice* (no. 59).

JOSHUA TREE

This renowned area is about a 4-hour drive south of Las Vegas. There are more routes in Joshua Tree National Park than in any other climbing area in the country (and perhaps the world). The weather tends to be a little drier than Las Vegas, but the temperatures are about the same. Spring and fall are the best seasons (and the most crowded).

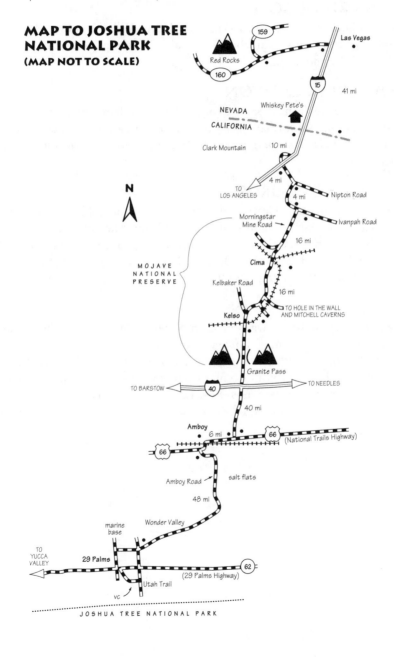

MAP TO JOSHUA TREE NATIONAL PARK (MAP NOT TO SCALE)

MOUNT CHARLESTON

If overhanging limestone in a mountainous setting appeals to you, this is the place. This is primarily a summertime area, although there is ice climbing here in the winter. Check out the new guidebook and articles in *Sport Climbing* (vol. 2, no. 4), *Climbing* (nos. 142, 149, 177), and *Rock & Ice* (nos. 57 and 64).

OWENS RIVER GORGE

About a 5-hour drive from Las Vegas (via Death Valley National Park), this popular area has its own guidebooks. See also *Climbing* (nos. 120, 126, 129) and *Rock & Ice* (no. 53).

SNOW CREEK CANYON

This sandstone area is near Saint George, Utah, less than 2 hours north of Las Vegas. Numerous routes have been done in the area and are described in a guidebook. See also *Climbing* (nos. 96, 102, 146), *Rock & Ice* (no. 63), and *Onsight* (no. 2).

VIRGIN RIVER GORGE

Located just north of Sin City on Interstate 15 in Arizona, this warm, dry lime-stone area has a bunch of hard routes to dangle on. The only drawback is the proximity to the interstate. See *Climbing* (nos. 127, 131, 148) and *Rock & Ice* (nos. 44 and 65) and the new guidebook, *Rock Climbing Arizona* by Stewart M. Green, Falcon Publishing (1999).

ZION

The spectacular sandstone walls of Zion National Park are less than 3 hours north of Las Vegas. Summer is hot and crowded, but spring and fall are perfect. There are lots of exciting canyoneering trips to do here, as well as big-wall free and aid routes. The park visitor center keeps a notebook with information on the climbs. See also *Climbing* (nos. 124, 129, 133, 138, 141, 180) and *Rock & Ice* (no. 45), and *Rock Climbing Utah* by Stewart M. Green, Falcon Publishing (1999).

ACCESS: It's every climber's concern

The Access Fund, a national, non-profit climbers' organization, works to keep climbing areas open and to conserve the climbing environment. Need help with closures? land acquisition? legal or land management issues? funding for trails and other projects? starting a local climbers' group? CALL US!

Climbers can help preserve access by being committed to leaving the environment in its natural state. Here are some simple guidelines:

• **STRIVE FOR ZERO IMPACT** especially in environmentally sensitive areas like caves. Chalk can be a significant impact on dark and porous rock—don't use it around historic rock art. Pick up litter, and leave trees and plants intact.

• **DISPOSE OF HUMAN WASTE PROPERLY** Use toilets whenever possible. If toilets are not available, dig a "cat hole" at least six inches deep and 200 feet from any water, trails, campsites, or the base of climbs. *Always pack out toilet paper.* On big wall routes, use a "poop tube" and carry waste up and off with you (the old "bag toss" is now illegal in many areas).

• **USE EXISTING TRAILS** Cutting switchbacks causes erosion. When walking off-trail, tread lightly, especially in the desert where cryptogamic soils (usually a dark crust) take thousands of years to form and are easily damaged. Be aware that "rim ecologies" (the clifftop) are often highly sensitive to disturbance.

• **BE DISCREET WITH FIXED ANCHORS** *Bolts are controversial and are not a convenience*—don't place 'em unless they are *really* necessary. Camouflage all anchors. Remove unsightly slings from rappel stations (better to use steel chain or welded cold shuts). Bolts sometimes can be used pro-actively to protect fragile resources—consult with your local land manager.

• **RESPECT THE RULES** and speak up when other climbers don't. Expect restrictions in designated wilderness areas, rock art sites, caves, and to protect wildlife, especially nesting birds of prey. *Power drills are illegal in wilderness and all national parks.*

• **PARK AND CAMP IN DESIGNATED AREAS** Some climbing areas require a permit for overnight camping.

• **MAINTAIN A LOW PROFILE** Leave the boom box and day-glo clothing at home—the less climbers are heard and seen, the better.

• **RESPECT PRIVATE PROPERTY** Be courteous to land owners. Don't climb where you're not wanted.

• **JOIN THE ACCESS FUND!** To become a member, make a tax-deductible donation of $25 or more.

The Access Fund

Preserving America's Diverse Climbing Resources
PO Box 17010 Boulder, CO 80308
303.545.6772 • www.accessfund.org

RATED ROUTE INDEX

5.0
☐ A-OK 55

5.3
☐ Chips and Salsa 72
☐ Costume Jewelry 212
☐ Penny Lane 19
☐ Solar Slab Gully 289
☐ You Are What You Eat 28

5.4
☐ Abbey Road 19
☐ Arachnoworld 229
☐ Buzz, Buzz 332
☐ Chameleon Pinnacle 393
☐ Guise and Gals 331
☐ Han Soloing 22
☐ Roman Hands 31
☐ Zen and the Art of Web
   Spinning 229

5.5
☐ C11H17NO3 242
☐ Climb Traveler 58
☐ Girls and Buoys 331
☐ Just in Case 181
☐ Magic Mirror 332
☐ Rising Moons 332
☐ Scanty Panty 75
☐ Snivler 229
☐ The Staircase 117
☐ Tonto 177

5.6
☐ Advance Romance 335
☐ Badger's Buttress 25
☐ Bonus Pullout Section 42
☐ Changelings 393
☐ Chicken Gumbo for Your
   Dumbo 16
☐ Cover My Buttress 75
☐ Doobie Dance 332
☐ First Grader 348
☐ Guys and Ghouls 33
☐ Heavy Spider Karma 229
☐ The Hex Files 78
☐ Human Chockstones 216
☐ Ignore the Man behind
   the Screen 217
☐ The Northeast Arête 202
☐ Panty Prow 76
☐ Physical Graffiti 30
☐ See Spot Run 99
☐ Shishka Bob 29
☐ Solar Slab 291
☐ Static 152

5.6+
☐ Carpetbagger 21
☐ Cat in the Hat 245
☐ Catwalk 306
☐ Soupy Sales 16
☐ Women and Children First 82

5.7
☐ Algae on Parade 332
☐ Back to Basics 348
☐ Bottoms up 35
☐ Con Jurors 395
☐ The Cookie Monster 244

☐ Cow Lick Co. Crag 35
☐ Crazy World (A4) 272
☐ Diamond Dance 70
☐ Ditch Day 85
☐ French Bulges 394
☐ From Soup to Nuts 18
☐ Geronimo 259
☐ Ghouls Just Wanna Have
   Fun 35
☐ Godzilla 78
☐ Group Therapy 162
☐ Happy Acres 36
☐ Healy's Haunted House 165
☐ Hefner 42
☐ High Scalin' 151
☐ Hole in the Pants 51
☐ Hop Route 207
☐ Johnny Vegas 293
☐ Ma and Pa in Kettle 29
☐ Mirage 394
☐ Morph Out! 394
☐ Ms. Adventure 155
☐ Nuttin' Could Be Finer 53
☐ Olive Oil 256
☐ Pillar Talk 170
☐ The Red and the Black 335
☐ Robin Trowel 214
☐ The Route to Mecca 21
☐ Ruta de Roja 24
☐ Sex in the Scrub Oak 218
☐ Shady Ladies 187
☐ Silk Panties 75
☐ Sir Climbalot 21
☐ Space Case 181
☐ Spiderline 183
☐ Split Crack 125
☐ Thong 75
☐ Tuna and Chips 72
☐ Tuna Cookies 72
☐ Tunnel Vision 162
☐ Van Allen Belt 188
☐ Walk to School 179
☐ Wok the Dog 65

5.7
☐ The Black Dagger 262
☐ Elementary Primer 99
☐ Kindergarten Cop 331
☐ Pauligk Pillar 242
☐ Radio Free Kansas 217
☐ Rodan 78
☐ Romper Room 332

5.8-
☐ Dark Shadows 237
☐ Frogland 344

5.8
☐ A-Cute Pain 103
☐ The Black Hole 230
☐ Black Magic 329
☐ Boxer Rebellion 75
☐ Brief Encounter 75
☐ The Bus Stops Here 227
☐ Carrie Fissure 23
☐ Chairman Mao's Little
   Red Book 100
☐ Classic Corner 24
☐ Cold September Corner 187

☐ Crack Bar 70
☐ Crack of Noon 143
☐ Crown Royal 344
☐ Ed MacMayonnaise 60
☐ Family Affair 43
☐ Fleet Street 19
☐ Fold-Out 204
☐ Fontanar de Rojo 24
☐ The Great Red Book 99
☐ Head Case 181
☐ Hip-Hoppin' with
   the Hutterites 137
☐ Human Cannonball 64
☐ Jonny Jamcrack 102
☐ Jubilant Song 390
☐ Ken Queasy 87
☐ Kick in the Balls 329
☐ The Life Chuckle 35
☐ Lizardry (TR) 70
☐ Lotta Balls 326
☐ Mo Hotta, Mo Betta 53
☐ Muckraker 19
☐ Neon Sunset 87
☐ Nevada Book 125
☐ Obie-One Keone 23
☐ Otters Are People Too 317
☐ Pad's Passion 70
☐ Parts Is Parts 153
☐ People Mover 117
☐ Petit Deceit 396
☐ Poundcake 143
☐ Power to Waste 326
☐ Ragged Edges 178
☐ Rainbow Buttress 302
☐ Red Vines 26
☐ Riding Hood 30
☐ Science Patrol 78
☐ Scumby 338
☐ Sore Sirs 395
☐ Spontaneous Enjoyment 35
☐ The Sport Chimney 50
☐ Sport Climbing Is
   Neither 108
☐ Stone Hammer 100
☐ Stuck on You 119
☐ Technicolor Sunrise 87
☐ There and Back Again 297
☐ They Call the
   Wind #!&% 218
☐ Trihardral 326
☐ Waterstreak 72
☐ Welcome to N.I.M.B.Y.
   Town 24
☐ When a Stranger Calls 244
☐ Who, Deany? 395
☐ Witches' Honor 106
☐ Zipperhead 87
☐ Zippy 312
☐ Zoroaster 48

5.8+
☐ Boodler 19
☐ Caliban 28
☐ Cantilever Corner 216
☐ Chasing Shadows 237
☐ Crimson Chrysalis 279
☐ David Copperhead 395
☐ Deez Guys 395

☐ Diet Delight 386
☐ Flight Path 217
☐ Frictiony Face, Panty Waist 122
☐ Ground-up Vocabulary 100
☐ Horndogger Select 289
☐ A Man in Every Pot 29
☐ Mojave Green 145
☐ Speed Racer 77
☐ Ultraman 77
☐ Valentine's Day 18
☐ Varnishing Point 227

5.9-
☐ Beulah's Book 293
☐ Buck's Muscle World 108
☐ Mother's Day 36
☐ A Simple Expediency 219

5.9
☐ Aeolian Wall, Original Route (A3+) 313
☐ Amazing Grace 199
☐ Arm Forces 394
☐ Battery Powered 153
☐ Battle Royale (A2) 272
☐ Black Licorice 26
☐ Black Track 172
☐ Bonaire 91
☐ Bridge of Sighs 214
☐ Bruja's Brew 329
☐ Burlesque 204
☐ Cactus Head 62
☐ Car Talk 219
☐ Chips Ahoy! 72
☐ Chrysler Crack 134
☐ Claw Hammer 60
☐ Climb Machine 58
☐ Clutch Cargo 77
☐ Community Pillar 252
☐ Couldn't Be Schmooter 53
☐ Coyote Moon 148
☐ The Darkroom 132
☐ Desert Solitaire (A3) 272
☐ Doin' the Good Drive 219
☐ Dukes of Hazard 250
☐ Epinephrine 375
☐ Family Circus 43
☐ Flying Pumpkin 24
☐ Friendship Route 331
☐ Ginger Cracks 281
☐ The Haj 21
☐ Hard Case 181
☐ Hit and Run 153
☐ Lady Wilson's Cleavage 321
☐ Lil' Red 31
☐ Looks Like Craps 151
☐ Lucky Nuts 326
☐ Magician's Hat 396
☐ The Misunderstanding 350
☐ Mom and Apple Pie 36
☐ Ms. October, 1995 42
☐ Mudterm 326
☐ P-Coat Junction 34
☐ Paiute Pillar 264
☐ Pending Project (A2) 19
☐ Possum Logic 172
☐ Question of Balance 99
☐ Quiggle's Wiggle 192
☐ Refried Brains 361
☐ Remote Control 234

☐ Ride the Tiger 241
☐ Rosie's Day Out 165
☐ Sensuous Mortician 204
☐ Shallow Fried Cracken 23
☐ Shell Game 396
☐ Sicktion 113
☐ The Singing Love Pen 18
☐ Slabotomy 390
☐ Sleeper 171
☐ Slight of Hand 396
☐ Smoke and Mirrors 394
☐ Spanning the Gap 216
☐ Spikes and Twine 126
☐ Split Infinitive 125
☐ Stick Right 220
☐ Stickball 219
☐ Tomato Amnesia 99
☐ Topless Twins 229
☐ Treacherous Journey 21
☐ True Lies 123
☐ Warlock 106
☐ Water Logged 188
☐ Working for Peanuts 51
☐ XTZ 144
☐ Zona Rosa 30

5.9+
☐ Aliens Have Landed 22
☐ Bengal 73
☐ The Black Orpheus 294
☐ Bon Ez 91
☐ Bush Pilots 229
☐ Common Bond of Circumstance 217
☐ Commuted Sentence 219
☐ Crabby Appleton 247
☐ Crude Behavior 93
☐ Crude Street Blues 93
☐ Electric Koolaid (TR) 86
☐ The Friar 286
☐ Frigid Air Buttress 202
☐ Ice Climb 182
☐ Lancaster Levels Luxor 34
☐ Lebanese JoJo 201
☐ Lewd, Crude, and Misconstrued 94
☐ Little Big Horn 175
☐ Long Walk on a Short Pier 119
☐ Magellanic Cloud 188
☐ Mister Masters 189
☐ Nadia's Nine 169
☐ Nature Is Fun 220
☐ Over the Hill to Grandmother's House 30
☐ Pending Disaster 19
☐ Pine Nuts 244
☐ Practice Crack 40
☐ Red Throbber Spire 234
☐ Roasted Ramen 139
☐ Slam Dancin' with the Amish 138
☐ Soylent Green Jeans 181
☐ Stemtation 312
☐ Straight Shooter 221
☐ Sumo Greatness 182
☐ Thermal Breakdown 93
☐ This Ain't No Disco 244
☐ Walking the Vertical Beach 96
☐ What's Eating You? 29

5.10-
☐ Belief in Proportion to the Evidence 217
☐ Black Magic Panties 206
☐ Blonde Dwarf 86
☐ Butt Floss (TR) 75
☐ Captain Crunch 176
☐ Chicken Lips 300
☐ Chicken Soup for the Soul(TR) 16
☐ Clyde Crashcup 217
☐ Cornucopia 340
☐ Crazy Girls 216
☐ Deguello 309
☐ Dirtbagger's Compensation 323
☐ Dream of Wild Turkeys 366
☐ Eagle Dance (A0) 303
☐ Early Times 370
☐ The Elephant Penis 220
☐ Falstaff 125
☐ The Figurine 39
☐ The Gobbler 369
☐ Gold Bikini and Cinnamon Bun Hairdo 23
☐ Gonzo Dogs 96
☐ Heatwave 176
☐ High Class Hoe 53
☐ High Wire 64
☐ Hook, Climb, and Whimper 279
☐ Horizontal Departure 46
☐ Hot Climb 176
☐ Kemosabe 176
☐ Knock the Bottom out of It 35
☐ Mac and Ronnie in Cheese 29
☐ No Laughing Matter 229
☐ N'Plus Ultra 170
☐ OB Button 247
☐ OB Fist 247
☐ P-Coat Sleeve 34
☐ Panty Line 75
☐ Pauline's Pentacle 245
☐ The Pocket Philosopher 172
☐ Ranger Danger 62
☐ Raptor 230
☐ Red Light 132
☐ Roasting Affair 183
☐ Rob Roy 331
☐ Rocky Road 25
☐ Romance Is a Heart Breakin' Affair 348
☐ Romeo Charlie 200
☐ A Rope, a Rubber Chicken, and a Vibrator 234
☐ Sand Felipe 353
☐ Sandblast 353
☐ Sheep Trail 178
☐ Simpatico 227
☐ Skewback (TR) 216
☐ Snapshot 132
☐ Son of Wilson 323
☐ Sour Mash 370
☐ Split Ends 125
☐ Swedish Erotica 126
☐ Tom Terrific 247
☐ Tricks Are for Kids 183
☐ Which Hunters? 106
☐ The Whiff 67

☐ Wholesome Fullback 354
☐ Woodrow 312

5.10
☐ #0 140
☐ Ain't No Saint 386
☐ All the Right Moves 340
☐ American Ninja 232
☐ Atman 48
☐ The Big Payback (A3) 276
☐ Big Top 65
☐ Black Betty 299
☐ Black Sun 383
☐ Blood Stains 32
☐ Bodiddly 178
☐ Brass Balls 230
☐ Burnt Toast 138
☐ Cabo San Looseness 352
☐ Carful of Clowns 64
☐ Cartwright Corner 252
☐ Centerfold 241
☐ Chicken Eruptus 178
☐ Children of the Sun 342
☐ Climb Bandits 60
☐ Cold Blue Steel 252
☐ Crawford's Corner 207
☐ Creepshow 249
☐ Crumbling Community 115
☐ Dense Pack 179
☐ Diablo (A2+) 129
☐ Dime Edging 145
☐ Dog Police 255
☐ Edge Dressing 237
☐ Edible Panties 76
☐ Elder Sibling (TR) 143
☐ Electric Orange Peeler 40
☐ Emerald City (A2) 272
☐ The Escalator 117
☐ Fairy Toast 138
☐ Fear and Loathing 211
☐ Friction Addiction 113
☐ Gemstone 212
☐ Gigantor 33
☐ Gin Ricky 330
☐ The Graduate 179
☐ Greased Lightning 199
☐ Grippitty Gravity 175
☐ Habeas Corpus 25
☐ Hidden Meaning (TR) 24
☐ High Anxiety 259
☐ Inti Watana 316
☐ Is It Soup Yet? 16
☐ Knotty Behavior 188
☐ Malice Alice 102
☐ Malicious Mischief 372
☐ Man's Best Friend 67
☐ Meyers Crack 48
☐ Miss Conception 350
☐ Mr. Freeze's Face 187
☐ Mugwump (TR) 21
☐ Music to My Fears 195
☐ The Negative 132
☐ The Next Century 241
☐ The Nightcrawler 262
☐ No Name 338
☐ Oakey Dokey 308
☐ One Stop in Tonopah 227
☐ Out of Control 232
☐ Panty Raid 76

☐ Pier-Less 216
☐ Powder Puff 40
☐ Power Failure 283
☐ Prescription Gription 113
☐ Real Domestic Chickens 335
☐ RF Gain 152
☐ Rock Warrior 365
☐ Runout Rodeo 96
☐ Sandstone Cowboy 100
☐ Scalawag 19
☐ Sea of Holes 230
☐ Shere Khan 73
☐ Short but Sweet 144
☐ Shut up and Dance 102
☐ Slot Machine 235
☐ Small Purchase 250
☐ Spark Plug 360
☐ Sterling Moss 182
☐ Stew on This 15
☐ Stick Left 220
☐ Stone Hammer II 104
☐ Strawberry Shubert 196
☐ The Swainbow Wall 271
☐ Swing Shift 199
☐ Tatanka (A3) 192
☐ Territorial Imperative 180
☐ Tie Me Tightly 188
☐ Tigger 73
☐ Tri-Burro Bridge 214
☐ Triassic Sands 353
☐ Tuckered Sparfish 176
☐ Unknown
　　(The Necromancer) 207
☐ Victoria's Secret (TR) 76
☐ Vile Pile 124
☐ The Walker Spur 244
☐ Weenie Juice 192
☐ Whipper 186
☐ Y2K 241
☐ Yellow Brick Road 368

5.10A
☐ Bigfoot 172
☐ Burros Might Fly 91
☐ Cat Walk 65
☐ Dancin' with a God 93
☐ Edward Silverhands 48
☐ Gelatin Pooch 108
☐ Innocent Bystander 154
☐ Pain in the Neck 103
☐ Playing Hooky 85
☐ Spotted Eagle 148
☐ Texas Tea 93
☐ Trigger Happy 153
☐ Vagabonds 91

5.10B
☐ April Fools 104
☐ Birthstone 104
☐ Black Gold 93
☐ Doctor's Orders 85
☐ First Born 143
☐ Fool's Gold 93
☐ Hero Worship 155
☐ It's a Bitch 67
☐ Low Tide 83
☐ Plastic People 124
☐ Pump First, Pay Later 108
☐ The Runaway 109
☐ Tremor 83

5.10C
☐ American Sportsman 109
☐ Burros Don't Gamble 91
☐ Cal. West 116
☐ Cool Whip 55
☐ Crankenstein 138
☐ Far Cry from Josh 117
☐ Grape Nuts 199
☐ Kokopelli 153
☐ Mirage II 159
☐ Money 71
☐ Mothers of Invention 36
☐ Panty-Mime 76
☐ The Prince of Darkness 366
☐ Quiet on the Set 60
☐ Roto-Hammer 104
☐ Running Amuck 108
☐ Sandstone Sandwich 237
☐ Some Assembly Required
　　153
☐ To Bolt or Toupee 115

5.10D
☐ Armed and Dangerous 154
☐ Baseboy 28
☐ Boulder Dash 26
☐ Brand New Bag 158
☐ Claimjumper's Special 49
☐ Cool Water Sandwich 55
☐ Crude Boys 91
☐ Dirty Little Girl 40
☐ Elbows of Mac and
　　Ronnie 29
☐ Flip the Switch 138
☐ Haunted Hooks 104
☐ Live Fast, Die Young 93
☐ Nightmare on
　　Crude Street 93
☐ Panty Shield 77
☐ Purple Haze 104
☐ Range of Motion 108
☐ Repeat Offender 154
☐ See Dick Fly 84
☐ Titty Litter 88
☐ The Warming 71

5.10+
☐ '34 Ford with Flames 309
☐ Abandoned Line 99
☐ Access Fun (TR) 24
☐ Ace of Hearts (TR) 18
☐ As the Toad Turns 348
☐ Bad Guys Approaching (A0)
　　262
☐ Bauble (TR) 212
☐ BCR 5L 91
☐ Blitzkrieg 192
☐ Breakaway 196
☐ Chalk Is Cheap 372
☐ Chilly Ones 225
☐ Chips Away 100
☐ Chocolate Flakes 250
☐ Clone Babies 250
☐ Desert Solitude 378
☐ Earth Juice 199
☐ Edge of the Sun 249
☐ False Perception 397
☐ Fear and Loathing II 96
☐ Fiddler on the Roof 369
☐ Five and Dime 250

☐ Flake Eyes 144
☐ Flakes of Wrath 239
☐ The Fox 32
☐ The Gift of the
    Wind Gods 312
☐ Goobies for Gumbies 165
☐ Haberdasher 26
☐ Iron Man 85
☐ Johnny Come Lately 370
☐ Kenny Laguna 348
☐ Killer Klowns 172
☐ Left Out 172
☐ Lone Star 377
☐ Mai Tai 331
☐ Mazatlan 351
☐ Men Are from Mars, Women
    Are from Venice 214
☐ Monkey Rhythm 143
☐ Mr. Natural of the Desert
    383
☐ Mushroom People 229
☐ Orange Clonus 222
☐ Our Father 356
☐ Party Line 129
☐ Perplexity 350
☐ Predator 123
☐ Rain Dance 344
☐ Red Heat 124
☐ Red Zinger 286
☐ Return to Forever 350
☐ Risky Business 238
☐ Sauron's Eye (A4) 267
☐ Serious Business 227
☐ Shit Howdy 29
☐ Show Burro 39
☐ Sick for Toys 377
☐ Side Effects 15
☐ Smooth as Silk 361
☐ Squelch 152
☐ Stout Roof 225
☐ Supernova 125
☐ That Wedged Feeling 120
☐ The Threat 174
☐ Tranquility Base 378
☐ Unimpeachable Groping
    283
☐ Unknown
    (The Necromancer) 207
☐ Velveeta 372
☐ The Whitehouse Effect 249

5.11-
☐ Bloodline 241
☐ Break Loose 128
☐ Calico Jack 139
☐ Captain Curmudgeon 176
☐ City Slickers 40
☐ Climb Warp 58
☐ Clipper 338
☐ Conz Crack 48
☐ Cut Loose 129
☐ Elephant Man 65
☐ Finger Fandango 309
☐ Go Greyhound 227
☐ Jam Session 183
☐ Jonny Rotten 102
☐ Lunar Escape 249
☐ Meat Puppet 62
☐ Mercedes 188
☐ Midnight Oil 250

☐ Moisture Brau 225
☐ Penthouse Pet 42
☐ Plan F 178
☐ Running 69
☐ Sandstone Samurai 363
☐ Sin City 183
☐ Slick Willy (A0) 318
☐ Spanky 31
☐ Spectrum 232
☐ Stand or Fall 67
☐ Teenage Mutant Ninja
    Turtles 151
☐ This Bud's for You 225
☐ Western Spaces 382
☐ Why Right 179
☐ Yellow Dog 62

5.11
☐ The Abdominizer 170
☐ Acid Jacks 180
☐ Archeoptryx 354
☐ Backlash 186
☐ Bighorn Buttress 172
☐ The Bindle 69
☐ Black Tongue 58
☐ Black Widow 299
☐ Bossa Nova 294
☐ Brain Damage 122
☐ Brown Recluse 267
☐ Buffalo Wall (A3) 189
☐ Cactus Massacre 62
☐ Calico Terror 123
☐ Chocolate Swirl 44
☐ Cocaine Hotline 69
☐ Cole Essence 354
☐ Crack 67
☐ Crawdad 62
☐ Crossfire 189
☐ Cutting Edge 361
☐ Dances with Beagles 305
☐ Dean's List 182
☐ The Delicate Sound of
    Thunder 356
☐ Desert Reality 338
☐ Desert Sportsman 140
☐ Eight Ball 69
☐ Ethical Behavior 89
☐ Excellent Adventure 238
☐ Forget Me Knot 222
☐ Free Base 69
☐ The Geezer 69
☐ Gnat Man on Ranch
    Hands 35
☐ Guccione 42
☐ Heart of Darkness 237
☐ High Noon 115
☐ Illusions of Grandstaff (TR)
    396
☐ Isis 60
☐ Ixtalan 352
☐ Levitation 29 303
☐ Lick It 39
☐ Lion Tamer (TR) 64
☐ Liquid God 96
☐ Lizard Locks 340
☐ Love Hurts 25
☐ Marshall Amp 131
☐ Meteor 186
☐ Monster Island 34

☐ Mr. Moto 120
☐ One Thing Leads to
    Another 69
☐ Only the Good Die Young
    358
☐ Outside the Envelope 69
☐ Ramen Pride 312
☐ Rap Bolters Need to Be
    Famous 139
☐ Reach the Beach 69
☐ Risk Brothers Roof 30
☐ Roman Meal (TR) 31
☐ Running Man 123
☐ Saltwater Taffy 44
☐ Sand Man (TR) 100
☐ Saved by Zero 69
☐ Seduction Line 338
☐ Seka's Soiled Panties 137
☐ Short Circuit 238
☐ The Skagg 69
☐ Smears for Fears 201
☐ Snow Blind 67
☐ Spell Me 395
☐ Tales from the Gripped 358
☐ Telecaster 132
☐ Telletubby Scandal 78
☐ Texas Hold'em 377
☐ A Thousand New
    Routes 115
☐ Turkish Taffy 44
☐ Unfinished Symphony 196
☐ Unknown (Ranch Hands
    Crag) 32
☐ Unknown
    (The Necromancer) 207
☐ Vernal Thaw (TR) 53
☐ White Tigers 73
☐ Winter Heat 53
☐ Yin and Yang 46
☐ Yodritch 125

5.11A
☐ Affliction for Friction 113
☐ Black Corridor,
    Route 4 Left 91
☐ Country Bumpkin 40
☐ Drilling Miss Daisy 42
☐ Fast Moving Train 157
☐ Fifi Hula 149
☐ Galloping Gal 124
☐ Hair Today, Gone
    Tomorrow 115
☐ Have a Beer with Fear 29
☐ The Lazy Fireman 220
☐ Meister's Edge 100
☐ Moments to Memories 157
☐ Nirvana 104
☐ Oils Well that Ends Well 94
☐ Payless Cashways 31
☐ Rebel without a Pause 94
☐ Red Sky Mining 157
☐ Repo Man 39
☐ Seventh Hour 118
☐ Shape of Things to Come
    143
☐ Sidewinder 221
☐ Special Guest Posers 97
☐ Spotted Owl 147
☐ Synthetic Society 124

☐ Time Off 141
☐ Totally Clips 76
☐ Yearnin' and Learnin' 154

5.11B
☐ Adoption 91
☐ Bad Reputation 154
☐ Blister in the Sun 151
☐ Caustic 28
☐ Cirque du Soleil 51
☐ A Day in the Life 108
☐ Desert Pickle 109
☐ Flying V 129
☐ Footloose 129
☐ Foreman Ferris 153
☐ Gift Rapped 157
☐ Glitter Gulch 103
☐ Good Mourning 143
☐ Gun Control 115
☐ Hurricane 116
☐ Idiots Rule 84
☐ James Brown 158
☐ Just in from L.A. 117
☐ Just Shut up and Climb 143
☐ Leveraged Buyout 146
☐ Liar's Poker 146
☐ Mexican Secret Agent Man 31
☐ Mr. Choad's Wild Ride 50
☐ Myxolidian 141
☐ One-Eyed Jacks 129
☐ Orange County 117
☐ Paradiddle Riddle 141
☐ Prime Ticket 60
☐ Red Storm Rising 157
☐ Sand Buckets 89
☐ Sand Wedge 88
☐ Sandstone Enema 94
☐ Scantily Clad Bimbo 118
☐ Scorpions 50
☐ Scudder Global 146
☐ Slabba Dabba Do 221
☐ Slave to the Grind 103
☐ Stonehenge 104
☐ Texas Lite Sweet 94
☐ Thunderbird 147
☐ Turtle Wax 50
☐ Under the Boardwalk 118
☐ Unknown (Ranch Hands Crag) 32
☐ Wheat Thick 169
☐ When the Cat's Away 157
☐ Why Left 179

5.11C
☐ Airlift 86
☐ Big Iron 171
☐ Black Flag 137
☐ Blanc Czech 62
☐ Bone Machine 84
☐ Buffalo Balls 172
☐ C.H.U.D. 140
☐ Cameo Appearance 60
☐ Comforts of Madness 138
☐ Disposable Blues 159
☐ Everybody's Slave 137
☐ The Felon 46
☐ Gridlock 108
☐ Headmaster Ritual 40

☐ Here Kitty, Kitty 67
☐ The Heteroclite 159
☐ Hooligans 134
☐ Hostile Takeover 146
☐ Jimmy Nap 120
☐ Land of the Free 183
☐ Life out of Balance 83
☐ Like Mom Used to Make 144
☐ Livin' on Borrowed Time 94
☐ The Max Flex 62
☐ Mind Field 89
☐ Native Son 143
☐ Pickled 28
☐ Pinkies for the Dean 146
☐ Play with Fire 48
☐ Poodle Chainsaw Massacre 67
☐ Sand Illusion 155
☐ Sister of Pain 103
☐ Star Search 60
☐ Sudden Impact 109
☐ Suffering Cats 88
☐ Swilderness Experience 31
☐ Tin Horn Posers 97
☐ Twentieth Century Ultra 145
☐ Unknown (Burlap Buttress) 344
☐ Unknown (Running Man Wall) 124

5.11D
☐ #1 140
☐ #2 140
☐ #3 140
☐ #6 140
☐ 911 86
☐ Arrowhead Arête 43
☐ Black Happy 50
☐ Blackened 50
☐ Circle Jerks 180
☐ Cujo 67
☐ Disguise the Limit 42
☐ GBH 137
☐ Golden Nugget 48
☐ Graveyard Waltz 124
☐ Hang Ten 70
☐ The Healer 143
☐ The Laying on of the Hands 89
☐ Messie Nessie 39
☐ New Traditionalists 123
☐ Nine Lives 88
☐ Northern Lights 125
☐ Peak Performance 50
☐ Pocket Rocket 83
☐ Quicksand 116
☐ Saddam's Mom 157
☐ Second Fiddle to a Dead Man 123
☐ Snack Crack 70
☐ Social Disorder 108
☐ Solar Flare 50
☐ Soul Power 158
☐ Synapse Collapse 45
☐ Tortugas Mutante 151
☐ Without a Paddle 255
☐ Yaak Crack 107

5.11+
☐ Animal Boy 99
☐ Autumnal Frost 53
☐ The Breathing Stone 378
☐ Cactus Root 62
☐ Captain Hook 176
☐ Chinese Handcuffs 340
☐ Circus Boy 64
☐ Climb Bomb 58
☐ Cloud Tower 276
☐ Corona Crack 225
☐ Dark Star 169
☐ The Dividing Line 36
☐ Eliminator Crack 309
☐ Fear This 29
☐ Fibonacci Wall 124
☐ Free Willy 318
☐ Fungus Folks 229
☐ Gold-Plated Garlic Press 40
☐ Gun Boy 178
☐ Home of the Brave 183
☐ Mind Bomb 174
☐ My Little Pony 372
☐ Rebel Yell 120
☐ Red Skies 69
☐ Resin Rose 109
☐ Resolution Arête 314
☐ Rojo 201
☐ Sonic Youth 137
☐ Sportin' a Woody 175
☐ Spring Break 189
☐ Straight Shot 330
☐ Stratocaster 131
☐ There Goes the Neighborhood 123
☐ Time's Up 262
☐ Twenty-nine Posers 222
☐ Water Dog 188
☐ When the Shit Hits the Fan 131
☐ Yucca (TR) 102

5.12-
☐ Afterburner 309
☐ American Ghostdance 363
☐ Americragger 120
☐ The Bristler 131
☐ Caligula 42
☐ Contempt of Court 25
☐ Crowd Pleaser 64
☐ Flame Ranger 126
☐ Gotham City 189
☐ Green Eagle 62
☐ Hodad 62
☐ Kisses Don't Lie 199
☐ Parental Guidance 238
☐ Ripcord 120
☐ Stukas over Disneyland 33
☐ Tarantula 189
☐ Violent Stems 338
☐ Whiplash 186

5.12
☐ Connect the Dots 159
☐ Dependent Variable 255
☐ Gay Nazis for Christ 62
☐ K-Day 340
☐ Lethal Weapon 239
☐ Midway 64

□ Nexus 158
□ Original Route,
  Rainbow Wall 267
□ Posby (TR) 222
□ Project (Stratocaster Wall)
  128
□ Project (The Trophy) 149
□ Satan in a Can 43
□ Sergeant Slaughter 276
□ Take the Skinheads
  Bowling 64
□ Tier of the Titans 126
□ Too Pumped to Pose (TR)
  222
□ Toxic Playboy 120
□ Unknown (The Trophy) 149
□ Velvet Elvis 60
□ Welcome to Red Rocks 242

5.12A
□ #4 140
□ Absolute Zero 159
□ Basement 119
□ Cannabis 45
□ Casino 70
□ Caught in the Crosshairs
  150
□ Chunder Bolt 48
□ Cowboy Café 132
□ Crude Control 91
□ Dodging a Bullet 150
□ Fear and Loathing III 109
□ Gimme Back My Bullets 50
□ Integrity of Desire 133
□ Jaws of Life 86
□ Judgment Day 49
□ KGB 45
□ Loki 137
□ Maneater 27
□ Matzoland 352
□ My Thai 70
□ One-Move Number 141
□ Pain Check 143
□ Presents of Mind 157
□ Pretty in Pink 97
□ Rafter Man 89
□ Rise and Whine 143
□ The Sands 70
□ Save the Heart to
  Eat Later 28
□ Serious Leisure 117
□ Sound of Power 115
□ Sputnik 147
□ Standing in the Shadows 83
□ Steep Thrills 50
□ Sunny and Steep 50
□ Sweet Pain 102
□ They Just Don't Make
  Outlaws Like They
  Used To 159
□ This Is the City 118
□ Titan Rocket 126
□ Tour de Pump 50
□ Unknown Arête 155
□ Viagra Falls 76
□ Where Egos Dare 143
□ Wizard of Odds 151

5.12B
□ #5 140
□ Abandon Ship 82
□ Aftershock 82
□ Agent Orange 137
□ Before Its Time 83
□ Big Damage 109
□ Boschton Marathon 122
□ Celebrity Roast 60
□ Churning in the Dirt 115
□ Climb and Punishment 40
□ Cling Free 118
□ Commando 124
□ Crimson Crimp 89
□ Death before Decaf 157
□ The Deep West 134
□ Every Mother's Nightmare
  85
□ Fear this Sport 28
□ Fidelity Select 146
□ Geometric Progression 118
□ Insecure Delusions 71
□ K-9 67
□ Keep Your Powder Dry 149
□ Land Shark 82
□ Lee Press-on 103
□ Lounge Tomato 138
□ Minstrel in the Gallery 108
□ Naked and Disfigured 84
□ Nevadatude 117
□ Onsight Flight 144
□ Party Down (TR) 129
□ Pier Pressure 119
□ Pigs in Zen 84
□ Plastic Pistol 134
□ Poseidon Adventure 81
□ Promises in the Dark 109
□ Sand Rail 89
□ Sandblaster 89
□ Smokin' 45
□ Southern Cross 151
□ Stand and Deliver 144
□ Stealin' 84
□ Stratocaster Direct 131
□ Thirsty Quail 118
□ Tropicana 70
□ Turbo Dog 50
□ Wedgie 76

5.12C
□ #.5 140
□ Almost, but Not Quite 119
□ Angler 82
□ Body English 109
□ Boobytrap 33
□ Choad Hard 129
□ The Choad Warrior 131
□ Computer Virus 155
□ Destiny 119
□ False Alarm 118
□ The Fiend 46
□ Flight Line 174
□ Gladiator 86
□ Glitch 107
□ The Grinch 157
□ Indian Giver 149
□ Jack Officers 32
□ New Wave Hookers 28

□ Poco Owes Me a Concert
  119
□ Purple Haze II 131
□ Ranch Hands 32
□ Stargazer 147
□ Supernova II 147
□ Swilderness Permit 31
□ Threadfin 82
□ The Trophy 149
□ Who Made Who 107

5.12D
□ Cavity Search 46
□ Cosmos 147
□ Desert Oasis 118
□ Drug Sniffing Pot-Bellied
  Pig 118
□ Flying Cowboys 134
□ The Gift 107
□ Man Overboard! 82
□ One Man's Kokopelli Is
  another Man's Side
  Show Bob 45
□ Pablo Diablo 129
□ Pet Shop Boy 149
□ Sand Boxing 89
□ Southern Comfort 151
□ Vision Quest 177
□ Where the Down Boys Go
  107
□ Wonderstuff 27

5.12+
□ Desert Crack 338
□ Love on the Rocks 25
□ Main Attraction 64
□ Rainbow Country 271
□ Rock Rastler 176
□ Tuscarora 297

5.13-
□ Desert Gold 338
□ Terminal Velocity 225

5.13
□ Meatlocker 150

5.13A
□ Freak Brothers 45
□ How Do Ya Like them
  Pineapples? 118
□ Master Beta 83
□ Midnight Cowboy 149
□ Nothing Shocking 107
□ Rubber Biscuit 89
□ Shadow Warrior 86
□ Shark Walk 149
□ SOS 82
□ Twilight of a Champion 149

5.13B
□ Barracuda 81
□ Beyond Reason 131
□ Monster Skank 115

5.13C
□ Sunsplash 115

INDEX

SYMBOLS
#.5 140
#0 140
#1 140
#2 140
#3 140
#4 140
#5 140
#6 140
'34 Ford with Flames 309
911 86

A
A-Cute Pain 103
A-OK 52, 55
Abandon Ship 82
Abandoned Line 99
Abbey Road 16, 18, 19
The Abdominizer 170
Absolute Zero 159
The Abutment 211, 214–217
   Bridge of Sighs 214
   Robin Trowel 214
Access Fun 24
Ace of Hearts 16, 18
Acid Jacks 180
Adoption 91, 92
Advance Romance 335
Aeolian Wall—Original Route
   285, 313
Affliction for Friction 113
Afterburner 284, 309, 310
Afterburner Cliff 309, 310
   '34 Ford with Flames 309
   Afterburner 309
   Deguello 309
   Eliminator Crack 309
   Finger Fandango 309
Aftershock 82
Agent Orange 137
Ain't No Saint 386, 388
Airlift 86
Alcohol Wall 328, 329–331
   Friendship Route 331
   Gin Ricky 330
   Mai Tai 331
   Rob Roy 331
   Straight Shot 330
Algae on Parade 332
Aliens Have Landed 22, 23
All the Right Moves 340
Almost, but Not Quite 119
Amazing Grace 199
American Ghostdance 363, 364
American Ninja 232
American Sportsman 109, 110
Americrag 119–122
   Americragger 120
   Jimmy Nap 120
   Mr. Moto 120
   Rebel Yell 120
   Stuck on You 119
   That Wedged Feeling 120
   Toxic Playboy 120

Americragger 120
Angel Food Wall 161–165
   Goobies for Gumbies 165
   Group Therapy 162
   Healy's Haunted House 165
   Tunnel Vision 162
Angler 82
Animal Boy 98, 99
April Fools 104, 105
Arachnoworld 228, 229
Archeoptryx 354
The Arena 85–86
   Gladiator 86
   Shadow Warrior 86
Arm Forces 394
Armed and Dangerous 154
Arrowhead Arête 43
As the Toad Turns 348
The Asylum 138
   Comforts of Madness 138
   Flip the Switch 138
   Lounge Tomato 138
Atman 47, 48
Autumnal Frost 52, 53
Avian Wall 147–148
   Coyote Moon 148
   Spotted Eagle 148
   Spotted Owl 147
   Thunderbird 147

B
B/W Wall 132–133
   The Darkroom 132
   The Negative 132
   Red Light 132
   Snapshot 132
Back to Basics 348
Backlash 186
Bad Guys Approaching 254,
   261, 262
Bad Reputation 154
Badger's Buttress 25
Barracuda 81, 82
Baseboy 27, 28
Basement 119
Battery Powered 153
Battle Royale 272
Bauble 210, 212, 213
BCR 5L 91
The Beach 151–152
   Looks Like Craps 151
   RF Gain 152
   Southern Comfort 151
   Southern Cross 151
   Squelch 152
   Static 152
   Wizard of Odds 151
Beer and Ice Gully 222–225
   Chilly Ones 225
   Corona Crack 225
   Moisture Brau 225
   Orange Clonus 222
   Posby 222
   Stout Roof 225

Terminal Velocity 225
   This Bud's for You 225
   Too Pumped to Pose 222
   Twenty-nine Posers 222
Before Its Time 83
Belief in Proportion to
   the Evidence 217, 218
Bengal 73
Beulah's Book 284, 287, 290,
   293
Bewitched 90
Beyond Reason 131
Big Damage 109, 110
Big Iron 171
The Big Payback 266, 276
Big Top 65
Bigfoot 172
Bighorn Buttress 172, 173
The Bindle 68, 69
Birthstone 104
Black Arch Wall 297–299
   Black Betty 299
   Black Widow 299
   There and Back Again 297
   Tuscarora 297
Black Betty 298, 299
Black Canyon of the
   Colorado 398
The Black Corridor 90–94
   Left Wall, Upper Level 93
      Black Gold 93
      Crude Behavior 93
      Crude Street Blues 93
      Dancin' with a God 93
      Fool's Gold 93
      Live Fast, Die Young 93
      Texas Tea 93
      Thermal Breakdown 93
   Left/South Wall, Lower Level 91
      BCR 5L 91
      Black Corridor Route 4
         Left 91
      Bon Ez 91
      Bonaire 91
      Crude Boys 91
      Crude Control 91
      Vagabonds 91
   Right Wall, Second Story 94
      Lewd, Crude, and
         Misconstrued 94
      Livin' on Borrowed Time 94
      Oils Well that Ends Well 94
      Rebel without a Pause 94
      Sandstone Enema 94
      Texas Lite Sweet 94
   Right/NorthWall, Basement 91
      Adoption 91
      Burros Don't Gamble 91
      Burros Might Fly 91
      Nightmare on Crude
         Street 93
Black Corridor Route 4 Left 91
The Black Dagger 254, 255, 262,
   263

Black Flag 137
Black Gold 93
Black Happy *49*, *50*
The Black Hole 230, *231*
Black Licorice 26
Black Magic 329
Black Magic Panties 206
The Black Orpheus *284*, *285*,
    294, *295*, *298*
    Descent *296*
Black Sun 383, *385*
Black Tongue 58, *59*
Black Track 172
Black Velvet Canyon *336*, 337–
    385
Black Velvet Wall 358–377
    American Ghostdance 363
    Chalk Is Cheap 372
    Cutting Edge 360
    Dream of Wild Turkeys 366
    Early Times 370
    Epinephrine 375
    Fiddler on the Roof 369
    The Gobbler 369
    Johnny Come Lately 370
    Lone Star 377
    Malicious Mischief 372
    My Little Pony 372
    The Prince of Darkness 366
    Refried Brains 361
    Rock Warrior 365
    Sandstone Samurai 363
    Smooth as Silk 361
    Sour Mash 370
    Spark Plug 360
    Texas Hold'em 377
    Velveeta 372
    Yellow Brick Road 368
Black Widow *284*, *298*, *299*
Blackened *49*, *50*
Blanc Czech 62, *63*
Blister in the Sun 151
Blister In The Sun Cliff 150–151
    Blister in the Sun 151
    High Scalin' 151
    Teenage Mutant Ninja
        Turtles 151
    Tortugas Mutante 151
Blitzkrieg 192
Blonde Dwarf 86, *87*
Blood Stains 32
Bloodline *240*, 241
Bodiddly 178
Body English 109, *110*
Bon Ez 91
Bonaire 91
Bone Machine 84
Bonus Pullout Section 42
Boobytrap 33
Boodler *18*, 19
Boschton Marathon 122
Boschton Marathon
    Block 122–123
    Boschton Marathon 122
    Brain Damage 122
    Frictiony Face, Panty Waist
        122
Bossa Nova 294, *298*
Bottoms up *33*, 35

Boulder Dash *23*, 26
Bowling Ball 64
    Take the Skinheads
        Bowling 64
Boxer Rebellion *74*, *75*
Brain Damage 122
Brand New Bag 158
Brass Balls 230
Brass Wall *209*, 227–232
    Arachnoworld 229
    The Black Hole 230
    Brass Balls 230
    The Bus Stops Here 227
    Bush Pilots 229
    Fungus Folks 229
    Go Greyhound 227
    Heavy Spider Karma 229
    Mushroom People 229
    No Laughing Matter 229
    One Stop in Tonopah 227
    Raptor 230
    Ripcord 230
    Sea of Holes 230
    Serious Business 227
    Simpatico 227
    Snivler 229
    Spectrum 232
    Topless Twins 229
    Varnishing Point 227
    Zen and the Art of Web
        Spinning 229
Break Loose 128
Breakaway *195*, *196*, *197*, *198*
The Breathing Stone 378, *383*
Bridge Mountain 201–232
    The Northeast Arête 202
    East Face
        Bauble 212
        Costume Jewelry 212
        Fear and Loathing 211
        Gemstone 212
        Tri-Burro Bridge 214
Bridge of Sighs 214
Brief Encounter *74*, *75*
The Bristler 131
Broast and Toast Cliff *135*,
    138–140
    Burnt Toast 138
    C.H.U.D. 140
    Calico Jack 139
    Desert Sportsman 140
    Fairy Toast 138
    Rap Bolters Need to Be
        Famous 139
    Roasted Ramen 139
Brown Recluse 266, 267, *268*
Brownstone Wall *255*, 259–264
    Bad Guys Approaching 262
    The Black Dagger 262
    High Anxiety 259
    The Nightcrawler 262
    Paiute Pillar 264
    Time's Up 262
Bruja's Brew 329
Buck's Muscle World 108
Buffalo Balls 172
Buffalo Wall 189, 189–192
    Blitzkrieg 192
    Buffalo Wall 189

Tatanka 192
The Bull Market 145–146
    Fidelity Select 146
    Hostile Takeover 146
    Leveraged Buyout 146
    Liar's Poker 146
    Pinkies for the Dean 146
    Scudder Global 146
    Twentieth Century Ultra 145
Burlap Buttress 340–344
    Children of the Sun 342
    K-Day 340
    Unknown 342, 344
Burlesque 204, *205*
Burnt Toast 138
Burros Don't Gamble 91
Burros Might Fly 91
The Bus Stops Here 227, *228*
Bush Pilots *228*, 229
Butt Floss *74*, *75*
Buzz, Buzz 332

C
C.H.U.D. 140
$C_{11}H_{17}NO_3$ 242, *243*
Cabo San Looseness 352
Cactus Head *61*, 62
Cactus Massacre *56*, 61–62
    Cactus Head 62
    Cactus Massacre 62
    Cactus Root 62
Cactus Root *61*, 62
Cal. West 116
Caliban *27*, 28
Calico Basin 15–55
Calico Jack 139
Calico Tank 150
Calico Terror 123
California Crags 116–117
    Cal. West 116
    The Escalator 117
    Far Cry from Josh 117
    Hurricane 116
    Just in from L.A. 117
    Nevadatude 117
    Orange County 117
    People Mover 117
    Quicksand 116
    Serious Leisure 117
    The Staircase 117
Caligula *41*, 42
Caligula Crag 41–42
    Bonus Pullout Section 42
    Caligula 42
    Disguise the Limit 42
    Guccione 42
    Hefner 42
    Ms. October, 1995 42
    Penthouse Pet 42
Cameo Appearance 60
Cannabis 45
Cannabis Crag 44–46
    Cannabis 45
    Cavity Search 46
    The Felon 46
    The Fiend 46
    Freak Brothers 45
    Horizontal Departure 46
    KGB 45

One Man's Kokopelli Is
    another Man's Side Show
    Bob 45
    Smokin' 45
    Synapse Collapse 45
Cannibal Crag 26, 27–30
    Baseboy 28
    Caliban 28
    Caustic 28
    Elbows of Mac and Ronnie 29
    Fear This 29
    Fear this Sport 28
    Have a Beer with Fear 29
    Ma and Pa in Kettle 29
    Mac and Ronnie in Cheese 29
    A Man in Every Pot 29
    Maneater 27
    New Wave Hookers 28
    Pickled 28
    Risk Brothers Roof 30
    Save the Heart to Eat Later 28
    Shishka Bob 29
    Shit Howdy 29
    What's Eating You? 29
    Wonderstuff 27
    You Are What You Eat 28
    Zona Rosa 30
Cantilever Corner 213, 216
Captain Crunch 176
Captain Curmudgeon 176
Captain Hook 176
Car Talk 218, 219
Carful of Clowns 64
Carpetbagger 18, 21
Carrie Fissure 23
Cartwright Corner 251, 252,
    253
The Case Face 180–182
    Hard Case 181
    Head Case 181
    Just in Case 181
    Soylent Green Jeans 181
    Space Case 181
    Sterling Moss 182
    Territorial Imperative 180
Casino 70
Cat in the Hat 208, 209, 245,
    246
Cat Walk (Dog Wall) 65, 66, 71
Catwalk (Oak Creek Canyon)
    285, 306, 307, 308
Caught in the Crosshairs 150
Caustic 27, 28
Cavity Search 46
Celebrity Roast 60
Centerfold 240, 241
Chairman Mao's Little Red Book
    98, 100
Chalk Is Cheap 372, 374
Chameleon Pinnacle 393
Changelings 393
Chasing Shadows 237
Chicken Eruptus 178
Chicken Gumbo for Your
    Dumbo 16
Chicken Lips 284, 300, 301
Chicken Soup for the Soul 16
Children of the Sun 342, 343
Chilly Ones 225

Chinese Handcuffs 340
Chips Ahoy! 71, 72
Chips and Salsa 71, 72
Chips Away 98, 100
Choad Hard 129
The Choad Warrior 131
Chocolate Flakes 250, 251, 253
Chocolate Swirl 44
Christmas Tree Pass 398, 399
Chrysler Crack 134
Chunder Bolt 48
Churning in the Dirt 115
Circle Jerks 180
Circus Boy 64
Circus Wall 56, 64–65
    Big Top 65
    Carful of Clowns 64
    Circus Boy 64
    Crowd Pleaser 64
    Elephant Man 65
    High Wire 64
    Human Cannonball 64
    Lion Tamer 64
    Main Attraction 64
    Midway 64
Cirque du Soleil 49, 51
City Slickers 40
Claimjumper's Special 49
Clark Mountain 398
Classic Corner 23, 24
Claw Hammer 60
Climb and Punishment 40
Climb Bandits 60
Climb Bomb 58, 59
Climb Bomb Cliff 56, 59
    Climb Bomb 58
    Climb Machine 58
    Climb Traveler 58
    Climb Warp 58
Climb Machine 58, 59
Climb Traveler 58, 59
Climb Warp 58, 59
Cling Free 118
Clipper 338
Clone Babies 250
Cloud Tower 254, 276–279,
    278, 281
    Cloud Tower 276
    Crimson Chrysalis 279
    Hook, Climb, and Whimper
        279
Clutch Cargo 77
Clyde Crashcup 217
Cocaine Hotline 68, 69
Cold Blue Steel 252
Cold September Corner 187
Cole Essence 354
Comforts of Madness 138
Commando 124
Common Bond of Circumstance
    217, 218
Common Time 141
    Myxolidian 141
    One-Move Number 141
    Paradiddle Riddle 141
    Time Off 141
Community Pillar 208, 252, 253
Commuted Sentence 218, 219
Computer Virus 155

Con Jurors 395
Connect the Dots 159
Contempt of Court 23, 25
Conundrum Crag 42–43
    Arrowhead Arête 43
    Drilling Miss Daisy 42
    Family Affair 43
    Satan in a Can 43
Conz Crack 48
The Cookie Monster 210, 243,
    244
Cool Water Sandwich 52, 55
Cool Whip 52, 55
Cornucopia 340, 341
Corona Crack 224, 225
Cosmos 147
Costume Jewelry 212
Costume Jewlery 210
Couldn't Be Schmooter 52, 53,
    54
Country Bumpkin 40
Cover My Buttress 73, 74, 75
Cow Lick Co. Crag 35
Cowboy Café 132
Coyote Moon 148
Crabby Appleton 208, 247
Crabby Appleton Area 247–249
    Crabby Appleton 247
    Creepshow 249
    Tom Terrific 247
    The Whitehouse Effect 249
Crack (The Fixx Cliff) 67, 68, 71
Crack Bar 70
Crack of Noon 143
Crankenstein 138
Crawdad 62, 63
Crawdad Canyon 398
Crawford's Corner 207
Crazy Girls 216
Crazy World 272, 274
Creepshow 249
Crimson Chrysalis 209, 254,
    255, 279, 280, 281
Crimson Crimp 89
Crossfire 189
Crowd Pleaser 64
Crown Royal 344, 345
Crude Behavior 93
Crude Boys 91
Crude Control 91
Crude Street Blues 93
Crumbling Community 115
Cujo 66, 67
Cut Loose 129
Cutting Edge 361

D
Dances with Beagles 300, 304,
    305
Dancin' with a God 93
Dark Shadows 208, 236, 237
    Edge Dressing 237
Dark Shadows Wall 234–239
    Chasing Shadows 237
    Dark Shadows 237
    Excellent Adventure 238
    Heart of Darkness 237
    Lethal Weapon 239
    Parental Guidance 238

Risky Business 238
Sandstone Sandwich 237
Short Circuit 238
Slot Machine 235
Dark Star 169
The Dark Thumb 183–185
   Home of the Brave 183
   Land of the Free 183
The Darkroom 132
David Copperhead 395
A Day in the Life 108
Dean's List 182
Death before Decaf 157
The Deep West 134
Deez Guys 395
Deguello 309, *310*
The Delicate Sound of Thunder 356
Dense Pack 179
Dependent Variable 255
Desert Crack 338
Desert Gold 338
Desert Oasis 118
Desert Pickle *90*, 109, *110*
Desert Reality 338, *339*
Desert Solitaire 272, *273*
Desert Solitude 378, *382*
Desert Sportsman 140
Destiny 119
Diablo 129
Diamond Dance 70
Dickies Cliff 32–34
   Boobytrap 33
   Gigantor 33
   Guys and Ghouls 33
   Lancaster Levels Luxor 34
   Monster Island 34
   Stukas over Disneyland 33
Diet Delight 386, *387*
Dime Edging 145
Dirtbagger's Compensation 323, *325*
Dirty Little Girl *38*, 40
Disguise the Limit *41*, 42
Disposable Blues 159
Ditch Day 85
The Dividing Line 36
Doctor's Orders 85
Dodging a Bullet 150
Dog Police *208*, 255
Dog Wall 65–67, *71*
   Cat Walk 65
   Cujo 67
   Here Kitty, Kitty 67
   It's a Bitch 67
   K-9 67
   Man's Best Friend 67
   Poodle Chainsaw Massacre 67
   Wok the Dog 65
Doin' the Good Drive 219
Doobie Dance 332
Dream of Wild Turkeys 366
Drilling Miss Daisy *42*, *43*
Drug Sniffing Pot-Bellied Pig 118
Dukes of Hazard 250, *251*, *253*

E
Eagle Dance *284*, *300*, 303, *304*
Eagle Wall Area 299–306

Chicken Lips 300
Dances with Beagles 305
Eagle Dance 303
Levitation 29 303
Rainbow Buttress 302
Early Times 370
Earth Juice 199
Ed MacMayonnaise 60
Edge Dressing *237*
Edge of the Sun 249
Edible Panties *73*, *74*, 76
Edward Silverhands 48
Eight Ball *68*, 69
Elbows of Mac and Ronnie 29
Elder Sibling 143
Electric Koolaid 86
Electric Orange Peeler *38*, 40
Elementary Primer 99
Elephant Man 65
The Elephant Penis *210*, 220
Eliminator Crack *284*, 309, *310*
Emerald City 272, *275*
Epinephrine *375*, *376*
The Escalator 117
Ethical Behavior 89
Ethics Wall 89
   Ethical Behavior 89
   The Laying on of the Hands 89
   Mind Field 89
   Rafter Man 89
Every Mother's Nightmare 85
Everybody's Slave 137
Excellent Adventure *236*, 238

F
Fairy Toast 138
False Alarm 118
False Perception 397
Falstaff 125
Family Affair 43
Family Circus 43
Far Cry from Josh 117
Fast Moving Train 157
Fear and Loathing *210*, 211, *213*
Fear and Loathing II *95*, *96*
Fear and Loathing III 109, *110*
Fear This 29
Fear this Sport *27*, *28*
The Felon 46
Fibonacci Wall 124
Fiddler on the Roof 369
Fidelity Select 146
The Fiend *45*, 46
Fifi Hula 149
The Figurine 39
Finger Fandango *284*, 309, *310*
First Born 143
First Creek Canyon *285*, *320*, 321–335
First Grader 348
First Pullout 57–78
Five and Dime 250
The Fixx Cliff *65*, 67–69, *71*
   The Bindle 69
   Cocaine Hotline 69
   Crack 67
   Eight Ball 69
   Free Base 69

The Geezer 69
One Thing Leads to Another 69
Outside the Envelope 69
Reach the Beach 69
Red Skies 69
Running 69
Saved by Zero 69
The Skagg 69
Snow Blind 67
Stand or Fall 67
The Whiff 67
Flake Eyes 144
Flakes of Wrath 239, *240*
Flame Ranger 126
Fleet Street 19
Flight Line 174
Flight Path *208*, *213*, 217
Flight Path Area *211*, 217–219
   Belief in Proportion to the Evidence 217
   Car Talk 219
   Common Bond of Circumstance 217
   Commuted Sentence 219
   Doin' the Good Drive 219
   Ignore the Man behind the Screen 217
   Radio Free Kansas 217
   Sex in the Scrub Oak 218
   A Simple Expediency 219
   They Call the Wind #!&% 218
Flip the Switch 138
Flying Cowboys 134
Flying Pumpkin *23*, 24
Flying V 129
Fold-Out 204
Fontanar de Rojo 24
Fool's Gold 93
Footloose 129
Foreman Ferris 153
Forget Me Knot *221*, 222
The Fox *26*, 32
Freak Brothers 45
Free Base *68*, 69, *71*
Free Willy *317*, 318
French Bulges 394
The Friar 286, *288*
Friction Addiction 113
Frictiony Face, Panty Waist 122
Friendship Route 331
Frigid Air Buttress 202–204
   Burlesque 204
   Frigid Air Buttress 202
Frogland 344, *346*, *347*
From Soup to Nuts *16*, 18
Front Corridor 113–115
   Affliction for Friction 113
   Churning in the Dirt 115
   Crumbling Community 115
   Friction Addiction 113
   Gun Control 115
   Hair Today, Gone Tomorrow 115
   High Noon 115
   Monster Skank 115
   Prescription Gription 113
   Sicktion 113

Sound of Power 115
Sunsplash 115
A Thousand New Routes 115
To Bolt or Toupee 115
Fungus Folks *228*, 229

G

The Gallery *90*, 107–108
Buck's Muscle World 108
A Day in the Life 108
Gelatin Pooch 108
The Gift 107
Glitch 107
Gridlock 108
Minstrel in the Gallery 108
Nothing Shocking 107
Pump First, Pay Later 108
Range of Motion 108
Running Amuck 108
The Sissy Traverse 107
Social Disorder 108
Sport Climbing Is Neither 108
Where the Down Boys Go 107
Who Made Who 107
Yaak Crack 107
Galloping Gal 124
Gateway Canyon *38*, *44*
Gay Nazis for Christ 62, *63*
GBH 137
The Geezer *68*, *69*
Gelatin Pooch 108
Gemstone *208*, *210–211*, 212, *213*
Geometric Progression 118
Geronimo *209*, *254*, 255, *259*, *260*
Ghouls Just Wanna Have Fun *33*, 35
The Gift 107
The Gift of the Wind Gods 312
Gift Rapped 157
Gigantor 33, *34*
Gimme Back My Bullets *49*, *50*
Gin Ricky 330
Ginger Buttress *209*, 279–283
Ginger Cracks 281
Power Failure 283
Unimpeachable Groping 283
Ginger Cracks *254*, 281, *282*
Girls and Buoys 331
Gladiator 86
Glitch *90*, 107
Glitter Gulch 103
Gnat Man Crag *33*, 34–35
Bottoms up 35
Ghouls Just Wanna Have Fun 35
Gnat Man on Ranch Hands 35
Knock the Bottom out of It 35
P-Coat Junction 34
P-Coat Sleeve 34
Gnat Man on Ranch Hands *33*, *34*, 35
Go Greyhound 227, *228*
The Gobbler 369
Godzilla 78
Gold Bikini and Cinnamon Bun Hairdo 23

Gold-Plated Garlic Press 40
Golden Nugget 48
Gonzo Dogs *95*, 96
Goobies for Gumbies 165
Good Mourning 143
Gotham City 189
The Graduate 179
Graduate Cliff 179–180
Walk to School 179
Grape Nuts 199
Graveyard Waltz 124
Greased Lightning 199
The Great Red Book 87, *98*, 99
Great Red Book Area 97–100
Abandoned Line 99
Animal Boy 99
Chairman Mao's Little Red Book 100
Chips Away 100
Elementary Primer 99
The Great Red Book 99
Ground-up Vocabulary 100
Question of Balance 99
Sandstone Cowboy 100
See Spot Run 99
Stone Hammer 100
Tomato Amnesia 99
The Great Red Roof 77
Green Eagle 62, *63*
Gridlock 108
The Grinch 157
Grippitty Gravity 175
Ground-up Vocabulary *98*, 100
Group Therapy 162, *164*
Guccione *41*, 42
Guise and Gals 331
Gun Boy 178
Gun Control 115
Guys and Ghouls 33, *34*

H

Habeas Corpus 25
Haberdasher 26
Hair Today, Gone Tomorrow 115
The Haj 21
The Hall of Fame 154–155
Armed and Dangerous 154
Bad Reputation 154
Computer Virus 155
Hero Worship 155
Innocent Bystander 154
Ms. Adventure 155
Repeat Offender 154
Sand Illusion 155
Unknown Arête 155
Yearnin' and Learnin' 154
Han Soloing 22
Hang Ten 70
Happy Acres *34*, 35–38, *36*
The Dividing Line 36
Happy Acres 36
The Life Chuckle 35
Mom and Apple Pie 36
Mother's Day 36
Mothers of Invention 36
Spontaneous Enjoyment 35
Haunted Hooks 104
Have a Beer with Fear 29

Head Case 181
Headmaster Ritual 40
The Healer 143
Healy's Haunted House 165, *166*
Heart of Darkness 237
Heatwave 176
Heavy Spider Karma *208*, *228*, 229
Hefner 42
Here Kitty, Kitty 66, *67*
Hero Worship 155
The Heteroclite 159
The Hex Files 78
Hidden Falls 169–176
Hidden Meaning 24
Hidden Wall 192
High Anxiety *259*, *261*
High Class Hoe *52*, *53*
High Noon 115
High Scalin' 151
High Wire 64
Hip-Hoppin' with the Hutterites 137
Hit and Run 153
Hodad 62, *63*
Hole in the Pants *51*, *52*
Holiday Wall 155–158
Death before Decaf 157
Fast Moving Train 157
Gift Rapped 157
The Grinch 157
Presents of Mind 157
Red Sky Mining 157
Red Storm Rising 157
Saddam's Mom 157
When the Cat's Away 157
Home of the Brave 183
Hook, Climb, and Whimper 279
Hooligans 134
Hop Route 207
Horizontal Departure 46
Horndogger Select *284*, *287*, 289
Hostile Takeover 146
Hot Climb 176
How Do Ya Like them Pineapples? 118
Human Cannonball 64
Human Chockstones *213*, 216
Hunter S. Thompson Dome *90*, 94–97
Fear and Loathing II 96
Gonzo Dogs 96
Liquid God 96
Pretty in Pink 97
Runout Rodeo 96
Walking the Vertical Beach 96
Hurricane 116

I

Ice Climb 182
Icebox Canyon *184*, 185–207
South Wall 192
Quiggle's Wiggle 192
Weenie Juice 192
Idiots Rule *82*, 84
Ignore the Man behind the Screen 217, *218*
Illusion Crags *392*, 393–397

Left Side 393–394
  Arm Forces 394
  Chameleon Pinnacle 393
  Changelings 393
  French Bulges 394
  Mirage 394
  Morph Out! 394
Main Cliff 394–398
  Con Jurors 395
  David Copperhead 395
  Deez Guys 395
  False Perception 397
  Illusions of Grandstaff 396
  Magician's Hat 396
  Petit Deceit 396
  Shell Game 396
  Slight of Hand 396
  Smoke and Mirrors 394
  Sore Sirs 395
  Spell Me 395
  Who, Deany? 395
Illusions of Grandstaff 396
Indecision Peak 326, *327*
  Mudterm 326
Indian Giver 149
Innocent Bystander 154
Insecure Delusions 71
Integrity of Desire 133
Inti Watana 316
Iron Man *82*, 85
Is It Soup Yet? 16
Isis *59*, 60
It's a Bitch *66, 67, 71*
Ixtalan *349, 352*

J
Jabba the Hut Rock 22–23
  Aliens Have Landed 22
  Carrie Fissure 23
  Gold Bikini and Cinnamon
    Bun Hairdo 23
  Han Soloing 22
  Obie-One Keone 23
  Shallow Fried Cracken 23
Jack Officers 32
Jackrabbit Buttress 256–259
  Geronimo 259
Jam Session 183
James Brown 158
James Brown Area 157–207
James Brown Wall 158
  Brand New Bag 158
  James Brown 158
  Soul Power 158
Jane's Wall 84–85
  Every Mother's Nightmare 85
  Idiots Rule 84
  Naked and Disfigured 84
  Pigs in Zen 84
  See Dick Fly 84
  Stealin' 84
Jaws of Life 86
Jimmy Nap 120
Johnny Come Lately 370
Johnny Vegas *284, 287, 290,*
  293
Jonny Jamcrack *101*, 102
Jonny Rotten 102
Joshua Tree 401

Jubilant Song *389*, 390
Judgment Day 49
Juniper Canyon 255–283
Just in Case 181
Just in from L.A. 117
Just Shut up and Climb 143
Just Walls 56

K
K-9 66, 67
K-Day 340
Keep Your Powder Dry 149
Kemosabe 176, *177*
Ken Queasy 87
Kenny Laguna 348
Keyhole Canyon 398, *400*
KGB 45
Kick in the Balls 329
Killer Klowns 172
Kindergarten Cop 331
Kisses Don't Lie 199
Kitty Crag 88
  Nine Lives 88
  Suffering Cats 88
  Titty Litter 88
Knock the Bottom out of It *33,*
  34, 35
Knotty Behavior 188
Kokopelli 153
The Kor Route *266, 267*

L
Lady Wilson's Cleavage 321,
  322
Lancaster Levels Luxor *33*, 34
Land of the Free 183
Land Shark 82
Las Vegas Limestone 400
The Laying on of the Hands 89
The Lazy Fireman 220
Lebanese JoJo 201
Lee Press-on 103
Left Out 172
Lethal Weapon *236*, 239
Leveraged Buyout 146
Levitation 29 *284, 300, 303, 304*
Lewd, Crude, and Misconstrued
  94
Liar's Poker 146
Lick It *38*, 39
The Life Chuckle 35
Life out of Balance 83
Like Mom Used to Make 144
Lil' Red 31
Lion Tamer 64
Liquid God *95*, 96
Little Big Horn 175
Live Fast, Die Young 93
Livin' on Borrowed Time 94
Lizard Locks 340
Lizardry 70
Loki 137
Lone Star 377, *379*
Long Walk on a Short Pier 119
Looks Like Craps 151
Lost Creek Canyon/Hidden Falls
  169–176
  The Abdominizer 170
  Big Iron 171

  Bigfoot 172
  Black Track 172
  Buffalo Balls 172
  Killer Klowns 172
  Left Out 172
  Lower Tier
    Captain Crunch 176
    Captain Curmudgeon 176
    Captain Hook 176
    Flight Line 174
    Heatwave 176
    Hot Climb 176
    Little Big Horn 175
    Mind Bomb 174
    Rock Rastler 176
    Sportin' a Woody 175
    The Threat 174
    Tuckered Sparfish 176
  N'Plus Ultra 170
  Pillar Talk 170
  Sleeper 171
  Upper Tier
    Bighorn Buttress 172
    Grippitty Gravity 175
    The Pocket Philosopher
    172
    Possum Logic 172
Lotta Balls 326, *328, 330*
Lotta Balls Wall 326–329
  Black Magic 329
  Bruja's Brew 329
  Kick in the Balls 329
  Lotta Balls 326
  Power to Waste 326
  Trihardral 326
Lounge Tomato 138
Love Hurts 25
Love on the Rocks 25
Low Tide 83
Lucky Nuts 326
Lunar Escape *208*, 249

M
Ma and Pa in Kettle 29
Mac and Ronnie in Cheese 29
Magellanic Cloud 188
Magic Bus 86–87
  Blonde Dwarf 86
  Electric Koolaid (TR) 86
  Ken Queasy 87
  Neon Sunset 87
  Technicolor Sunrise 87
  Zipperhead 87
Magic Mirror 332
Magic Triangle Area 249–252
  Cartwright Corner 252
  Chocolate Flakes 250
  Clone Babies 250
  Cold Blue Steel 252
  Community Pillar 252
  Dependent Variable 255
  Dog Police 255
  Dukes of Hazard 250
  Edge of the Sun 249
  Five and Dime 250
  Lunar Escape 249
  Midnight Oil 250
  Small Purchase 250
  Without a Paddle 255

Magician's Hat 396
Mai Tai 331
Main Attraction 64
Malice Alice 102
Malicious Mischief 372
A Man in Every Pot 29
Man Overboard! 82
Maneater 27
Man's Best Friend 66, 67, 71
Marshall Amp 131
The Marshmallow 145
  Dime Edging 145
  Mojave Green 145
Mass Production Wall 152–153
  Battery Powered 153
  Foreman Ferris 153
  Hit and Run 153
  Kokopelli 153
  Parts Is Parts 153
  Some Assembly Required 153
  Trigger Happy 153
Master Beta 83
Matzoland 352
The Max Flex 62, 63
Mazatlan 351
Meat Puppet 62, 63
Meat Puppets Wall 56, 62
  Blanc Czech 62
  Crawdad 62
  Gay Nazis for Christ 62
  Green Eagle 62
  Hodad 62
  The Max Flex 62
  Meat Puppet 62
  Ranger Danger 62
  Yellow Dog 62
Meatlocker 150
Meister's Edge 90, 100, 101–102
Meister's Edge Area
  Jonny Jamcrack 102
  Jonny Rotten 102
  Malice Alice 102
  Meister's Edge 100
  Sand Man 100
  Shut up and Dance 102
  Yucca 102
Men Are from Mars, Women
  Are from Venice 214
Mercedes 188
Mescalito 209
  East Face 239–245
    Bloodline 241
    C11H17NO3 242
    Centerfold 241
    The Cookie Monster 244
    Flakes of Wrath 239
    Negro Blanco 239
    The Next Century 241
    Pauligk Pillar 242
    Pauline's Pentacle 245
    Pine Nuts 244
    Ride the Tiger 241
    This Ain't No Disco 244
    The Walker Spur 244
    Welcome to Red Rocks 242
    When a Stranger Calls 244
    Y2K 241
  South Face 245–247
    Cat in the Hat 245

OB Button 247
OB Fist 247
Messie Nessie 39
Meteor 186
Mexican Secret Agent Man 31
Meyers Crack 48
Meyers Cracks 48–49
  Conz Crack 48
  Meyers Crack 48
Midnight Cowboy 149
Midnight Oil 250
Midway 64
Mind Bomb 174
Mind Field 89
Minstrel in the Gallery 108
Mirage 394
Mirage II 159
Miss Conception 350
Mister Masters 189
The Misunderstanding 350
Mo Hotta, Mo Betta 52, 53
Moderate Mecca 15–21
  Abbey Road 19
  Ace of Hearts 18
  Boodler 19
  Carpetbagger 21
  Chicken Gumbo for Your
    Dumbo 16
  Chicken Soup for the Soul
    (TR) 16
  Fleet Street 19
  From Soup to Nuts 18
  The Haj 21
  Is It Soup Yet? 16
  Muckraker 19
  Mugwump 21
  Pending Disaster 19
  Pending Project 19
  Penny Lane 19
  The Route to Mecca 21
  Scalawag 19
  Side Effects 15
  The Singing Love Pen 18
  Sir Climbalot 21
  Soupy Sales 16
  Stew on This 15
  Treacherous Journey 21
  Valentine's Day 18
Moisture Brau 224, 225
Mojave Green 145
Mom and Apple Pie 36
Moments to Memories 157
Moneky Bars Boulder 38
Money 71
Monkey Rhythm 143
Monster Island 33, 34
Monster Skank 115
The Monument
  All the Right Moves 340
  Chinese Handcuffs 340
  Clipper 338
  Cornucopia 340
  Desert Crack 338
  Desert Gold 338
  Desert Reality 338
  Lizard Locks 340
  No Name 338
  Scumby 338
  Seduction Line 338

Violent Stems 338
Morph Out! 394
Mother's Day 34, 36
Mothers of Invention 36
Mount Charleston 402
Mount Wilson 285, 309–318,
  321–323
  Dirtbagger's Compensation
    323
  East Face
    Aeolian Wall—Original
      Route 313
    The Gift of the Wind Gods
      312
    Inti Watana 316
    Resolution Arête 314
    Woodrow 312
  Lady Wilson's Cleavage 321
  Son of Wilson 323
The Monument 338–340
Mr. Choad's Wild Ride 49, 50
Mr. Freeze's Face 187
Mr. Moto 120
Mr. Natural of the Desert 383,
  385
Ms. Adventure 155
Ms. October, 1995 41, 42
Muckraker 16, 18, 19
Mudterm 326
Mugwump 21
Mushroom People 221, 228, 229
Music to My Fears 195
My Little Pony 372, 373
My Thai 70
Myxolidian 141

N
Nadia's Niche 169
  Dark Star 169
  Nadia's Nine 169
  Wheat Thick 169
Nadia's Nine 169
Naked and Disfigured 84
Native Son 143
Nature Is Fun 208, 220
The Necromancer 204–207
  Black Magic Panties 206
  Crawford's Corner 207
  Fold-Out 204
  Hop Route 207
  Sensuous Mortician 204
The Negative 132
Negro Blanco 239, 240
Neon Sunset 87
Nevada Book 125
Nevadatude 117
New Traditionalists 123
New Wave Hookers 27, 28
Next Century 209
The Next Century 208, 210,
  240, 241
Next Wall
  Connect the Dots 159
  The Heteroclite 159
  Mirage II 159
  Nexus 158
  They Just Don't Make
    Outlaws Like They Used
    To 159

Nexus 158
The Nightcrawler *254*, *255*, *261*, 262
Nightmare on Crude Street *92*, 93
Nine Lives 88
Nirvana 104
No Laughing Matter *221*, *228*, 229
No Name 338
The Northeast Arête 202
Northern Lights 125
Nothing Shocking 107
N'Plus Ultra 170
Numbers Crag 140–141
  #.5 140
  #0 140
  #1 140
  #2 140
  #3 140
  #4 140
  #5 140
  #6 140
Nuttin' Could Be Finer *52*, *53*

O
Oak Creek Canyon 285–318
  Upper Oak Creek Canyon *306–309*
Oakey Dokey 298, 308
The Oasis *65*, 69–71
  Casino 70
  Crack Bar 70
  Diamond Dance 70
  Hang Ten 70
  Insecure Delusions 71
  Lizardry 70
  Money 71
  My Thai 70
  Pad's Passion 70
  The Sands 70
  Snack Crack 70
  Tropicana 70
  The Warming 71
OB Button 247
OB Fist 247
Obie-One Keone 23
The Observatory *90*, 104–106
  Warlock 106
  Which Hunters? 106
  Witches' Honor 106
Oils Well that Ends Well 94
Old School 44
Olive Oil *254*–*255*, *256*, *257*–*258*
One Man's Kokopelli Is another Man's Side Show Bob 45
One Stop in Tonopah *227*, *228*
One Thing Leads to Another *68*, 69
One-Eyed Jacks 129
One-Move Number 141
Only the Good Die Young 358
Onsight Flight 144
Orange Clonus 222, *223*
Orange County 117
Original Route, Rainbow Wall *254*, *266*, *267*, *270*, *281*
Otters Are People Too 317

Our Father 356
Out of Control 232
Out Of Control Area 232–234
  American Ninja 232
  Out of Control 232
  Red Throbber Spire 234
  Remote Control 234
  A Rope, a Rubber Chicken, and a Vibrator 234
Outhouse Wall 183
  Jam Session 183
  Roasting Affair 183
  Sin City 183
  Spiderline 183
  Tricks Are for Kids 183
Outside the Envelope *68*, 69
Over the Hill to Grandmother's House 30
Owens River Gorge 402

P
P-Coat Junction *33*, 34
P-Coat Sleeve *33*, 34
Pablo Diablo 129
Pad's Passion 70
Pain Check 143
Pain in the Neck 103
Paiute Pillar *254*, *264*, *265*
Panty Line *73*, *74*, *75*
Panty Prow *73*, 76
Panty Raid 73–74, *76*
Panty Shield *73*, 77
Panty Wall *65*, 73–77
  Boxer Rebellion 75
  Brief Encounter 75
  Butt Floss 75
  Cover My Buttress 75
  Edible Panties 76
  Panty Line 75
  Panty Prow 76
  Panty Raid 76
  Panty Shield 77
  Panty-Mime 76
  Scanty Panty 75
  Silk Panties 75
  Thong 75
  Totally Clips 76
  Viagra Falls 76
  Victoria's Secret 76
  Wedgie 76
Panty-Mime *73*, 76
Paradiddle Riddle 141
Parental Guidance 236, 238
Parts Is Parts 153
Party Down 129
Party Line 129
Pauligk Pillar *240*, *242*, *243*
Pauline's Pentacle 245
Payless Cashways *26*, 31
Peak Performance *49*, *50*
Pending Disaster *16*, *18*, 19
Pending Project 19
Penny Lane 19
Penthouse Pet *41*, *42*
People Mover 117
Perplexity 350
Pet Shop Boy 149
Petit Deceit 396
Physical Graffiti 30

Pickled *27*, 28
The Pier 117–119
  Almost, but Not Quite 119
  Basement 119
  Cling Free 118
  Desert Oasis 118
  Destiny 119
  Drug Sniffing Pot-Bellied Pig 118
  False Alarm 118
  Geometric Progression 118
  How Do Ya Like them Pineapples? 118
  Long Walk on a Short Pier 119
  Pier Pressure 119
  Poco Owes Me a Concert 119
  Scantily Clad Bimbo 118
  Seventh Hour 118
  Thirsty Quail 118
  This Is the City 118
  Under the Boardwalk 118
Pier Pressure 119
Pier-Less 216
Pigs in Zen 84
Pillar Talk 170
Pine Creek Canyon 209–252
  North Fork 232–245
  South Fork 245–252
Pine Nuts *208*, *243*, 244
Pinkies for the Dean 146
Plan F 178
Plastic People 124
Plastic Pistol 134
Play with Fire 48
The Playground 39–40
  Lower Tier *39*
    Lick It 39
    Show Burro 39
  Middle Tier 39
    Dirty Little Girl 40
    Electric Orange Peeler 40
    Gold-Plated Garlic Press 40
    Messie Nessie 39
    Practice Crack 40
    Repo Man 39
  Upper Tier 40
    City Slickers 40
    Climb and Punishment 40
    Country Bumpkin 40
    Headmaster Ritual 40
    Powder Puff 40
Playing Hooky 85
The Pocket Philosopher 172
Pocket Rocket *82*, *83*
Poco Owes Me a Concert 119
Poodle Chainsaw Massacre 66, 67
Posby 222, *224*
Poseidon Adventure 81
Poser Crag *90*, 97
  Special Guest Posers 97
  Tin Horn Posers 97
Possum Logic 172
Poundcake 143
Powder Puff 40
Power Failure *209*, *254*–*255*, *281*, 283
Power to Waste 326

Practice Crack *38*, 40
Predator 123
Prescription Gription 113
Presents of Mind 157
Pretty in Pink *95*, 97
Prime Ticket 60
The Prince of Darkness 366
Promises in the Dark 109, *110*
Pump First, Pay Later 108
Purple Haze 104
Purple Haze II 131

Q
Question of Balance *98*, 99
Quicksand 116
Quiet on the Set 60
Quiggle's Wiggle 192, *193*

R
Radio Free Kansas 217, *218*
Rafter Man 89
Ragged Edges 178
Ragged Edges Cliff 176–179
    Bodiddly 178
    Chicken Eruptus 178
    Dense Pack 179
    Gun Boy 178
    Kemosabe 176
    Plan F 178
    Ragged Edges 178
    Sheep Trail 178
    Tonto 177
    Vision Quest 177
    Why Left 179
    Why Right 179
Rain Dance 344
Rainbow Buttress *284–285, 300,*
    302, 304
Rainbow Country 271
Rainbow Mountain *255, 281,*
    285
Rainbow Wall *209, 255,* 264–
    276
    Battle Royale 272
    The Big Payback 276
    Brown Recluse 267
    Crazy World 272
    Desert Solitaire 272
    Emerald City 272
    The Kor Route 267
    Original Route 267
    Rainbow Country 271
    Sauron's Eye 267
    Sergeant Slaughter 276
    The Swainbow Wall 271
Ramen Pride *311*, 312
Ramen Pride Cliff 309–312
    Ramen Pride 312
    Stemtation 312
    Zippy 312
Ranch Hands 32
Ranch Hands Crag 31–32
    Blood Stains 32
    The Fox 32
    Jack Officers 32
    Mexican Secret Agent Man 31
    Payless Cashways 31
    Ranch Hands 32
    Roman Hands 31

Roman Meal 31
Spanky 31
Swilderness Experience 31
Swilderness Permit 31
Unknown 32
Range of Motion *90*, 108
Ranger Danger 62, *63*
Rap Bolters Need to Be Famous
    139
Raptor 230
Reach the Beach *68*, 69
Real Domestic Chickens 335
Rebel without a Pause *92*, 94
Rebel Yell 120
The Red and the Black *334, 335*
Red Heat 124
Red Light 132
Red Skies *68*, 69
Red Sky Mining 157
Red Spring Rock *23,* 24–27
    Access Fun 24
    Badger's Buttress 25
    Black Licorice 26
    Boulder Dash 26
    Classic Corner 24
    Contempt of Court 25
    Flying Pumpkin 24
    Fontanar de Rojo 24
    Habeas Corpus 25
    Haberdasher 26
    Hidden Meaning 24
    Love Hurts 25
    Red Vines 26
    Rocky Road 25
    Ruta de Roja 24
    Welcome to N.I.M.B.Y. Town
        24
Red Spring Rocks
    Love on the Rocks 25
Red Storm Rising 157
Red Throbber Spire *208*, 234,
    235
Red Vines *23*, 26
Red Zinger 286
Refried Brains 361, *362*
Refrigerator Wall 192–199
    Amazing Grace 199
    Breakaway 196
    Earth Juice 199
    Grape Nuts 199
    Greased Lightning 199
    Kisses Don't Lie 199
    Music to My Fears 195
    Strawberry Shubert 196
    Swing Shift 199
    Unfinished Symphony 196
Remote Control *208*, 234
Repeat Offender 154
Repo Man 39
Rescue Wall 86
    911 86
    Airlift 86
    Jaws of Life 86
Resin Rose 109
Resolution Arête *284, 285,* 314,
    315
Return to Forever 350
RF Gain 152
Ride the Tiger *240, 241*

Riding Hood 30
Riding Hood Wall *26,* 30–31
    Lil' Red 31
    Over the Hill to
        Grandmother's House 30
    Physical Graffiti 30
    Riding Hood 30
Ripcord *208,* 230, *231*
Rise and Whine 143
Rising Moons 332, *333*
Risk Brothers Roof *26,* 30
Risky Business *236, 238*
Roasted Ramen 139
Roasting Affair 183
Rob Roy 331
Robin Trowel 214
Rock Rastler 176
Rock Warrior 365
Rocky Road 25
Rodan 78
Rojo 201
Roman Hands 31
Roman Meal 31
Romance Is a Heart Breakin'
    Affair 348
Romeo Charlie 200
Romper Room 332
Romper Room Area 331–335
    Algae on Parade 332
    Buzz, Buzz 332
    Doobie Dance 332
    Girls and Buoys 331
    Guise and Gals 331
    Kindergarten Cop 331
    Magic Mirror 332
    Rising Moons 332
    Romper Room 332
A Rope, a Rubber Chicken, and
    a Vibrator 234
Rose Tower 256
    Olive Oil 256
Rosie's Day Out 165
Roto-Hammer 104
The Route to Mecca *18, 21*
Rubber Biscuit 89
The Runaway 109, *110*
Running *68*, 69
Running Amuck 108
Running Man 123
Running Man Wall 123–126
    Calico Terror 123
    Commando 124
    Falstaff 125
    Fibonacci Wall 124
    Flame Ranger 126
    Galloping Gal 124
    Graveyard Waltz 124
    Nevada Book 125
    New Traditionalists 123
    Northern Lights 125
    Plastic People 124
    Predator 123
    Red Heat 124
    Running Man 123
    Second Fiddle to a Dead Man
        123
    Spikes and Twine 126
    Split Crack 125
    Split Ends 125

Split Infinitive 125
Supernova 125
Swedish Erotica 126
Synthetic Society 124
There Goes the Neighborhood 123
Tier of the Titans 126
Titan Rocket 126
True Lies 123
Unknown 124
Vile Pile 124
Yodritch 125
Running Man Wall Area 120–133
Runout Rodeo 95, 96
Ruta de Roja 24

S

Saddam's Mom 157
Saltwater Taffy 44
Sand Boxing 89
Sand Buckets 89
Sand Felipe 353
Sand Illusion 155
Sand Man 100, 101
Sand Rail 89
Sand Wedge 88
Sandblast 353
Sandblaster 89
The Sandbox 88–89
    Crimson Crimp 89
    Rubber Biscuit 89
    Sand Boxing 89
    Sand Buckets 89
    Sand Rail 89
    Sand Wedge 88
    Sandblaster 89
The Sands 70
Sandstone Cowboy 100
Sandstone Enema 94
Sandstone Quarry 112, 113–159
    Central 133–144
    East 113–120
    North 144–150
    Northeast 150–157
Sandstone Samurai 363
Sandstone Sandwich 236, 237
Sandy Corridor 133–134
    Chrysler Crack 134
    The Deep West 134
    Flying Cowboys 134
    Integrity of Desire 133
    Plastic Pistol 134
Satan in a Can 43
Satellite Wall 147
    Cosmos 147
    Sputnik 147
    Stargazer 147
    Supernova II 147
Sauron's Eye 266, 267, 269
Save the Heart to Eat Later 27, 28
Saved by Zero 68, 69
Scalawag 16, 18, 19, 20
Scantily Clad Bimbo 118
Scanty Panty 74, 75
Science Patrol 78
Scorpions 49, 50
Scudder Global 146

Scumby 338
Sea of Holes 230, 231
Second Fiddle to a Dead Man 123
Second Pullout 81
Seduction Line 338
See Dick Fly 82, 84
See Spot Run 98, 99
Seka's Soiled Panties 137
Sensuous Mortician 204
Sergeant Slaughter 254, 266, 276, 277
Serious Business 227, 228
Serious Leisure 117
Seventh Hour 118
Sex in the Scrub Oak 218
Shadow Warrior 86
Shady Ladies 187
Shallow Fried Cracken 23
Shape of Things to Come 143
Shark Walk 149
Sheep Trail 178
Shell Game 396
Shere Khan 73
Shishka Bob 29
Shit Howdy 26, 29
Short but Sweet 144
Short Circuit 236, 238
Show Burro 39
Shut up and Dance 101, 102
Sick for Toys 377, 381
Sicktion 113
Side Effects 15, 16
Sidewinder 221
Silk Panties 73, 74, 75
Simpatico 227, 228
A Simple Expediency 218, 219
Sin City 183
The Singing Love Pen 18
Sir Climbalot 21
The Sissy Traverse 107
Sister of Pain 103
The Skagg 68, 69
Skewback 216
Slabba Dabba Do 221
Slabotomy 390
Slam Dancin' with the Amish 138
Slave to the Grind 92, 103
Sleeper 171
Slick Willy 317, 318
Slight of Hand 396
Slippery Peak Apron 335–338
    Advance Romance 335
    Real Domestic Chickens 335
    Red and the Black, The 335
Slot Machine 235, 236
Small Purchase 208, 250
Smears for Fears 200, 201
Smears For Fears Area 199–201
    Lebanese JoJo 201
    Rojo 201
    Romeo Charlie 200
    Smears for Fears 201
Smoke and Mirrors 394
Smokin' 45
Smooth as Silk 361
Snack Crack 70
Snapshot 132

Snivler 228, 229
Snow Blind 67, 68
Snow Creek Canyon 402
Social Disorder 108
Solar Flare 49, 50
Solar Slab 285, 287, 291, 292
Solar Slab Area 286–297
    Beulah's Book 293
    The Black Orpheus 294
    Bossa Nova 294
    The Friar 286
    Horndogger Select 289
    Johnny Vegas 293
    Red Zinger 286
    Solar Slab 291
    Solar Slab Gully 289
Solar Slab Gully 287, 289, 290
Some Assembly Required 153
Son of Wilson 323, 324
Sonic Youth 134, 136, 137
Sonic Youth Cliff 134–138
    Agent Orange 137
    Black Flag 137
    Crankenstein 138
    Everybody's Slave 137
    GBH 137
    Hip-Hoppin' with the Hutterites 137
    Hooligans 134
    Loki 137
    Seka's Soiled Panties 137
    Slam Dancin' with the Amish 138
    Sonic Youth 137
Sore Sirs 395
SOS 82
Soul Power 158
Sound of Power 115
Soupy Sales 16
Sour Mash 370, 371
Southern Comfort 151
Southern Cross 151
Soylent Green Jeans 181
Space Case 181
Spanky 31
Spanning the Gap 213, 216
Spark Plug 360
Special Guest Posers 87, 97
Spectrum 232, 233
Speed Racer 77
Spell Me 395
Spiderline 183
Spikes and Twine 126
Split Crack 125
Split Ends 125
Split Infinitive 125
Spontaneous Enjoyment 35
The Sport Chimney 49, 50
Sport Climbing Is Neither 108
Sportin' a Woody 175
Spotted Eagle 148
Spotted Owl 147
Spring Break 189
Sputnik 147
Squelch 152
The Staircase 117
Stand and Deliver 144
Stand or Fall 67, 68
Standing in the Shadows 83

Star Search 60
Stargazer 147
Static 152
Stealin' 84
Steep Thrills *49, 50*
Stemtation *311*, 312
Sterling Moss 182
Stew on This 15, *16*
Stick Gully 219–220
    The Elephant Penis 220
    Nature Is Fun 220
    Stick Left 220
    Stick Right 220
    Stickball 219
Stick Left *210*, 220
Stick Right *210*, 220
Stickball *210*, 219
Stone Hammer *98*, 100
Stone Hammer II 104
Stone Wall *90*, 103–104
    April Fools 104
    Birthstone 104
    Haunted Hooks 104
    Nirvana 104
    Purple Haze 104
    Roto-Hammer 104
    Stone Hammer II 104
    Stonehenge 104
Stonehenge 104
Stout Roof *224*, 225
Straight Shooter 221
Straight Shooter Wall 220–222
    Forget Me Knot 222
    The Lazy Fireman 220
    Sidewinder 221
    Slabba Dabba Do 221
    Straight Shooter 221
Straight Shot 330
Stratocaster *90*, 131
Stratocaster Direct *130*, 131
Stratocaster Wall 126–132
    Beyond Reason 131
    Break Loose 128
    The Bristler 131
    Choad Hard 129
    The Choad Warrior 131
    Cowboy Café 132
    Cut Loose 129
    Diablo 129
    Flying V 129
    Footloose 129
    Marshall Amp 131
    One-Eyed Jacks 129
    Pablo Diablo 129
    Party Line 129
    Project 128
    Purple Haze II 131
    Stratocaster 131
    Stratocaster Direct 131
    Telecaster 132
    When the Shit Hits the Fan 131
Strawberry Shubert 196
Stuck on You 119
Stukas over Disneyland 33
Sudden Impact 109, *110*
Suffering Cats 88
Sumo Greatness 182
Sumo Greatness Slab 182

Dean's List 182
Ice Climb 182
Sumo Greatness 182
Sunny and Steep *49*, 50
Sunny and Steep Crag *44*, 49–51
    Black Happy 50
    Blackened 50
    Cirque du Soleil 51
    Claimjumper's Special 49
    Gimme Back My Bullets 50
    Mr. Choad's Wild Ride 50
    Peak Performance 50
    Scorpions 50
    Solar Flare 50
    The Sport Chimney 50
    Steep Thrills 50
    Sunny and Steep 50
    Tour de Pump 50
    Turbo Dog 50
    Turtle Wax 50
    Working for Peanuts 51
Sunnyside Crag 185–189
    Backlash 186
    Cold September Corner 187
    Crossfire 189
    Gotham City 189
    Knotty Behavior 188
    Magellanic Cloud 188
    Mercedes 188
    Meteor 186
    Mr. Freeze's Face 187
    Mister Masters 189
    Shady Ladies 187
    Spring Break 189
    Tarantula 189
    Tie Me Tightly 188
    Van Allen Belt 188
    Water Dog 188
    Water Logged 188
    Whiplash 186
    Whipper 186
Sunsplash 115
Supernova 125, 162
Supernova II 147
The Swainbow Wall 271
Swedish Erotica 126
Sweet Pain *92*, 102
Sweet Pain Wall *90*, 102–103
    A-Cute Pain 103
    Glitter Gulch 103
    Lee Press-on 103
    Pain in the Neck 103
    Sister of Pain 103
    Slave to the Grind 103
    Sweet Pain 102
The Sweet Spot 159–161
    Absolute Zero 159
    Disposable Blues 159
Swilderness Experience 31
Swilderness Permit 31
Swing Shift 199
Swirly Cliff 44
    Chocolate Swirl 44
    Old School 44
    Saltwater Taffy 44
    Turkish Taffy 44
Synapse Collapse 45
Synthetic Society 124

T
Take the Skinheads Bowling 64
Tales from the Gripped 358, *359*
Tarantula 189
Tatanka *191*, 192
Technicolor Sunrise 87
Teenage Mutant Ninja Turtles 151
Telecaster 132
Telletubby Scandal 78
Terminal Velocity *208*, 224, 225, *226*
Territorial Imperative 180
Texas Hold'em 377, *378*
Texas Lite Sweet 94
Texas Tea 93
That Wedged Feeling 120
There and Back Again 284, 297, *298*
There Goes the Neighborhood 123
Thermal Breakdown 93
They Call the Wind #!&% 218
They Just Don't Make Outlaws Like They Used To 159
Thirsty Quail 118
This Ain't No Disco *243*, 244
This Bud's for You *224*, 225
This Is the City 118
Thong *73*, 74, *75*
A Thousand New Routes 115
Threadfin 82
The Threat 174
Thunderbird 147
Tie Me Tightly 188
Tier of the Titans 126
Tiger Stripe Wall 72–73
    Bengal 73
    Shere Khan 73
    Tigger 73
    White Tigers 73
Tigger 73
Time Off 141
Time's Up *254*, 261, 262
Tin Horn Posers 97
Titan Rocket 126
Titty Litter 88
To Bolt or Toupee 115
Tom Terrific 247, *248*
Tomato Amnesia *98*, 99
Tonto 177
Too Pumped to Pose 222, *224*
Topless Twins *221*, 228, 229
Tortugas Mutante 151
Totally Clips *74*, 76
Tour de Pump *49*, 50
Toxic Playboy 120
Tranquility Base 378, *382*
Treacherous Journey 21
Tremor *82*, 83
Tri-Burro Bridge *208*, 210, 214, *215*
Triassic Sands 353
Tricks Are for Kids 183
Trigger Happy 153
Trihardral 326
The Trophy *146*, 148–150, *149*
    Caught in the Crosshairs 150
    Dodging a Bullet 150

Fifi Hula 149
Indian Giver 149
Keep Your Powder Dry 149
Meatlocker 150
Midnight Cowboy 149
Pet Shop Boy 149
Project 149
Shark Walk 149
The Trophy 149
Twilight of a Champion 149
Unknown 149
Tropicana 70
Truancy Cliff 85
　Ditch Day 85
　Doctor's Orders 85
　Iron Man 85
　Playing Hooky 85
True Lies 123
Trundle Wall 83–84
　Before Its Time 83
　Bone Machine 84
　Life out of Balance 83
　Master Beta 83
　Pocket Rocket 83
　Standing in the Shadows 83
Tsunami Wall 81–83
　Abandon Ship 82
　Aftershock 82
　Angler 82
　Barracuda 81
　Land Shark 82
　Low Tide 83
　Man Overboard! 82
　Poseidon Adventure 81
　SOS 82
　Threadfin 82
　Tremor 83
　Women and Children First 82
Tuckered Sparfish 176
Tuna and Chips 71, 72
Tuna and Chips Wall 65, 71–72
　Chips Ahoy! 72
　Chips and Salsa 72
　Tuna and Chips 72
　Tuna Cookies 72
　Waterstreak 72
Tuna Cookies 71, 72
Tunnel Vision 162, 163
Turbo Dog 49, 50
Turkish Taffy 44
Turtle Wax 49, 50
Turtlehead 44
Tuscarora 284, 297, 298–299
Twentieth Century Ultra 145
Twenty-nine Posers 222, 224
Twilight of a Champion 149
The Twinkie 144
　Flake Eyes 144
　Like Mom Used to Make 144
　Short but Sweet 144

U
Ultraman 77
Ultraman Wall 65, 77–78
　Clutch Cargo 77
　Godzilla 78
　The Hex Files 78
　Rodan 78
　Science Patrol 78

Speed Racer 77
Telletubby Scandal 78
Ultraman 77
Under the Boardwalk 118
Unfinished Symphony 196
Unimpeachable Groping 283
Universal City 56, 60
　Cameo Appearance 60
　Celebrity Roast 60
　Ed MacMayonnaise 60
　Prime Ticket 60
　Quiet on the Set 60
　Star Search 60
Unknown Arête 155

V
Vagabonds 91
Valentine's Day 16–17, 18
Van Allen Belt 188
Varnishing Point 221, 227, 228
Velveeta 372
Velvet Elvis 59, 60
Velvet Elvis Crag 56, 58–60
　Black Tongue 58
　Claw Hammer 60
　Climb Bandits 60
　Isis 60
　Velvet Elvis 60
Vernal Thaw 52, 53
Viagra Falls 74, 76
Victoria's Secret 76
Vile Pile 124
Violent Stems 338
Virgin River Gorge 402
Vision Quest 177

W
Wake Up Wall 141–144
　Crack of Noon 143
　Elder Sibling 143
　First Born 143
　Good Mourning 143
　The Healer 143
　Just Shut up and Climb 143
　Monkey Rhythm 143
　Native Son 143
　Onsight Flight 144
　Pain Check 143
　Poundcake 143
　Rise and Whine 143
　Shape of Things to Come 143
　Stand and Deliver 144
　Where Egos Dare 143
　XTZ 144
Walk to School 179
The Walker Spur 243, 244
Walking the Vertical Beach 95, 96
Wall of Confusion 90, 109
　American Sportsman 109
　Big Damage 109
　Body English 109
　Desert Pickle 109
　Fear and Loathing III 109
　Promises in the Dark 109
　Resin Rose 109
　The Runaway 109
　Sudden Impact 109
Warlock 90, 106

The Warming 71
Water Dog 188
Water Logged 188
Waterstreak 71, 72
Wedgie 74, 76
Weenie Juice 192
Welcome to N.I.M.B.Y. Town 24
Welcome to Red Rocks 240, 242, 243
Western Spaces 382, 384
Western Spaces Wall 377–393
　Black Sun 383
　The Breathing Stone 378
　Desert Solitude 378
　Mr. Natural of the Desert 383
　Sick for Toys 377
　Tranquility Base 378
　Western Spaces 382
What's Eating You? 29
Wheat Thick 169
When a Stranger Calls 243, 244
When the Cat's Away 157
When the Shit Hits the Fan 131
Where Egos Dare 143
Where the Down Boys Go 107
Which Hunters? 106
The Whiff 67, 68
Whiplash 186
Whipper 186
Whiskey Peak 344–358
　Archeoptryx 354
　As the Toad Turns 348
　Back to Basics 348
　Cabo San Looseness 352
　Cole Essence 354
　Crown Royal 344
　The Delicate Sound of Thunder 356
　First Grader 348
　Frogland 344
　Ixtalan 352
　Kenny Laguna 348
　Matzoland 352
　Mazatlan 351
　Miss Conception 350
　The Misunderstanding 350
　Only the Good Die Young 358
　Our Father 356
　Perplexity 350
　Rain Dance 344
　Return to Forever 350
　Romance Is a Heart Breakin' Affair 348
　Sand Felipe 353
　Sandblast 353
　Tales from the Gripped 358
　Triassic Sands 353
　Wholesome Fullback 354
White Rock Spring Area 160, 161–165
White Rock Springs Peak 165–169
　Rosie's Day Out 165
White Tigers 73
The Whitehouse Effect 249
Who, Deany? 395
Who Made Who 107

Wholesome Fullback 354, *355*, *357*
Why Left 179
Why Right 179
Willow Spring *168*, 169–183
Willy's Coulior 317–318
    Free Willy 318
    Otters Are People Too 317
    Slick Willy 318
Windy Canyon 386–390
    Ain't No Saint 386
    Diet Delight 386
    Jubilant Song 390
    Slabotomy 390
Winter Heat *52*, 53
Winter Heat Wall *44*, 51–55
    A-OK 55
    Autumnal Frost 53
    Cool Water Sandwich 55
    Cool Whip 55
    Couldn't Be Schmooter 53
    High Class Hoe 53
    Hole in the Pants 51
    Mo Hotta, Mo Betta 53
    Nuttin' Could Be Finer 53
    Vernal Thaw 53
    Winter Heat 53
Witches' Honor *90,* 106
Without a Paddle 255
Wizard of Odds 151
Wok the Dog 65, 66
Women and Children First 82
Wonderstuff 27
Woodrow 312
Working for Peanuts *49*, 51

X
XTZ 144

Y
Y2K *240*, 241
Yaak Crack *90*, 107
Yearnin' and Learnin' 154
Yellow Brick Road 368
Yellow Dog 62, *63*
Yin and Yang 46, *46–48*
    Atman 48
    Yin and Yang 46
    Zoroaster 48
Yodritch 125
You Are What You Eat 27, 28
Yucca 102

Z
Zen and the Art of Web Spinning *228*, 229
Zion 402
Zipperhead 87
Zippy *311*, 312
Zona Rosa 30
Zoroaster 48